CONTENTS

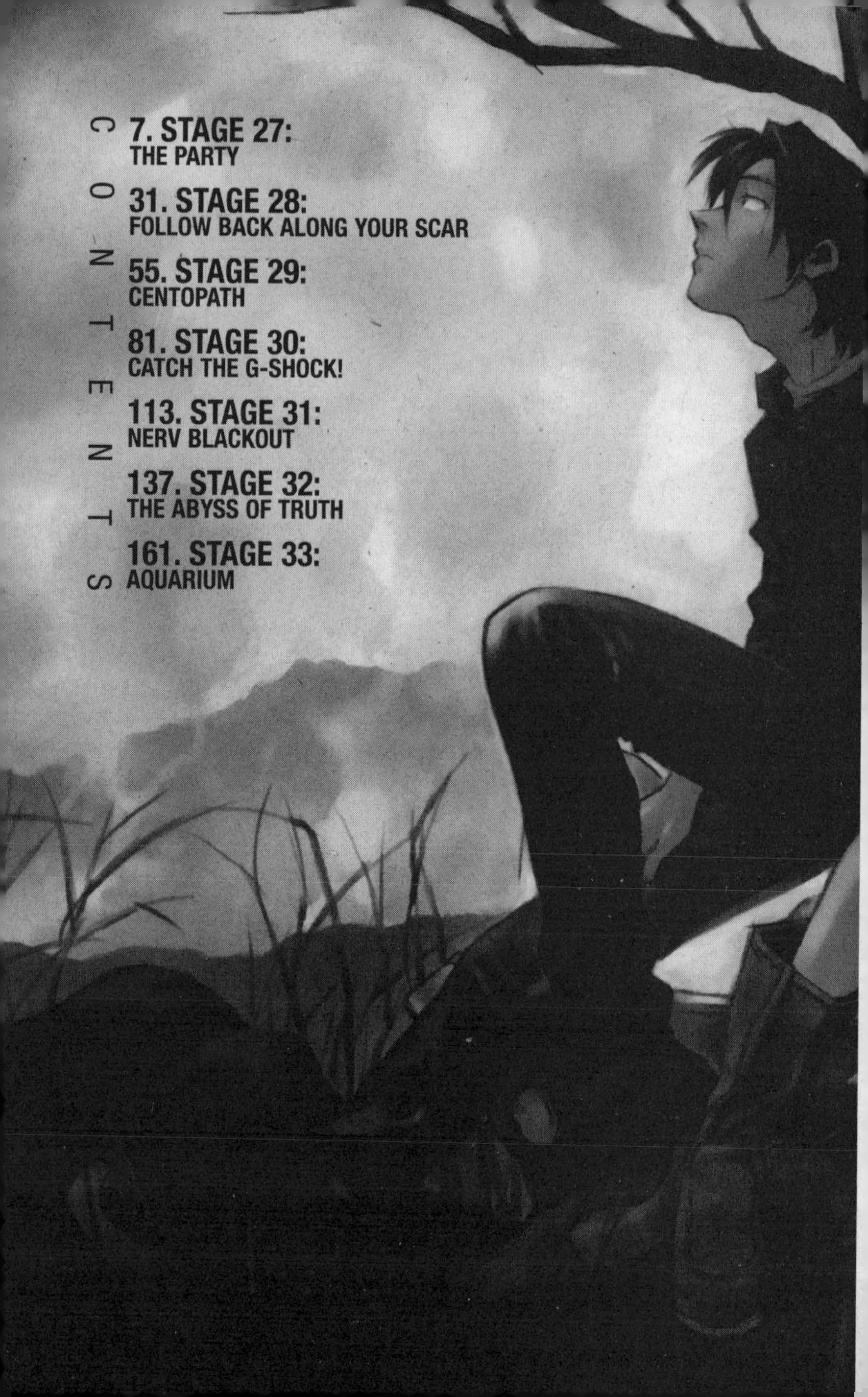

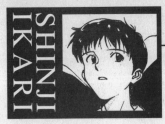

SHINJI IKARI

EVA PILOT, NERV
MIDDLE SCHOOL STUDENT
Age: 14

Shinji was the "Third Child" chosen to pilot the monstrous Evangelion series: biomechanical units developed by the clandestine UN paramilitary agency known as NERV to fight entities code-named "Angels." Both resentful of his father, supreme commander Gendo Ikari, and desperate for his approval, Shinji has already defeated four Angels despite having no previous knowledge of NERV or combat.

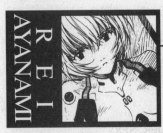

REI AYANAMI

EVA PILOT, NERV
MIDDLE SCHOOL STUDENT
Age: 14

Rei is the "First Child" to be chosen to pilot an Evangelion, and first to use it in combat, sustaining severe injuries in Unit-01 while fighting the Third Angel. Although Rei barely expresses emotion, she at first regarded Shinji as an interloper. Since she and Shinji fought the Fifth Angel together, they have grown closer, yet Shinji is still mystified at how Rei relates to Gendo in a way he himself cannot.

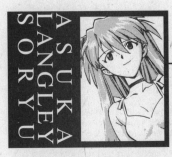

ASUKA LANGLEY SORYU

EVA UNIT-02 PILOT, NERV
MIDDLE SCHOOL STUDENT
Age: 14

Asuka is a United States citizen of mixed Japanese and German ancestry. A boastfully "superior" product of eugenic breeding, Shinji knows that she tries to hide both her bratty nature and pain over the loss of her mother. Asuka is the "second Child" to be identified as qualified to pilot an Evangelion by the obscure Marduk Agency, and was assigned to Eva Unit-02. Attracted by Ryoji Kaji.

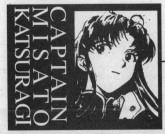

CAPTAIN MISATO KATSURAGI

OPERATIONS CHIEF, NERV
Age: 29

Even though Capt. Katsuragi is third in command at NERV, after Commander Gendo and Sub-Commander Fuyutsuki, and oversees the Eva pilots in combat in her role as tactical planner, there are many things about the organization that have been kept from her. A carouser and slob in her off-hours, Misato has become surrogate family for Shinji, with whom she shares an apartment.

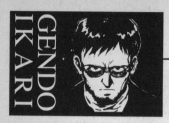

GENDO IKARI

SUPREME COMMANDER, NERV
Age: 48

Shinji's father; this ruthless and enigmatic man is the guiding force behind the development of NERV's Evangelion system. He is also the man entrusted to carry out the even more secret Instrumentality Project. Gendo was an absent father, entrusting Shinji's upbringing to his uncle and aunt.

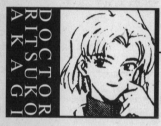

DOCTOR RITSUKO AKAGI

CHIEF SCIENTIST, NERV
Age: 30

Technical supervisor for NERV's "Project E (Evangelion)," Dr. Akagi is a polymath genius who rode the wave of scientific revolution that followed the cracking of the human genetic code at the end of the 20th century. Her disciplines include physics, biotechnology and computer science. Dr. Akagi was a friend of Misato's in college.

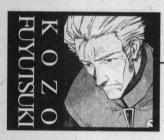

KOZO FUYUTSUKI

SUB-COMMANDER, NERV
Age: UNCERTAIN—ABOUT 60

Gendo's second-in-command and right-hand man. Before the Second Impact, Fuyutsuki was a biology professor in Kyoto, Japan, during which time he first met Gendo, who married his prize student. He and Dr. Akagi may be the only ones at NERV besides Gendo to know the complete story behind Evangelion and the Instrumentality Project.

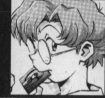

KENSUKE AIDA

MIDDLE SCHOOL STUDENT
Age: 14

A devoted fan of military affairs, Aida plays war games in army costume out in the country, habitually carries a Sony camcorder to capture shots of hardware or combat, and engages in computer hacking to acquire information for his "mania." He has expressed the wish that someone like Misato would "order him around."

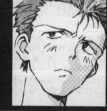

TOJI SUZUHARA

MIDDLE SCHOOL STUDENT
Age: 14

Best friend of Aida; speaks with a pronounced accent from his home town, Osaka. His father and grandfather are both part of NERV's research labs. At first he blamed Shinji (and punched him out) for injuries his sister suffered due to "collateral damage" from the first battle in Tokyo-3 against the Angels; now both Aida and he are friends with Unit-01's pilot.

NEON GENESIS EVANGELION
VIZ MEDIA EDITION VOLUME FIVE

STORY AND ART BY
YOSHIYUKI SADAMOTO

ORIGINAL CONCEPT BY
GAINAX

ENGLISH ADAPTATION
FRED BURKE AND CARL GUSTAV HORN

TRANSLATION
LILLIAN OLSEN

LETTERING
WAYNE TRUMAN

GRAPHIC DESIGN
VERONICA CASSON

EDITORS
MEGAN BATES AND CARL GUSTAV HORN

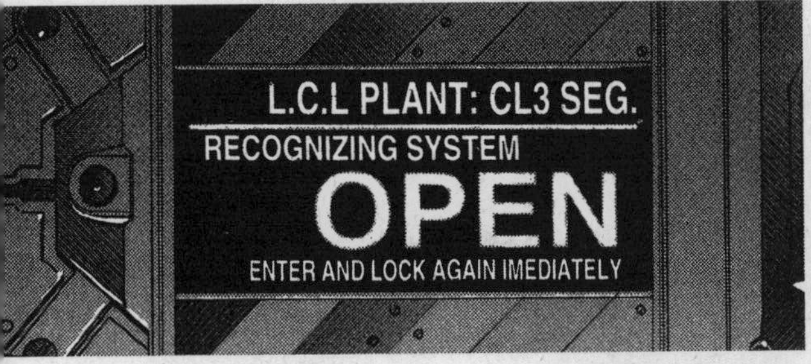

L.C.L PLANT: CL3 SEG.
RECOGNIZING SYSTEM
OPEN
ENTER AND LOCK AGAIN IMEDIATELY

MANAGING EDITOR
ANNETTE ROMAN

EDITORIAL DIRECTOR
ELIZABETH KAWASAKI

EDITOR IN CHIEF
ALVIN LU

SR. DIRECTOR OF ACQUISITIONS
RIKA INOUYE

SR. VP OF MARKETING
LIZA COPPOLA

EXEC. VP OF SALES & MARKETING
JOHN EASUM

PUBLISHER
HYOE NARITA

PUBLISHED BY VIZ MEDIA, LLC P.O. BOX 77064 SAN FRANCISCO, CA 94107

VIZ MEDIA EDITION
10 9 8 7 6 5 4 3 2
FIRST PRINTING JULY 2004
SECOND PRINTING JUNE 2006

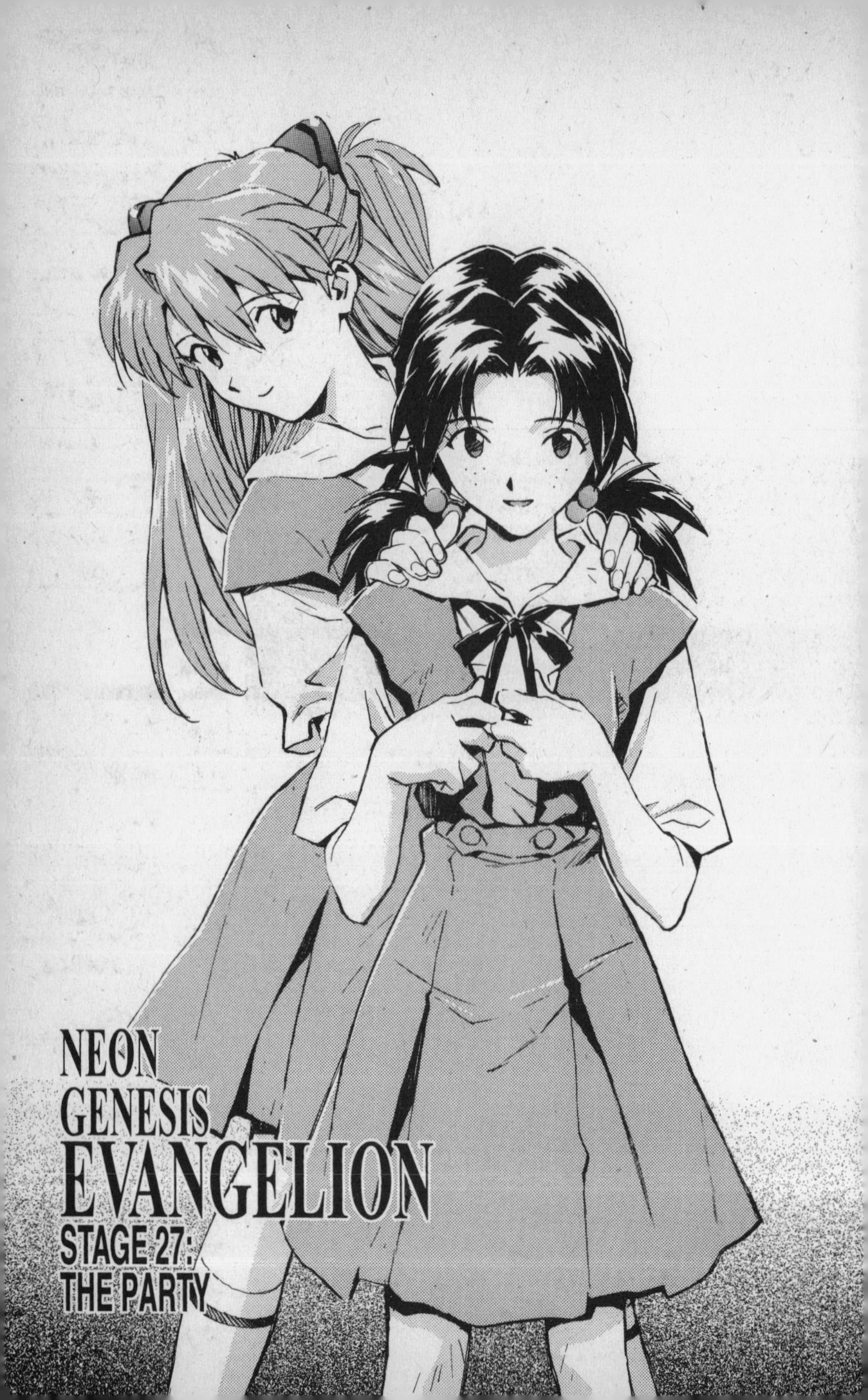
NEON
GENESIS
EVANGELION
STAGE 27:
THE PARTY

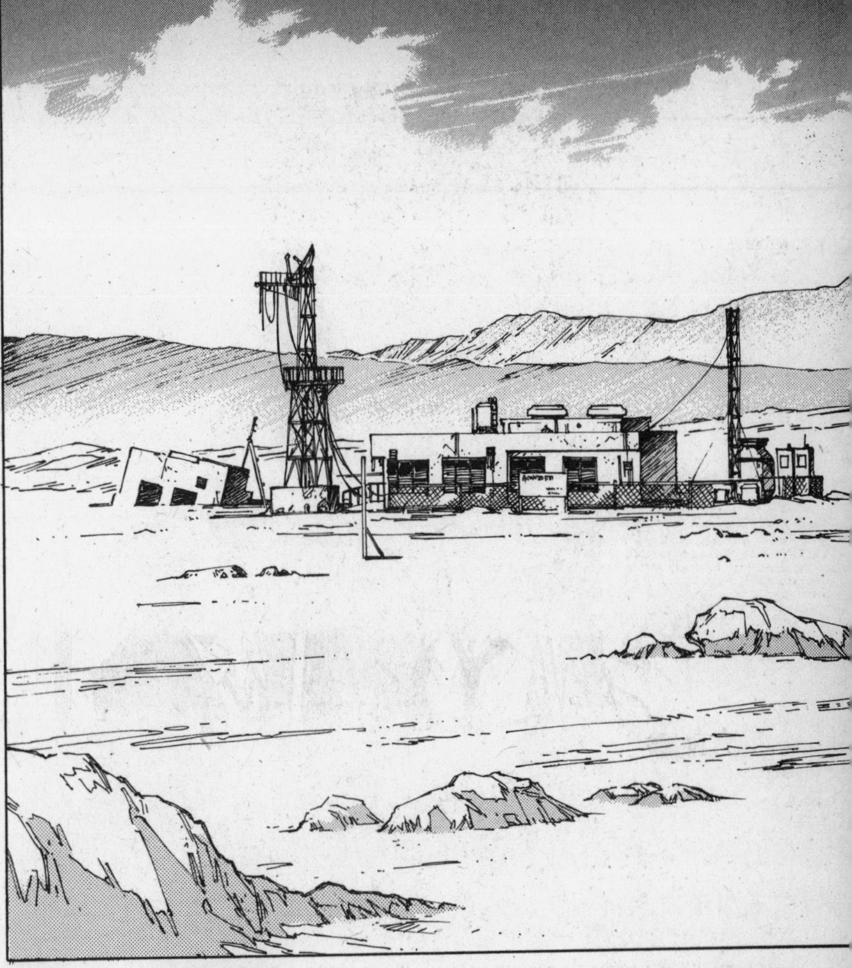

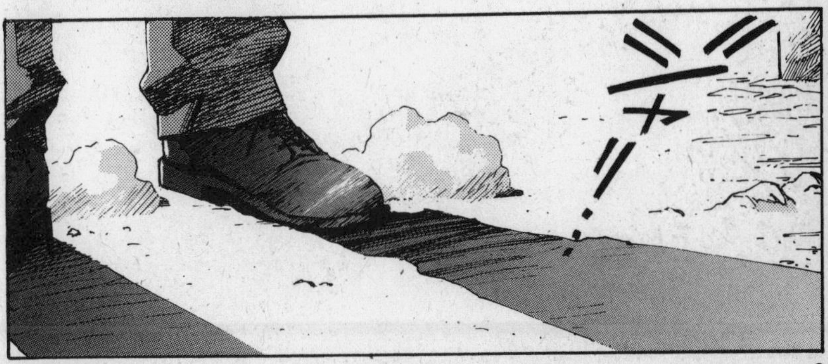
ジャリ…

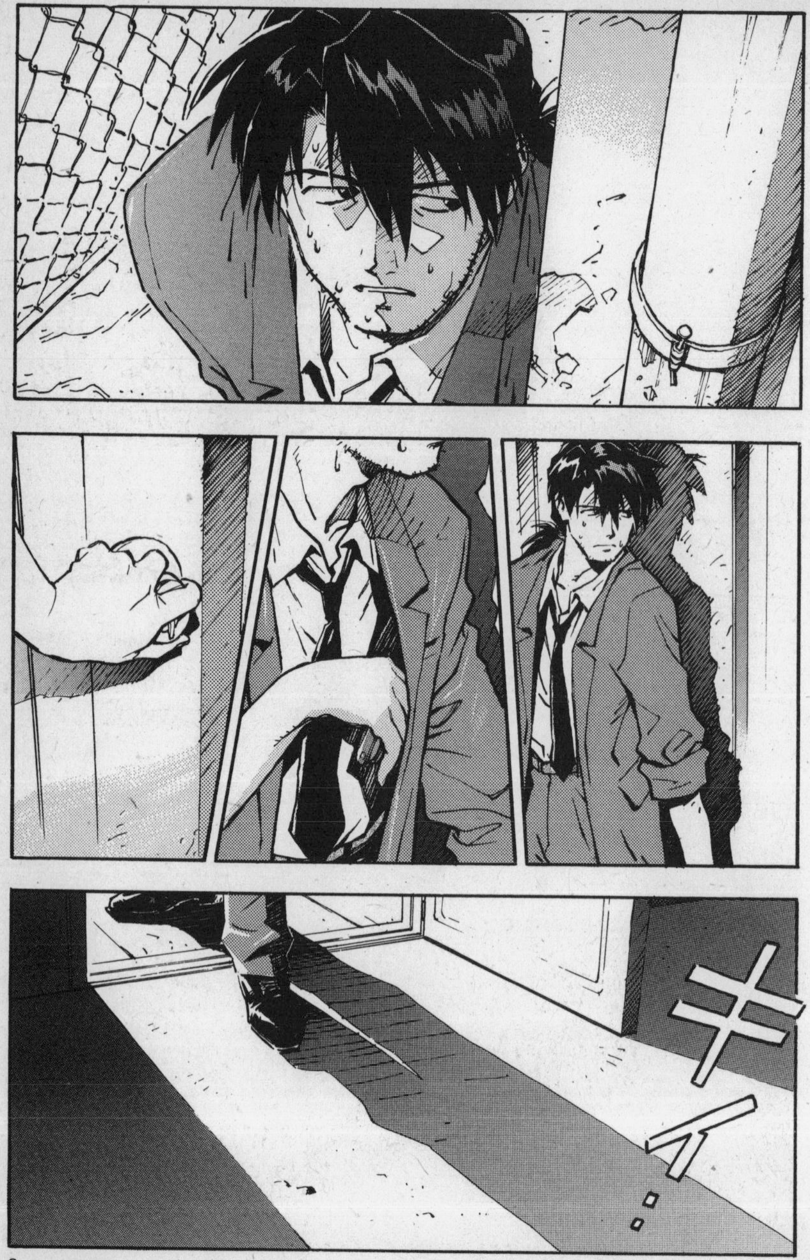
キィ…

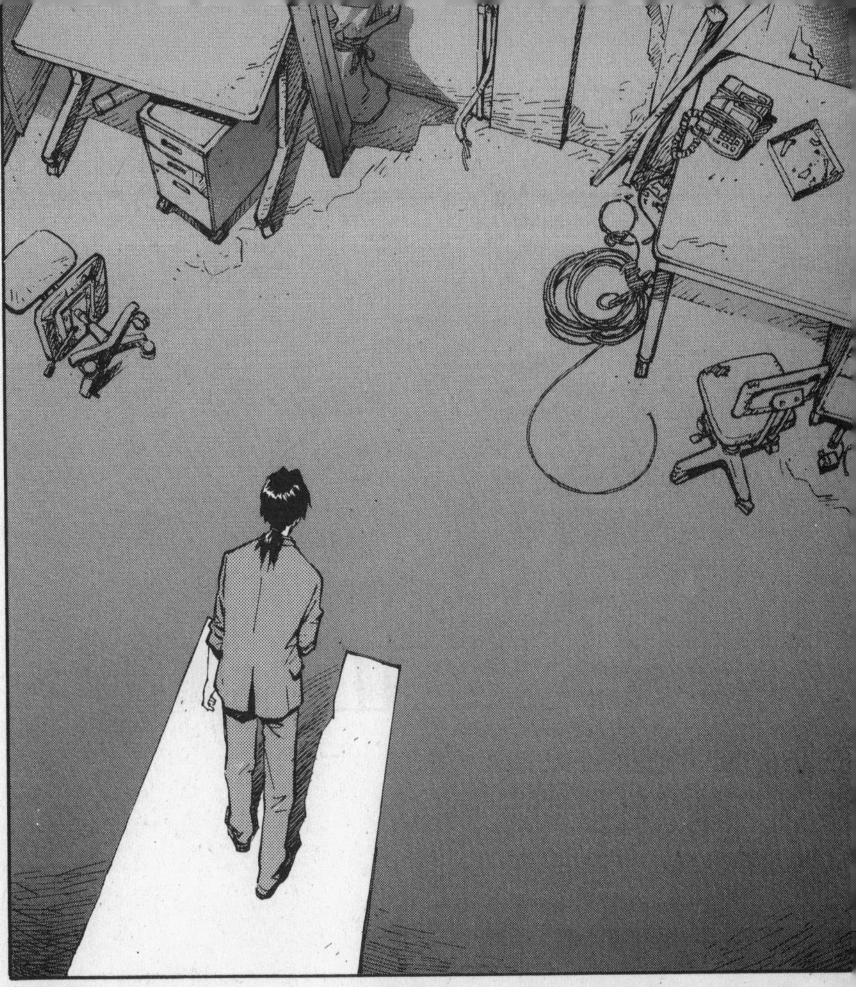

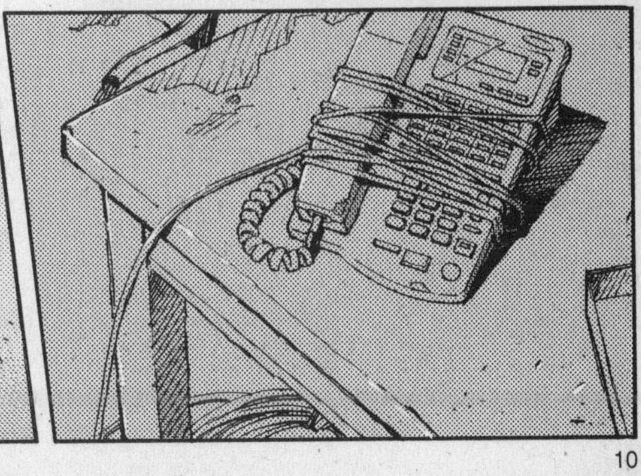

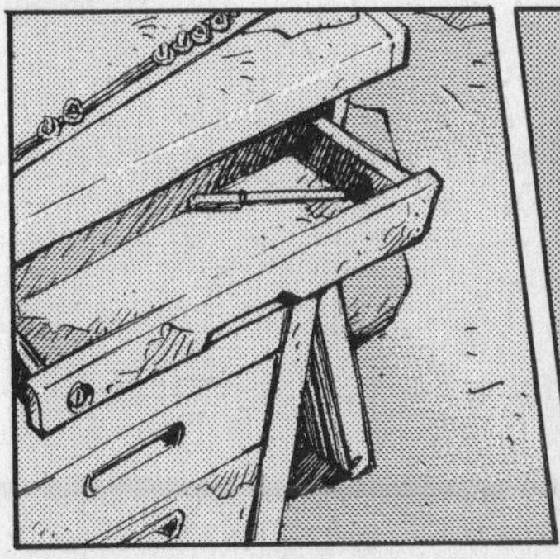

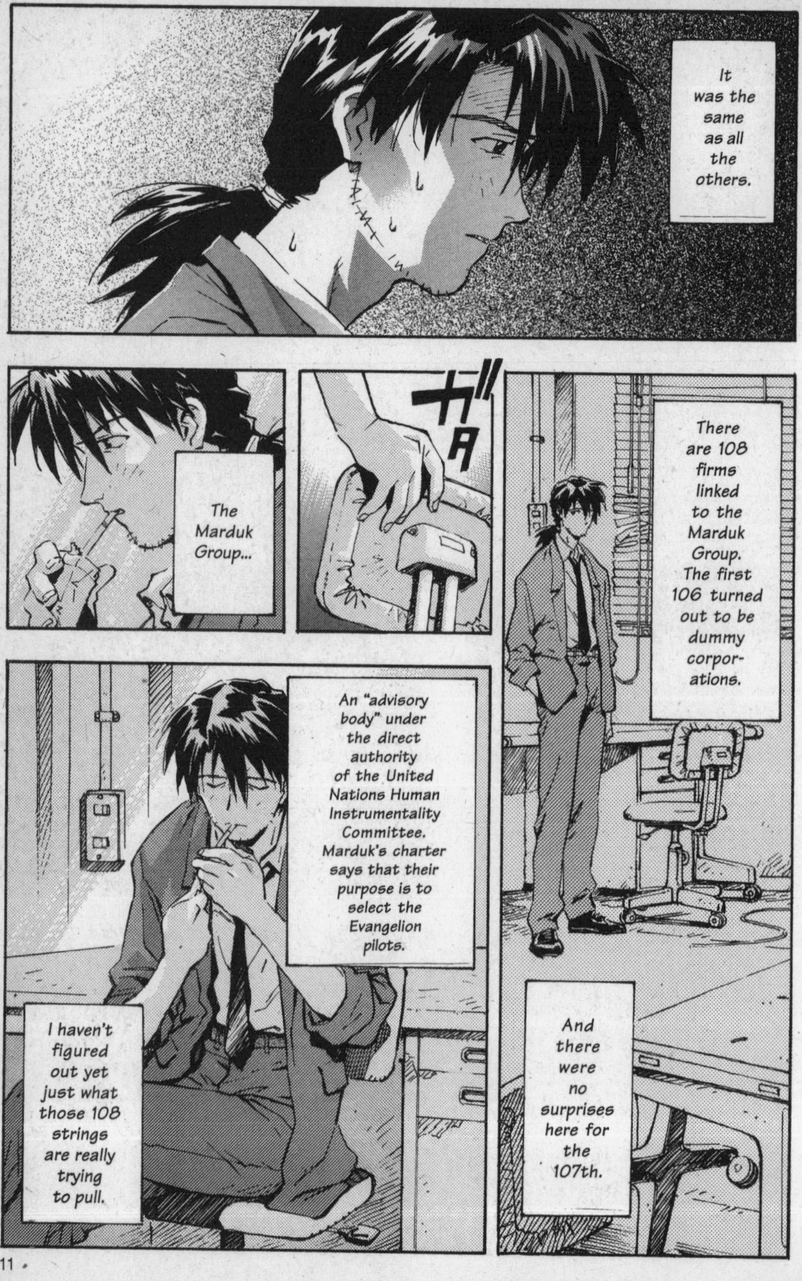

It was the same as all the others.
There are 108 firms linked to the Marduk Group. The first 106 turned out to be dummy corporations.
And there were no surprises here for the 107th.
ガタ
The Marduk Group...
An "advisory body" under the direct authority of the United Nations Human Instrumentality Committee. Marduk's charter says that their purpose is to select the Evangelion pilots.
I haven't figured out yet just what those 108 strings are really trying to pull.

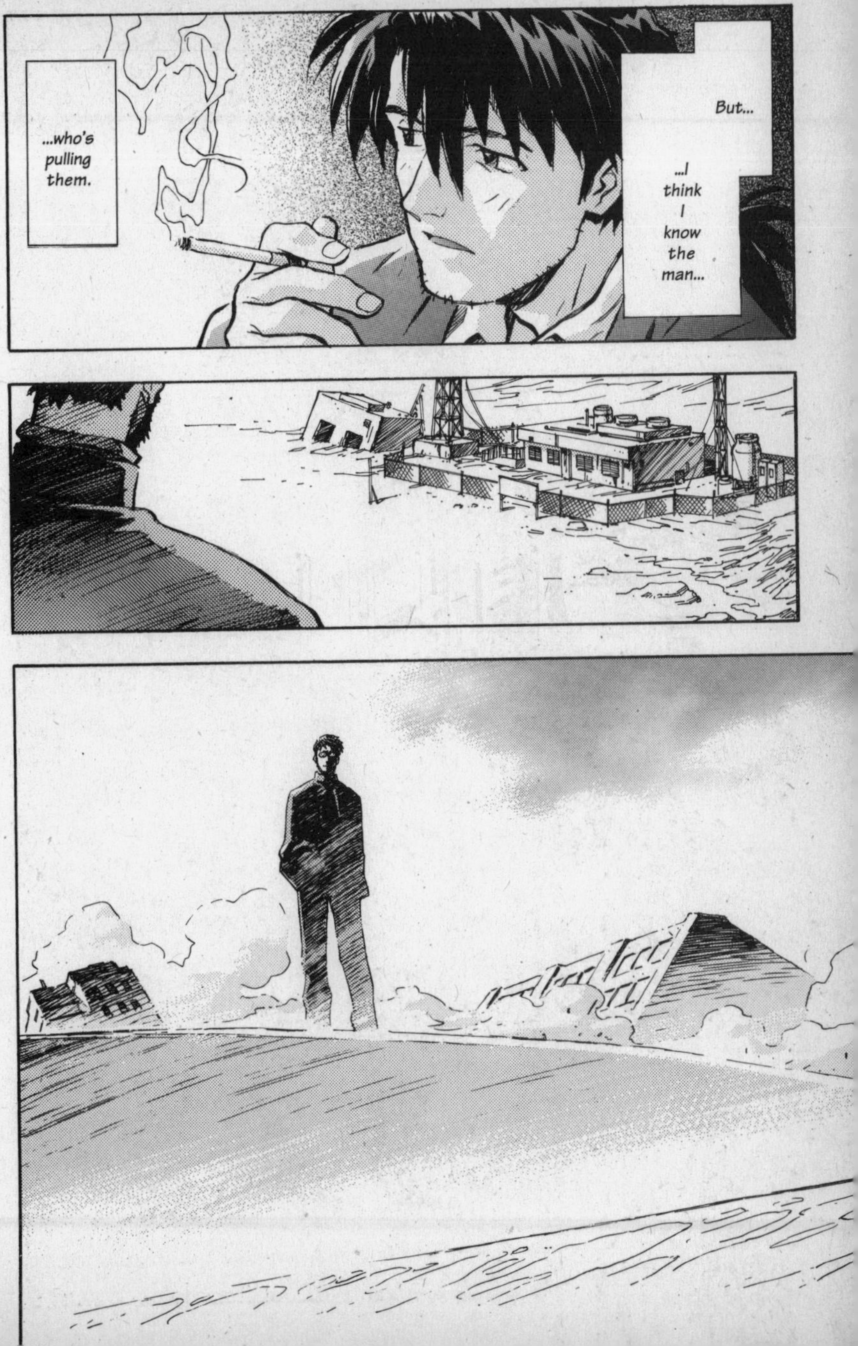
But...
...I think I know the man...
...who's pulling them.

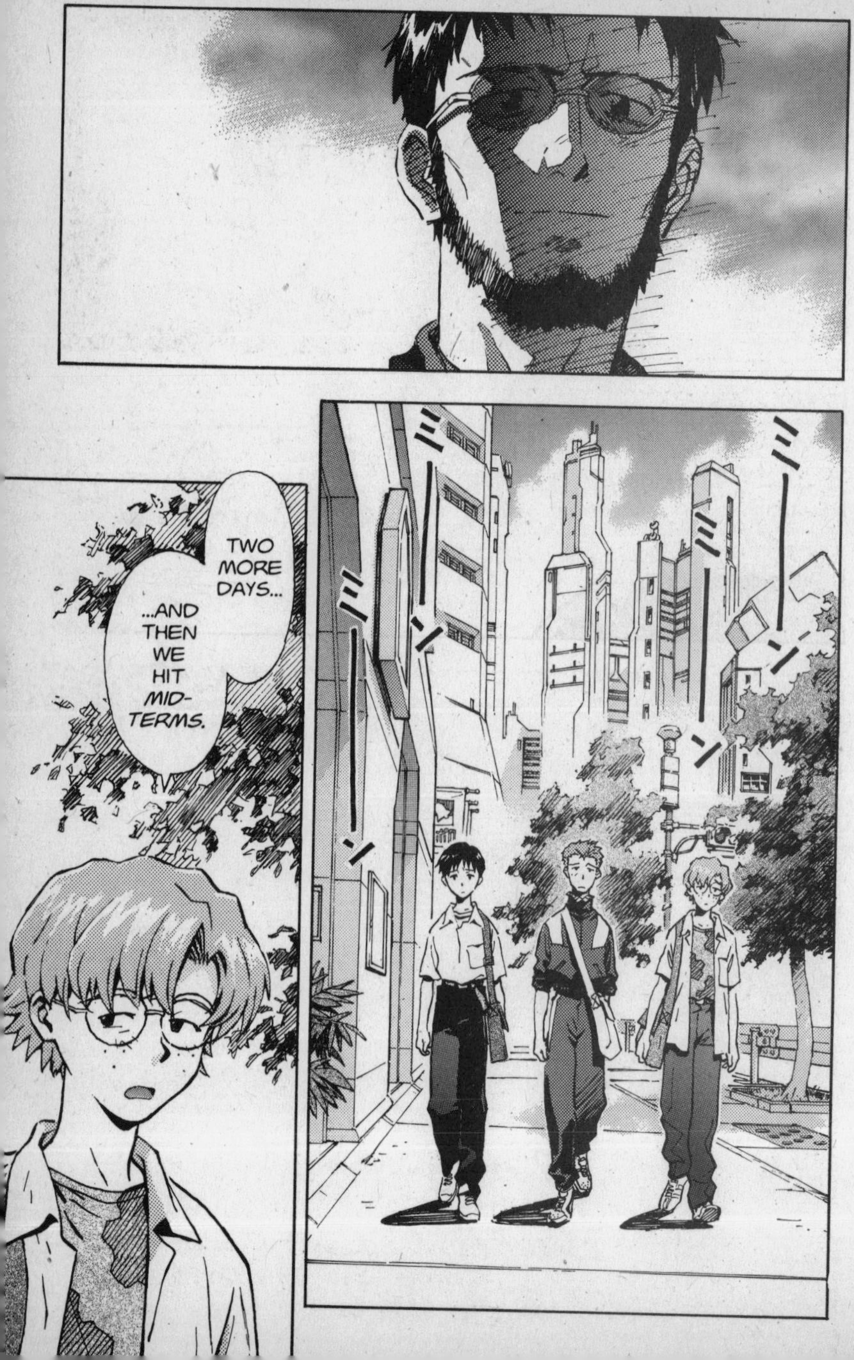
ミーン
ミーン
ミーン
ミーン
TWO MORE DAYS...
...AND THEN WE HIT MID-TERMS.

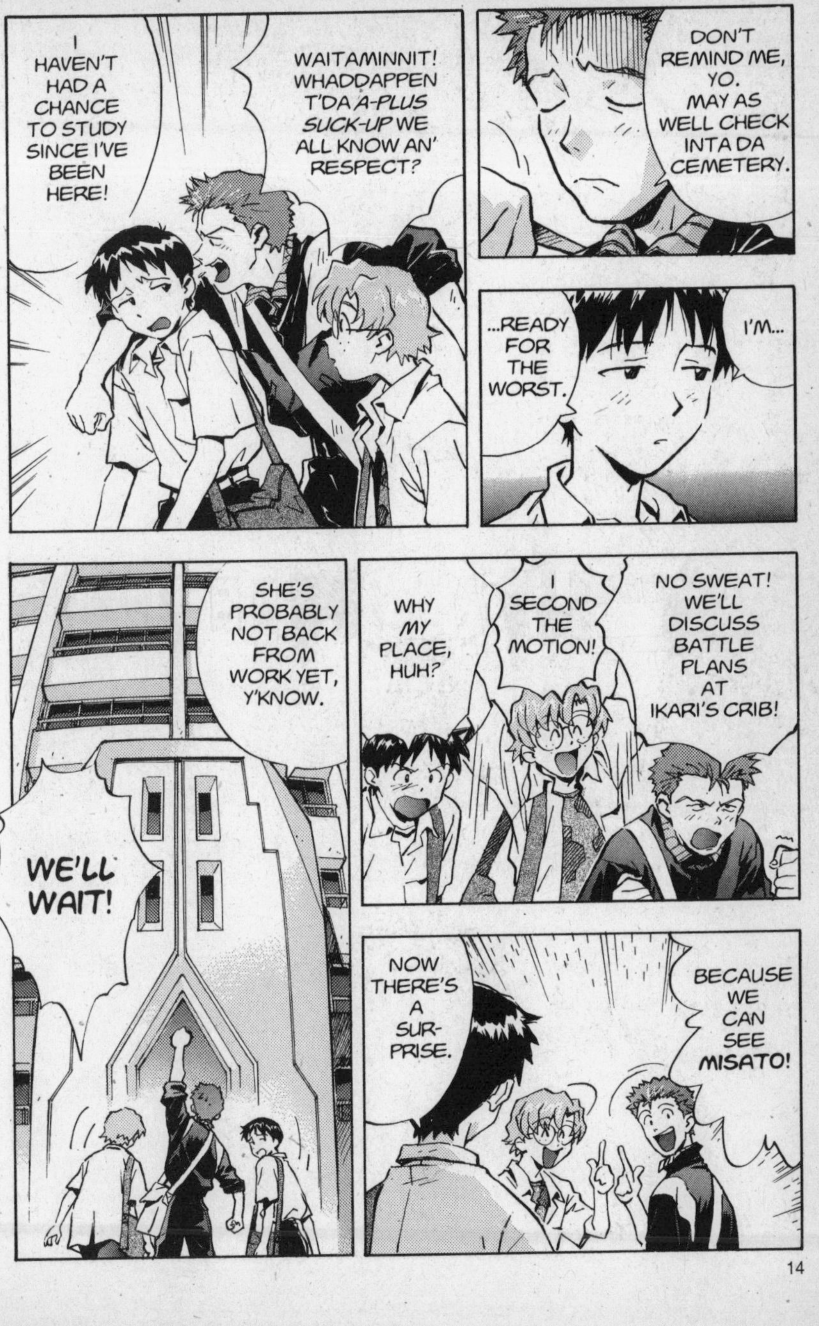
I HAVEN'T HAD A CHANCE TO STUDY SINCE I'VE BEEN HERE!
WAITAMINNIT! WHADDAPPEN T'DA A-PLUS SUCK-UP WE ALL KNOW AN' RESPECT?
DON'T REMIND ME, YO. MAY AS WELL CHECK INTA DA CEMETERY.
I'M...
...READY FOR THE WORST.
NO SWEAT! WE'LL DISCUSS BATTLE PLANS AT IKARI'S CRIB!
I SECOND THE MOTION!
WHY MY PLACE, HUH?
BECAUSE WE CAN SEE MISATO!
NOW THERE'S A SUR-PRISE.
SHE'S PROBABLY NOT BACK FROM WORK YET, Y'KNOW.
WE'LL WAIT!

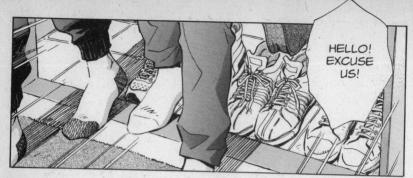

HELLO! EXCUSE US!

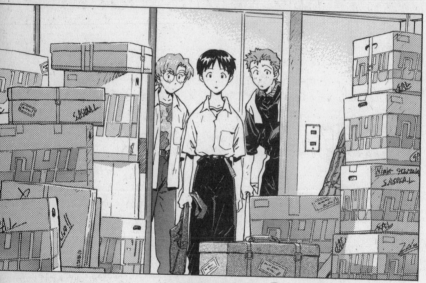

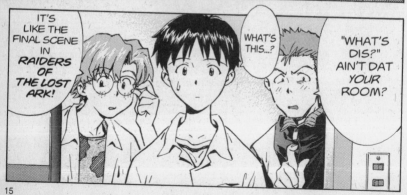

IT'S LIKE THE FINAL SCENE IN *RAIDERS OF THE LOST ARK!*

WHAT'S THIS...?

"WHAT'S DIS?" AIN'T DAT *YOUR* ROOM?

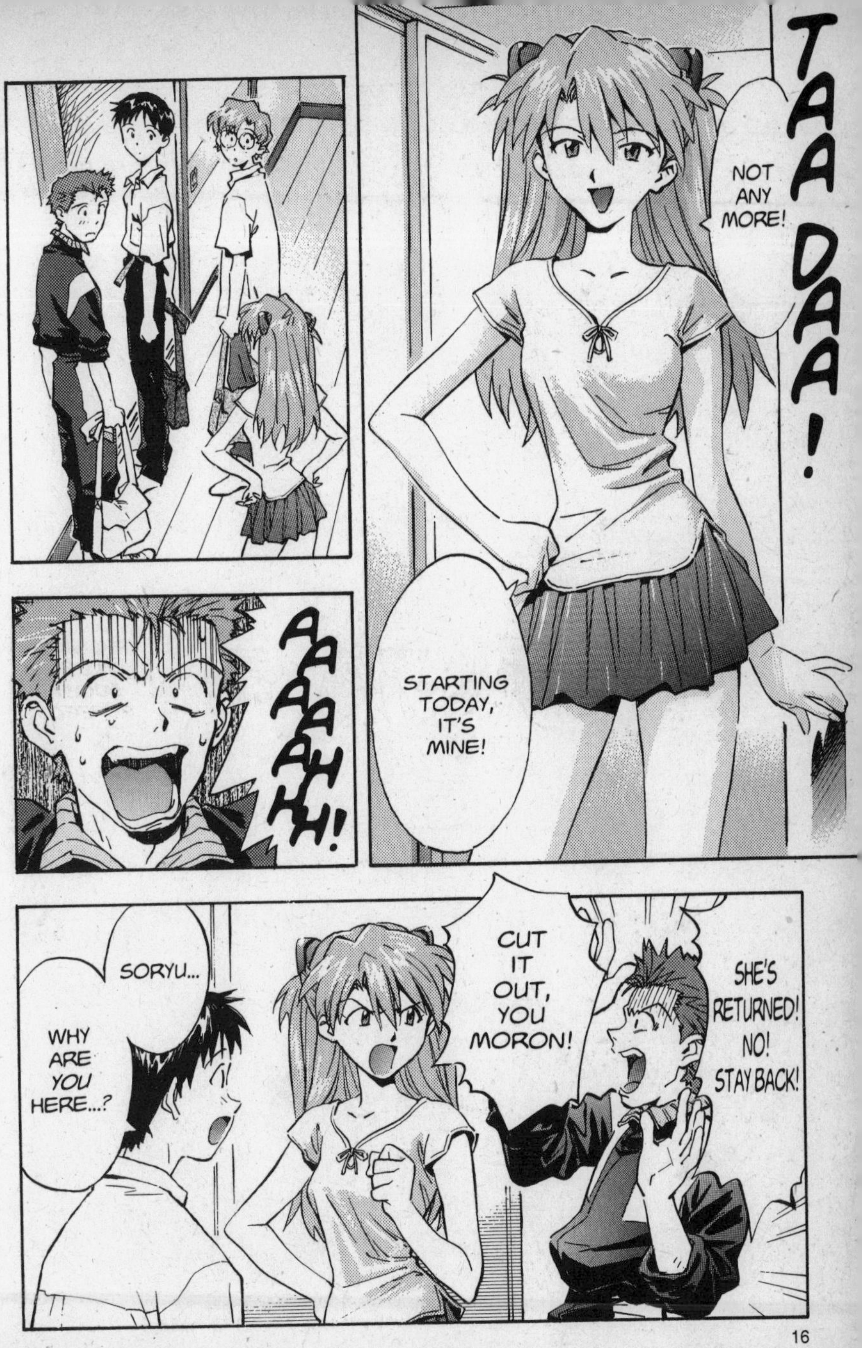
TAA DAAA!
NOT ANY MORE!
STARTING TODAY, IT'S MINE!
AAAAAHH!
SHE'S RETURNED! NO! STAY BACK!
CUT IT OUT, YOU MORON!
SORYU...
WHY ARE YOU HERE...?

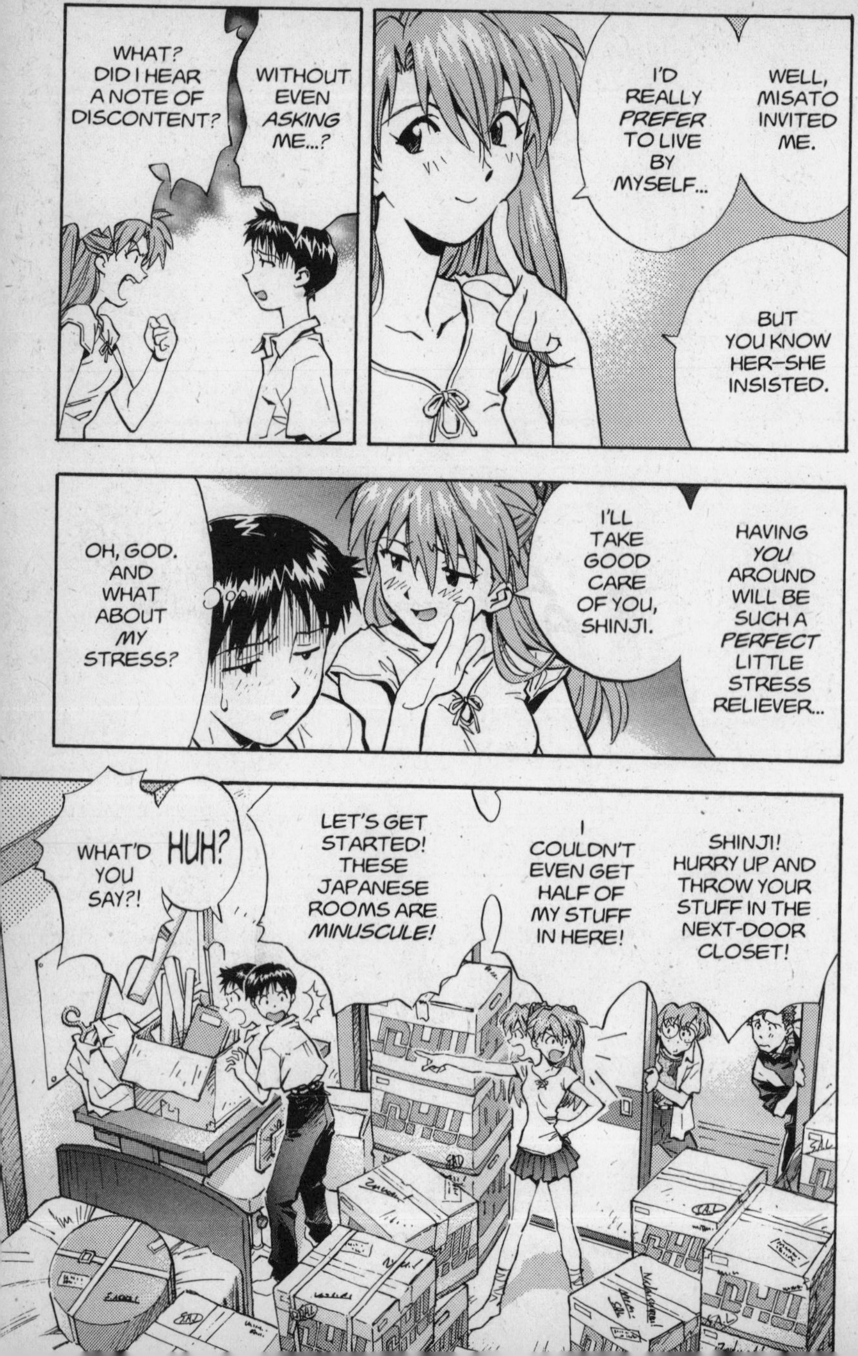
WELL, MISATO INVITED ME.
I'D REALLY *PREFER* TO LIVE BY MYSELF...
BUT YOU KNOW HER–SHE INSISTED.
WITHOUT EVEN *ASKING* ME...?
WHAT? DID I HEAR A NOTE OF DISCONTENT?
HAVING *YOU* AROUND WILL BE SUCH A *PERFECT* LITTLE STRESS RELIEVER...
I'LL TAKE GOOD CARE OF YOU, SHINJI.
OH, GOD. AND WHAT ABOUT *MY* STRESS?
SHINJI! HURRY UP AND THROW YOUR STUFF IN THE NEXT-DOOR CLOSET!
I COULDN'T EVEN GET HALF OF *MY STUFF* IN HERE!
LET'S GET STARTED! THESE JAPANESE ROOMS ARE *MINUSCULE!*
HUH?
WHAT'D YOU SAY?!

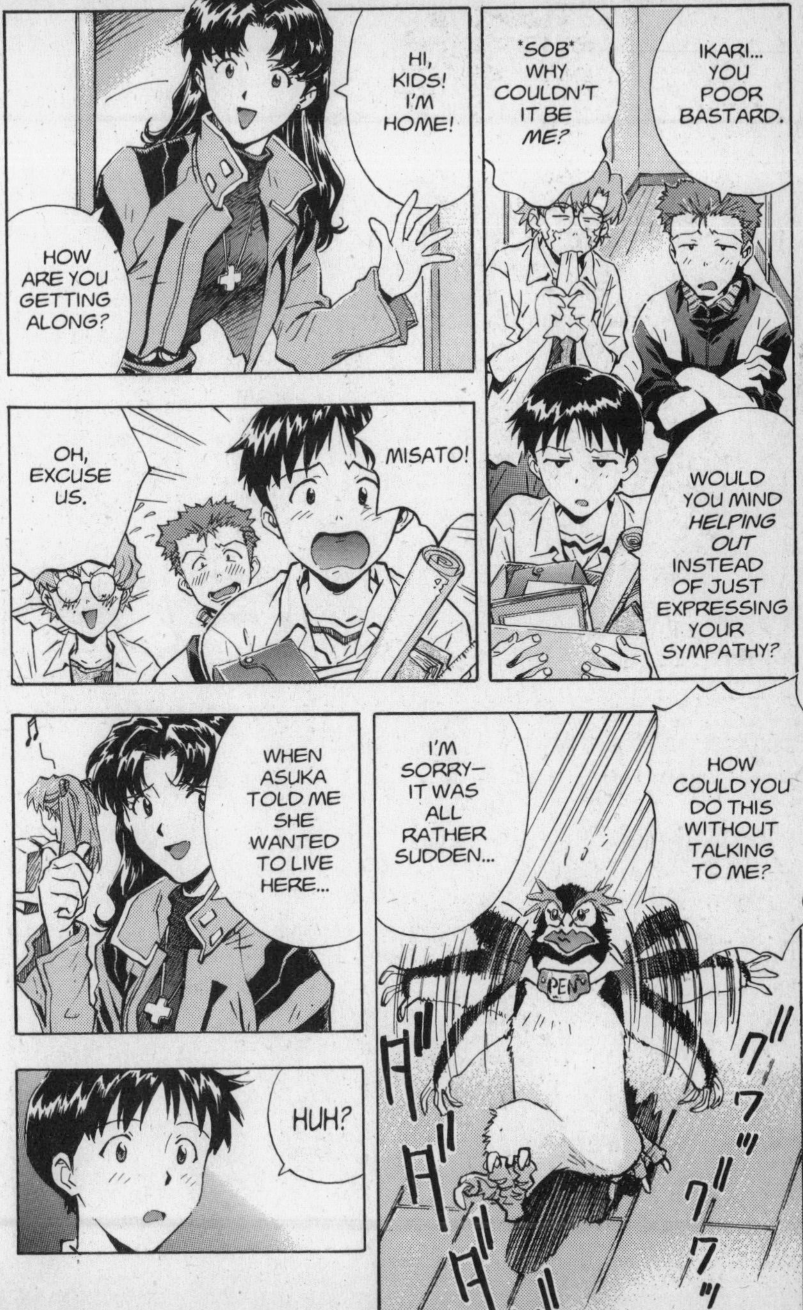
IKARI... YOU POOR BASTARD.
SOB WHY COULDN'T IT BE ME?
WOULD YOU MIND HELPING OUT INSTEAD OF JUST EXPRESSING YOUR SYMPATHY?
HI, KIDS! I'M HOME!
HOW ARE YOU GETTING ALONG?
MISATO!
OH, EXCUSE US.
HOW COULD YOU DO THIS WITHOUT TALKING TO ME?
I'M SORRY— IT WAS ALL RATHER SUDDEN...
WHEN ASUKA TOLD ME SHE WANTED TO LIVE HERE...
HUH?
PEN

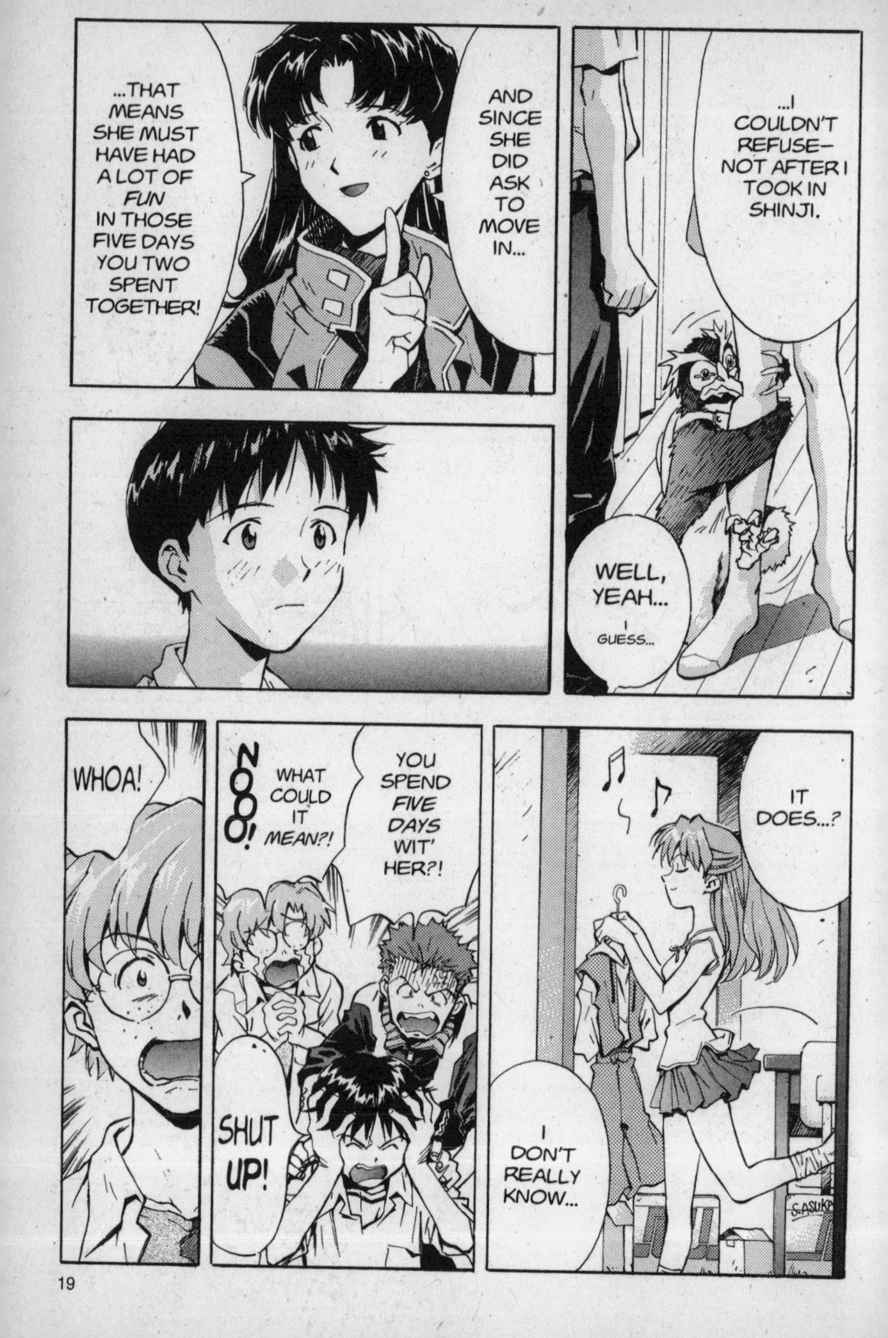
...I COULDN'T REFUSE— NOT AFTER I TOOK IN SHINJI.
WELL, YEAH... I GUESS...
AND SINCE SHE DID ASK TO MOVE IN...
...THAT MEANS SHE MUST HAVE HAD A LOT OF *FUN* IN THOSE FIVE DAYS YOU TWO SPENT TOGETHER!
IT DOES...?
I DON'T REALLY KNOW...
YOU SPEND *FIVE DAYS* WIT' HER?!
WHAT COULD IT *MEAN?!*
NOOO!
SHUT UP!
WHOA!
S.ASUKA

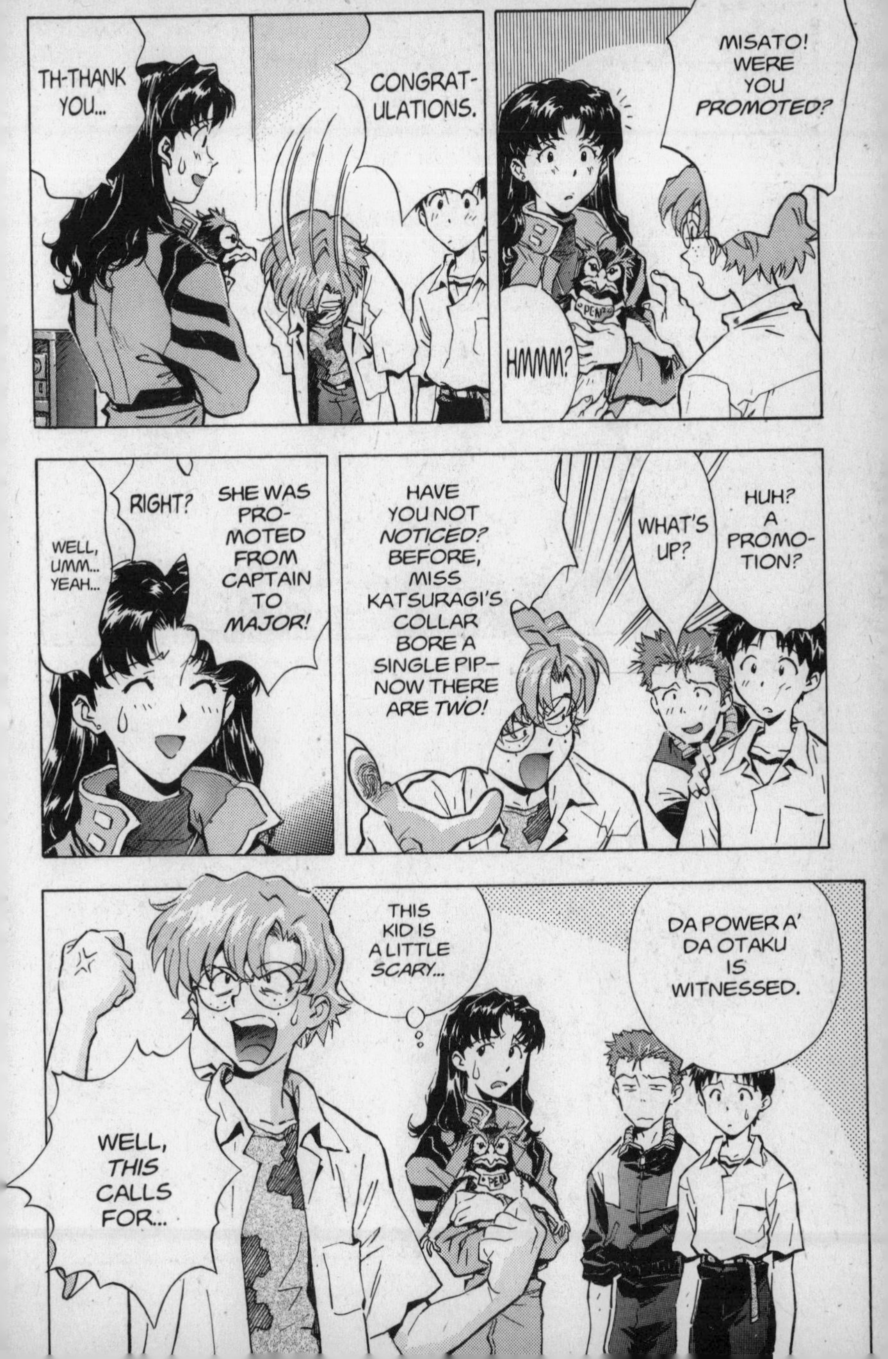
MISATO! WERE YOU *PROMOTED?*
HMMM?
CONGRAT-ULATIONS.
TH-THANK YOU...
HUH? A PROMO-TION?
WHAT'S UP?
HAVE YOU NOT *NOTICED?* BEFORE, MISS KATSURAGI'S COLLAR BORE A SINGLE PIP—NOW THERE ARE *TWO!*
SHE WAS PRO-MOTED FROM CAPTAIN TO *MAJOR!*
RIGHT?
WELL, UMM... YEAH...
DA POWER A' DA OTAKU IS WITNESSED.
THIS KID IS A LITTLE *SCARY...*
WELL, *THIS* CALLS FOR...

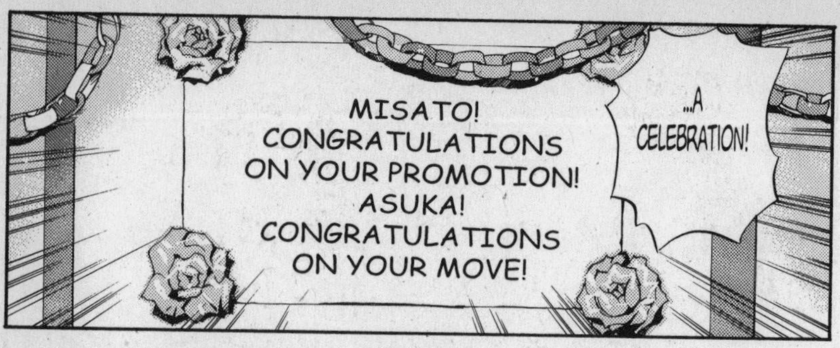
MISATO! CONGRATULATIONS ON YOUR PROMOTION! ASUKA! CONGRATULATIONS ON YOUR MOVE!
...A CELEBRATION!

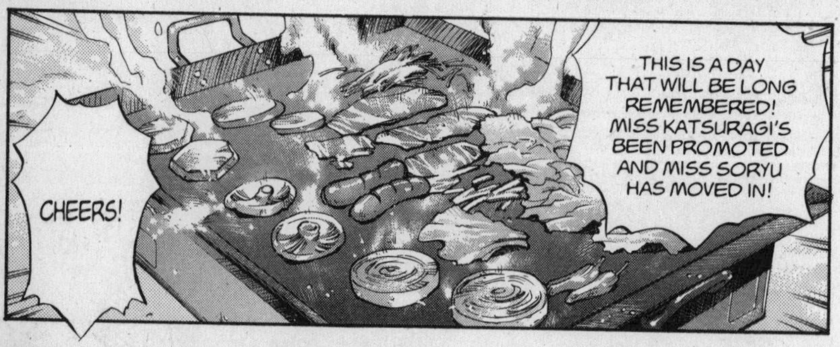
THIS IS A DAY THAT WILL BE LONG REMEMBERED! MISS KATSURAGI'S BEEN PROMOTED AND MISS SORYU HAS MOVED IN!
CHEERS!

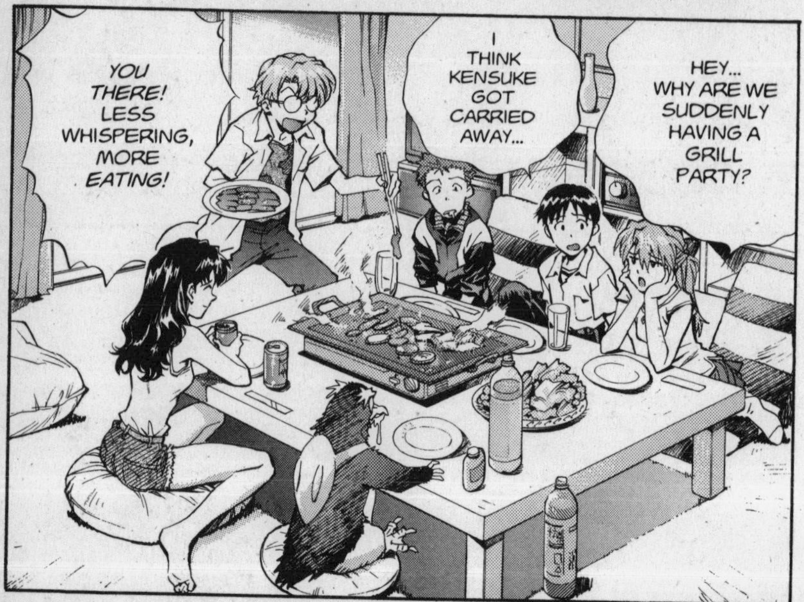
HEY... WHY ARE WE SUDDENLY HAVING A GRILL PARTY?
I THINK KENSUKE GOT CARRIED AWAY...
YOU THERE! LESS WHISPERING, MORE EATING!

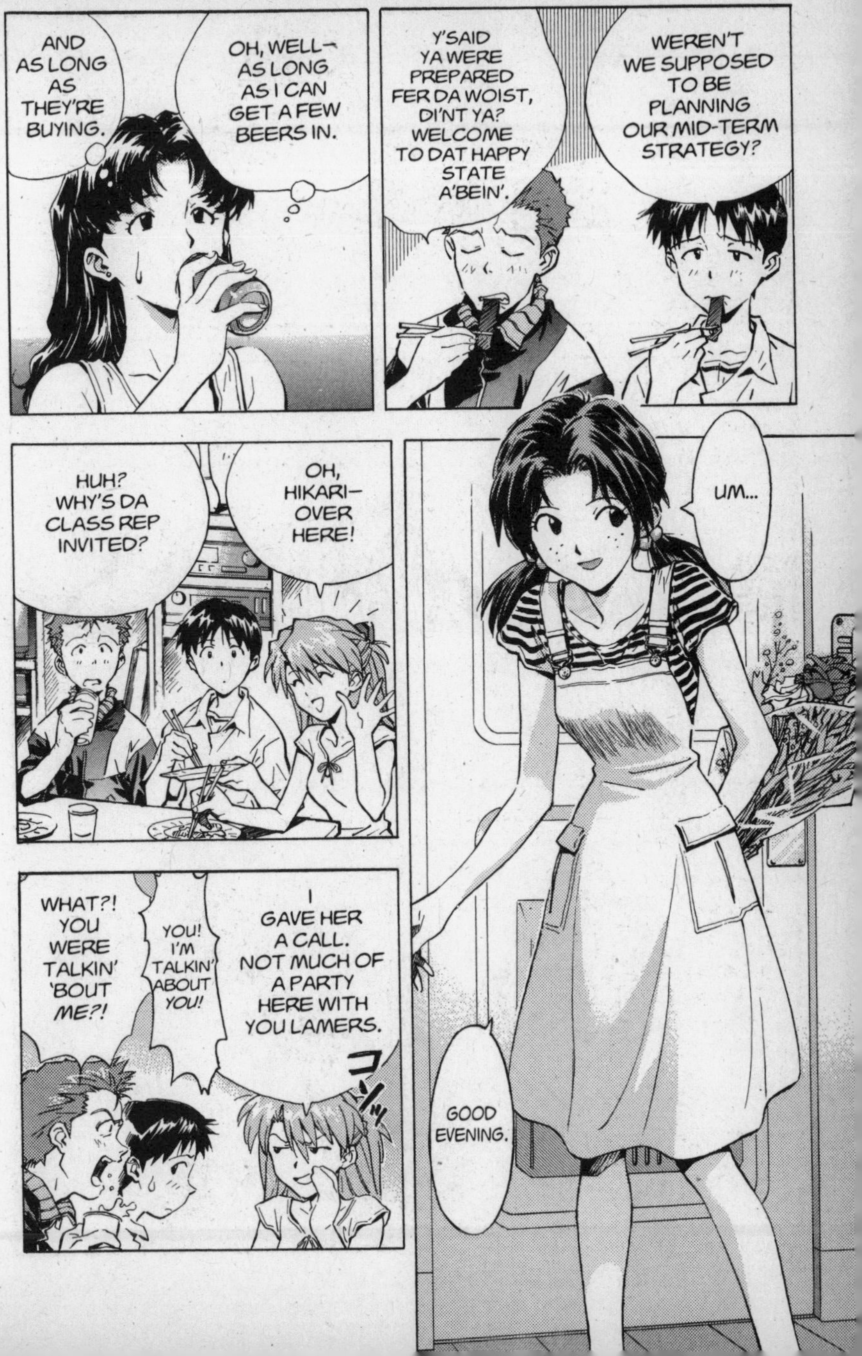
WEREN'T WE SUPPOSED TO BE PLANNING OUR MID-TERM STRATEGY?
Y'SAID YA WERE PREPARED FER DA WOIST, DI'NT YA? WELCOME TO DAT HAPPY STATE A'BEIN'.
OH, WELL— AS LONG AS I CAN GET A FEW BEERS IN.
AND AS LONG AS THEY'RE BUYING.
UM...
GOOD EVENING.
OH, HIKARI— OVER HERE!
HUH? WHY'S DA CLASS REP INVITED?
I GAVE HER A CALL. NOT MUCH OF A PARTY HERE WITH YOU LAMERS.
YOU! I'M TALKIN' ABOUT YOU!
WHAT?! YOU WERE TALKIN' 'BOUT ME?!

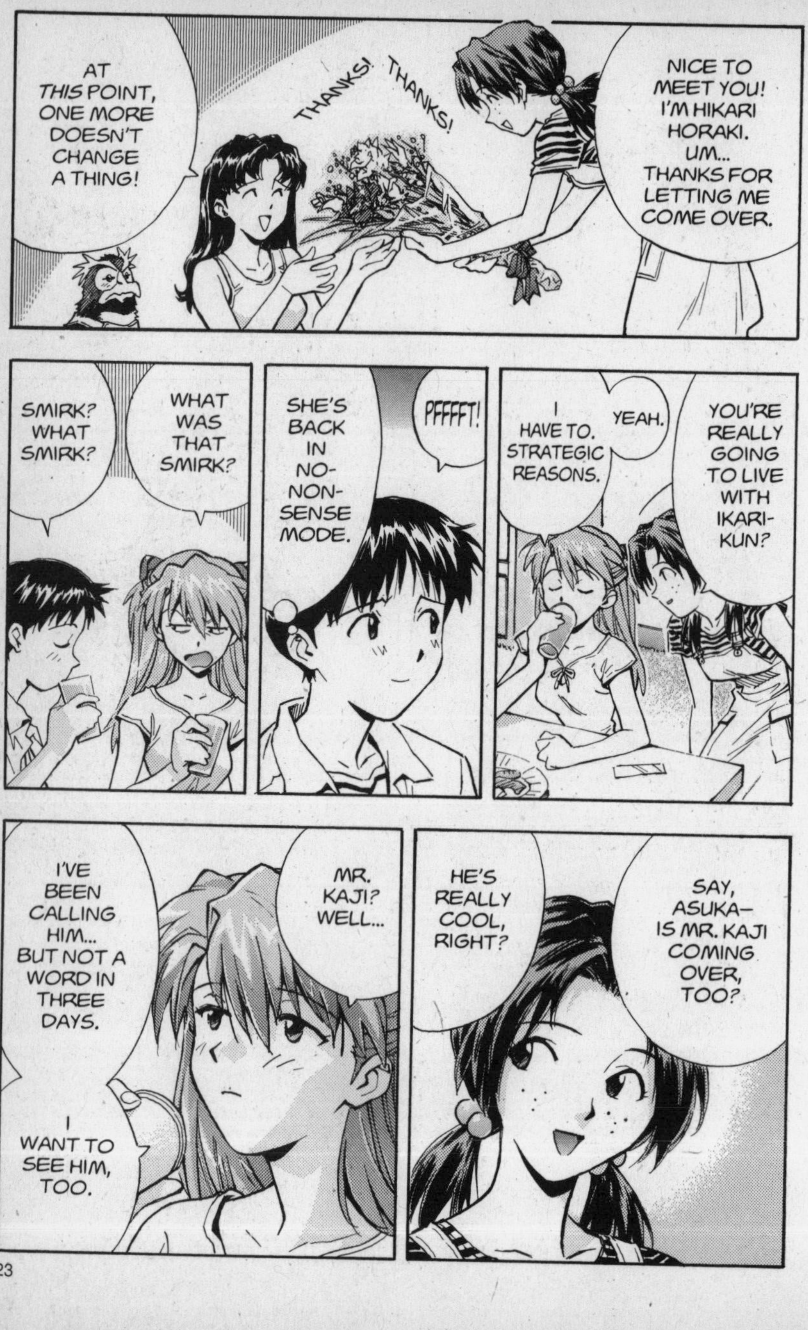
NICE TO MEET YOU! I'M HIKARI HORAKI. UM... THANKS FOR LETTING ME COME OVER.
THANKS! THANKS!
AT THIS POINT, ONE MORE DOESN'T CHANGE A THING!
YOU'RE REALLY GOING TO LIVE WITH IKARI-KUN?
YEAH.
I HAVE TO. STRATEGIC REASONS.
PFFFFT!
SHE'S BACK IN NO-NONSENSE MODE.
WHAT WAS THAT SMIRK?
SMIRK? WHAT SMIRK?
SAY, ASUKA— IS MR. KAJI COMING OVER, TOO?
HE'S REALLY COOL, RIGHT?
MR. KAJI? WELL...
I'VE BEEN CALLING HIM... BUT NOT A WORD IN THREE DAYS.
I WANT TO SEE HIM, TOO.

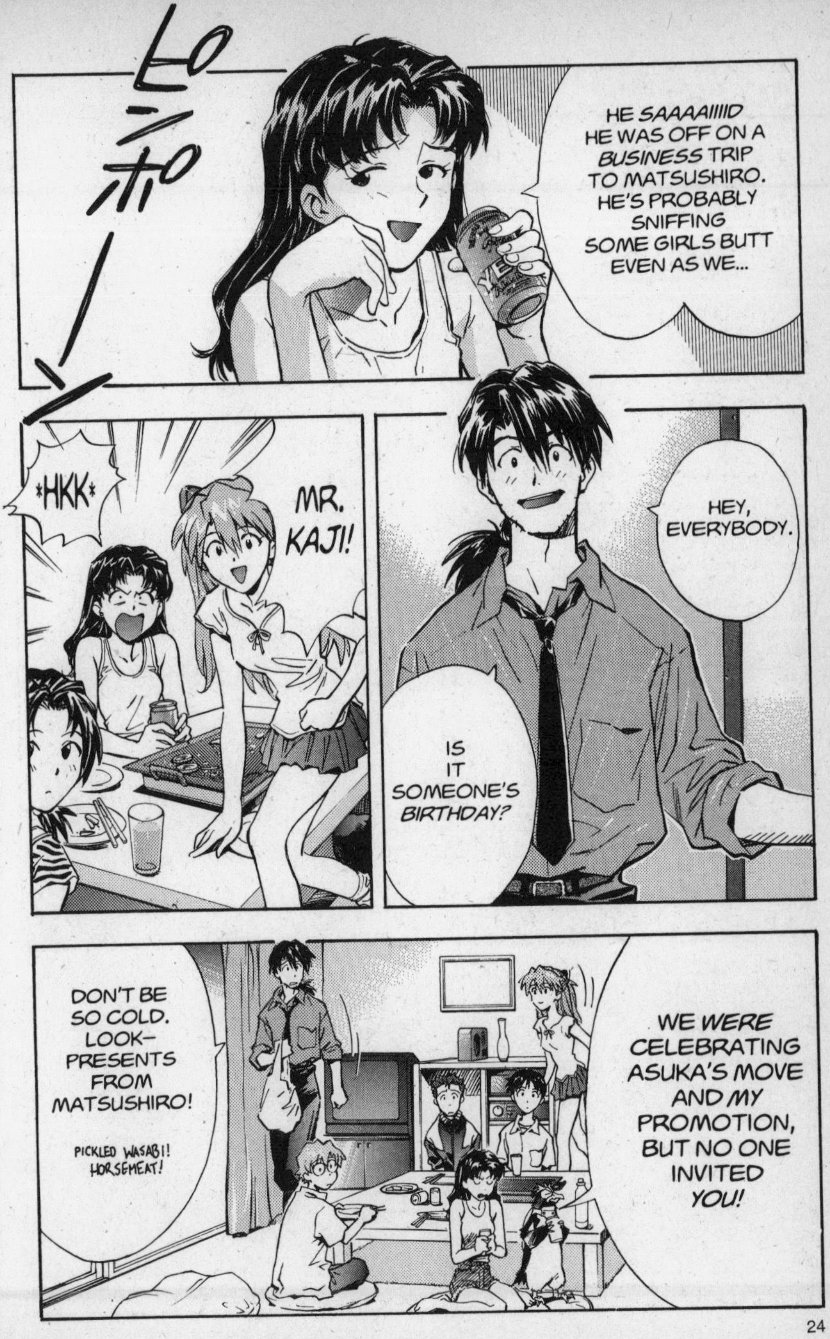

HE SAAAAIIIID HE WAS OFF ON A BUSINESS TRIP TO MATSUSHIRO. HE'S PROBABLY SNIFFING SOME GIRLS BUTT EVEN AS WE...
ピンポーン
HEY, EVERYBODY.
IS IT SOMEONE'S BIRTHDAY?
MR. KAJI!
HKK
WE WERE CELEBRATING ASUKA'S MOVE AND MY PROMOTION, BUT NO ONE INVITED YOU!
DON'T BE SO COLD. LOOK—PRESENTS FROM MATSUSHIRO!
PICKLED WASABI! HORSEMEAT!

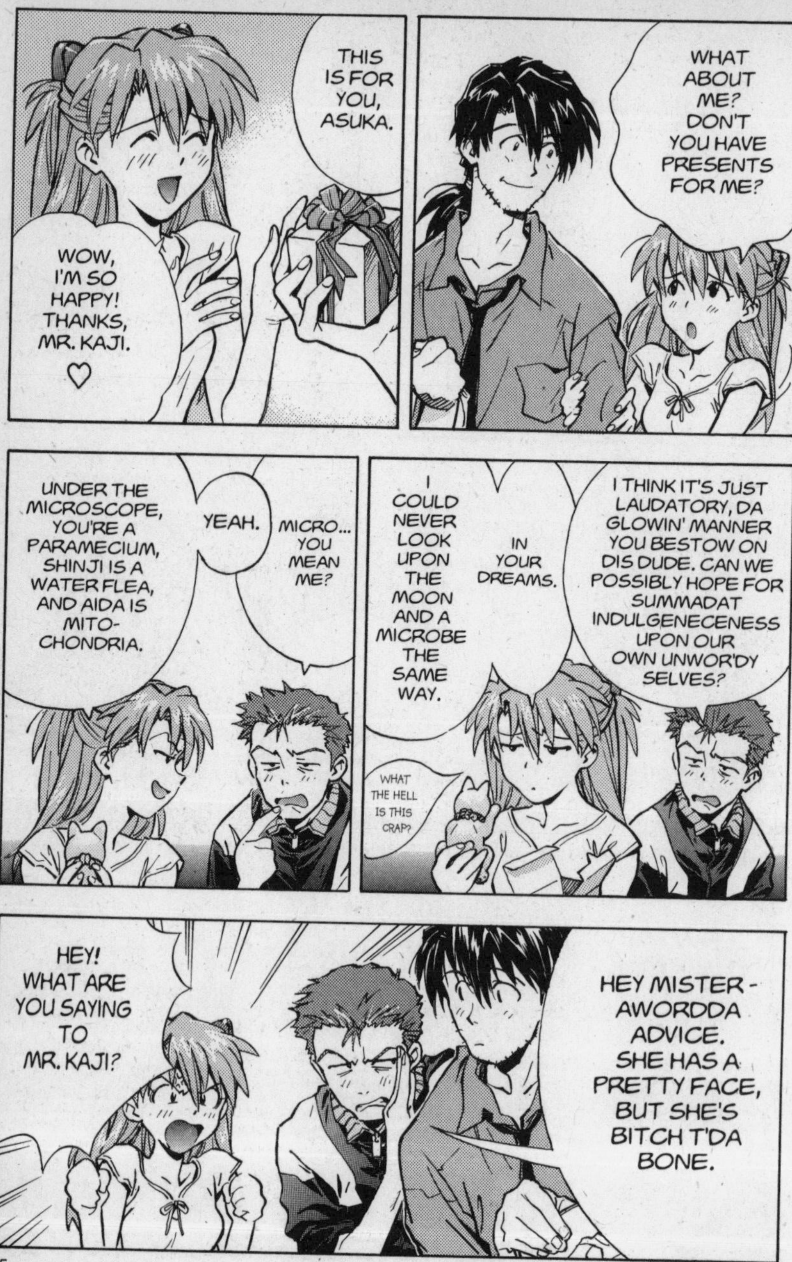
THIS IS FOR YOU, ASUKA.
WOW, I'M SO HAPPY! THANKS, MR. KAJI. ♡
WHAT ABOUT ME? DON'T YOU HAVE PRESENTS FOR ME?
UNDER THE MICROSCOPE, YOU'RE A PARAMECIUM, SHINJI IS A WATER FLEA, AND AIDA IS MITO-CHONDRIA.
YEAH.
MICRO... YOU MEAN ME?
I COULD NEVER LOOK UPON THE MOON AND A MICROBE THE SAME WAY.
IN YOUR DREAMS.
I THINK IT'S JUST LAUDATORY, DA GLOWIN' MANNER YOU BESTOW ON DIS DUDE. CAN WE POSSIBLY HOPE FOR SUMMADAT INDULGENECENESS UPON OUR OWN UNWOR'DY SELVES?
WHAT THE HELL IS THIS CRAP?
HEY MISTER - AWORDDA ADVICE. SHE HAS A PRETTY FACE, BUT SHE'S BITCH T'DA BONE.
HEY! WHAT ARE YOU SAYING TO MR. KAJI?

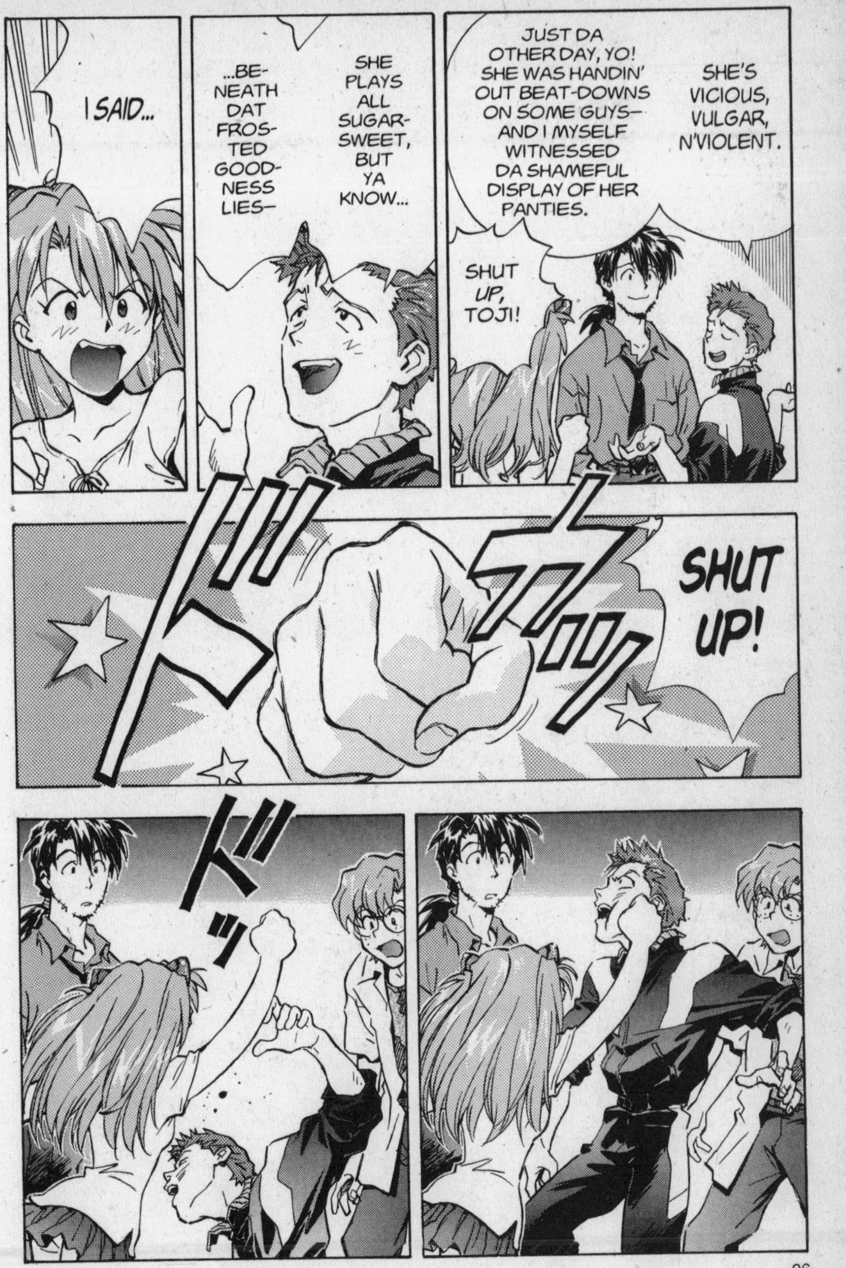
SHE'S VICIOUS, VULGAR, N'VIOLENT.
JUST DA OTHER DAY, YO! SHE WAS HANDIN' OUT BEAT-DOWNS ON SOME GUYS— AND I MYSELF WITNESSED DA SHAMEFUL DISPLAY OF HER PANTIES.
SHUT UP, TOJI!
SHE PLAYS ALL SUGAR-SWEET, BUT YA KNOW...
...BE-NEATH DAT FROS-TED GOOD-NESS LIES—
I SAID...
SHUT UP!

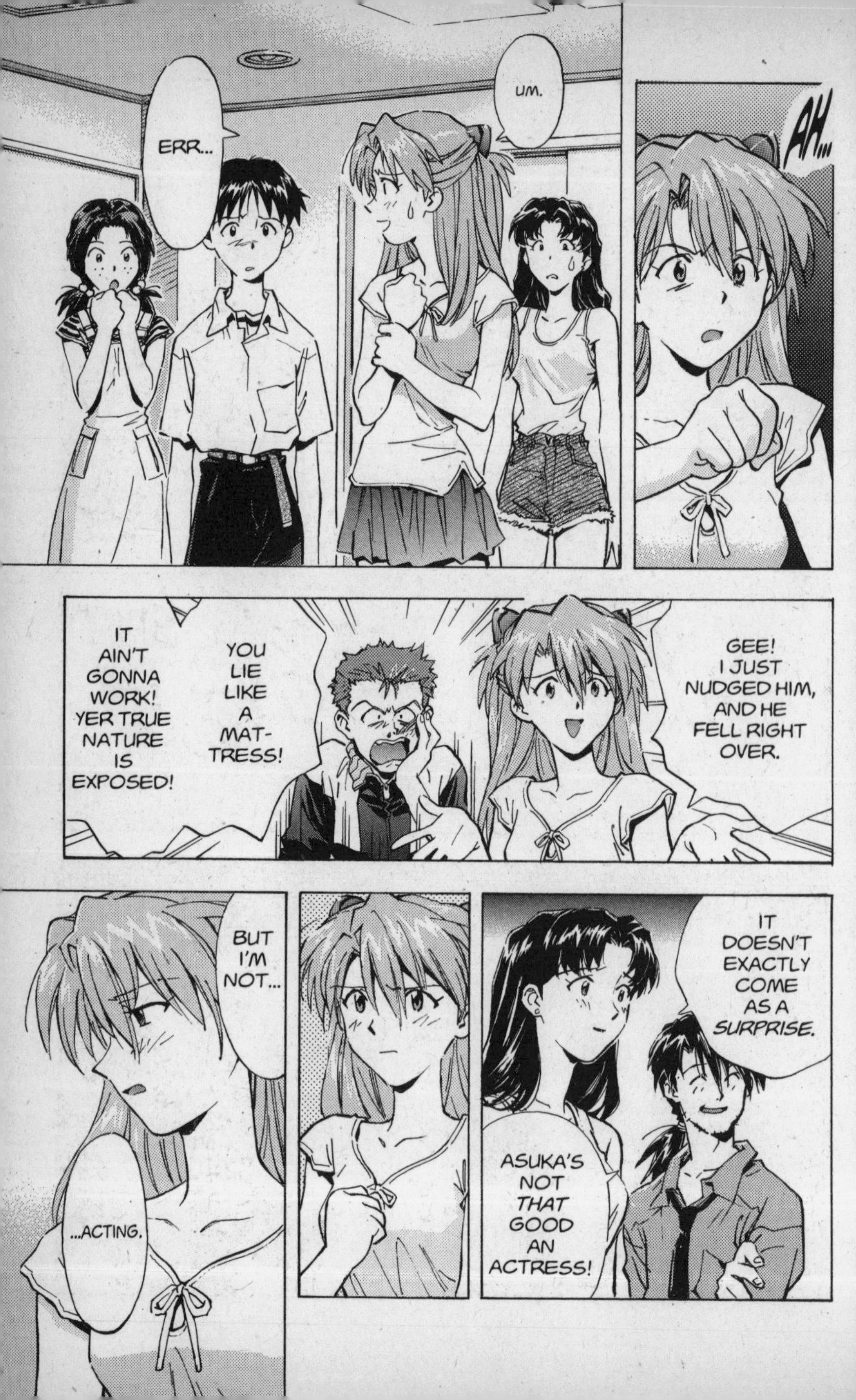
AH...
UM.
ERR...
GEE! I JUST NUDGED HIM, AND HE FELL RIGHT OVER.
YOU LIE LIKE A MAT-TRESS!
IT AIN'T GONNA WORK! YER TRUE NATURE IS EXPOSED!
IT DOESN'T EXACTLY COME AS A SURPRISE.
ASUKA'S NOT THAT GOOD AN ACTRESS!
BUT I'M NOT...
...ACTING.

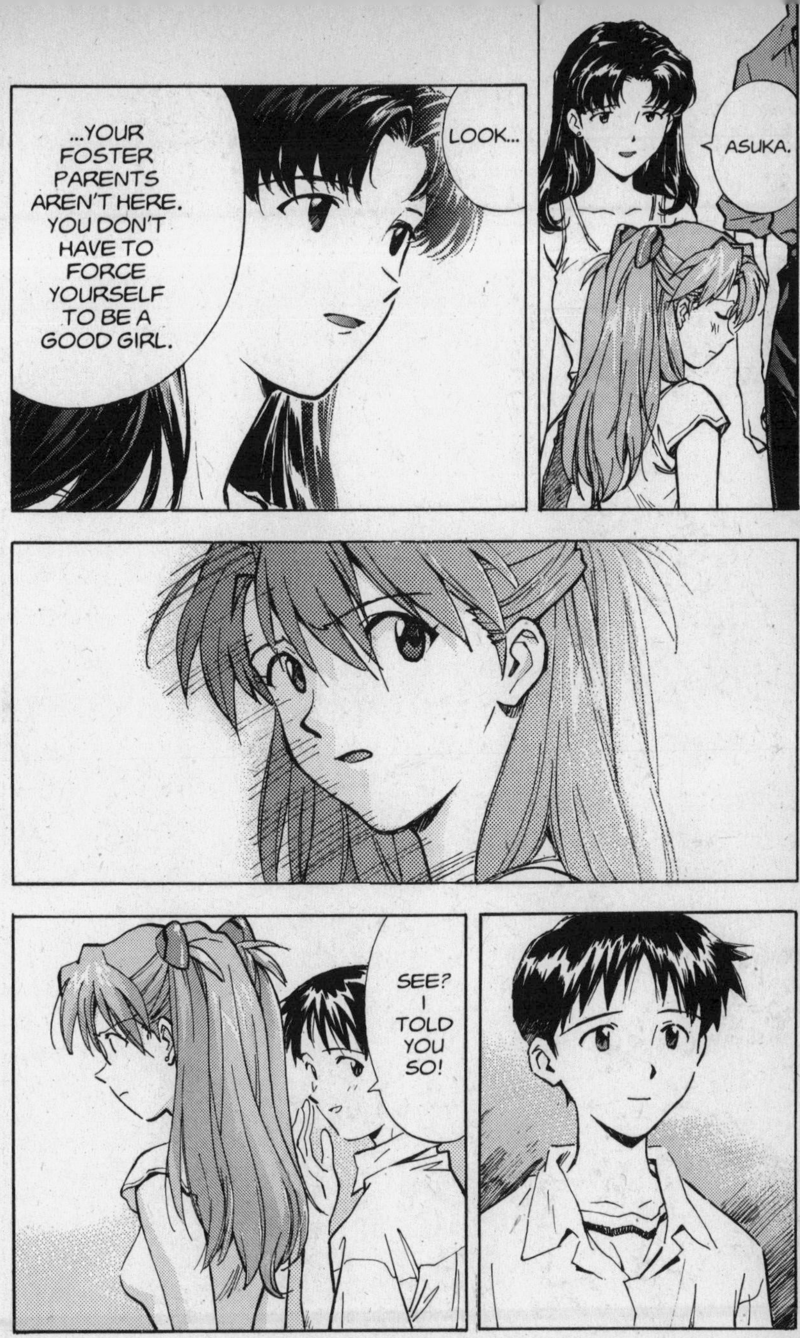
ASUKA.
LOOK...
...YOUR FOSTER PARENTS AREN'T HERE. YOU DON'T HAVE TO FORCE YOURSELF TO BE A GOOD GIRL.
SEE? I TOLD YOU SO!

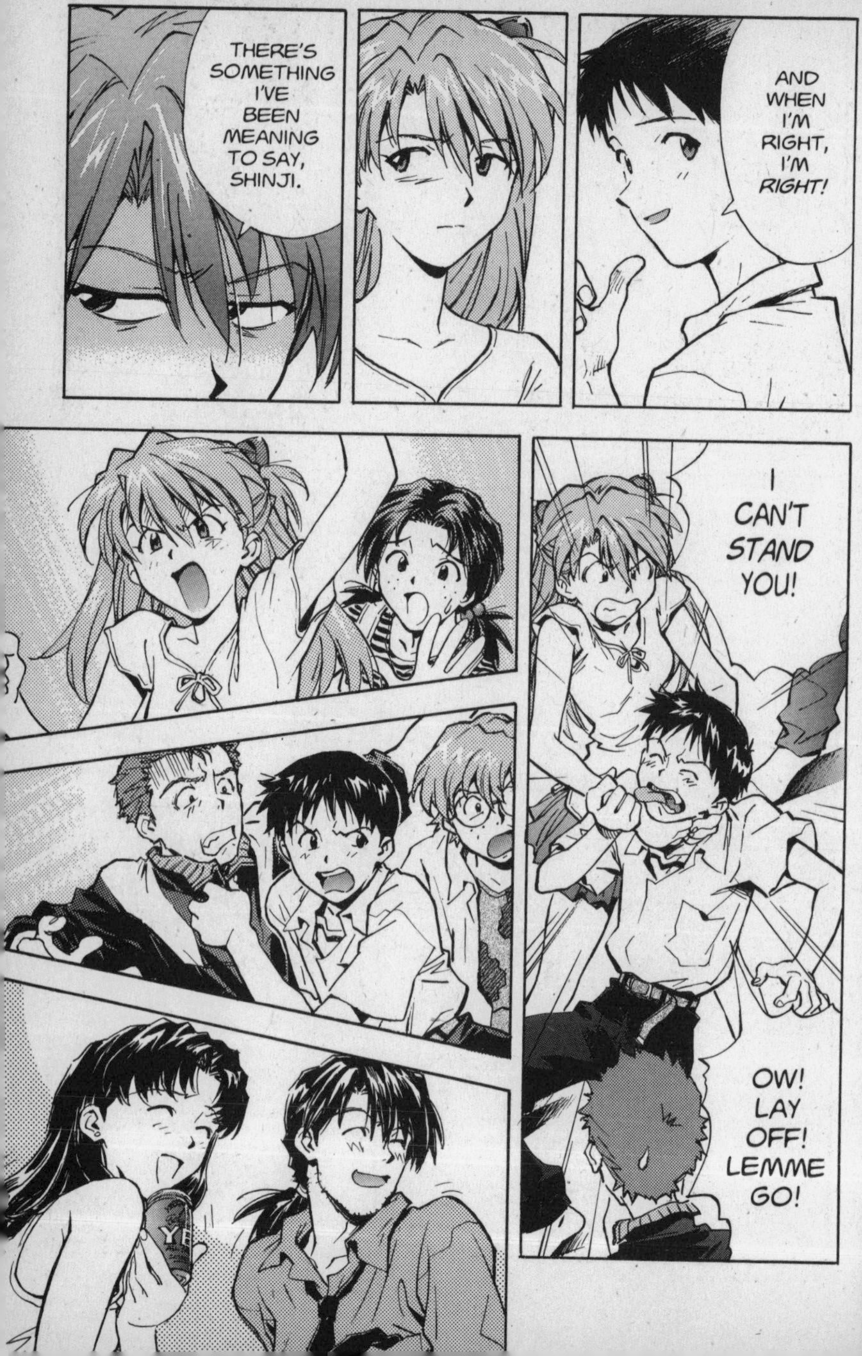
AND WHEN I'M RIGHT, I'M RIGHT!
THERE'S SOMETHING I'VE BEEN MEANING TO SAY, SHINJI.
I CAN'T STAND YOU!
OW! LAY OFF! LEMME GO!

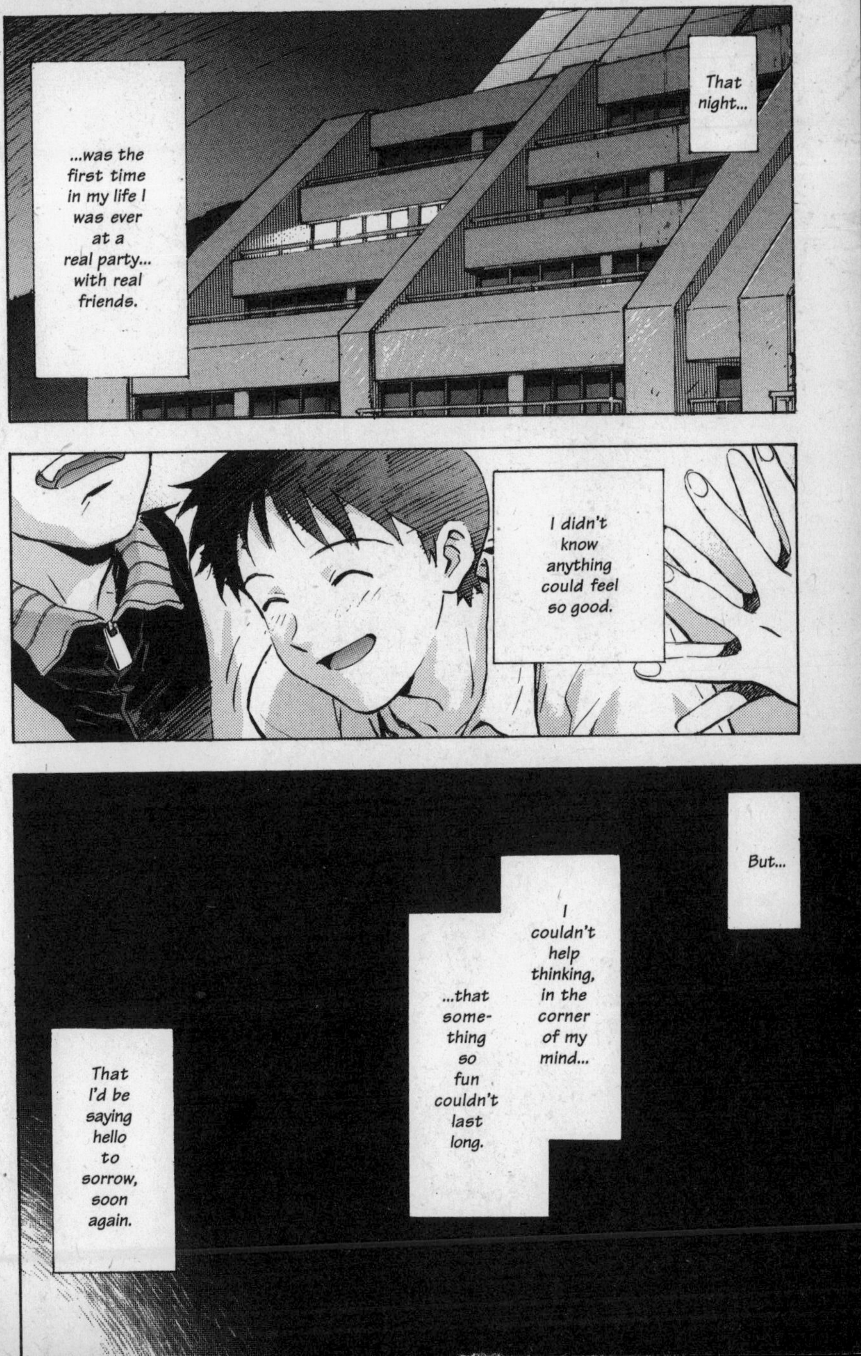
That night...
...was the first time in my life I was ever at a real party... with real friends.
I didn't know anything could feel so good.
But...
I couldn't help thinking, in the corner of my mind...
...that something so fun couldn't last long.
That I'd be saying hello to sorrow, soon again.

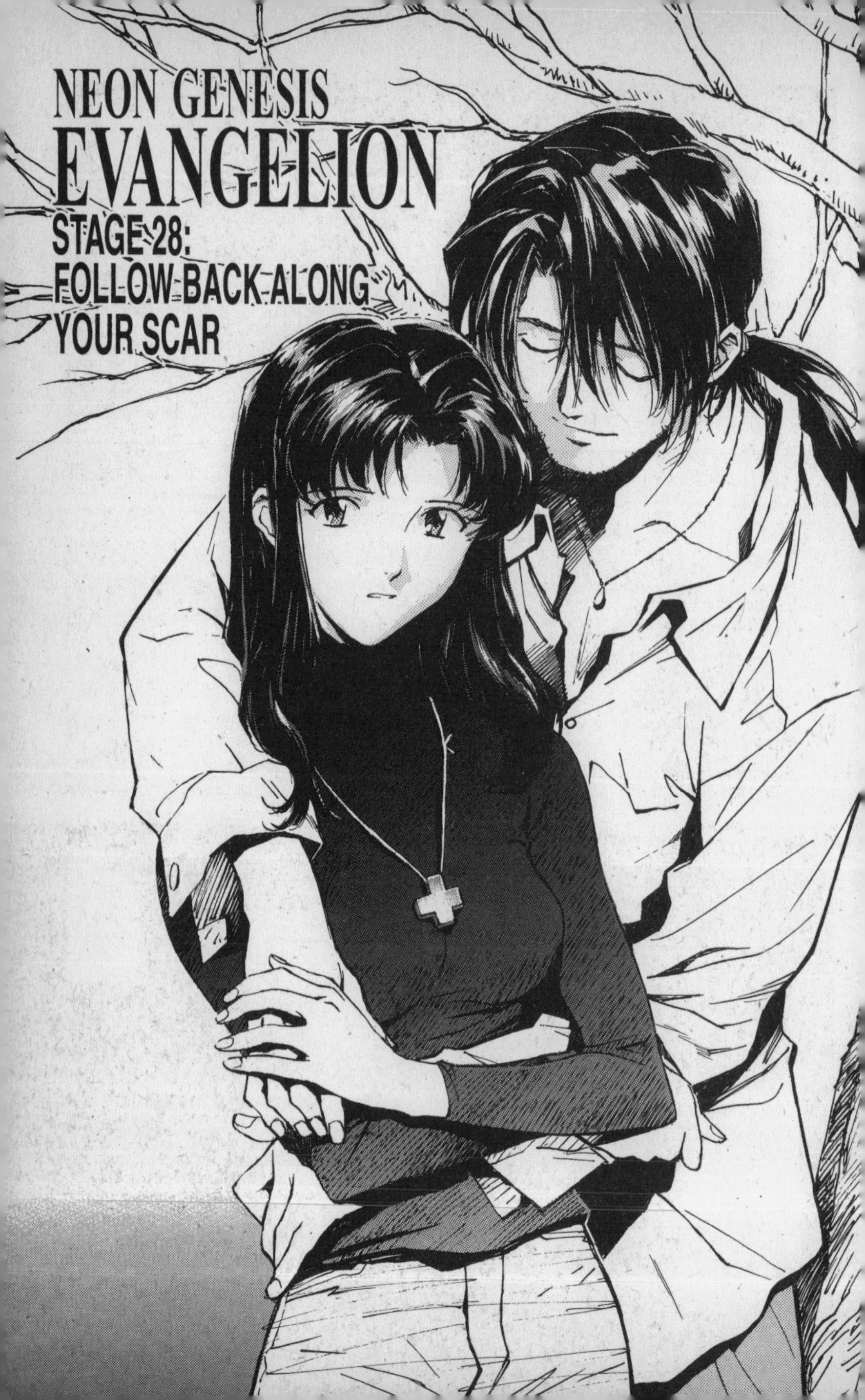
NEON GENESIS
EVANGELION
STAGE 28:
FOLLOW BACK ALONG
YOUR SCAR

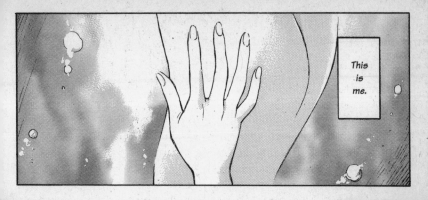

This
is
me.

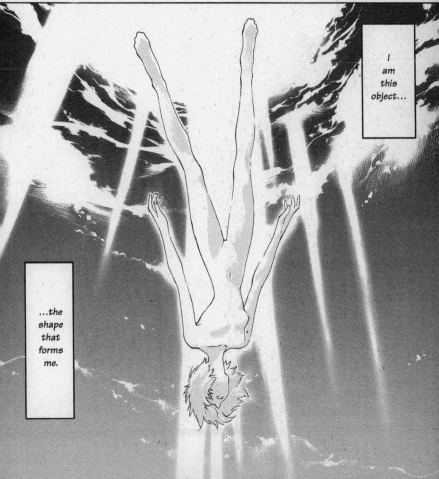

I
am
this
object...

...the
shape
that
forms
me.

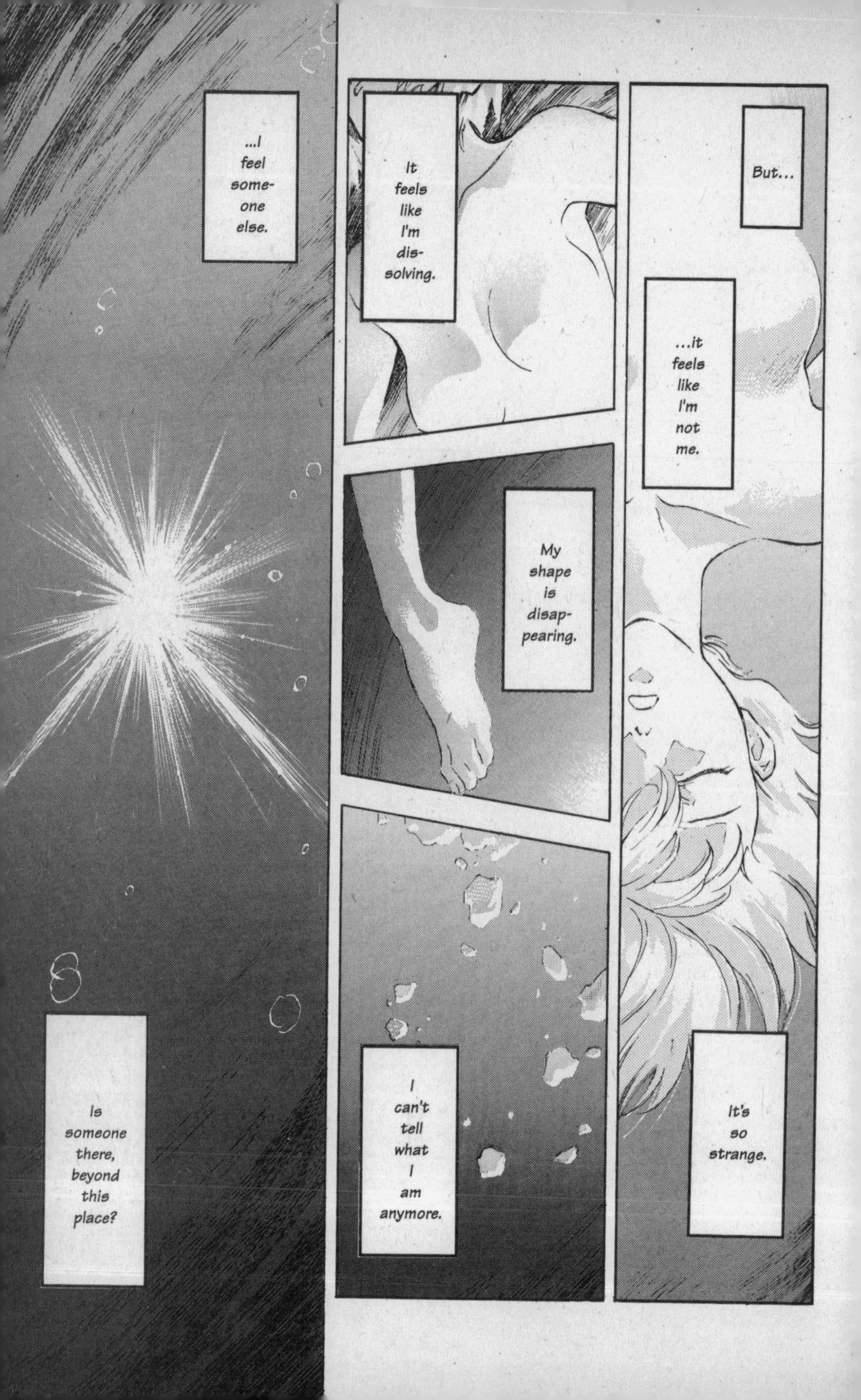
But...
...it feels like I'm not me.
It's so strange.
It feels like I'm dis-solving.
My shape is disap-pearing.
I can't tell what I am anymore.
...I feel some-one else.
Is someone there, beyond this place?

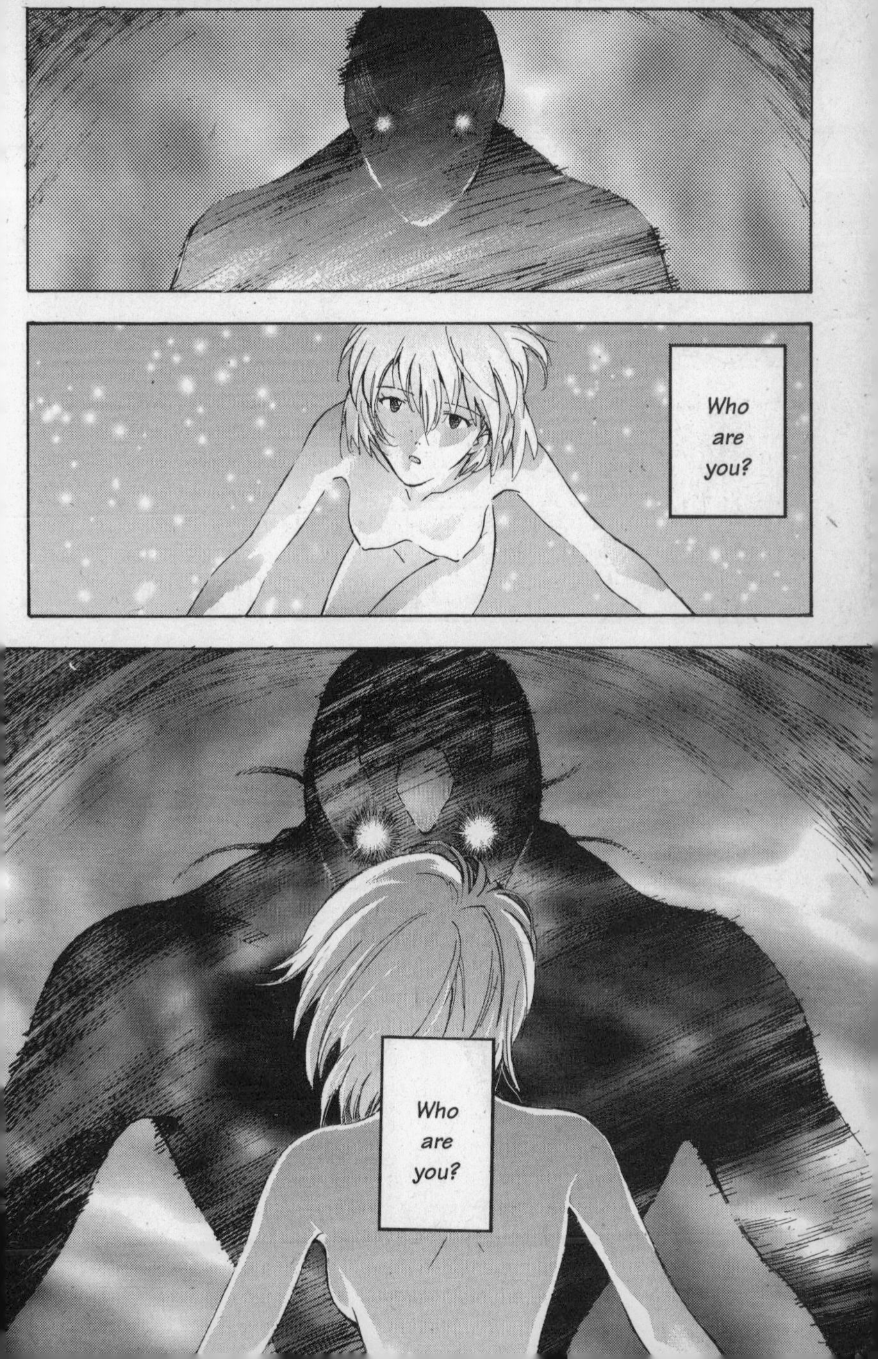
Who are you?
Who are you?

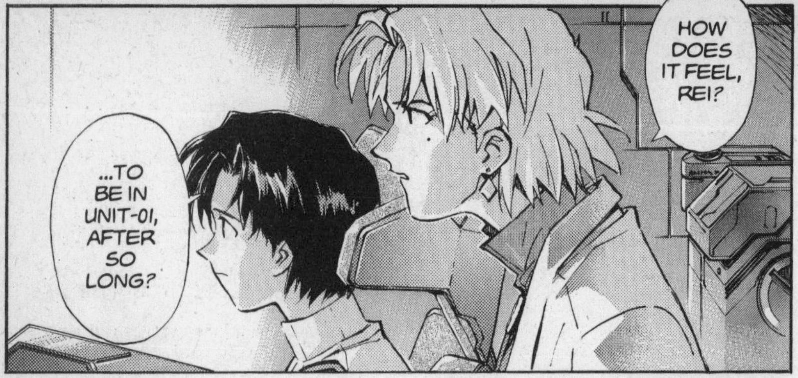
HOW DOES IT FEEL, REI?
...TO BE IN UNIT-01, AFTER SO LONG?
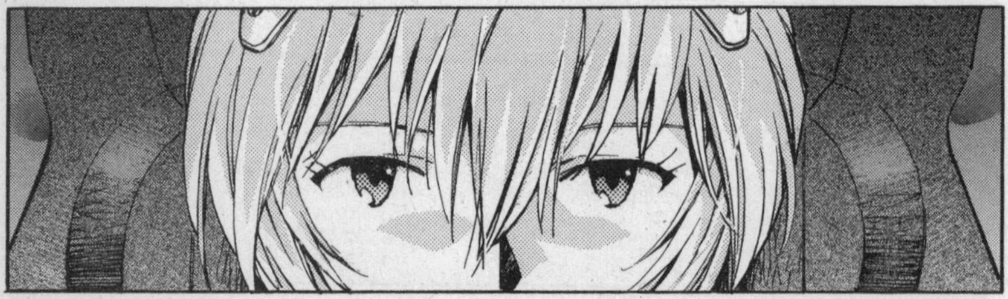
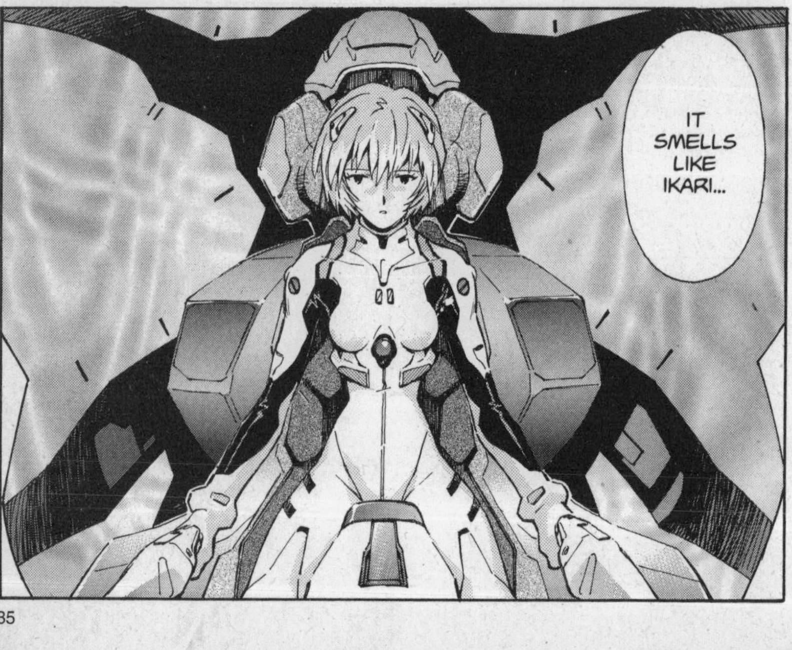
IT SMELLS LIKE IKARI...

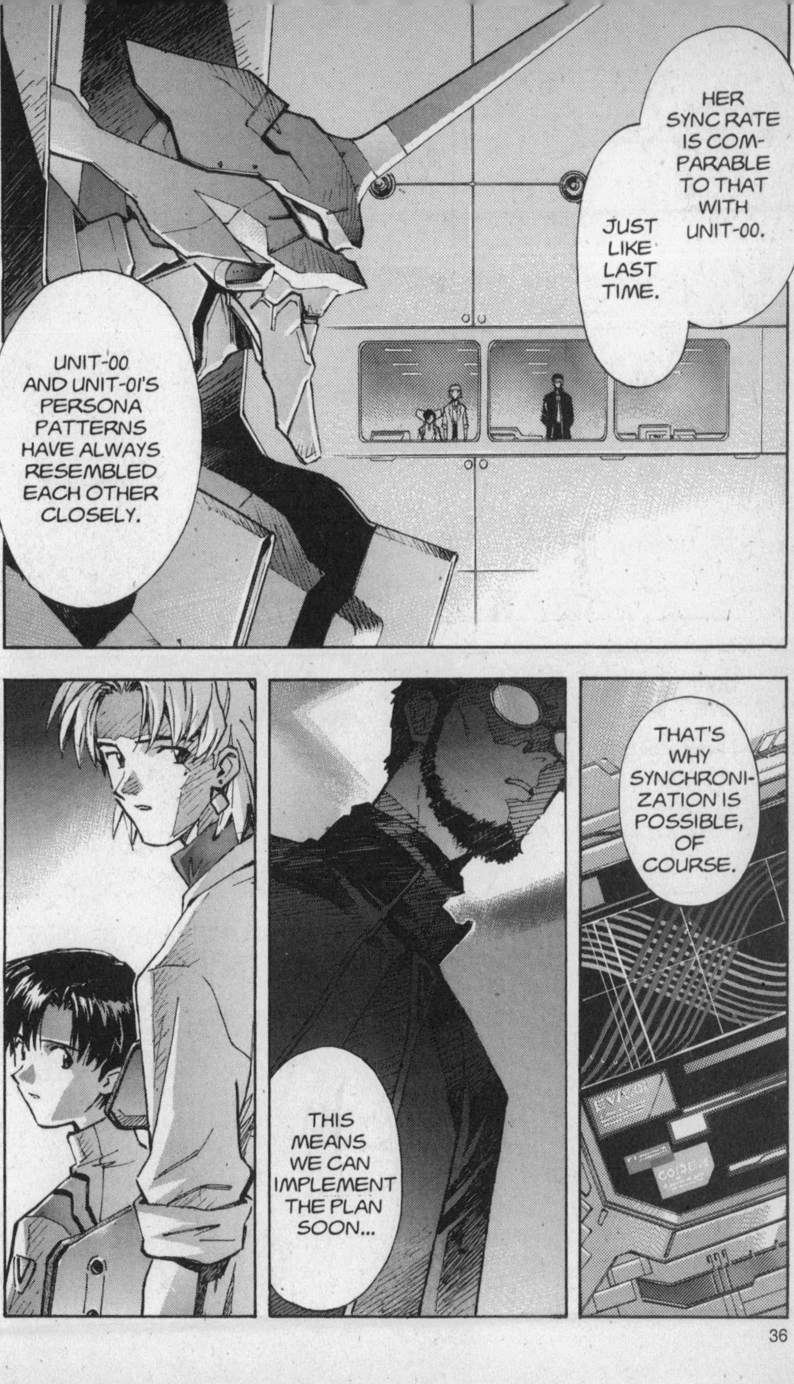
HER SYNC RATE IS COMPARABLE TO THAT WITH UNIT-00.
JUST LIKE LAST TIME.
UNIT-00 AND UNIT-01'S PERSONA PATTERNS HAVE ALWAYS RESEMBLED EACH OTHER CLOSELY.
THAT'S WHY SYNCHRONIZATION IS POSSIBLE, OF COURSE.
THIS MEANS WE CAN IMPLEMENT THE PLAN SOON...

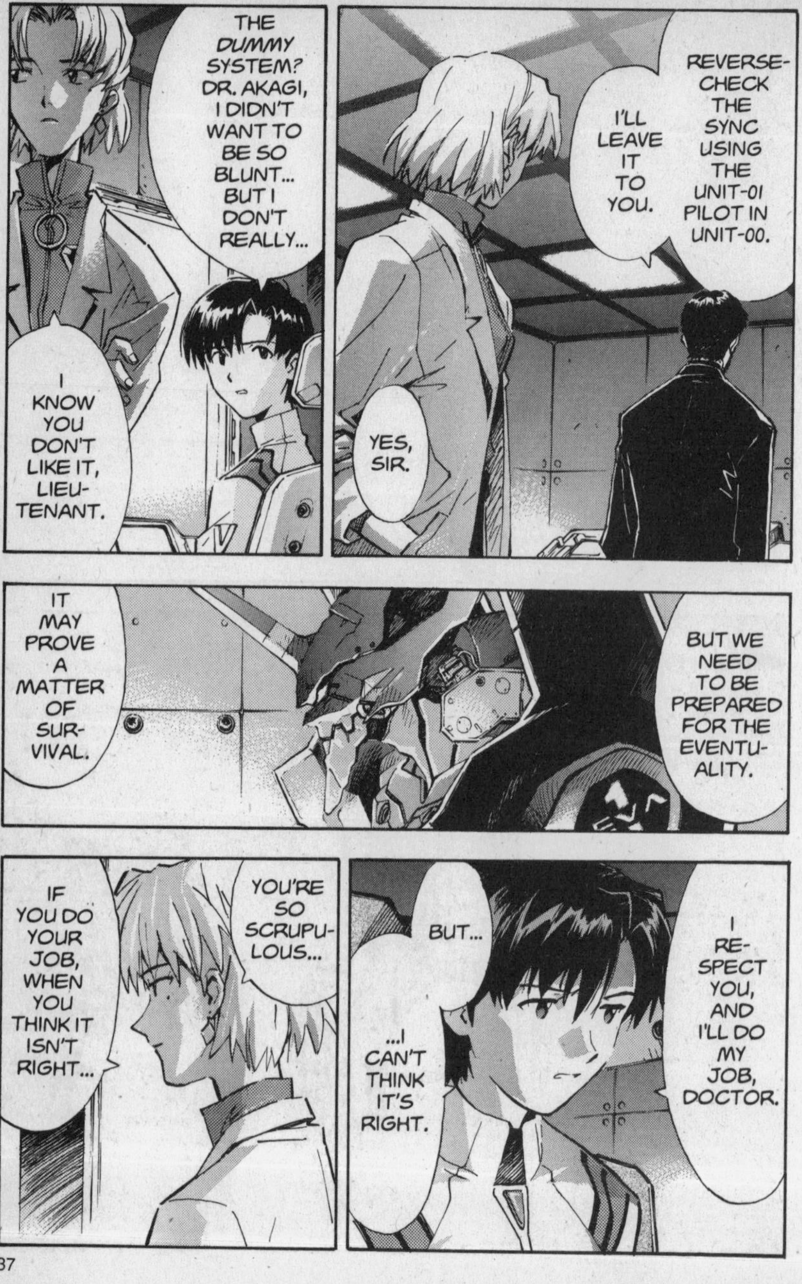
REVERSE-CHECK THE SYNC USING THE UNIT-01 PILOT IN UNIT-00.
I'LL LEAVE IT TO YOU.
YES, SIR.
THE *DUMMY* SYSTEM? DR. AKAGI, I DIDN'T WANT TO BE SO BLUNT... BUT I DON'T REALLY...
I KNOW YOU DON'T LIKE IT, LIEUTENANT.
BUT WE NEED TO BE PREPARED FOR THE EVENTUALITY.
IT MAY PROVE A MATTER OF SURVIVAL.
I RESPECT YOU, AND I'LL DO MY JOB, DOCTOR.
BUT...
...I CAN'T THINK IT'S RIGHT.
YOU'RE SO SCRUPULOUS...
IF YOU DO YOUR JOB, WHEN YOU THINK IT ISN'T RIGHT...

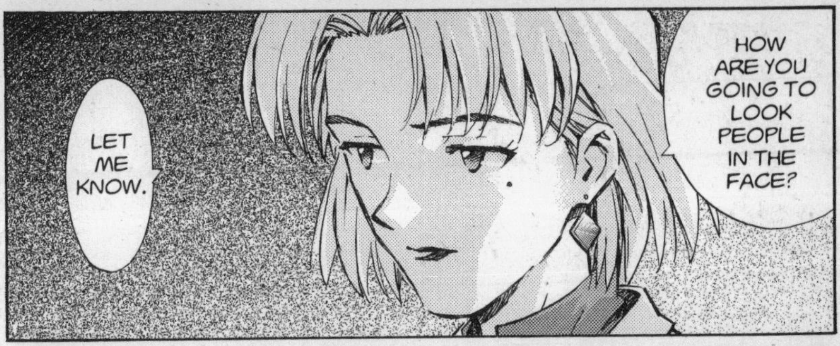
HOW ARE YOU GOING TO LOOK PEOPLE IN THE FACE?
LET ME KNOW.
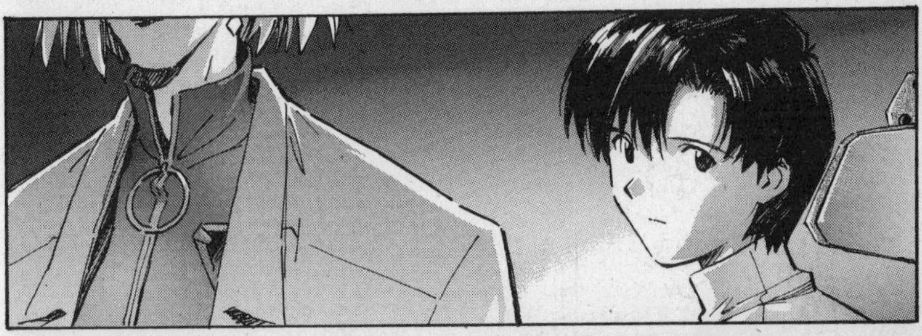
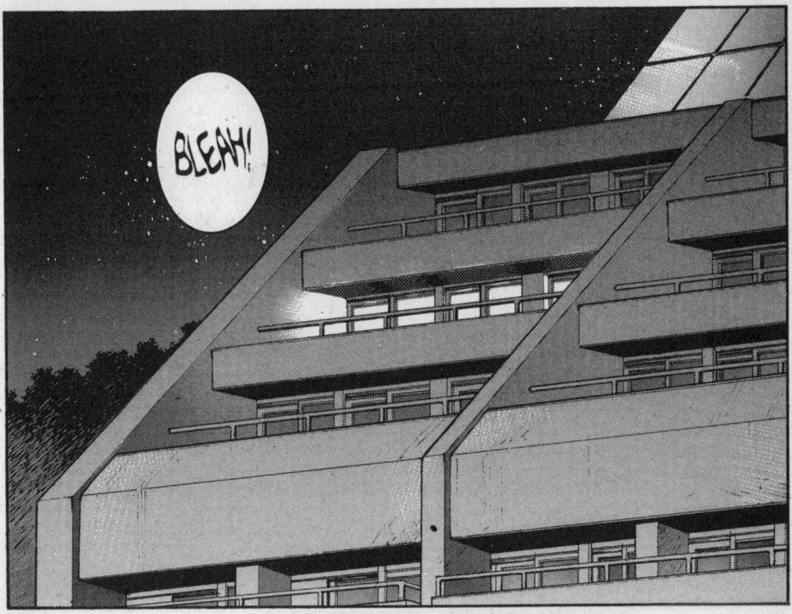
BLEAH!

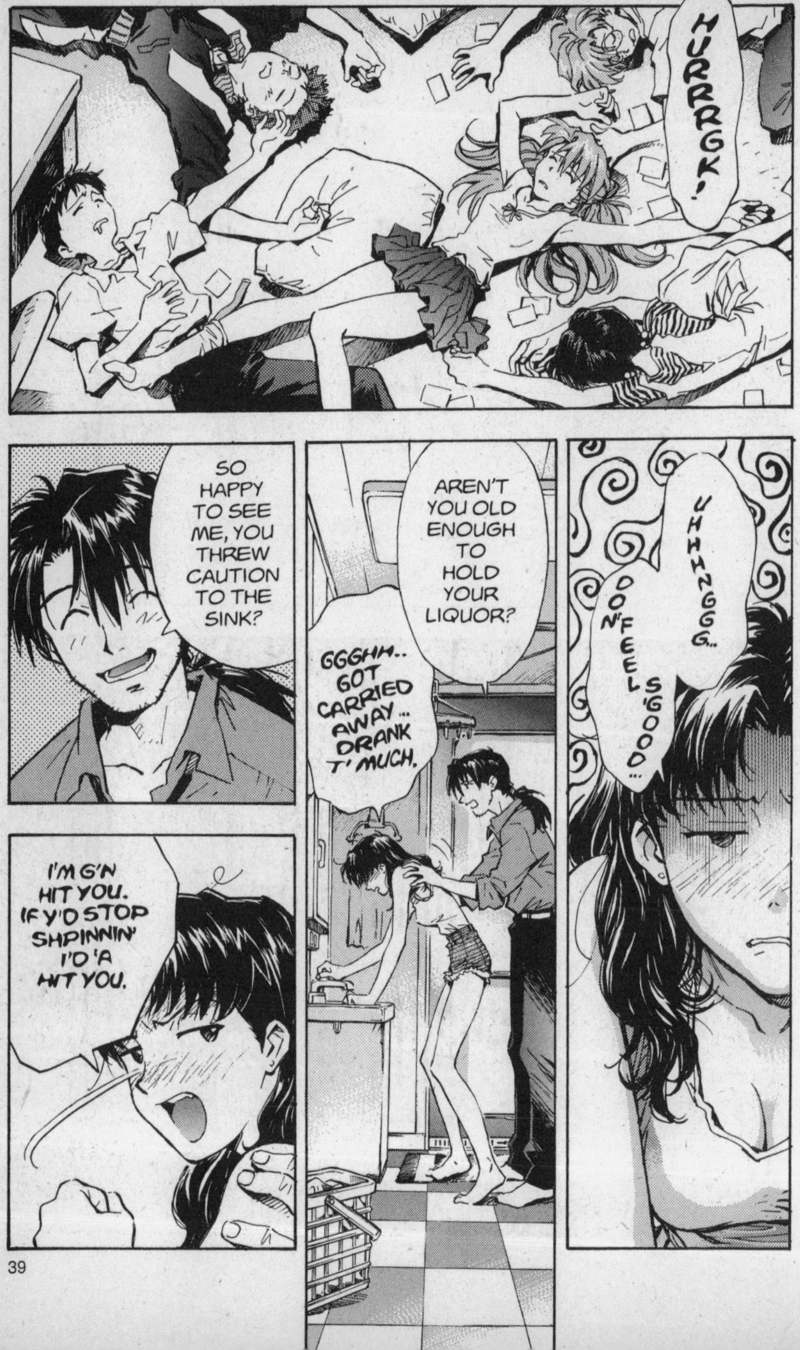
HURRRGK!
UHHHNGGG...
DON' FEEL S'GOOOD...
AREN'T YOU OLD ENOUGH TO HOLD YOUR LIQUOR?
GGGHH.. GOT CARRIED AWAY... DRANK T'MUCH.
SO HAPPY TO SEE ME, YOU THREW CAUTION TO THE SINK?
I'M G'N HIT YOU. IF Y'D STOP SHPINNIN' I'D 'A HIT YOU.

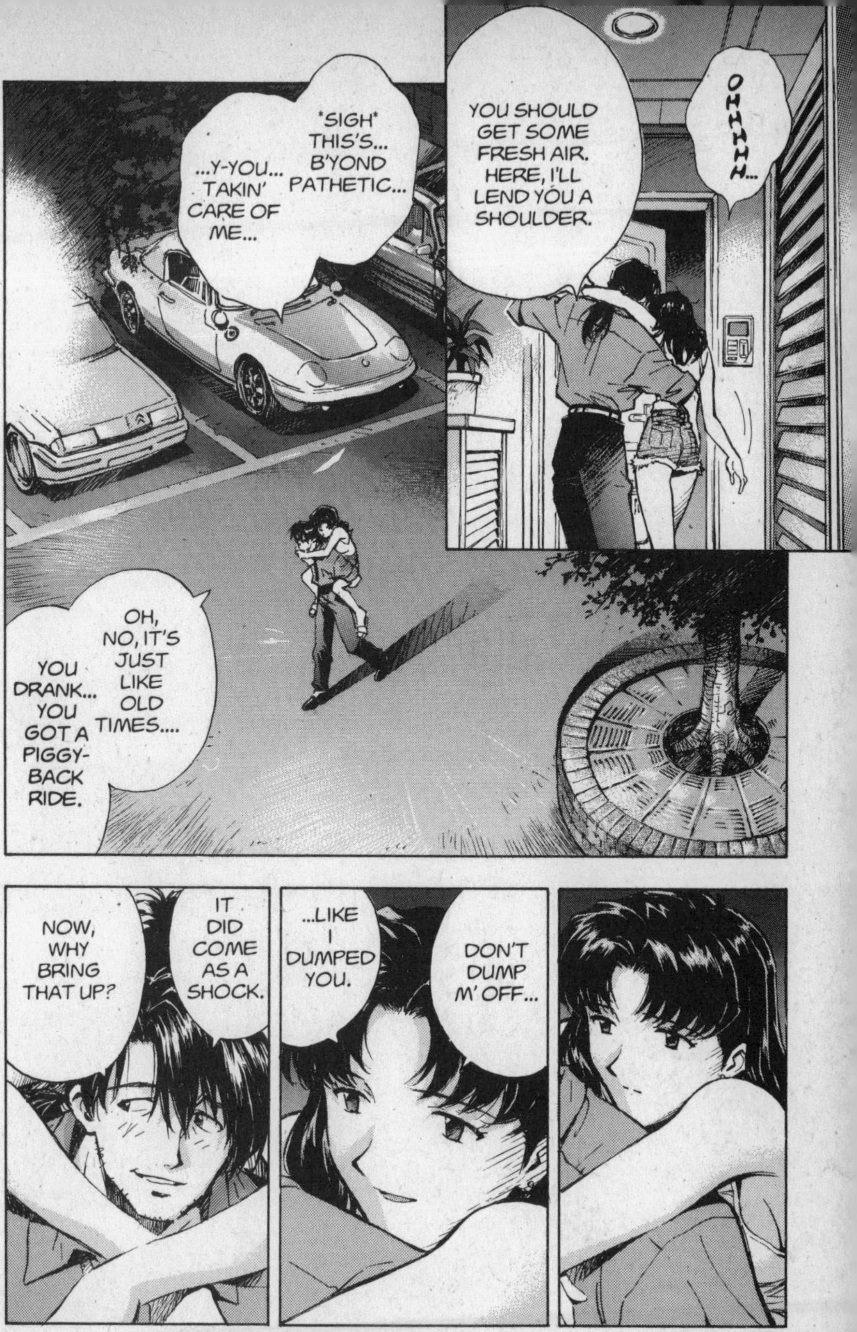
OHHHHH...
YOU SHOULD GET SOME FRESH AIR. HERE, I'LL LEND YOU A SHOULDER.
SIGH THIS'S... B'YOND PATHETIC...
...Y-YOU... TAKIN' CARE OF ME...
OH, NO, IT'S JUST LIKE OLD TIMES....
YOU DRANK... YOU GOT A PIGGY-BACK RIDE.
DON'T DUMP M' OFF...
...LIKE I DUMPED YOU.
IT DID COME AS A SHOCK.
NOW, WHY BRING THAT UP?

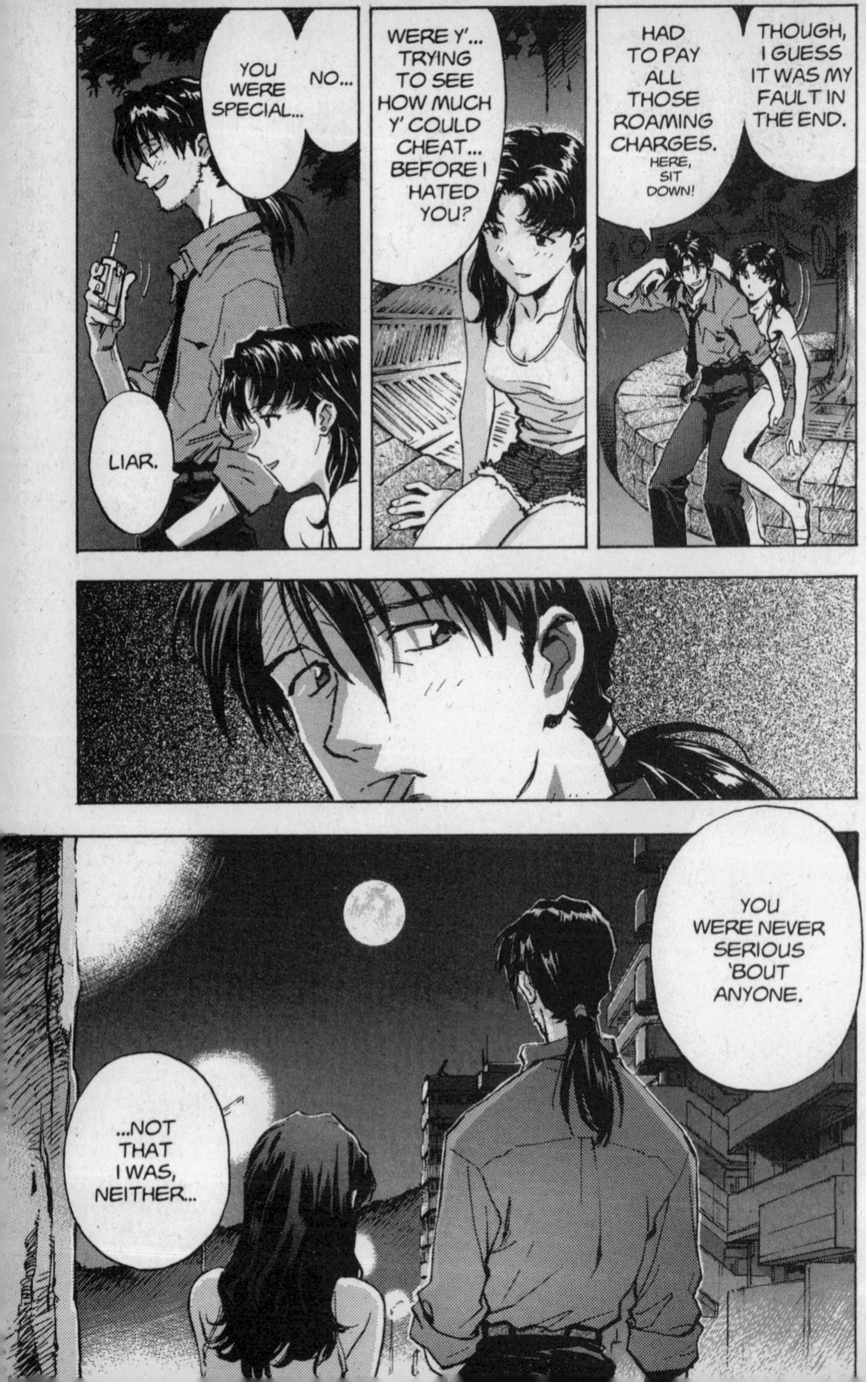
THOUGH, I GUESS IT WAS MY FAULT IN THE END.
HAD TO PAY ALL THOSE ROAMING CHARGES.
HERE, SIT DOWN!
WERE Y'... TRYING TO SEE HOW MUCH Y' COULD CHEAT... BEFORE I HATED YOU?
NO...
YOU WERE SPECIAL...
LIAR.
YOU WERE NEVER SERIOUS 'BOUT ANYONE.
...NOT THAT I WAS, NEITHER..

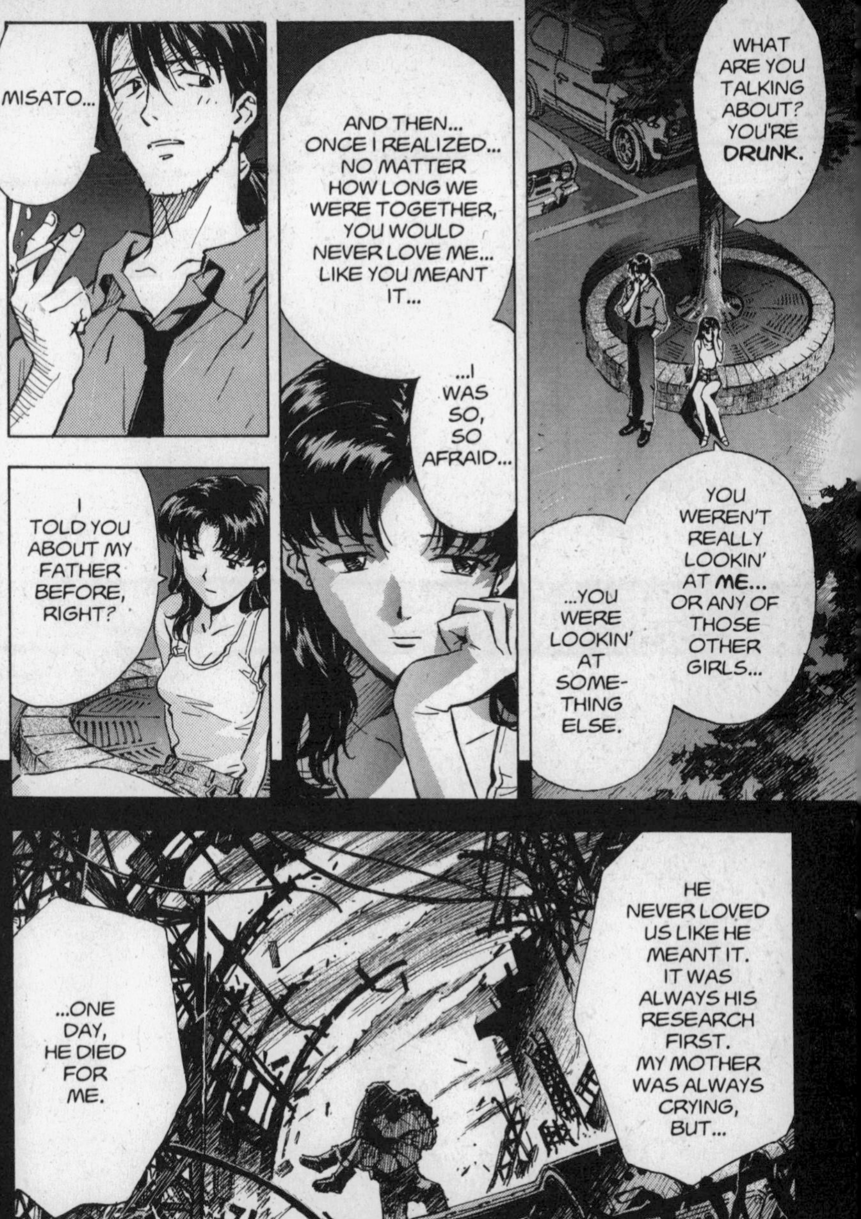
WHAT ARE YOU TALKING ABOUT? YOU'RE DRUNK.
YOU WEREN'T REALLY LOOKIN' AT ME... OR ANY OF THOSE OTHER GIRLS...
...YOU WERE LOOKIN' AT SOME-THING ELSE.
AND THEN... ONCE I REALIZED... NO MATTER HOW LONG WE WERE TOGETHER, YOU WOULD NEVER LOVE ME... LIKE YOU MEANT IT...
...I WAS SO, SO AFRAID...
MISATO...
I TOLD YOU ABOUT MY FATHER BEFORE, RIGHT?
HE NEVER LOVED US LIKE HE MEANT IT. IT WAS ALWAYS HIS RESEARCH FIRST. MY MOTHER WAS ALWAYS CRYING, BUT...
...ONE DAY, HE DIED FOR ME.

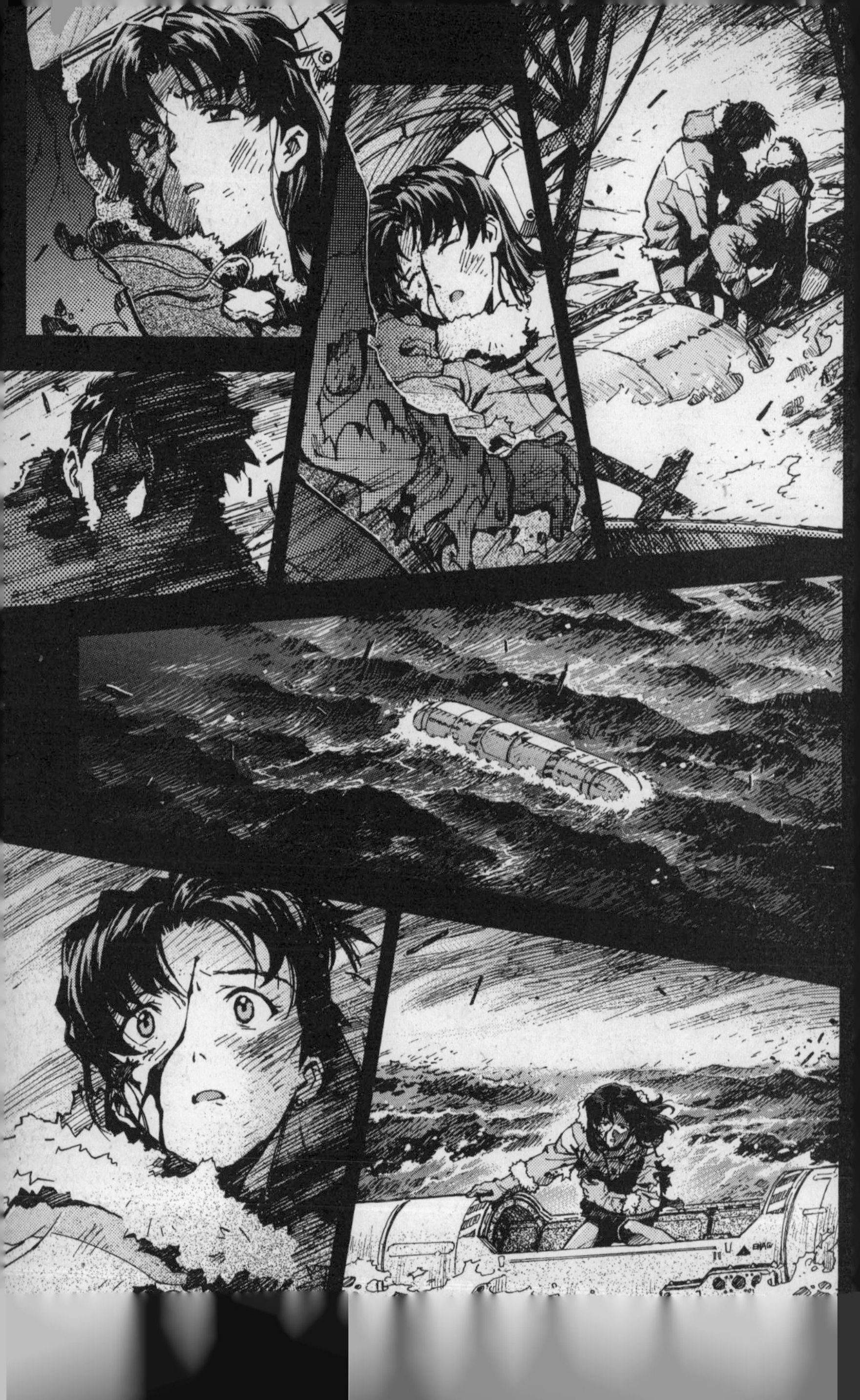

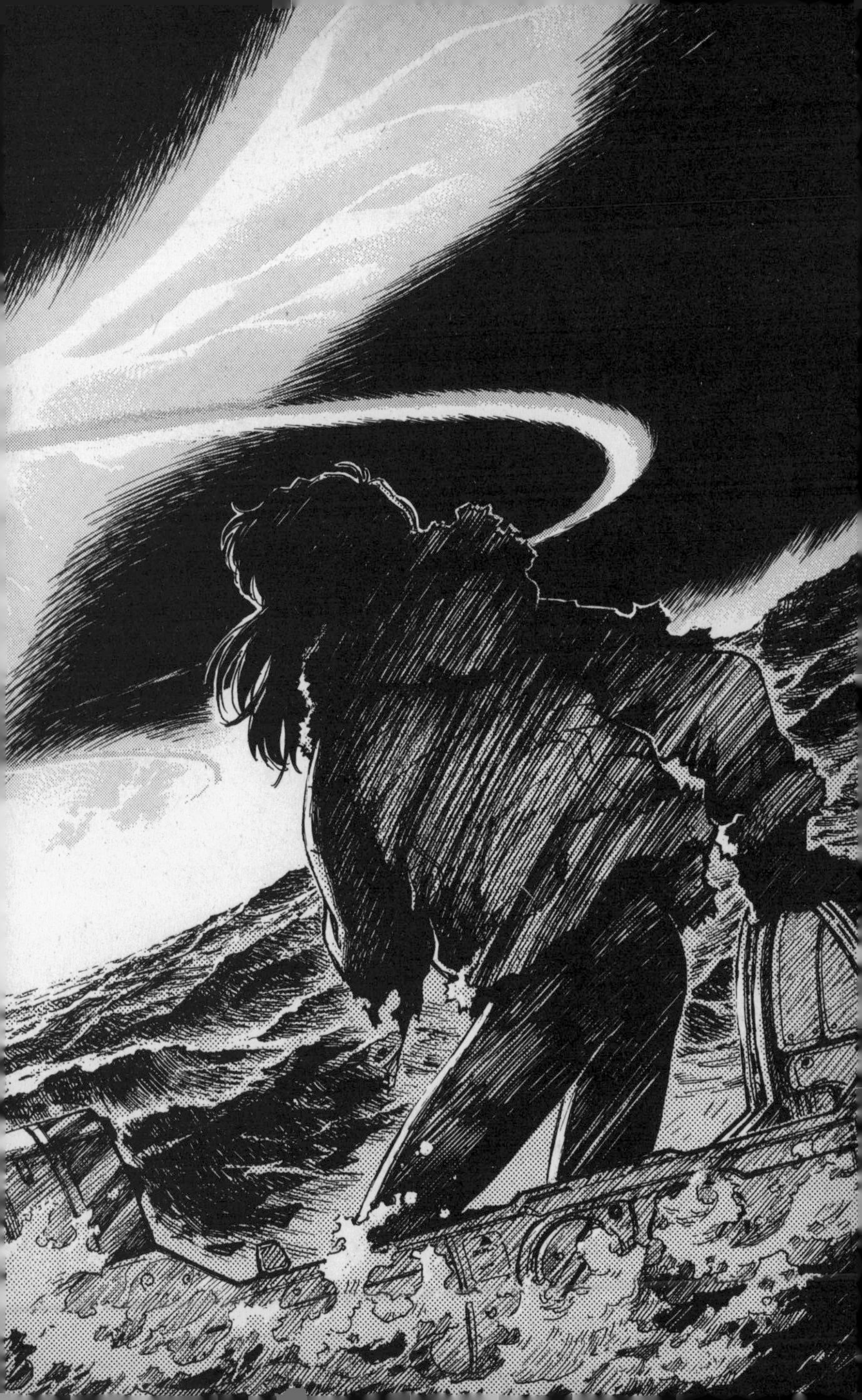

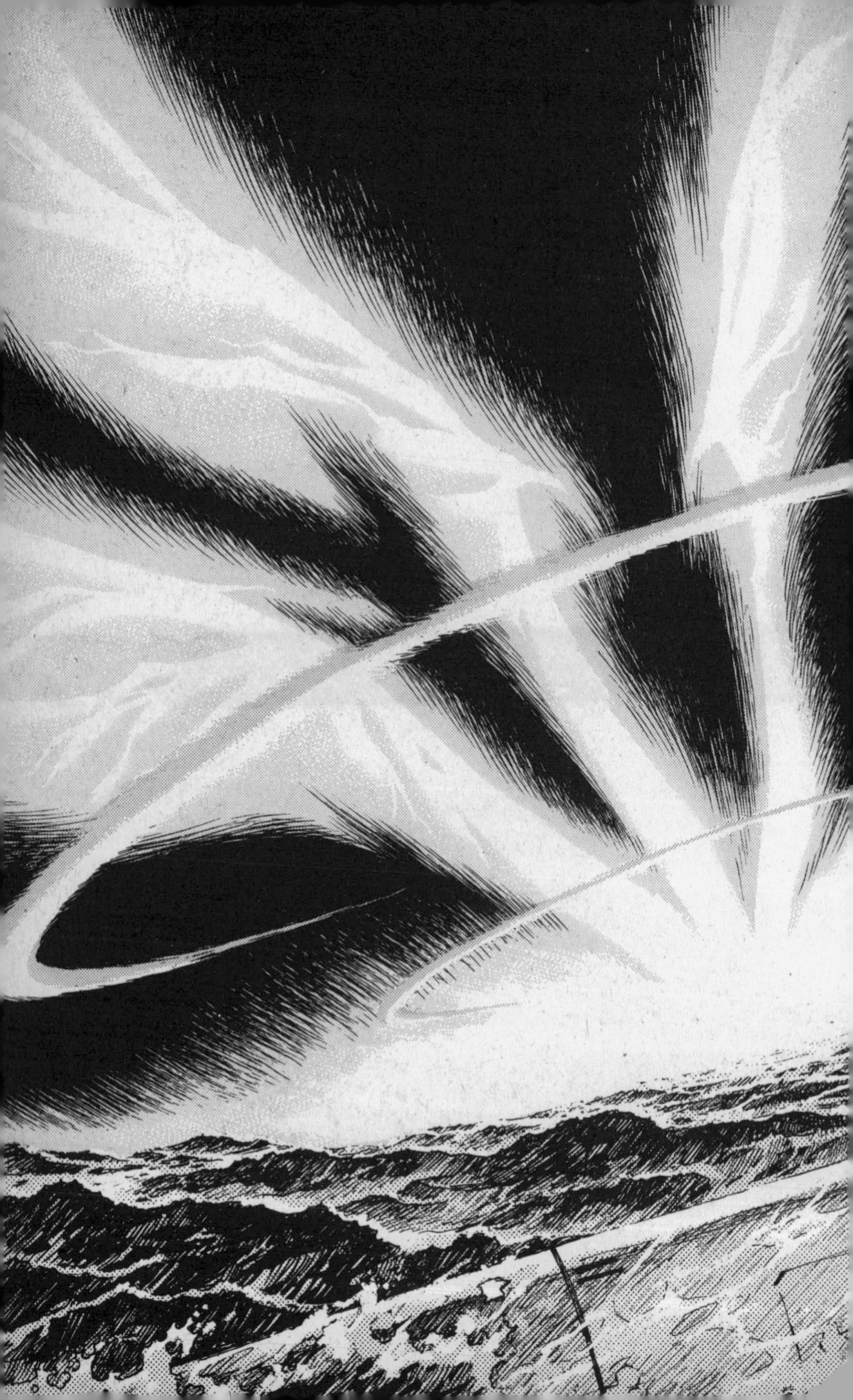

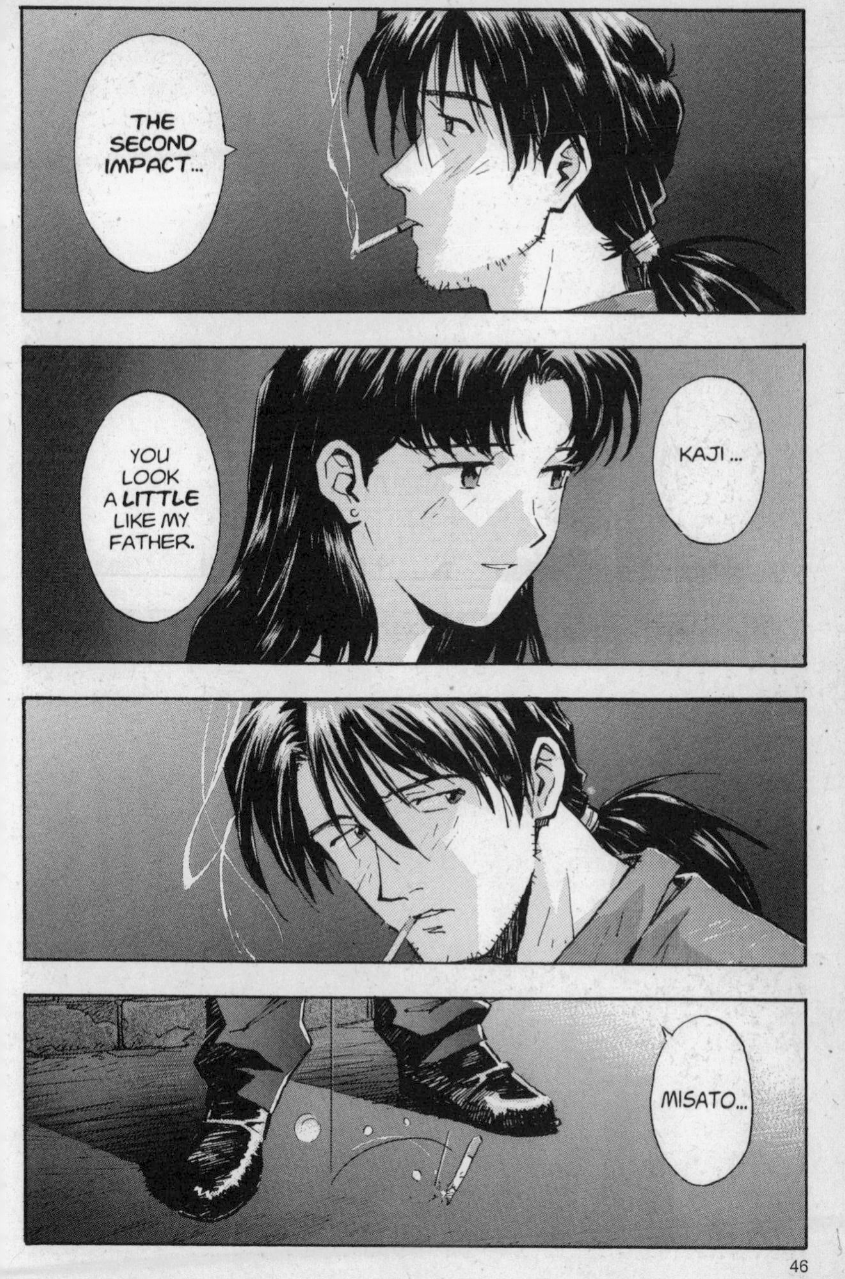
THE SECOND IMPACT...
KAJI...
YOU LOOK A LITTLE LIKE MY FATHER.
MISATO...

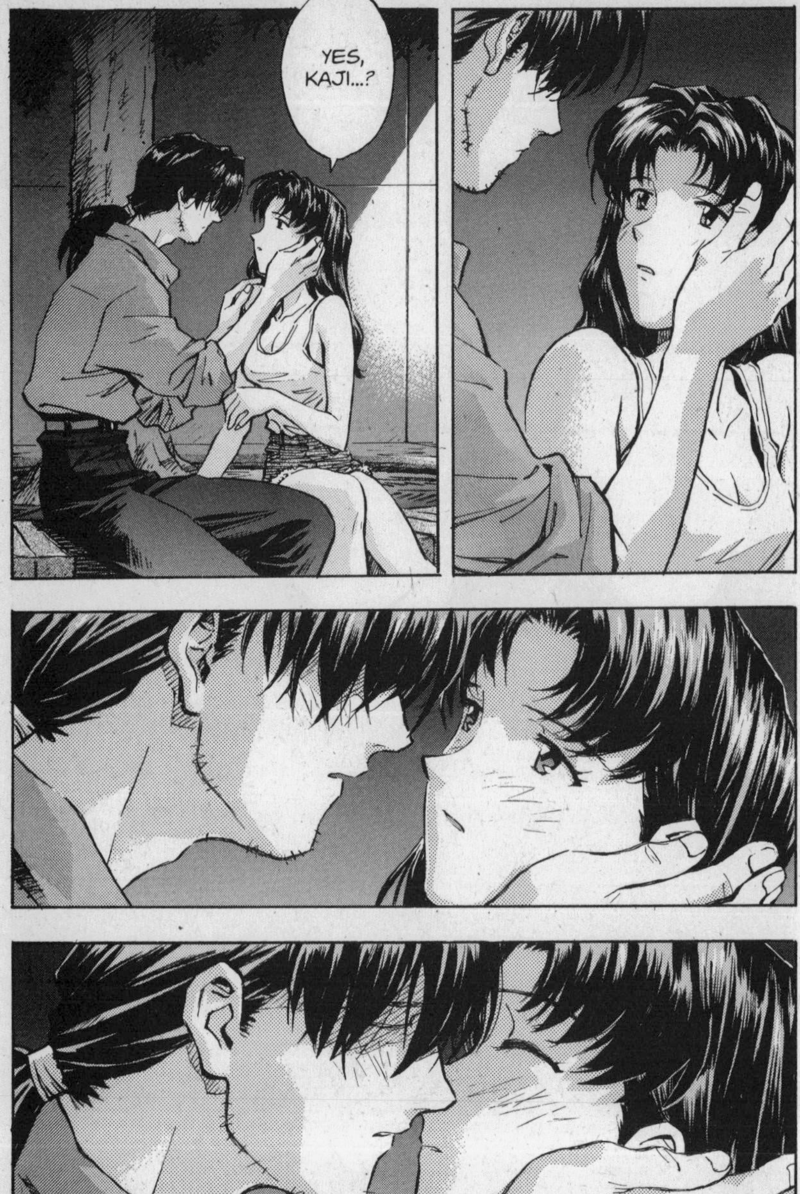
YES, KAJI...?

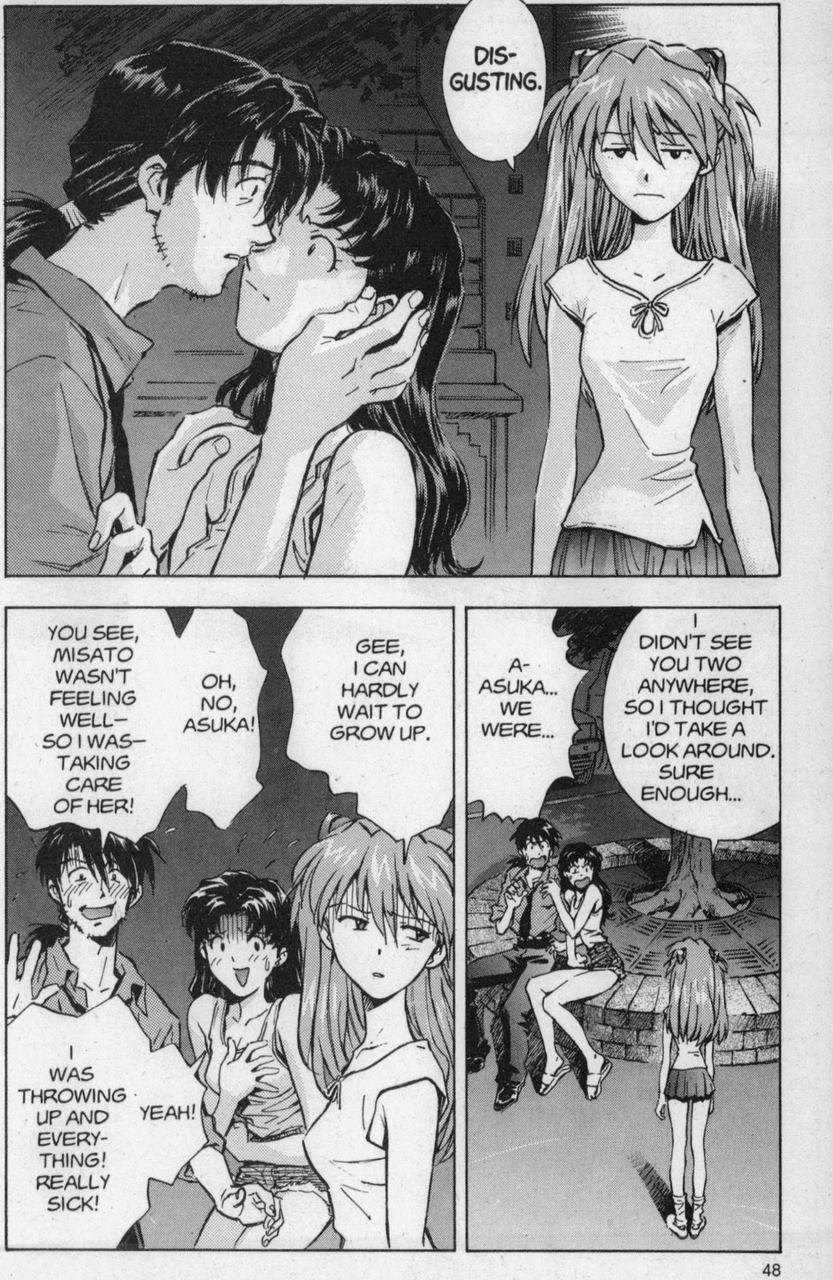
DIS-GUSTING.
I DIDN'T SEE YOU TWO ANYWHERE, SO I THOUGHT I'D TAKE A LOOK AROUND. SURE ENOUGH...
A- ASUKA... WE WERE...
GEE, I CAN HARDLY WAIT TO GROW UP.
OH, NO, ASUKA!
YOU SEE, MISATO WASN'T FEELING WELL— SO I WAS— TAKING CARE OF HER!
YEAH!
I WAS THROWING UP AND EVERY-THING! REALLY SICK!

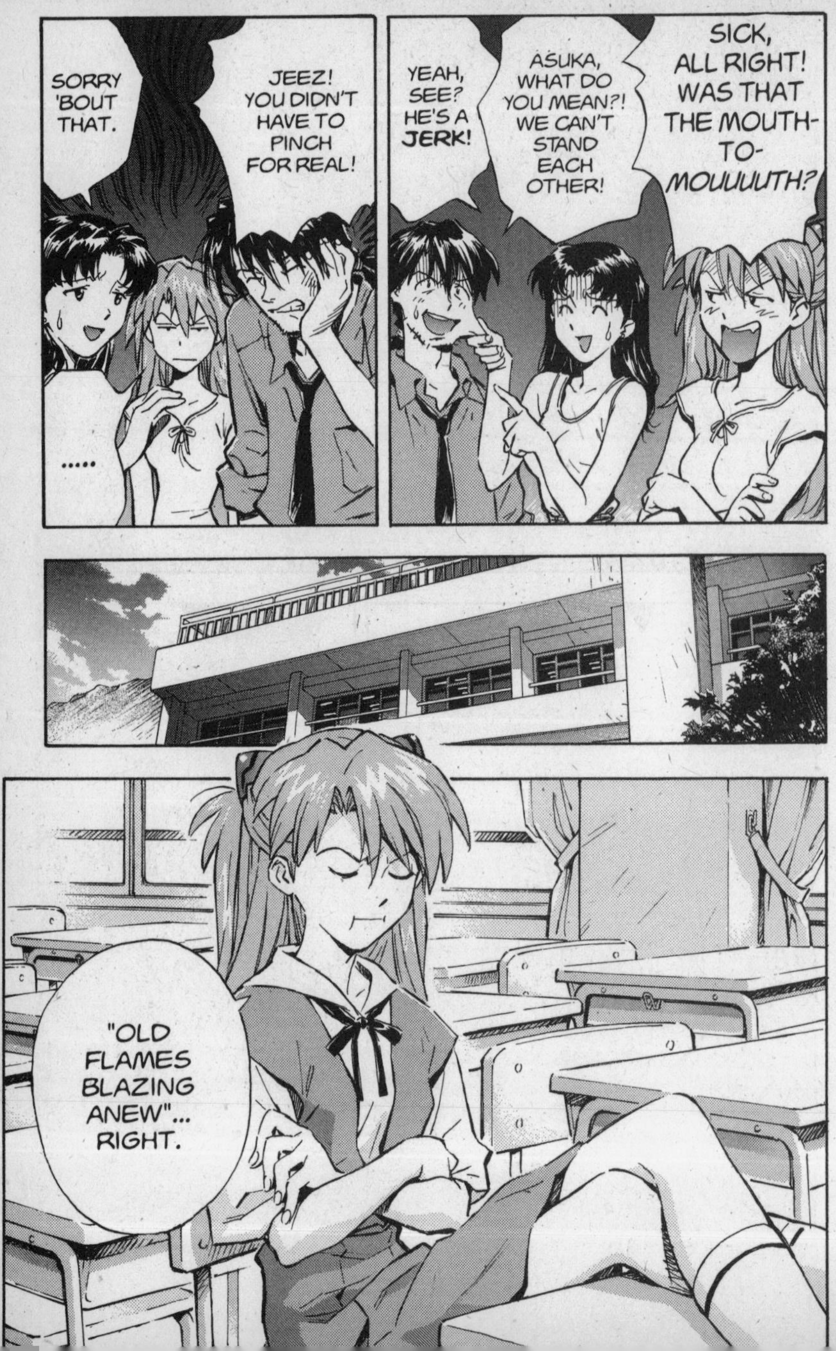
SICK, ALL RIGHT! WAS THAT THE MOUTH-TO-MOUUUUTH?
ASUKA, WHAT DO YOU MEAN?! WE CAN'T STAND EACH OTHER!
YEAH, SEE? HE'S A **JERK**!
JEEZ! YOU DIDN'T HAVE TO PINCH FOR REAL!
SORRY 'BOUT THAT.
.....
"OLD FLAMES BLAZING ANEW"... RIGHT.

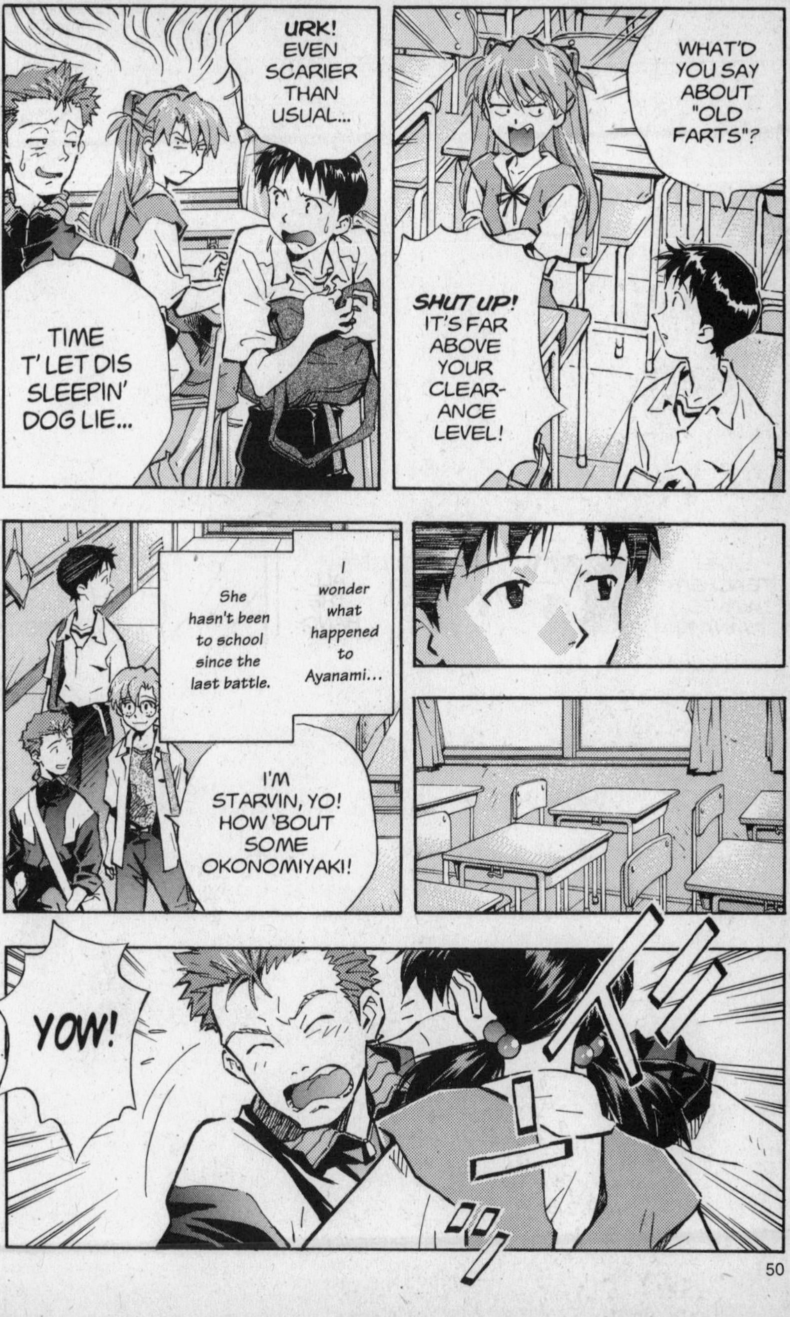
WHAT'D YOU SAY ABOUT "OLD FARTS"?
SHUT UP! IT'S FAR ABOVE YOUR CLEARANCE-ANCE LEVEL!
URK! EVEN SCARIER THAN USUAL...
TIME T' LET DIS SLEEPIN' DOG LIE...
I wonder what happened to Ayanami...
She hasn't been to school since the last battle.
I'M STARVIN, YO! HOW 'BOUT SOME OKONOMIYAKI!
YOW!

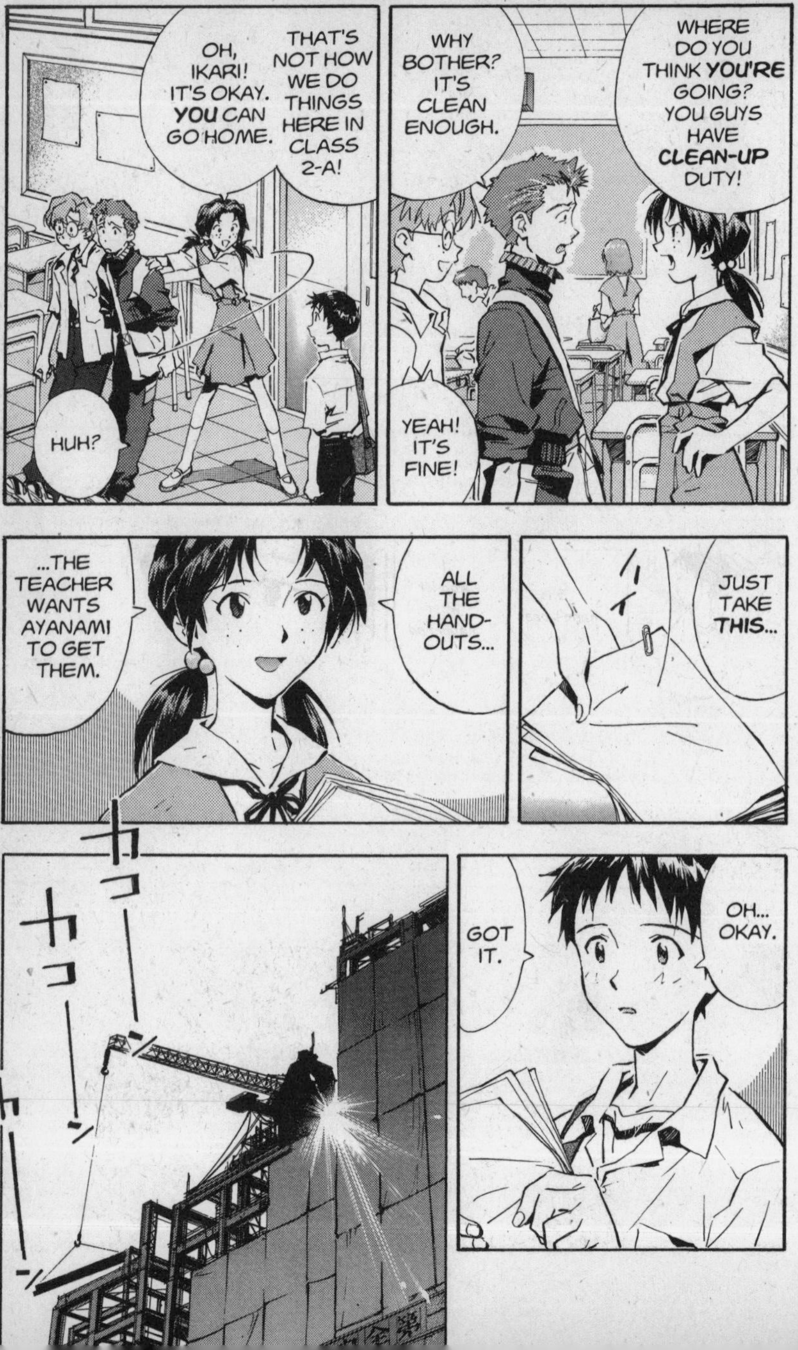
WHERE DO YOU THINK YOU'RE GOING? YOU GUYS HAVE CLEAN-UP DUTY!
WHY BOTHER? IT'S CLEAN ENOUGH.
YEAH! IT'S FINE!
THAT'S NOT HOW WE DO THINGS HERE IN CLASS 2-A!
OH, IKARI! IT'S OKAY. YOU CAN GO HOME.
HUH?
JUST TAKE THIS...
ALL THE HAND-OUTS...
...THE TEACHER WANTS AYANAMI TO GET THEM.
OH... OKAY.
GOT IT.
カコーン
カコーン
カーン

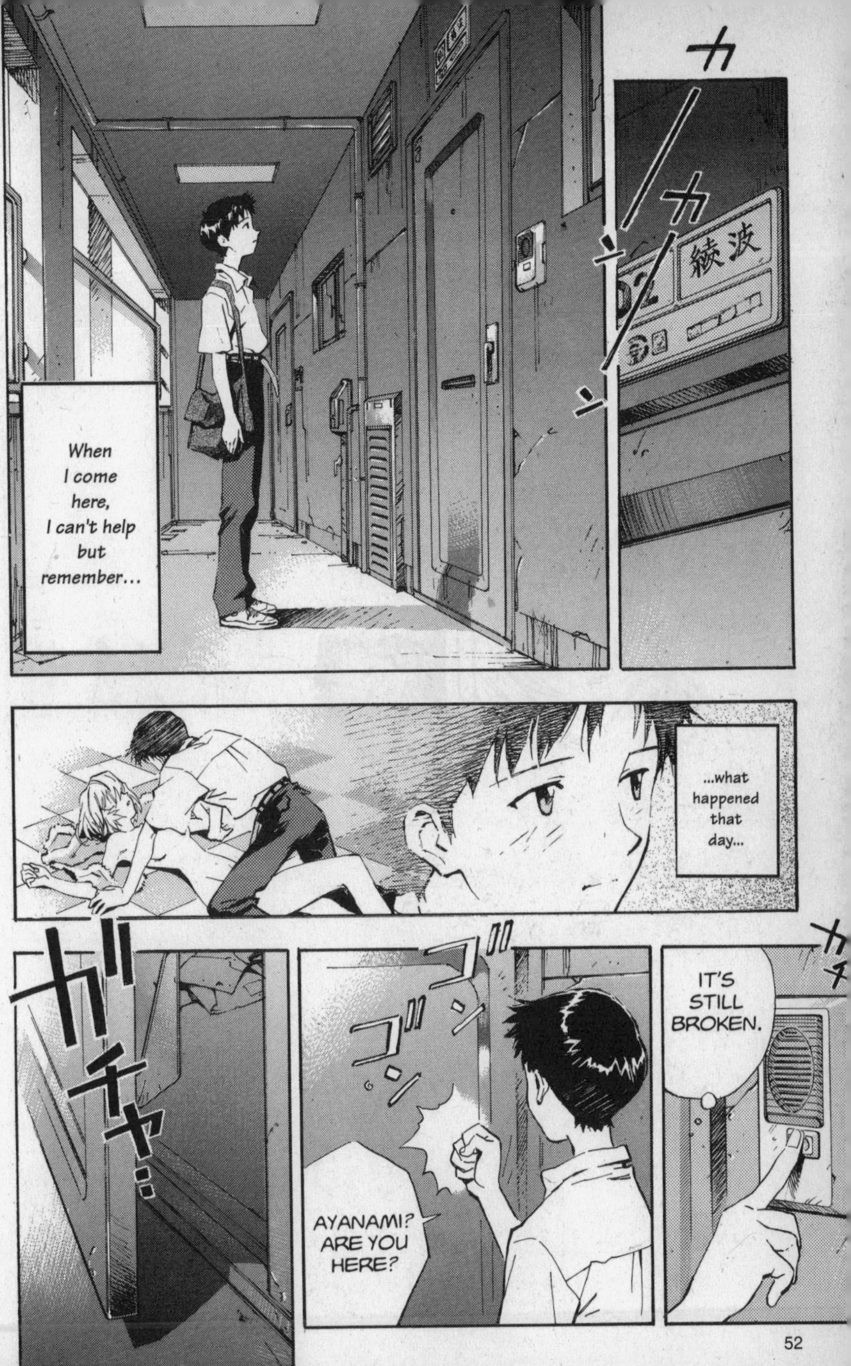
綾波
When I come here, I can't help but remember…
...what happened that day...
IT'S STILL BROKEN.
AYANAMI? ARE YOU HERE?

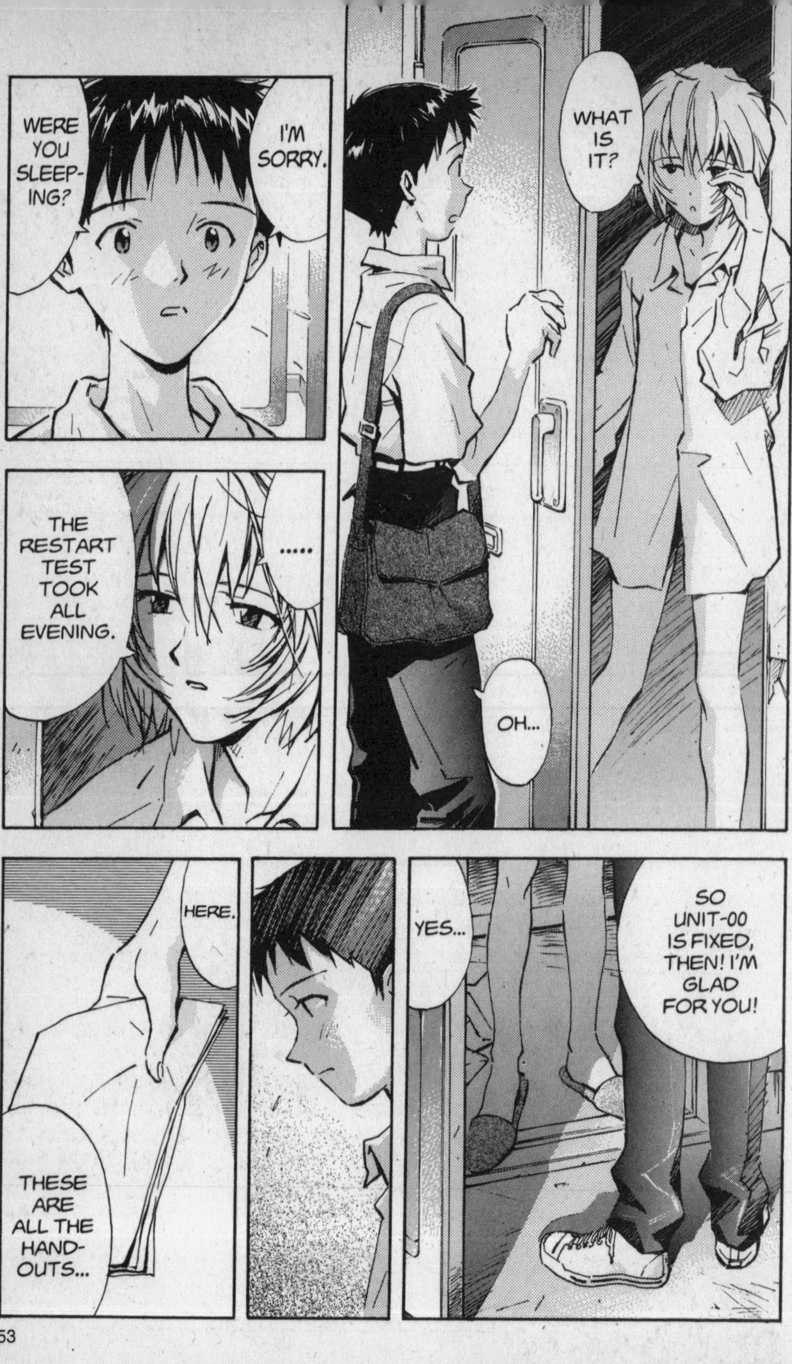
WHAT IS IT?
I'M SORRY.
WERE YOU SLEEPING?
.....
THE RESTART TEST TOOK ALL EVENING.
OH...
SO UNIT-00 IS FIXED, THEN! I'M GLAD FOR YOU!
YES...
HERE.
THESE ARE ALL THE HANDOUTS...

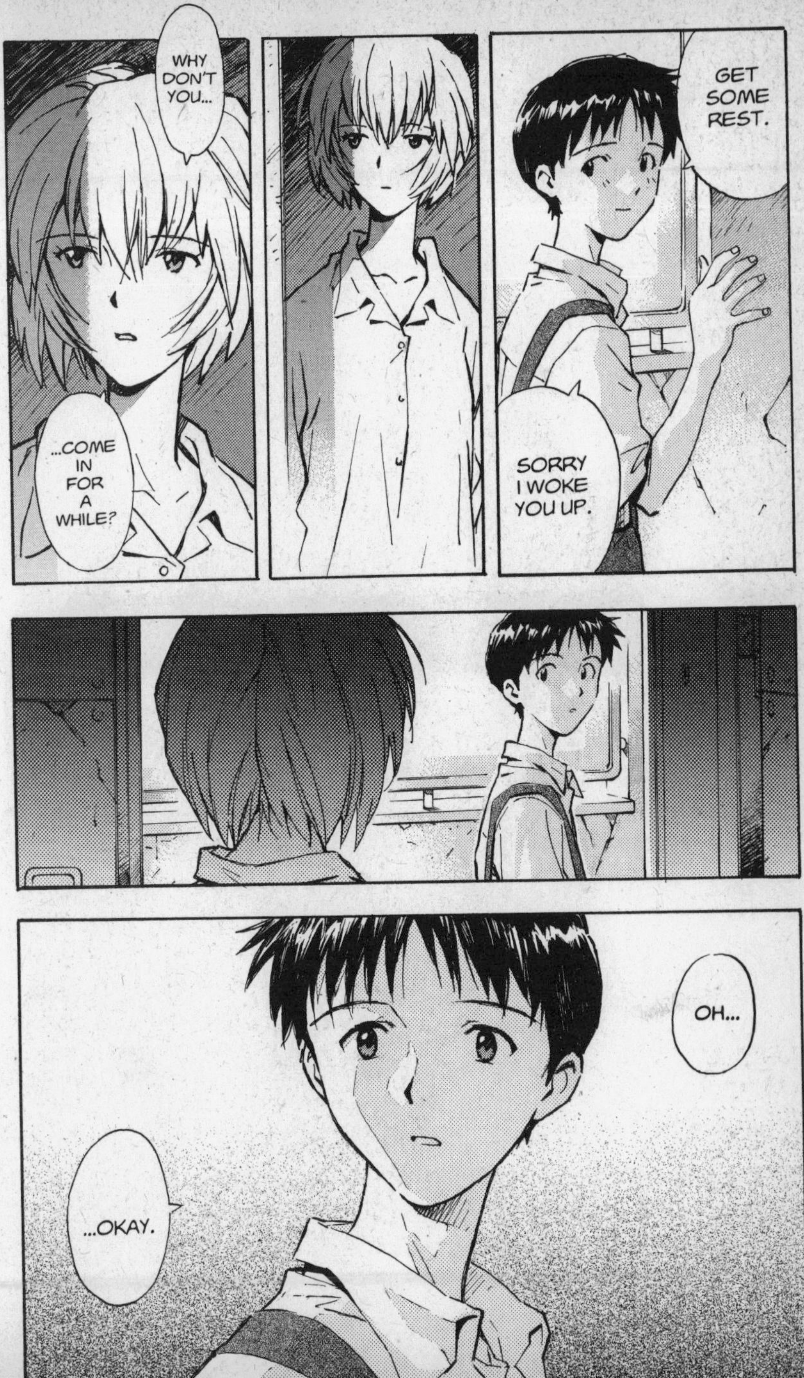
GET SOME REST.
SORRY I WOKE YOU UP.
WHY DON'T YOU...
...COME IN FOR A WHILE?
OH...
...OKAY.

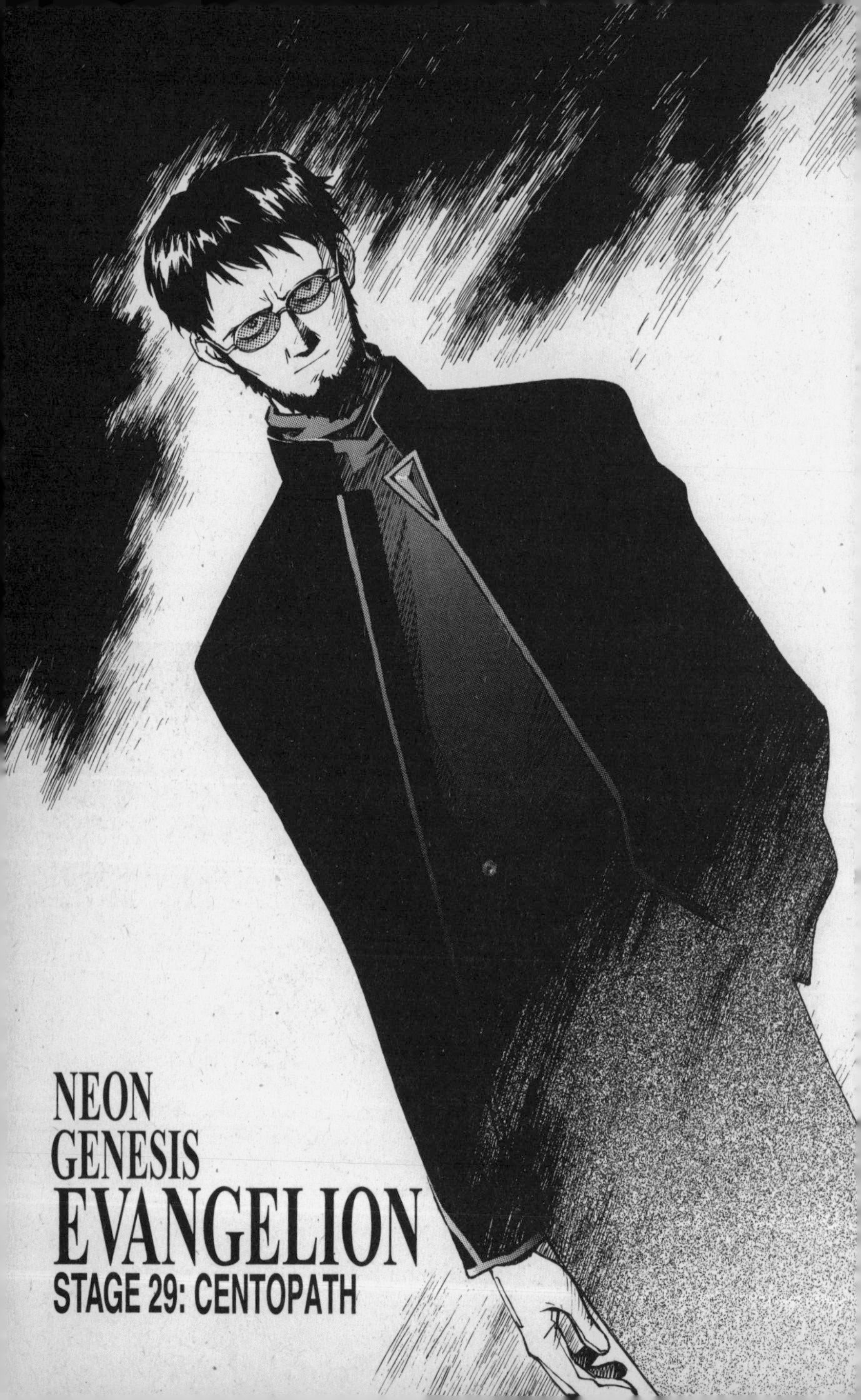

NEON GENESIS EVANGELION

STAGE 29: CENTOPATH

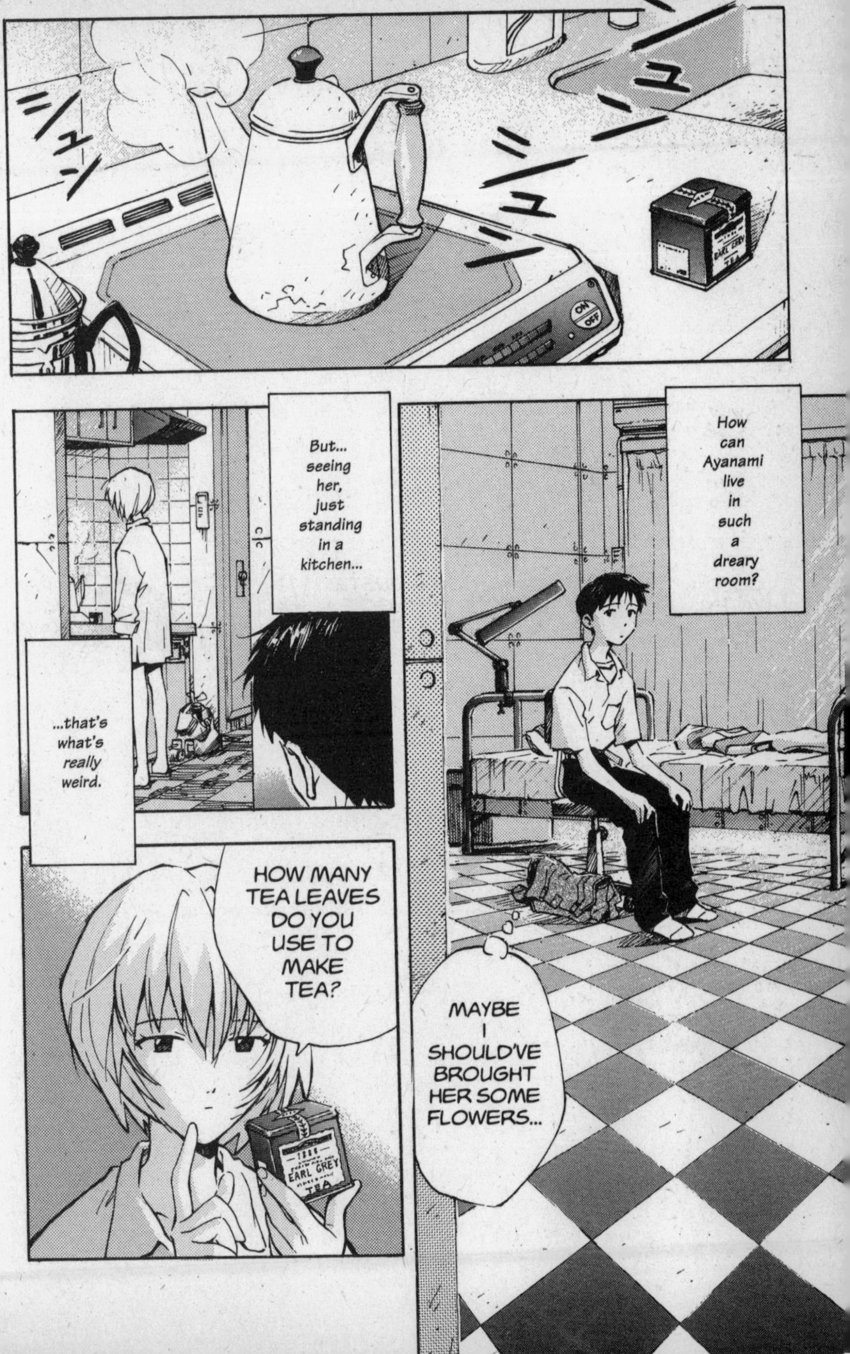

How can Ayanami live in such a dreary room?
MAYBE I SHOULD'VE BROUGHT HER SOME FLOWERS...
But... seeing her, just standing in a kitchen...
...that's what's really weird.
HOW MANY TEA LEAVES DO YOU USE TO MAKE TEA?
EARL GREY TEA

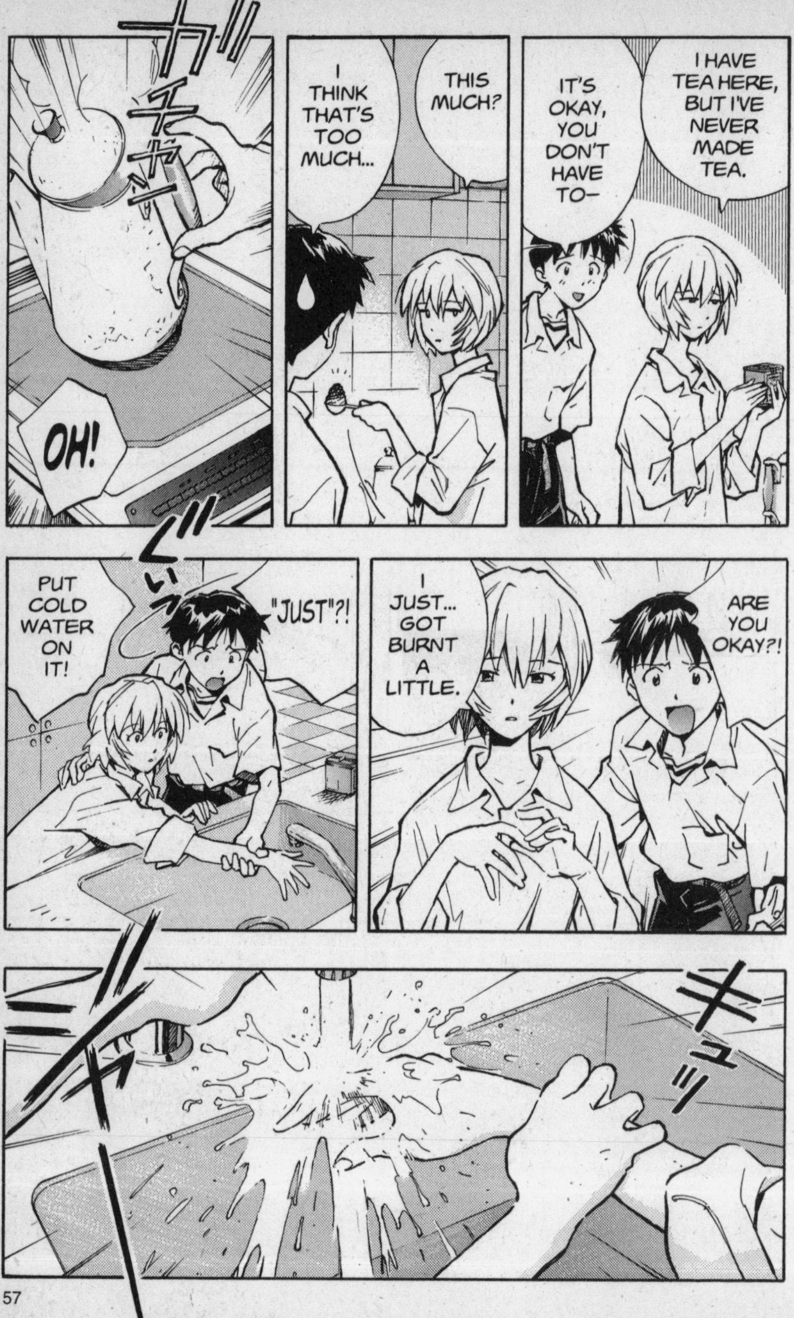
I HAVE TEA HERE, BUT I'VE NEVER MADE TEA.
IT'S OKAY, YOU DON'T HAVE TO—
THIS MUCH?
I THINK THAT'S TOO MUCH...
OH!
ARE YOU OKAY?!
I JUST... GOT BURNT A LITTLE.
"JUST"?!
PUT COLD WATER ON IT!

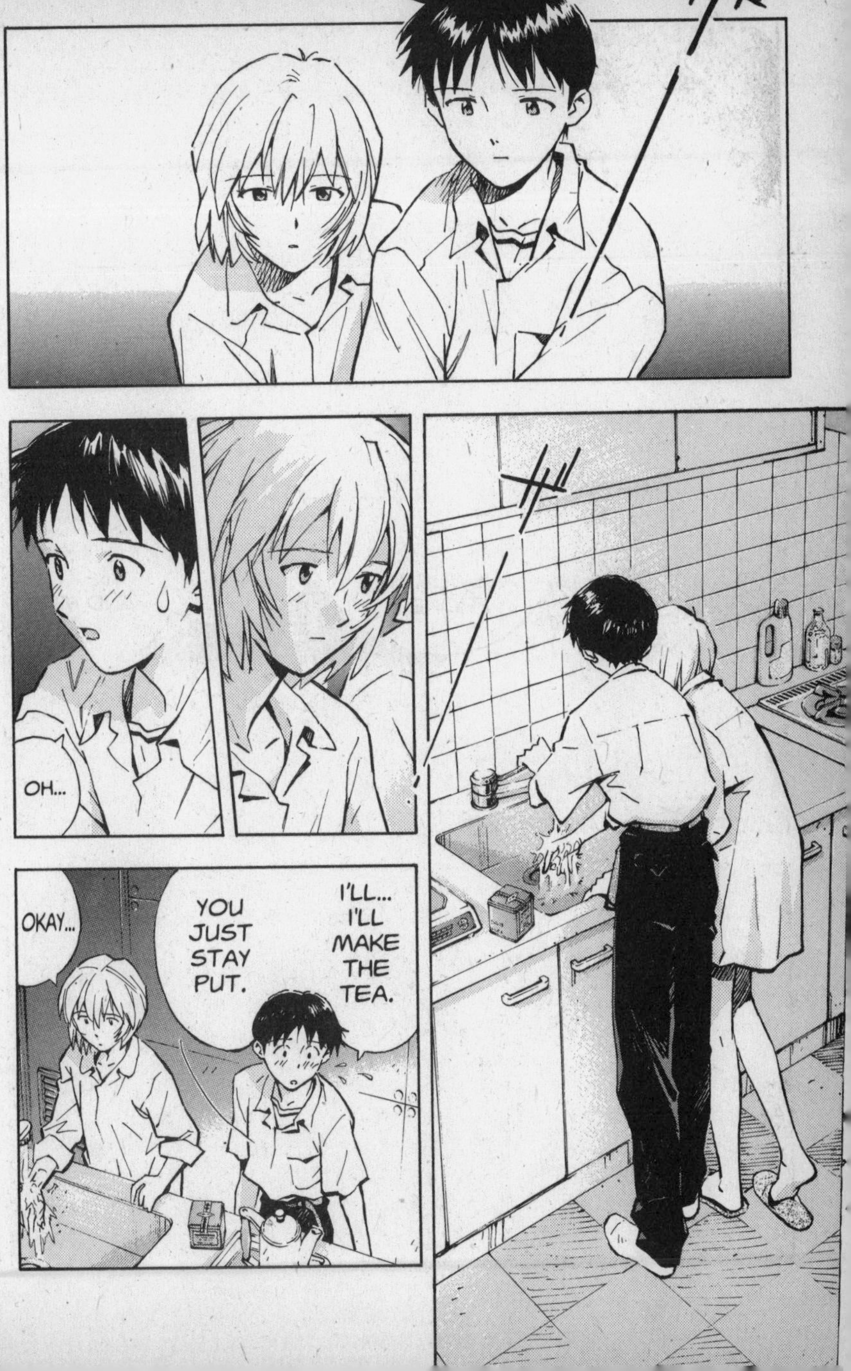
OH...
I'LL... I'LL MAKE THE TEA.
YOU JUST STAY PUT.
OKAY...

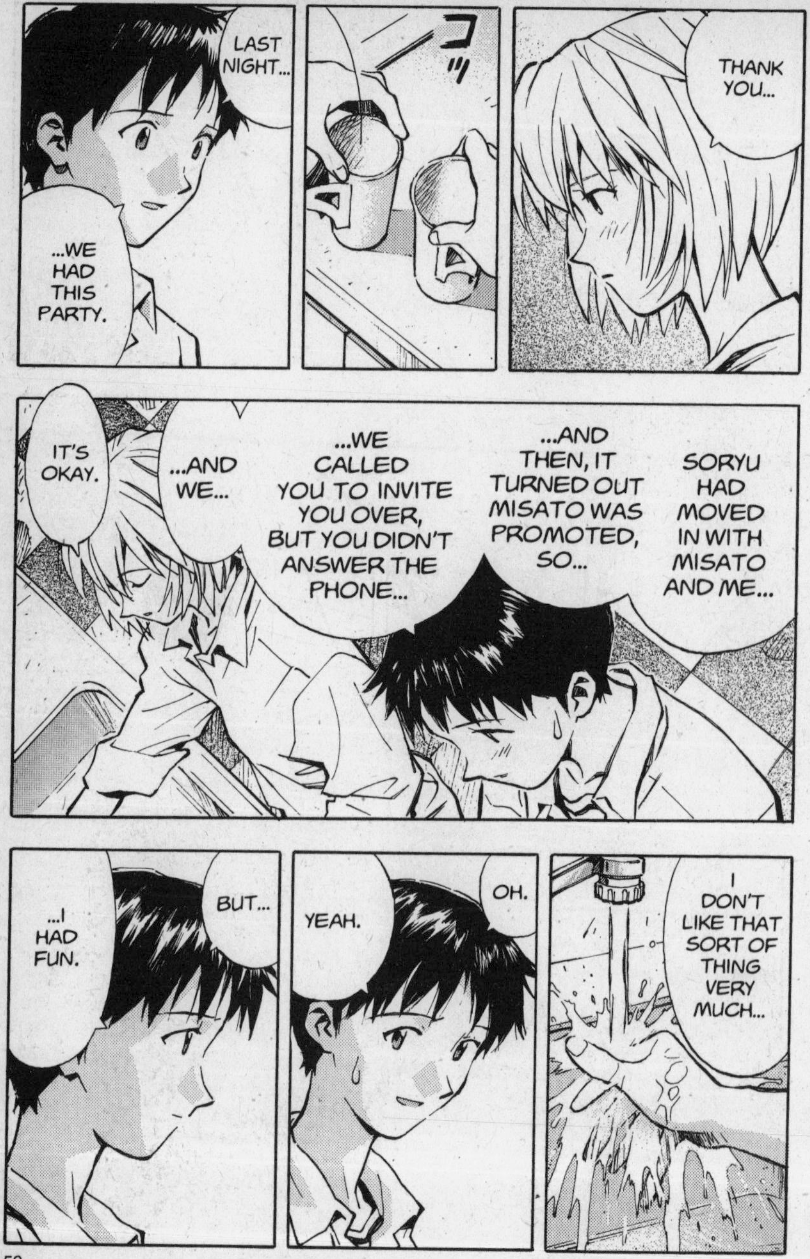
THANK YOU...
コッ
LAST NIGHT...
...WE HAD THIS PARTY.
SORYU HAD MOVED IN WITH MISATO AND ME...
...AND THEN, IT TURNED OUT MISATO WAS PROMOTED, SO...
...WE CALLED YOU TO INVITE YOU OVER, BUT YOU DIDN'T ANSWER THE PHONE...
...AND WE...
IT'S OKAY.
I DON'T LIKE THAT SORT OF THING VERY MUCH...
OH.
YEAH.
BUT...
...I HAD FUN.

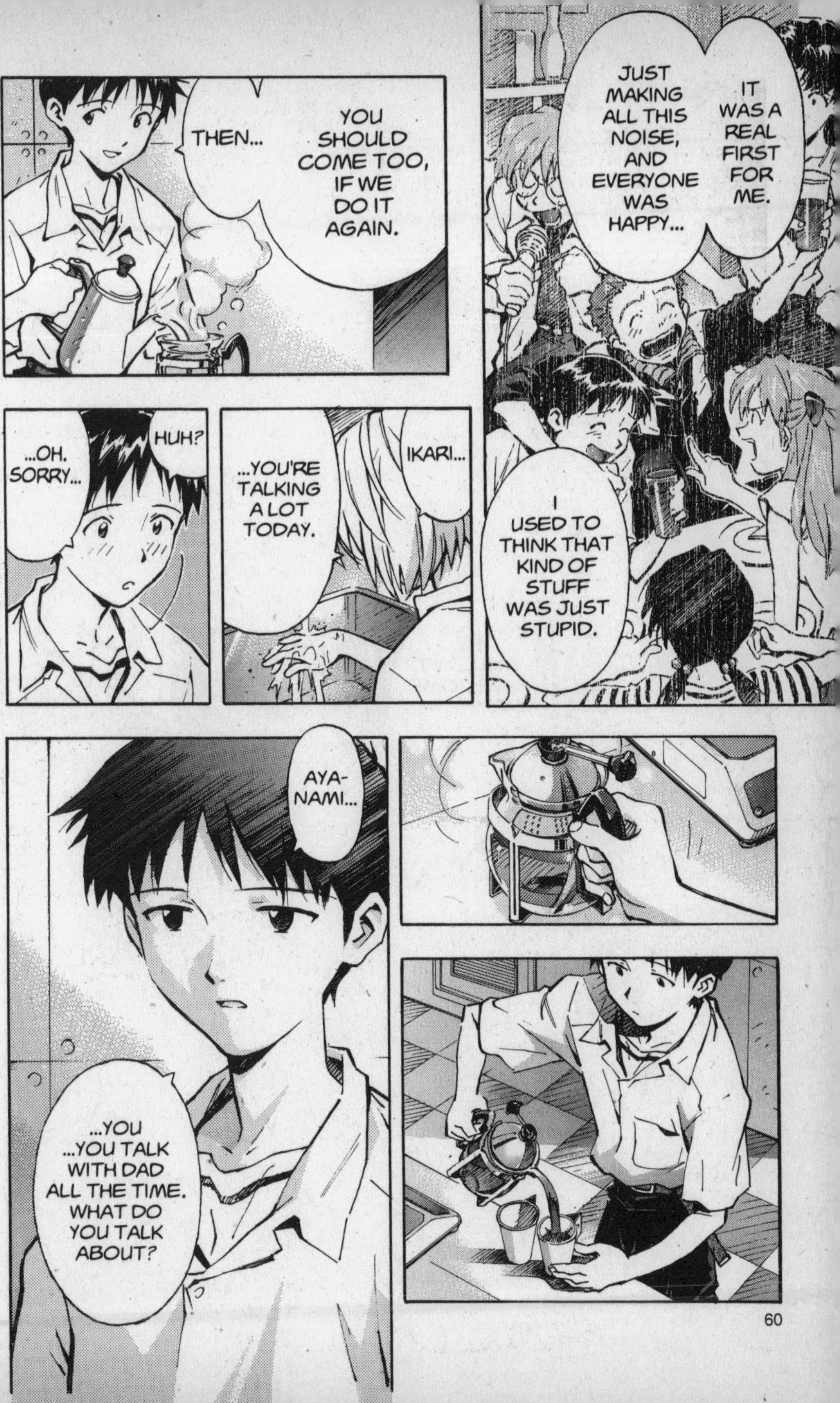
IT WAS A REAL FIRST FOR ME.
JUST MAKING ALL THIS NOISE, AND EVERYONE WAS HAPPY...
I USED TO THINK THAT KIND OF STUFF WAS JUST STUPID.
THEN...
YOU SHOULD COME TOO, IF WE DO IT AGAIN.
IKARI...
...YOU'RE TALKING A LOT TODAY.
HUH?
...OH. SORRY...
AYA-NAMI...
...YOU ...YOU TALK WITH DAD ALL THE TIME. WHAT DO YOU TALK ABOUT?

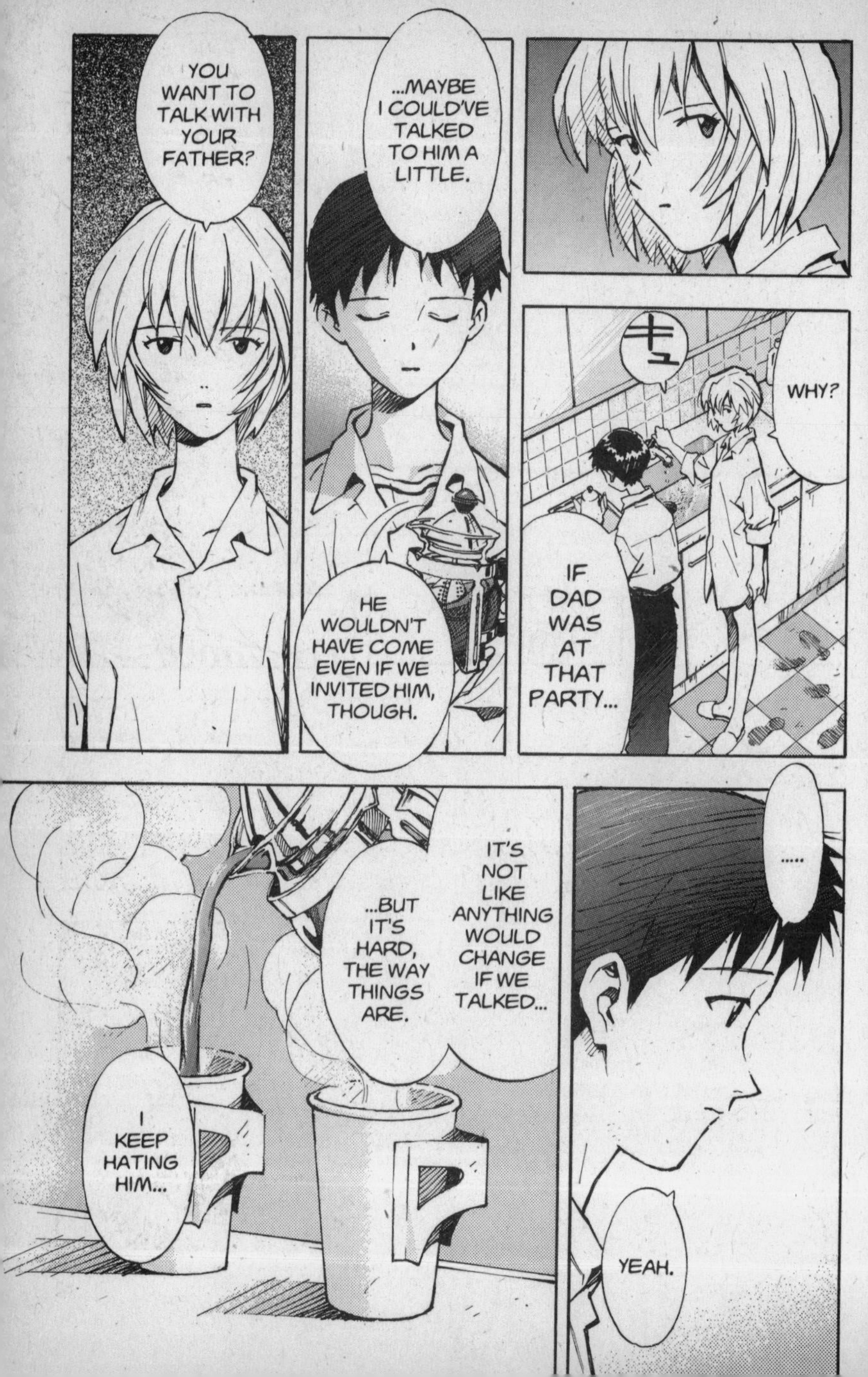
キュ
WHY?
IF DAD WAS AT THAT PARTY...
...MAYBE I COULD'VE TALKED TO HIM A LITTLE.
HE WOULDN'T HAVE COME EVEN IF WE INVITED HIM, THOUGH.
YOU WANT TO TALK WITH YOUR FATHER?
.....
YEAH.
IT'S NOT LIKE ANYTHING WOULD CHANGE IF WE TALKED...
...BUT IT'S HARD, THE WAY THINGS ARE.
I KEEP HATING HIM...

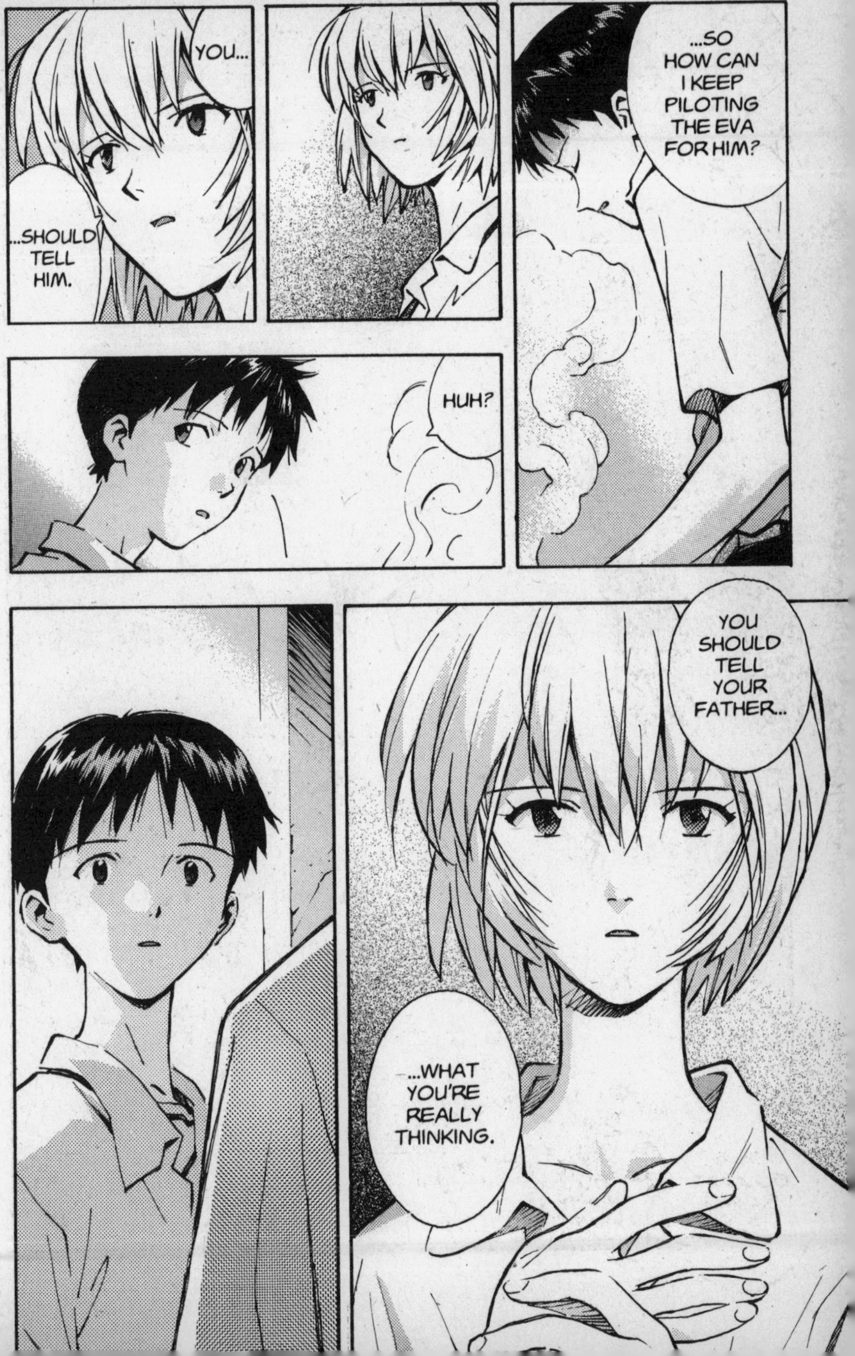
...SO HOW CAN I KEEP PILOTING THE EVA FOR HIM?
YOU...
...SHOULD TELL HIM.
HUH?
YOU SHOULD TELL YOUR FATHER...
...WHAT YOU'RE REALLY THINKING.

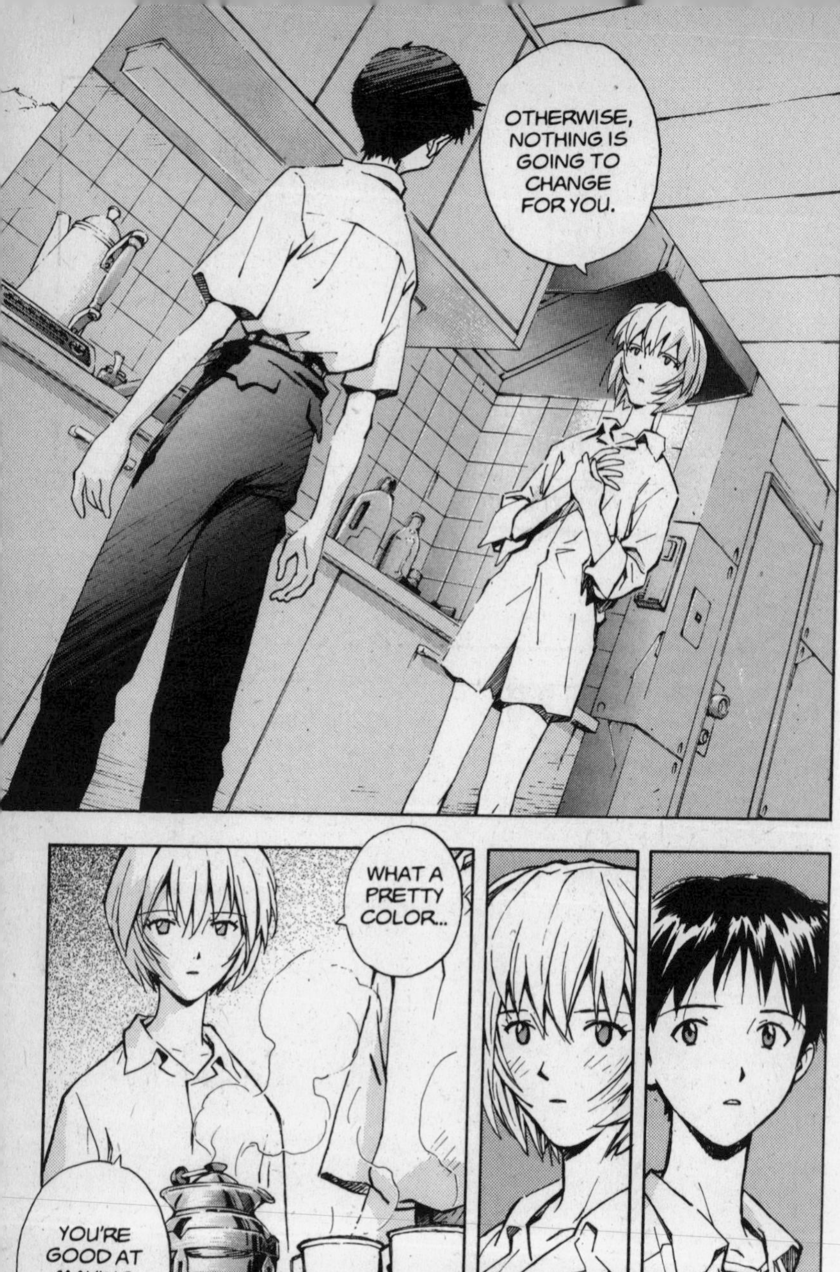
OTHERWISE, NOTHING IS GOING TO CHANGE FOR YOU.
WHAT A PRETTY COLOR...
YOU'RE GOOD AT MAKING TEA.

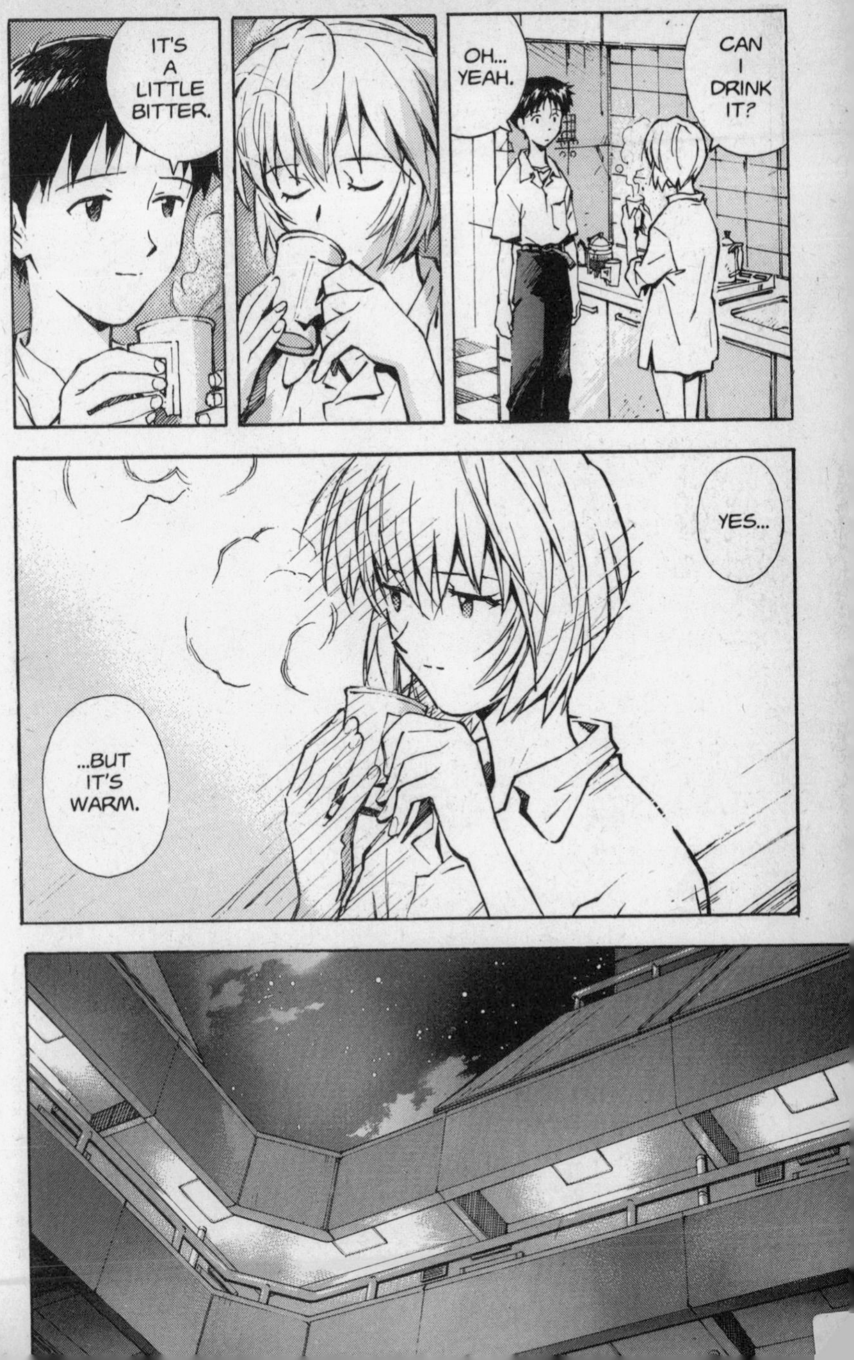
CAN I DRINK IT?
OH... YEAH.
IT'S A LITTLE BITTER.
YES...
...BUT IT'S WARM.

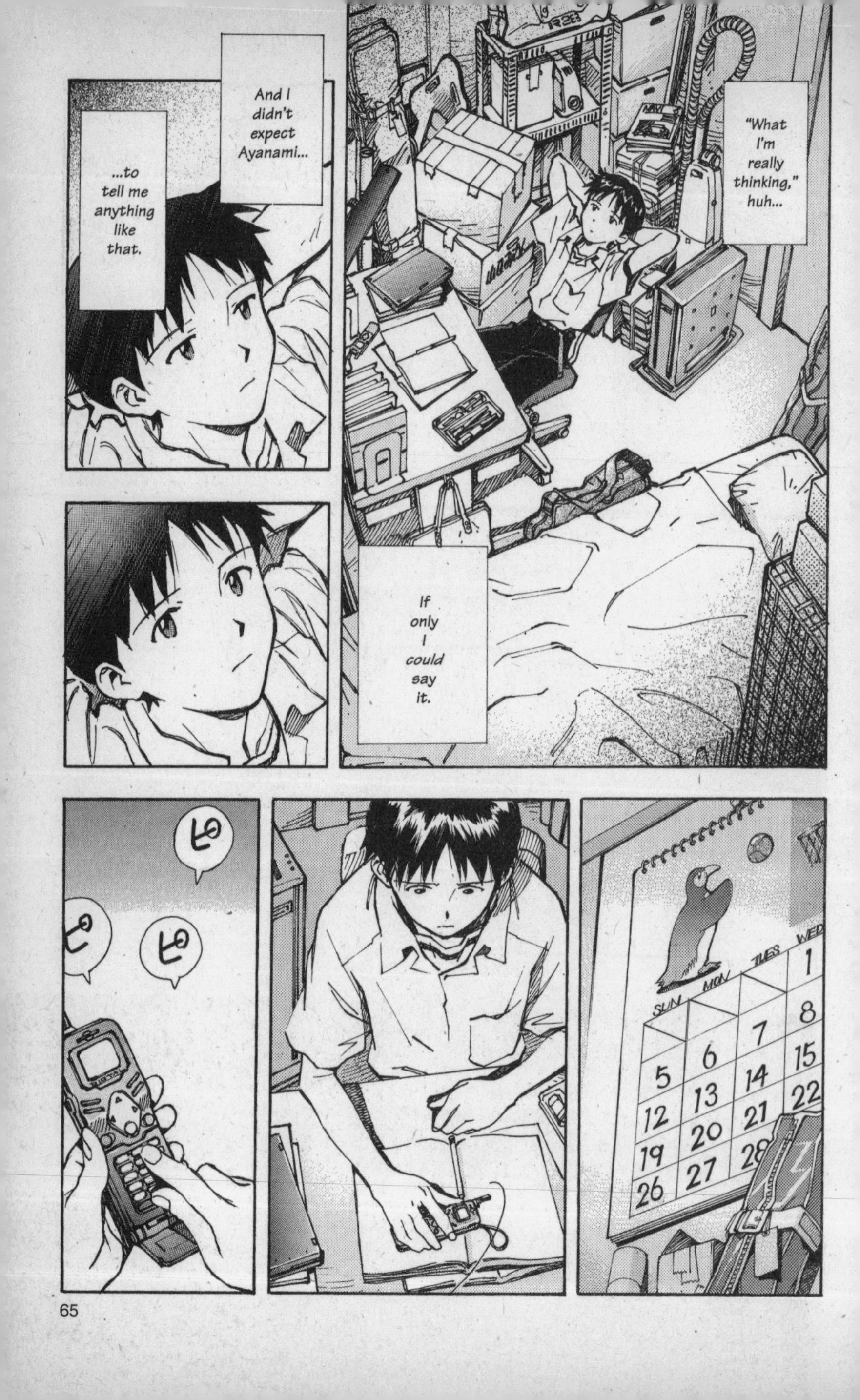
"What I'm really thinking," huh...
If only I could say it.
And I didn't expect Ayanami...
...to tell me anything like that.
SUN
MON
TUES
WED
ピ
ピ
ピ

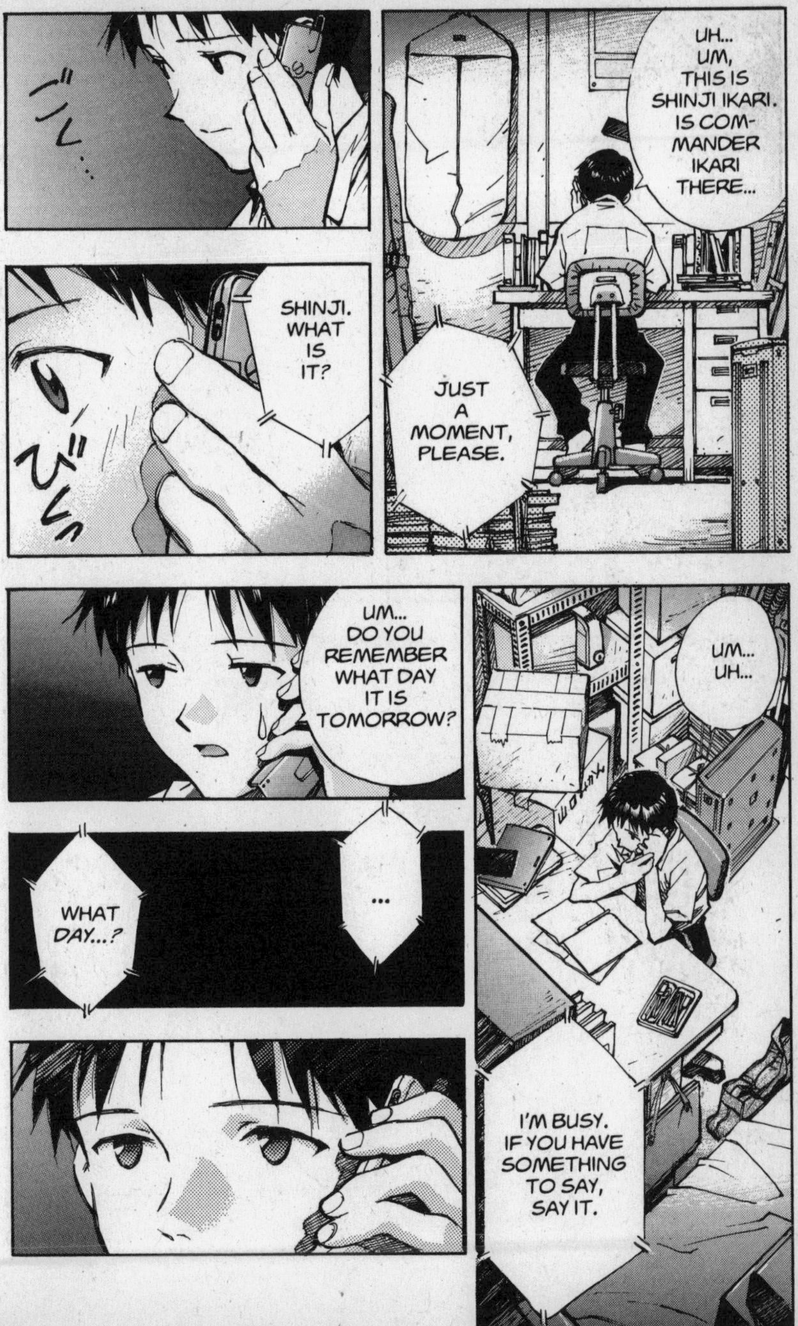
UH... UM, THIS IS SHINJI IKARI. IS COMMANDER IKARI THERE...
JUST A MOMENT, PLEASE.
SHINJI. WHAT IS IT?
UM... UH...
I'M BUSY. IF YOU HAVE SOMETHING TO SAY, SAY IT.
UM... DO YOU REMEMBER WHAT DAY IT IS TOMORROW?
...
WHAT DAY...?

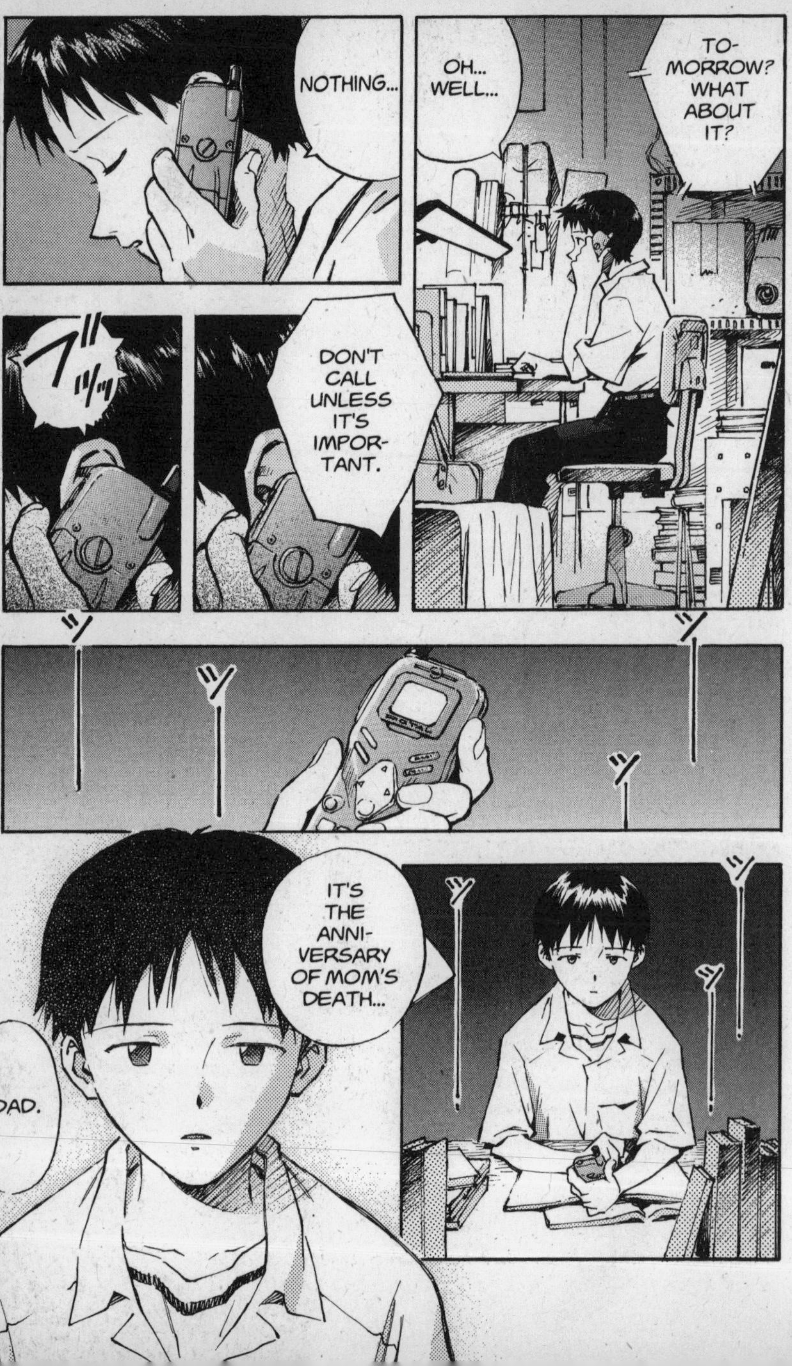
TO-MORROW? WHAT ABOUT IT?
OH... WELL...
NOTHING...
DON'T CALL UNLESS IT'S IMPOR-TANT.
IT'S THE ANNI-VERSARY OF MOM'S DEATH...
...DAD.

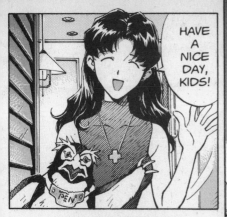

HAVE A NICE DAY, KIDS!

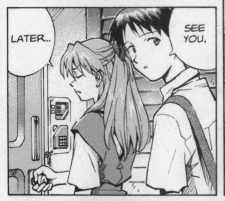

LATER...

SEE YOU.

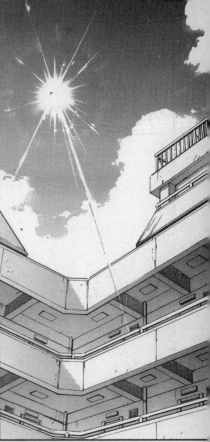

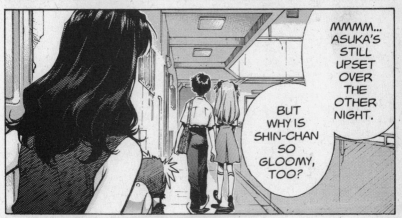

MMMM... ASUKA'S STILL UPSET OVER THE OTHER NIGHT.

BUT WHY IS SHIN-CHAN SO GLOOMY, TOO?

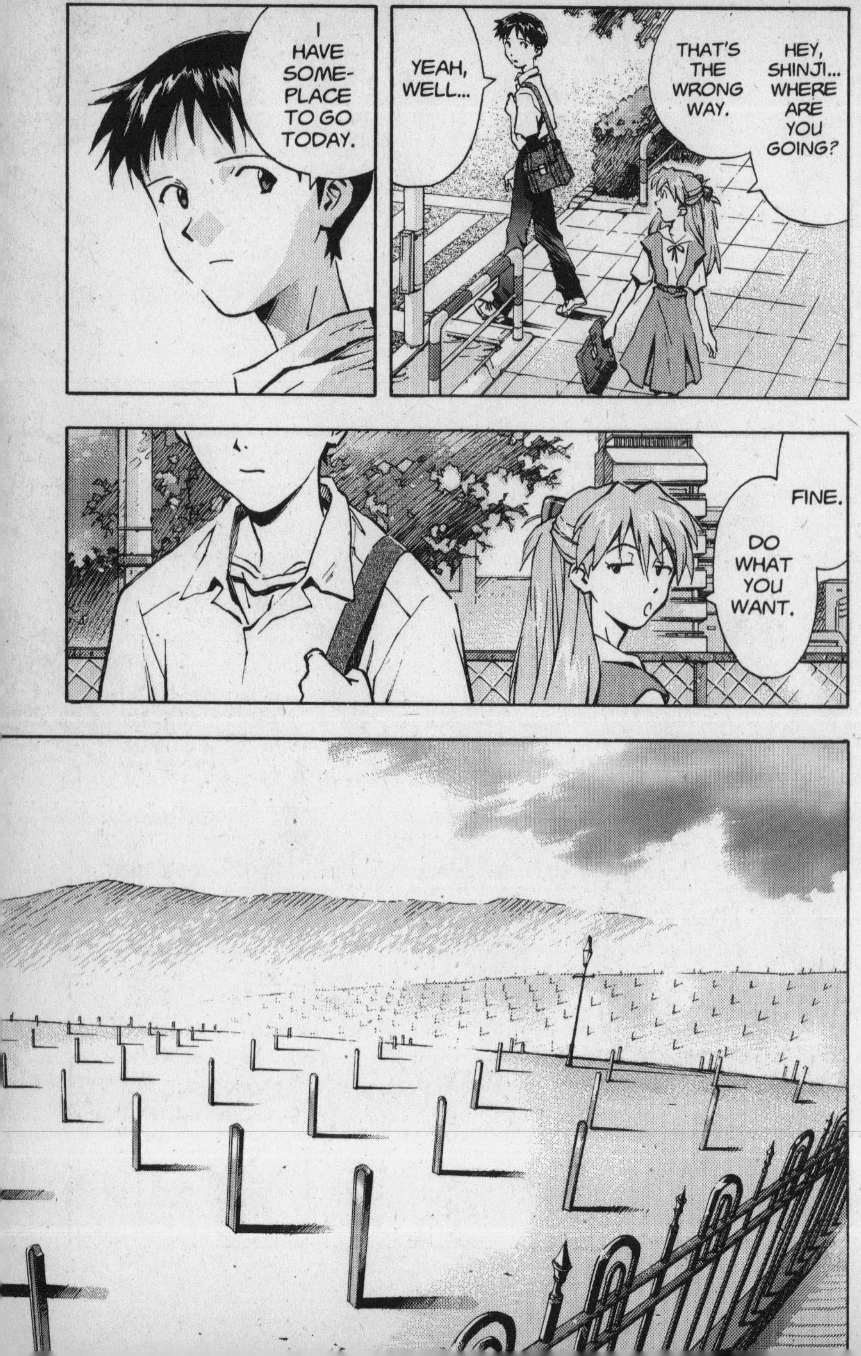
HEY, SHINJI... WHERE ARE YOU GOING?
THAT'S THE WRONG WAY.
YEAH, WELL...
I HAVE SOME-PLACE TO GO TODAY.
FINE.
DO WHAT YOU WANT.

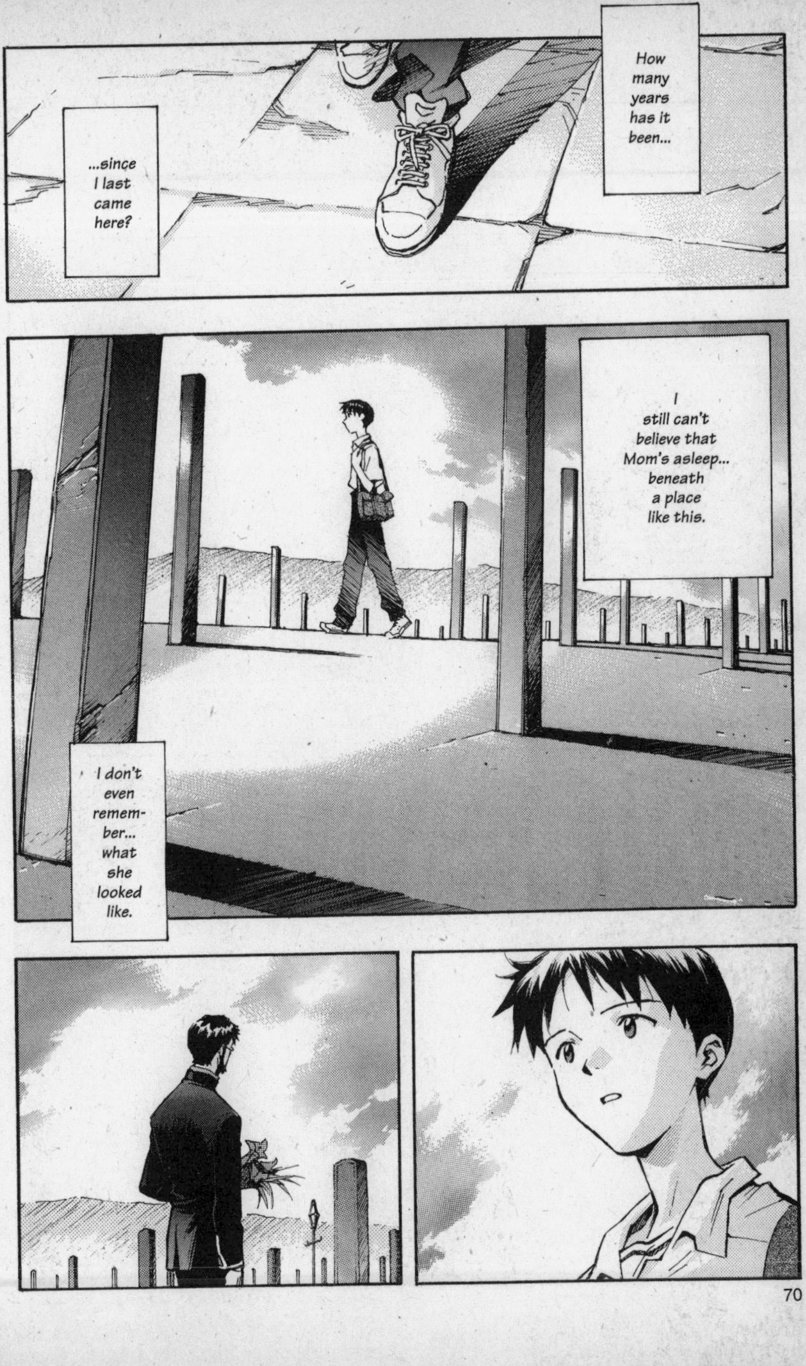
How many years has it been...
...since I last came here?
I still can't believe that Mom's asleep... beneath a place like this.
I don't even remem-ber... what she looked like.

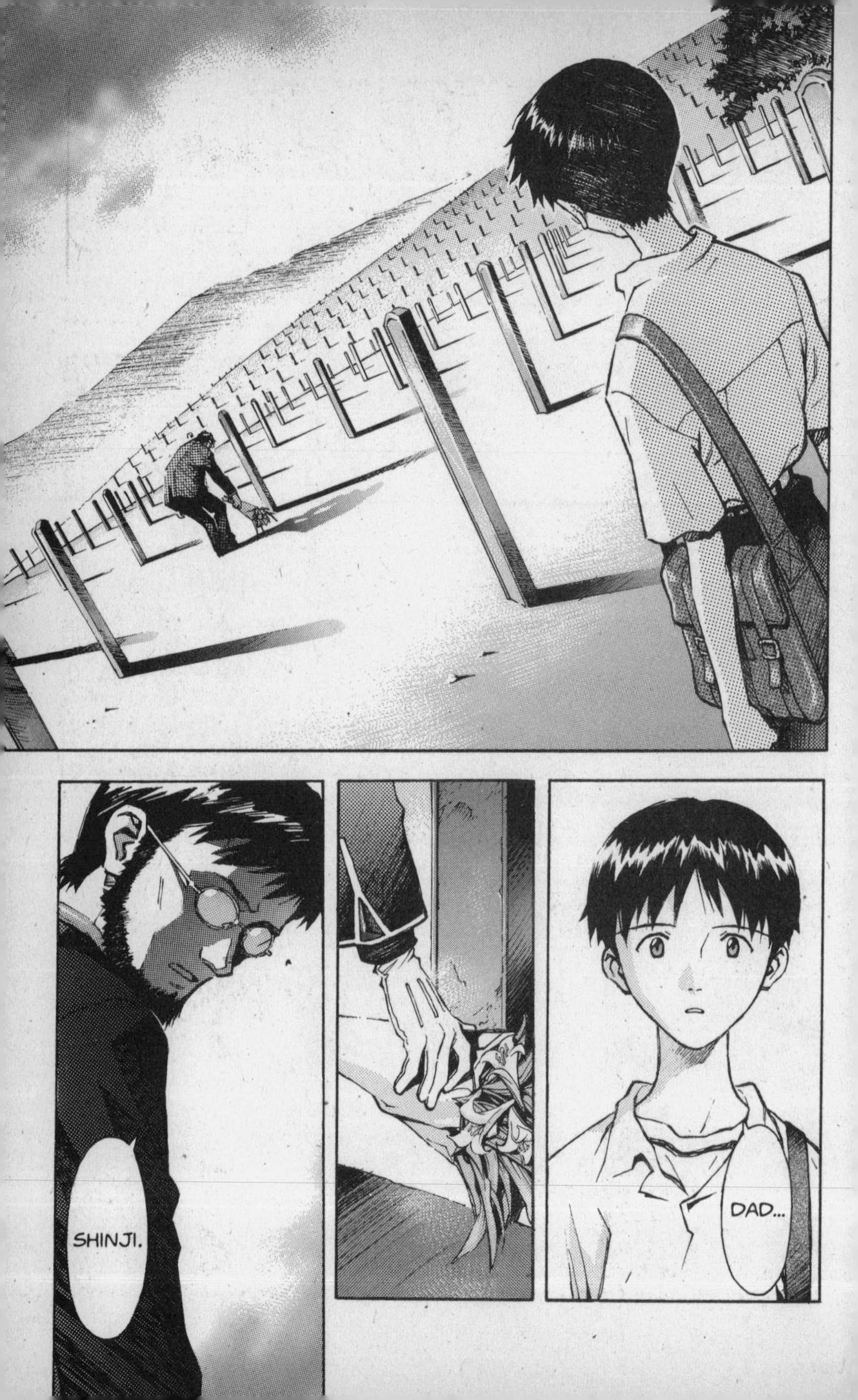
DAD...
SHINJI.

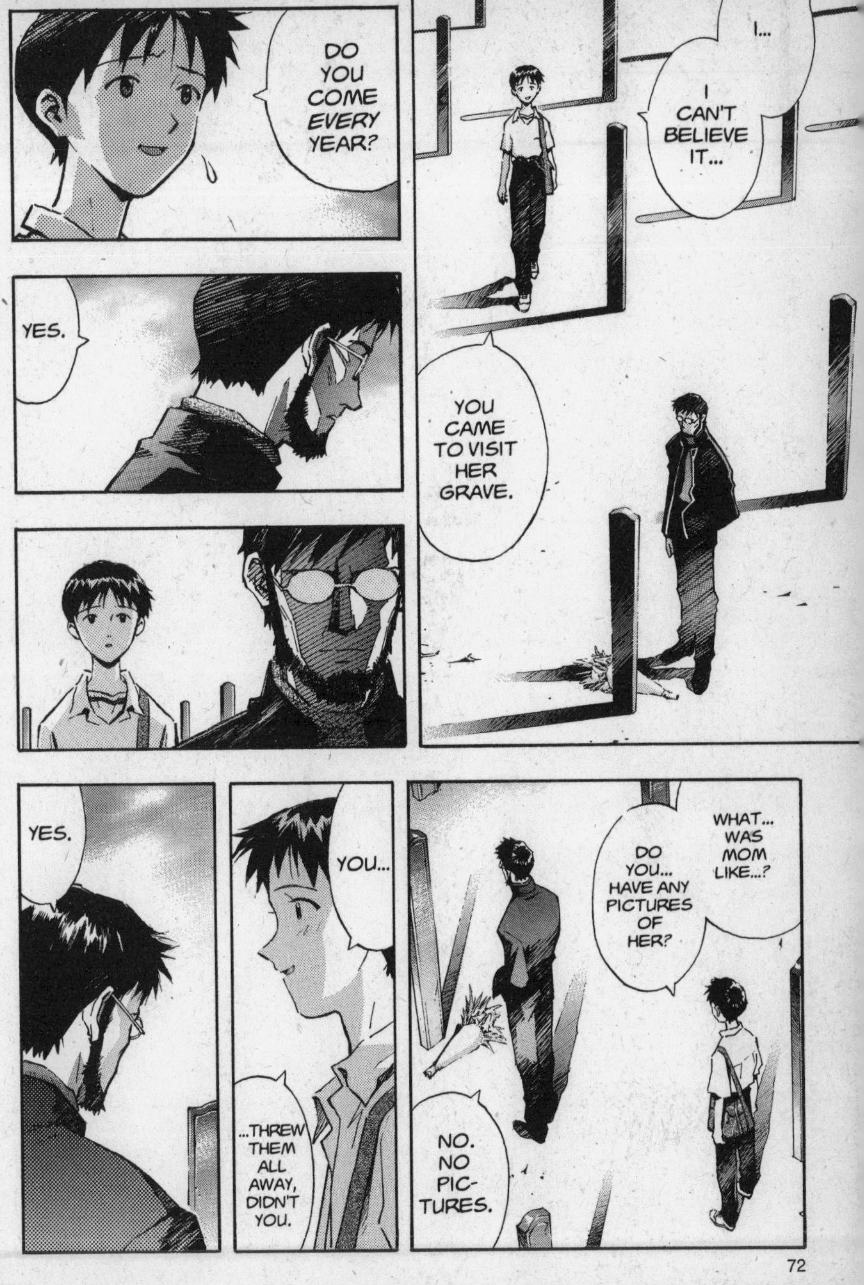
I...
I CAN'T BELIEVE IT...
YOU CAME TO VISIT HER GRAVE.
DO YOU COME EVERY YEAR?
YES.
WHAT... WAS MOM LIKE...?
DO YOU... HAVE ANY PICTURES OF HER?
NO. NO PIC- TURES.
YOU...
...THREW THEM ALL AWAY, DIDN'T YOU.
YES.

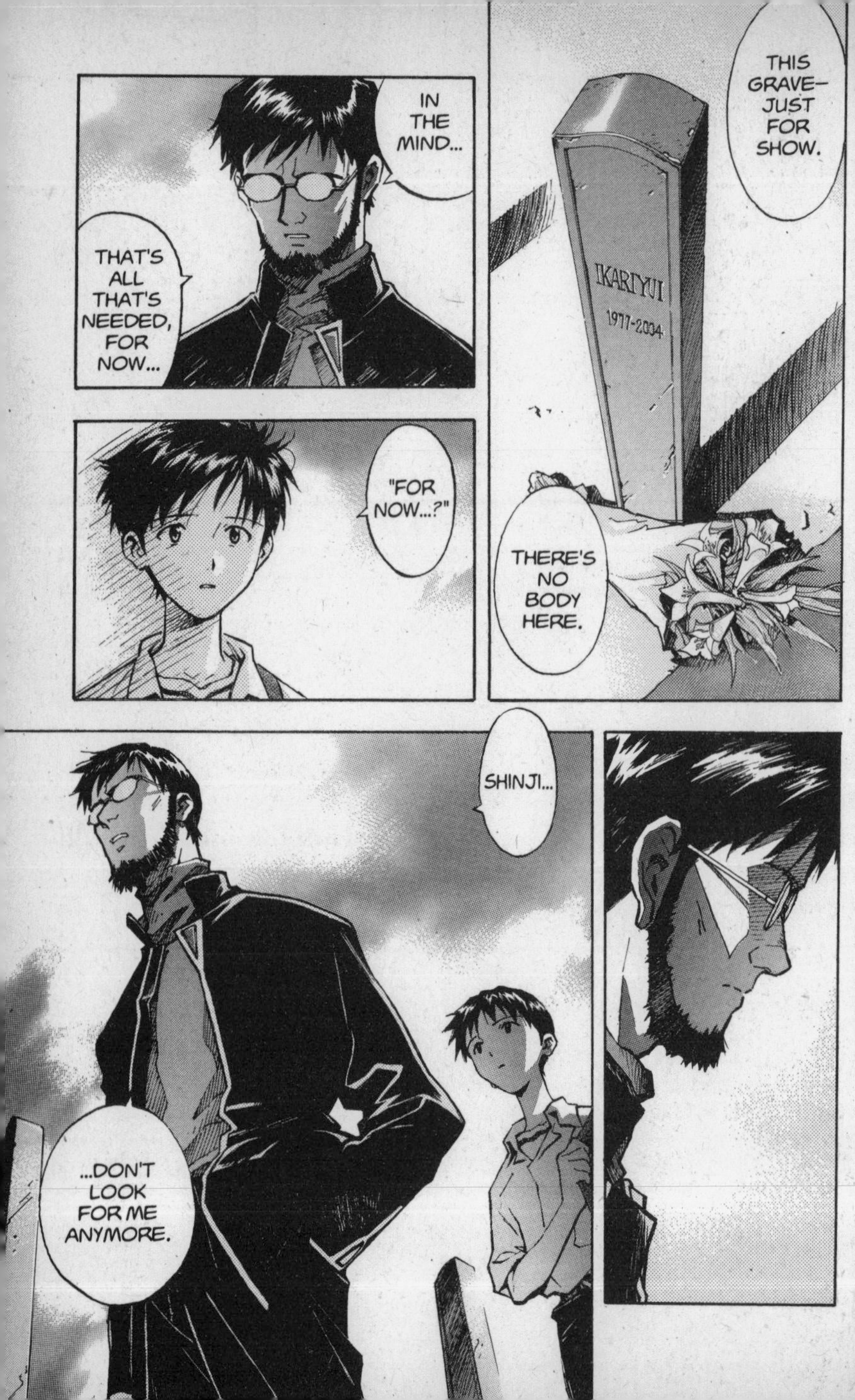
THIS GRAVE— JUST FOR SHOW.
IKARI YUI
1977-2004
THERE'S NO BODY HERE.
IN THE MIND...
THAT'S ALL THAT'S NEEDED, FOR NOW...
"FOR NOW...?"
SHINJI...
...DON'T LOOK FOR ME ANYMORE.

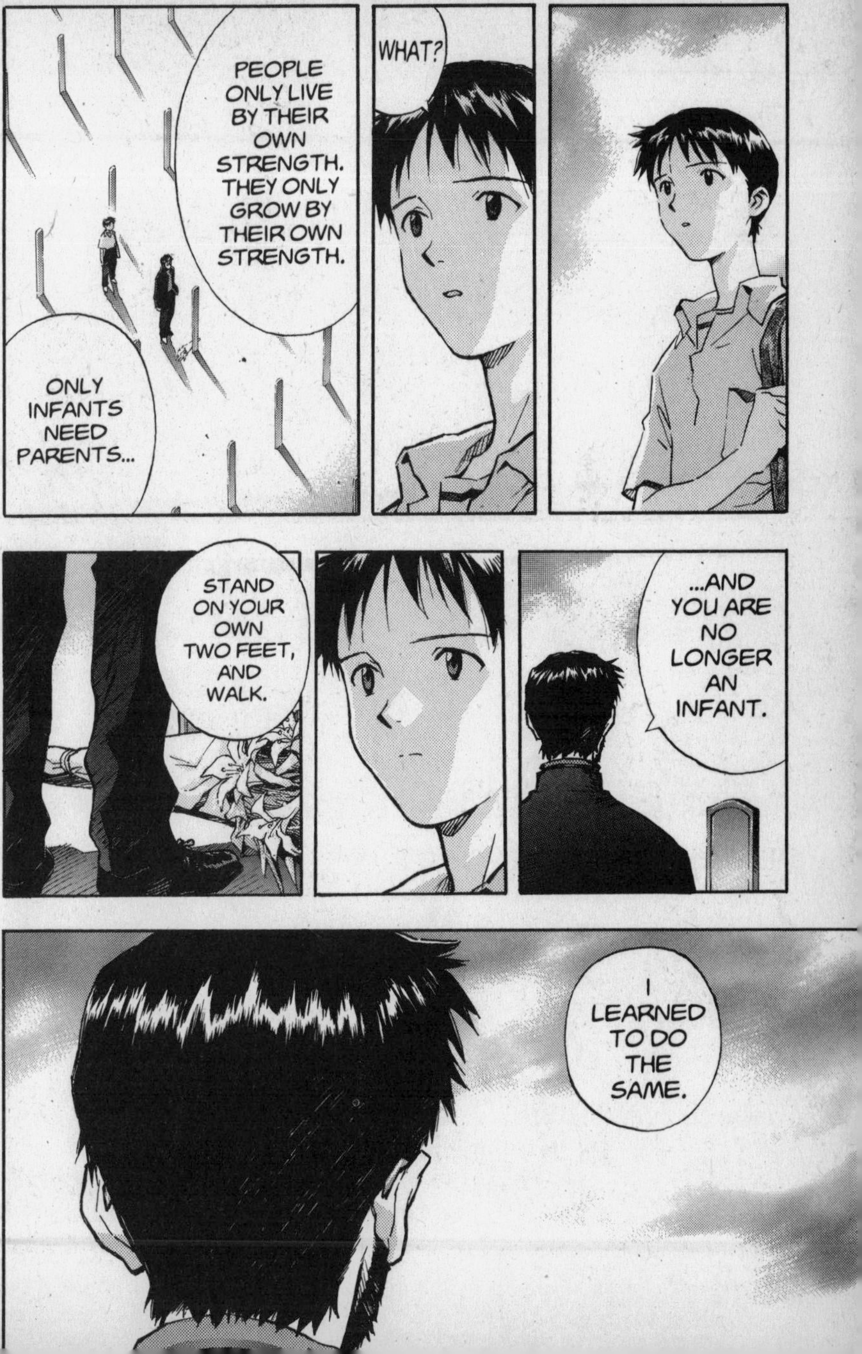
WHAT?
PEOPLE ONLY LIVE BY THEIR OWN STRENGTH. THEY ONLY GROW BY THEIR OWN STRENGTH.
ONLY INFANTS NEED PARENTS...
...AND YOU ARE NO LONGER AN INFANT.
STAND ON YOUR OWN TWO FEET, AND WALK.
I LEARNED TO DO THE SAME.

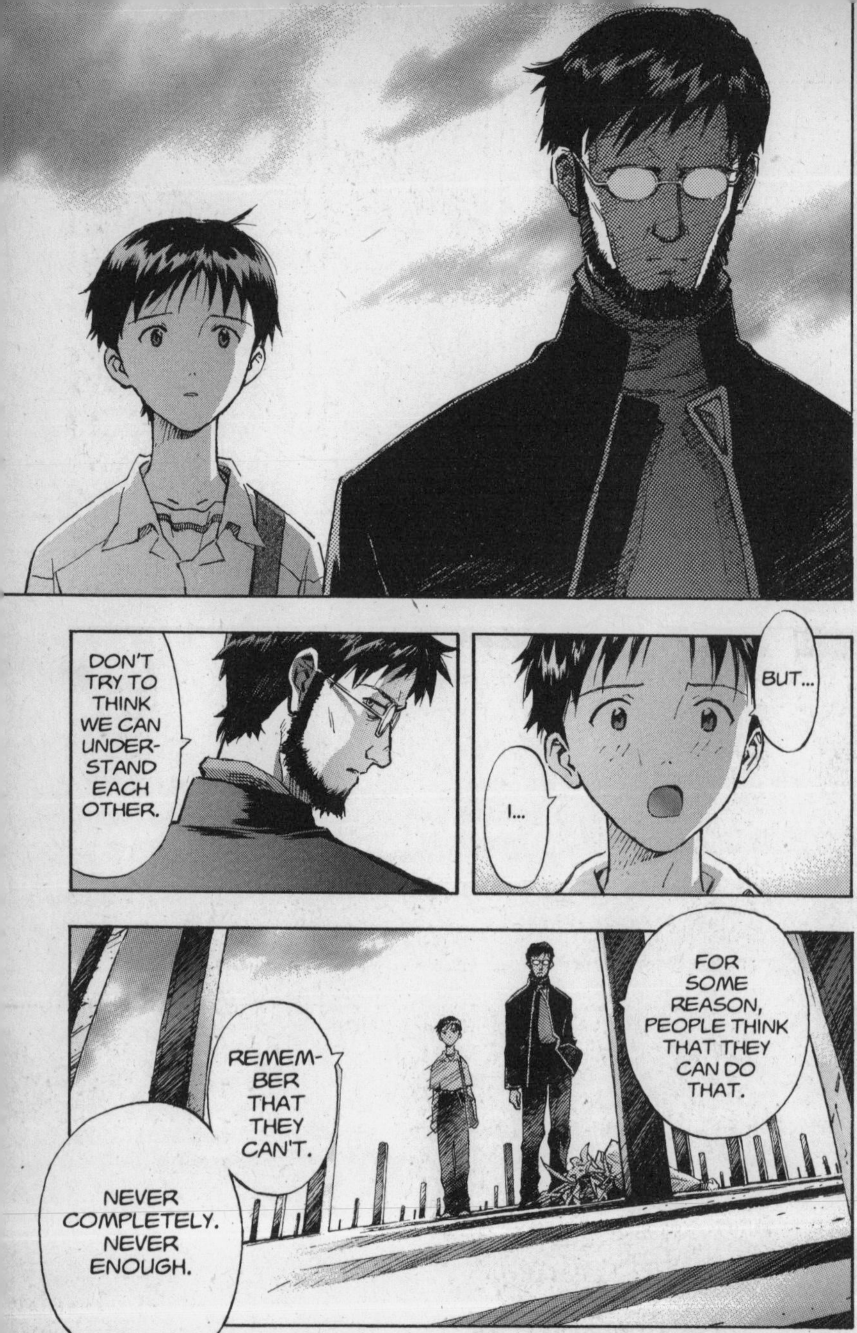
BUT...
I...
DON'T TRY TO THINK WE CAN UNDER-STAND EACH OTHER.
FOR SOME REASON, PEOPLE THINK THAT THEY CAN DO THAT.
REMEM-BER THAT THEY CAN'T.
NEVER COMPLETELY. NEVER ENOUGH.

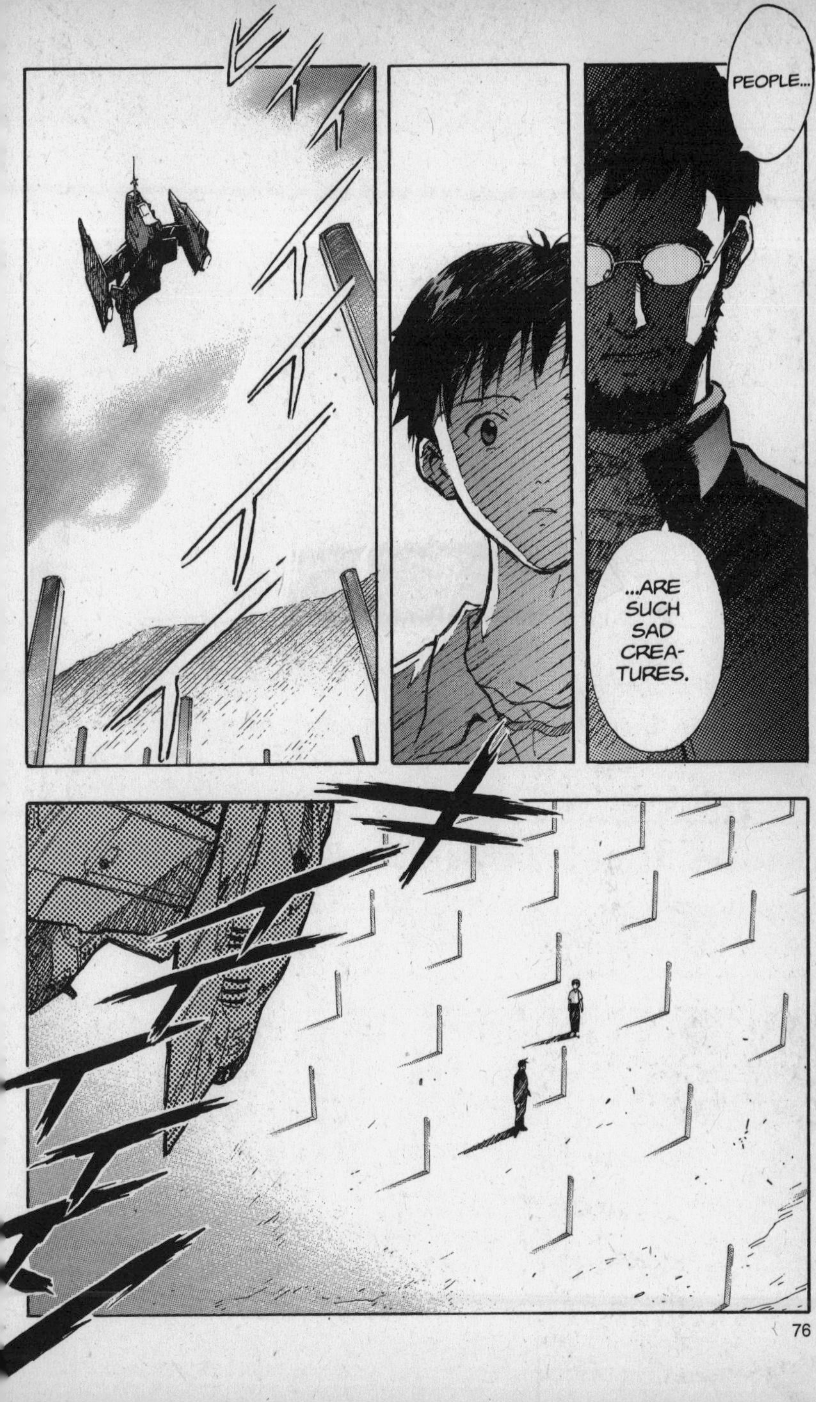
PEOPLE...
...ARE SUCH SAD CREA-TURES.

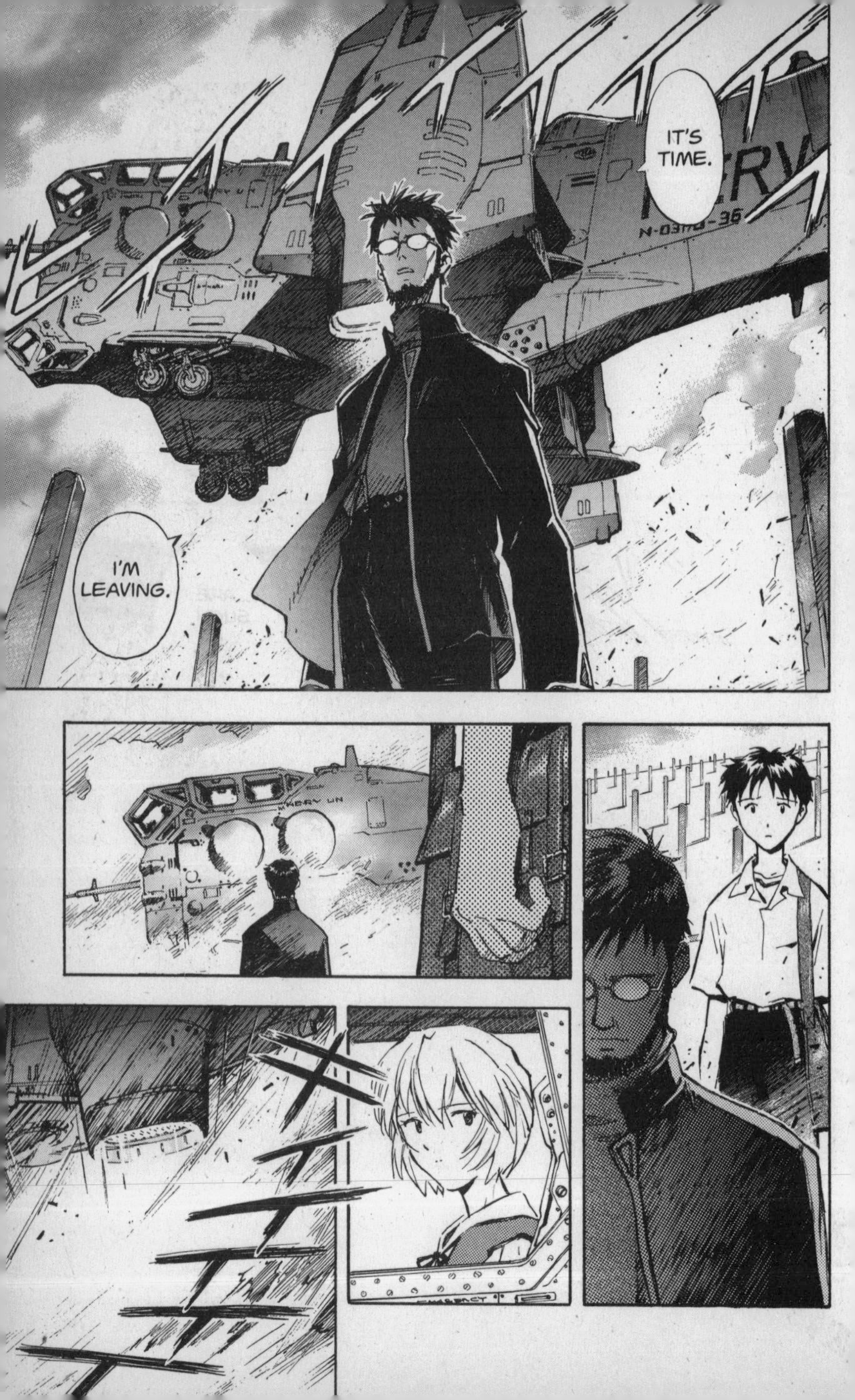
IT'S TIME.
I'M LEAVING.

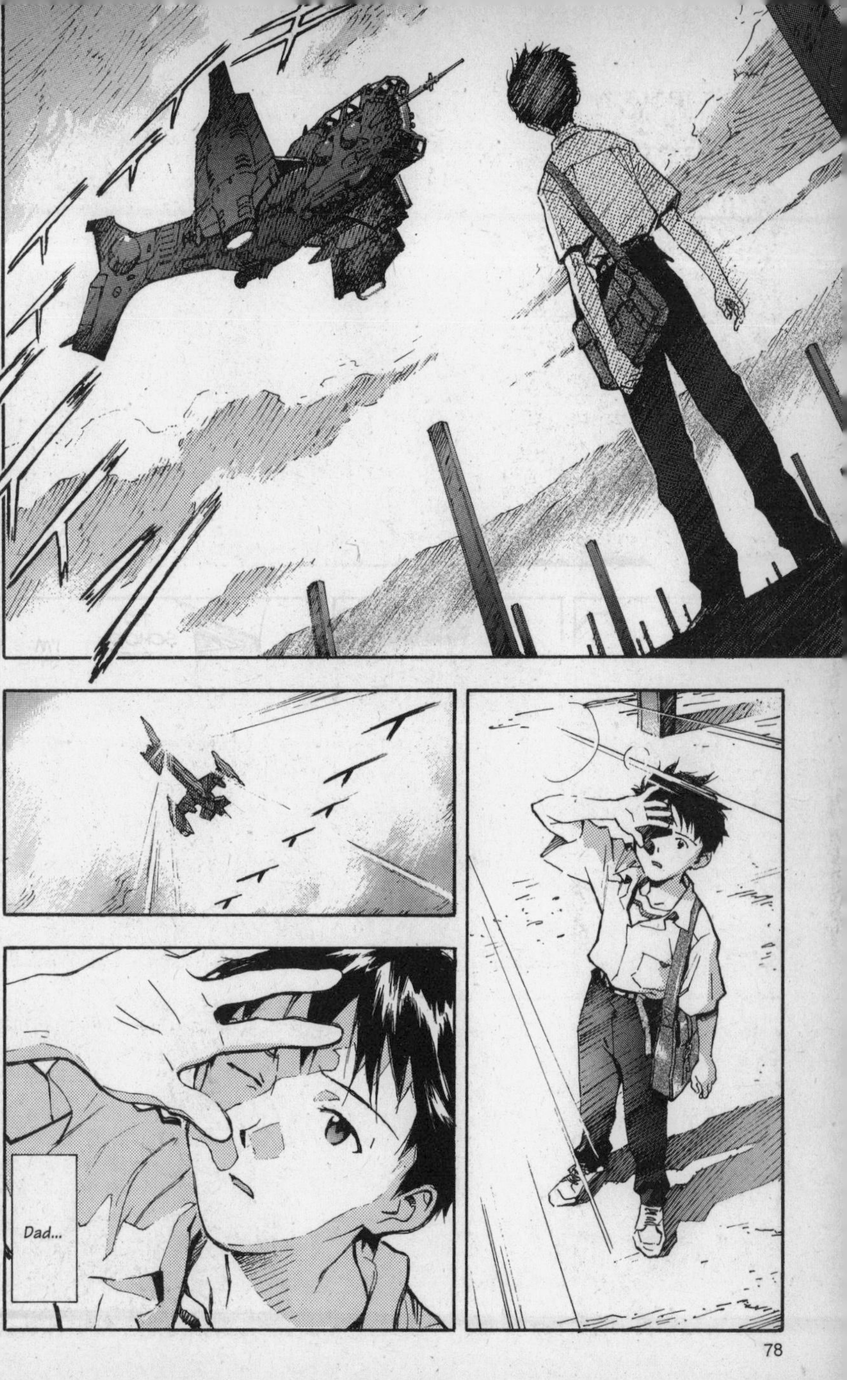
Dad...

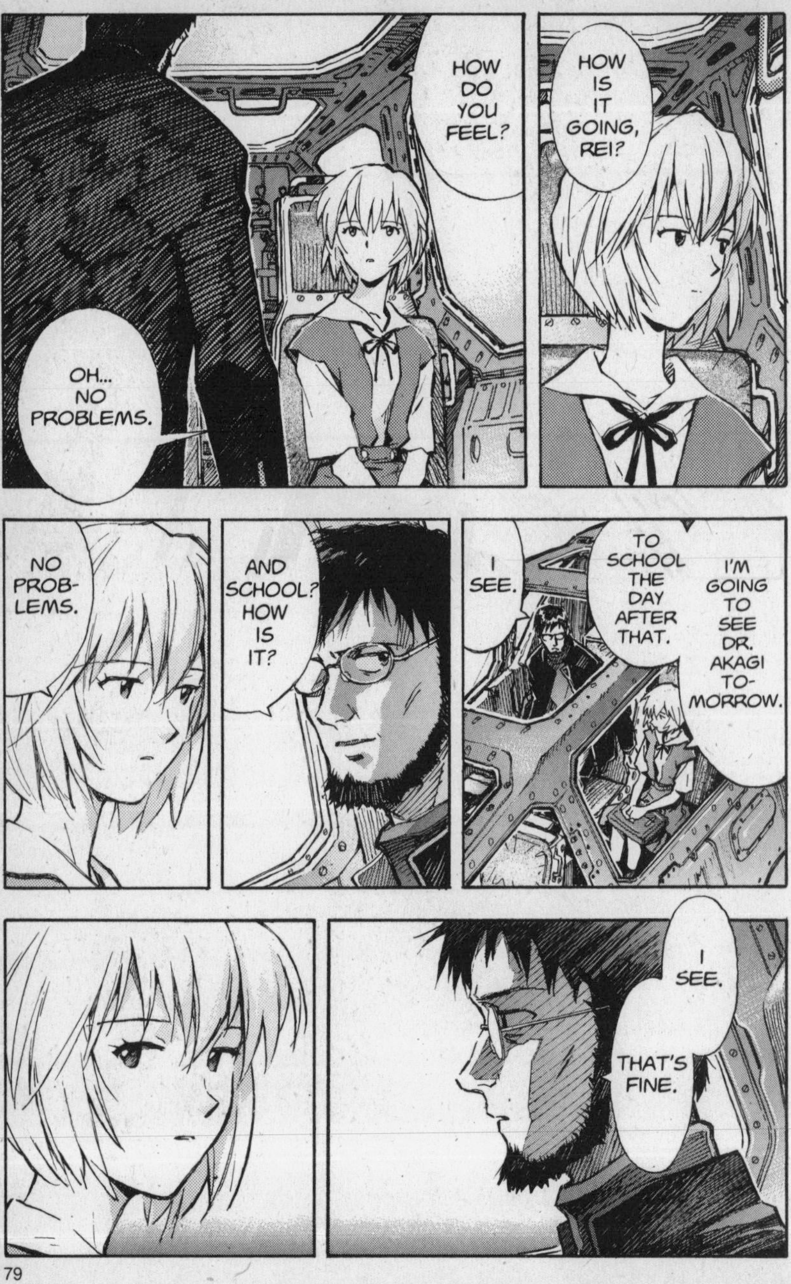
HOW IS IT GOING, REI?
HOW DO YOU FEEL?
OH... NO PROBLEMS.
I'M GOING TO SEE DR. AKAGI TO-MORROW.
TO SCHOOL THE DAY AFTER THAT.
I SEE.
AND SCHOOL? HOW IS IT?
NO PROB-LEMS.
I SEE.
THAT'S FINE.

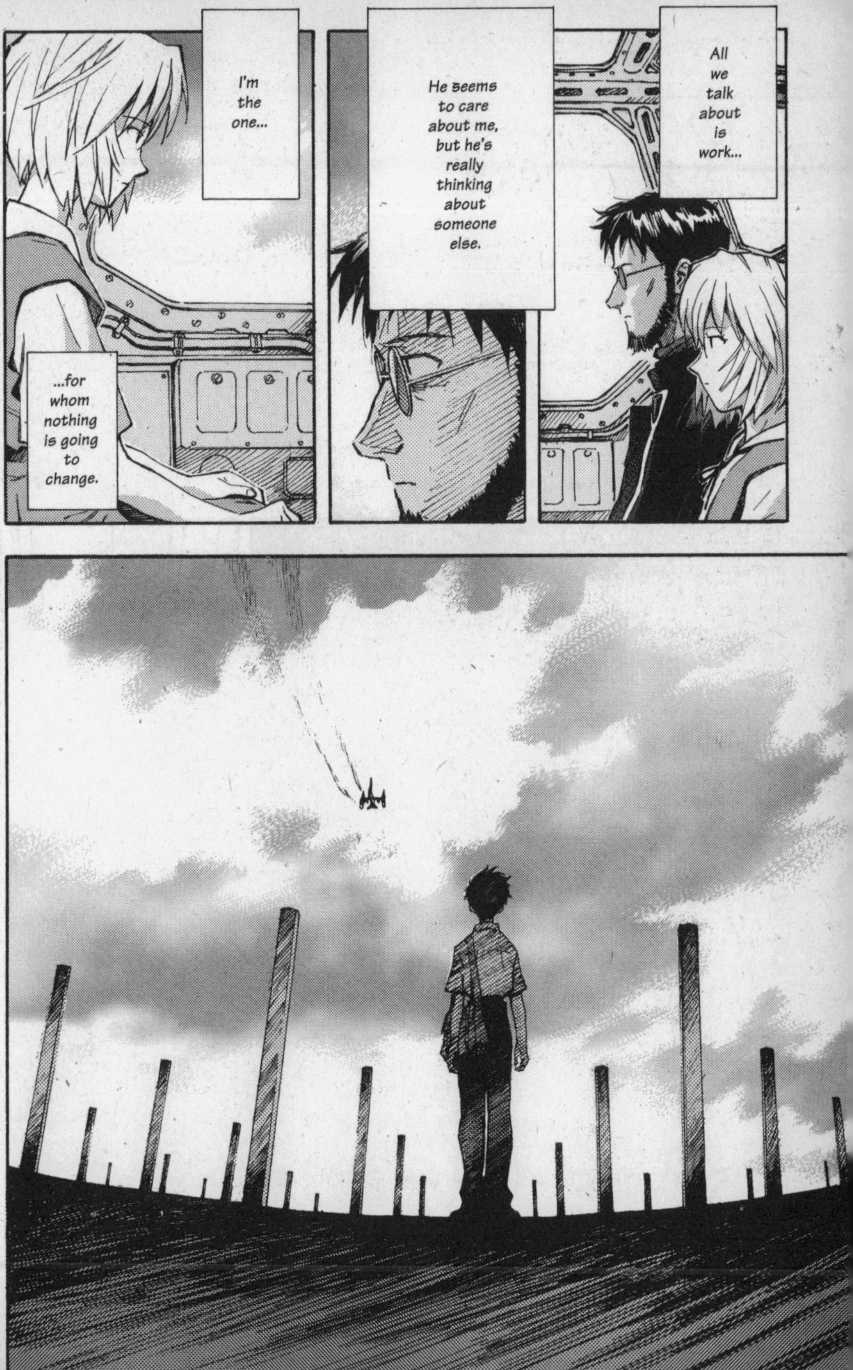
All we talk about is work...
He seems to care about me, but he's really thinking about someone else.
I'm the one...
...for whom nothing is going to change.

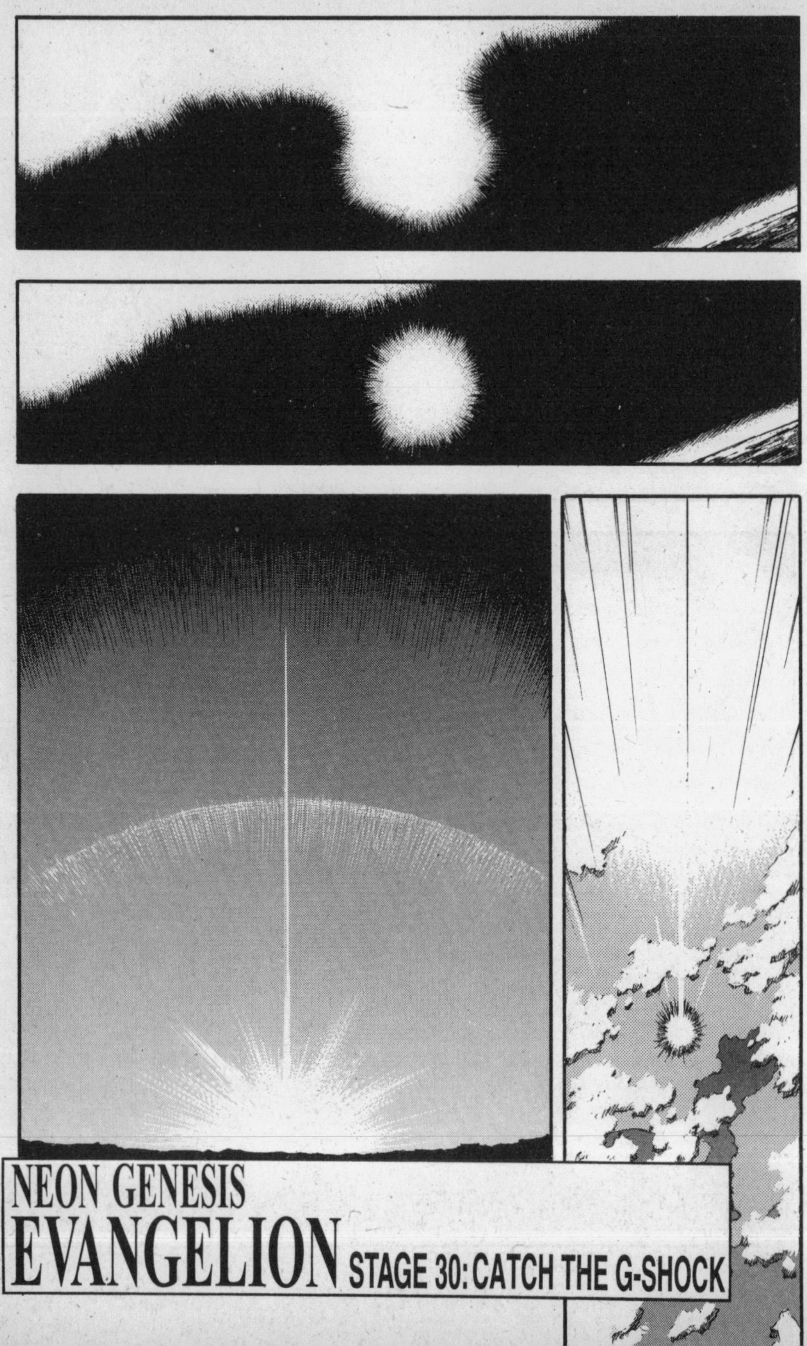
NEON GENESIS
EVANGELION
STAGE 30: CATCH THE G-SHOCK

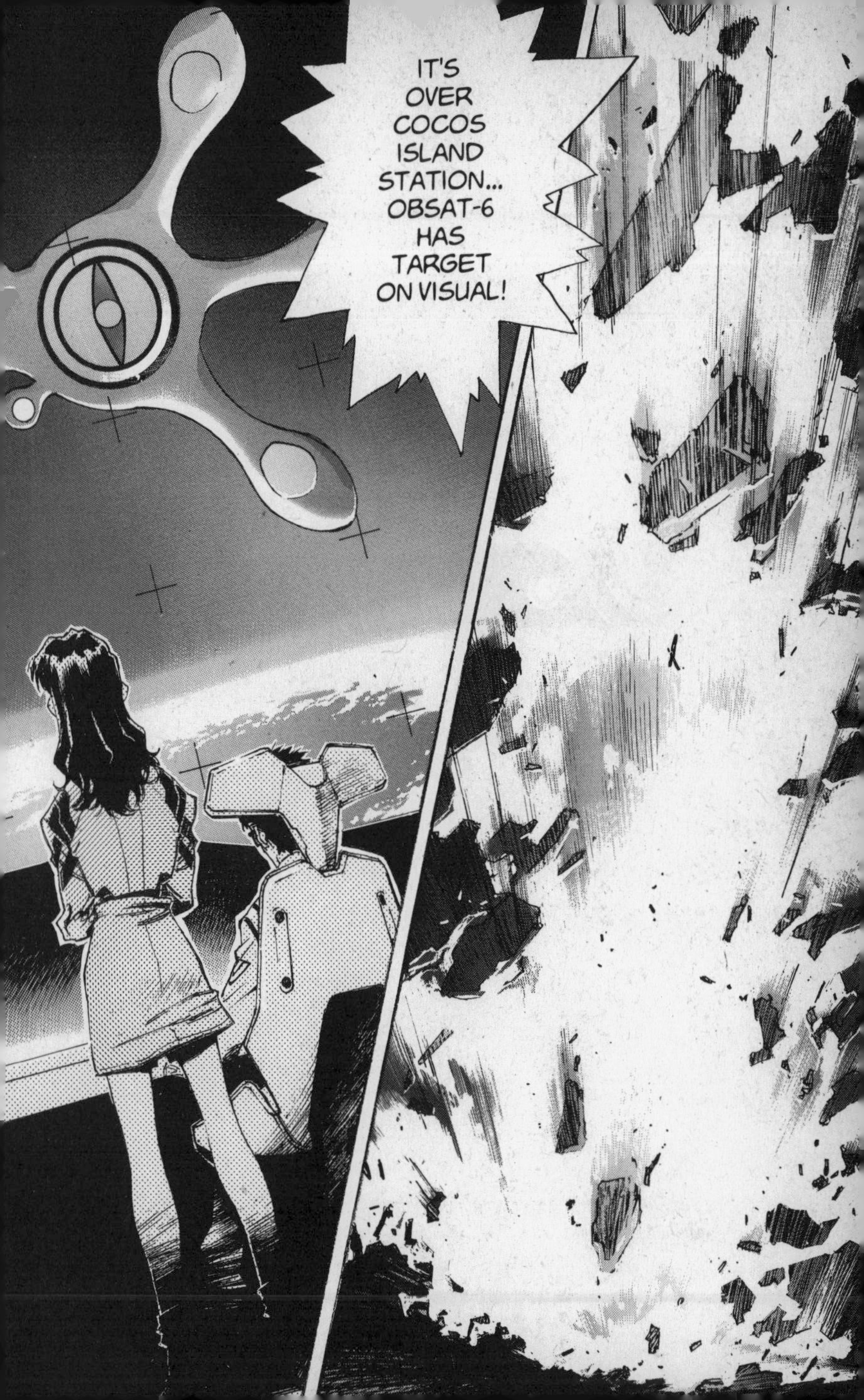
IT'S OVER COCOS ISLAND STATION... OBSAT-6 HAS TARGET ON VISUAL!

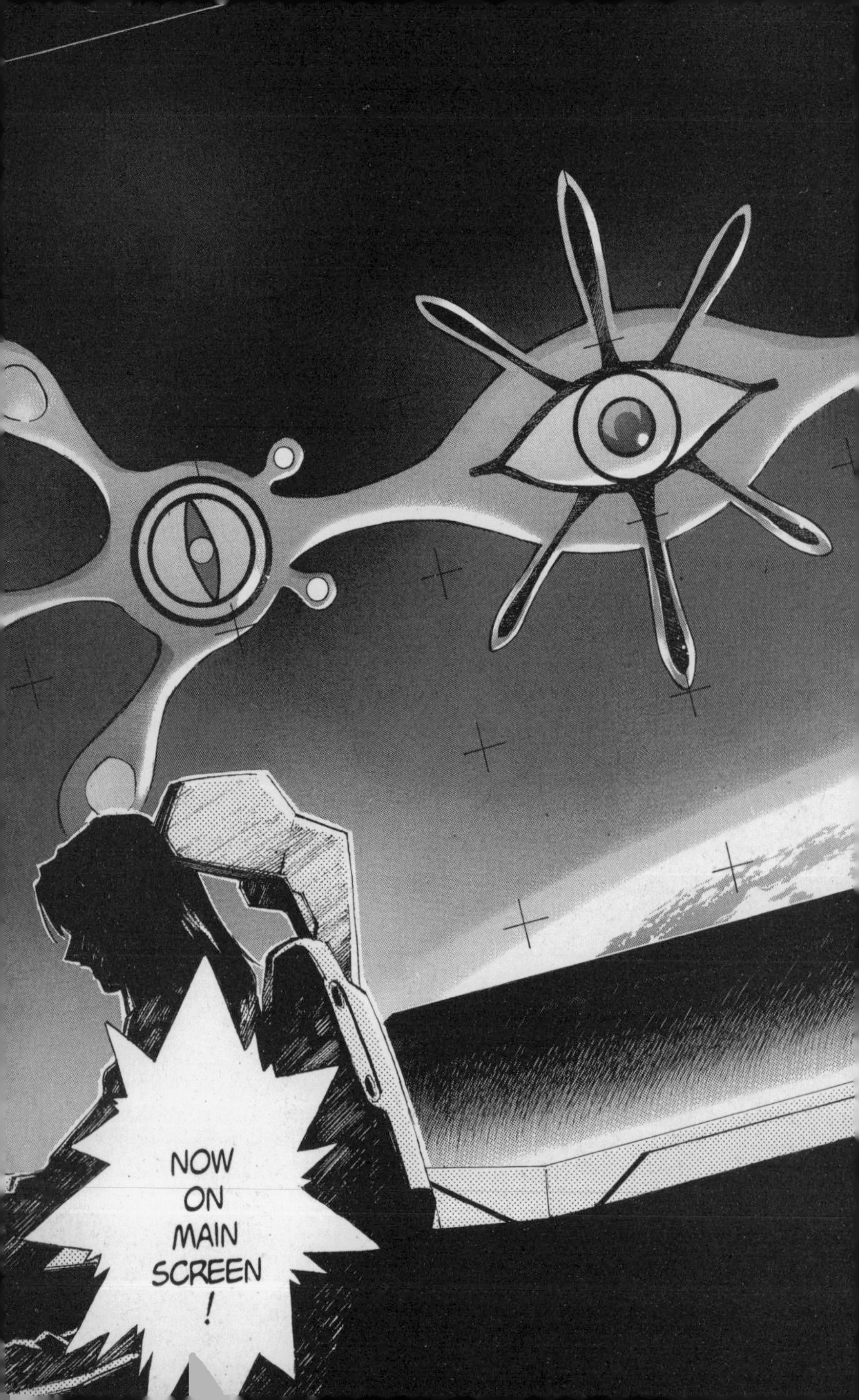
NOW ON MAIN SCREEN !

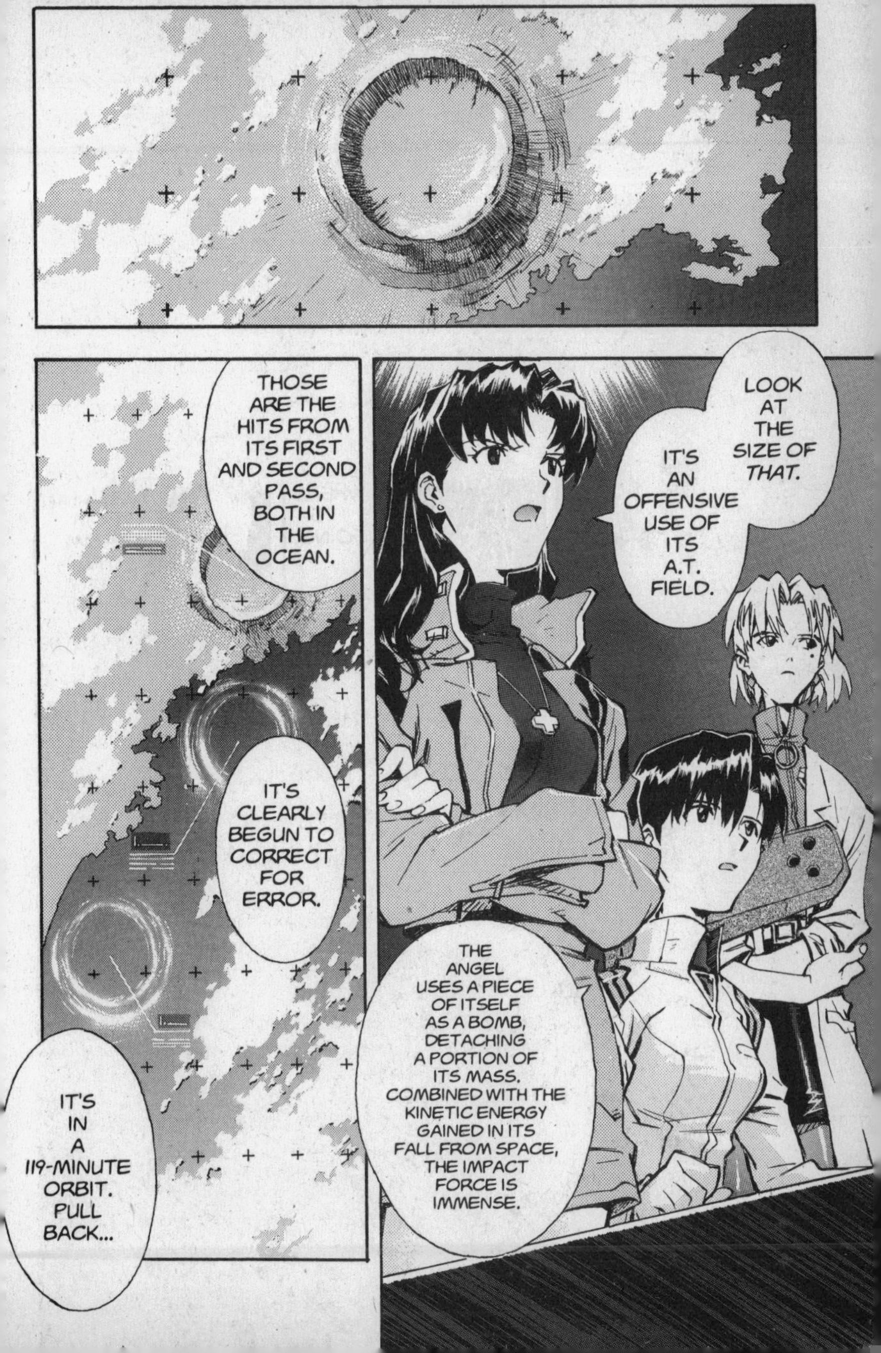
LOOK AT THE SIZE OF THAT.
IT'S AN OFFENSIVE USE OF ITS A.T. FIELD.
THE ANGEL USES A PIECE OF ITSELF AS A BOMB, DETACHING A PORTION OF ITS MASS. COMBINED WITH THE KINETIC ENERGY GAINED IN ITS FALL FROM SPACE, THE IMPACT FORCE IS IMMENSE.
THOSE ARE THE HITS FROM ITS FIRST AND SECOND PASS, BOTH IN THE OCEAN.
IT'S CLEARLY BEGUN TO CORRECT FOR ERROR.
IT'S IN A 119-MINUTE ORBIT. PULL BACK...

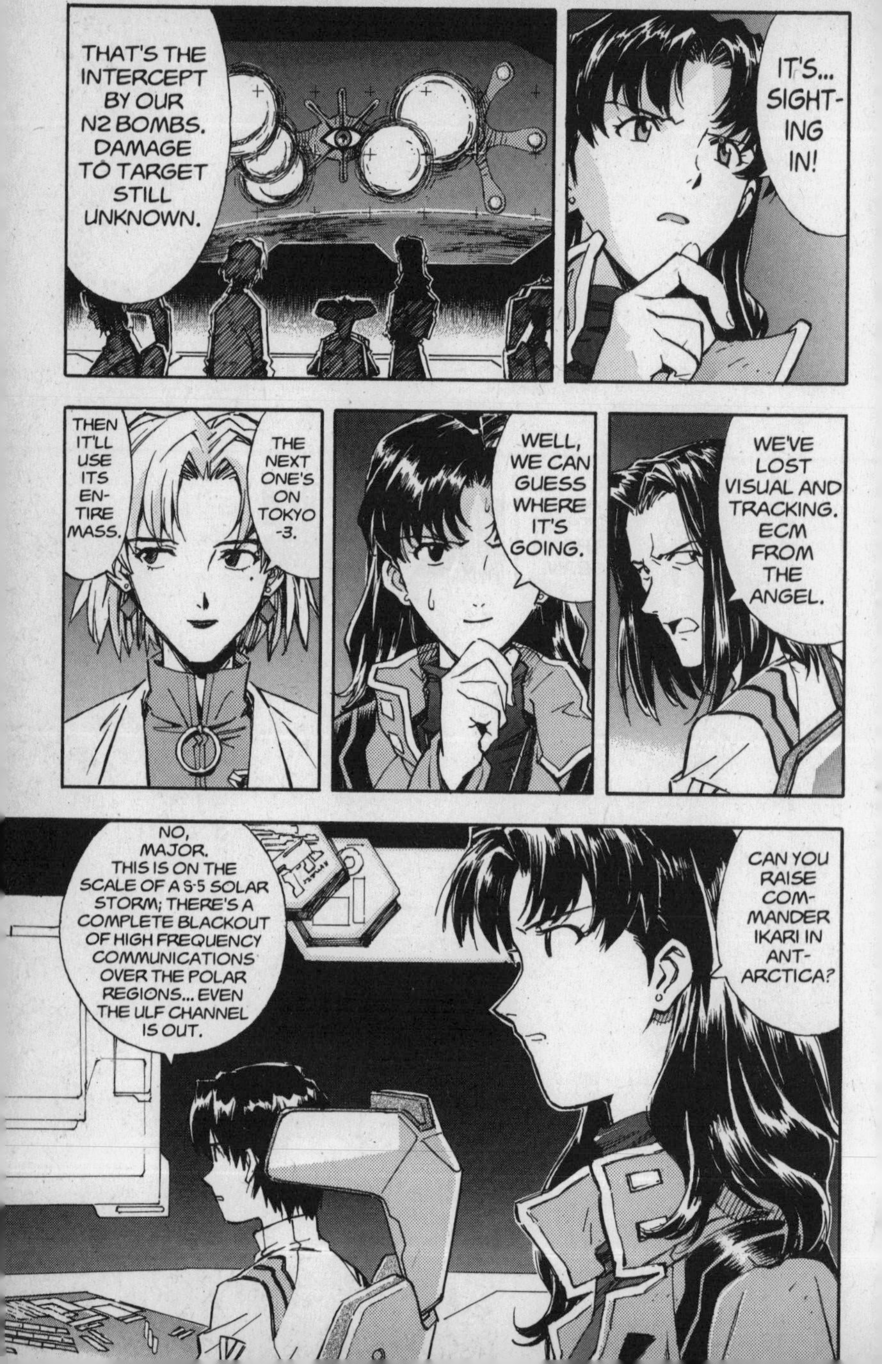
IT'S... SIGHTING IN!
THAT'S THE INTERCEPT BY OUR N2 BOMBS. DAMAGE TO TARGET STILL UNKNOWN.
WE'VE LOST VISUAL AND TRACKING. ECM FROM THE ANGEL.
WELL, WE CAN GUESS WHERE IT'S GOING.
THE NEXT ONE'S ON TOKYO-3.
THEN IT'LL USE ITS ENTIRE MASS.
CAN YOU RAISE COMMANDER IKARI IN ANTARCTICA?
NO, MAJOR. THIS IS ON THE SCALE OF A S-5 SOLAR STORM; THERE'S A COMPLETE BLACKOUT OF HIGH FREQUENCY COMMUNICATIONS OVER THE POLAR REGIONS... EVEN THE ULF CHANNEL IS OUT.

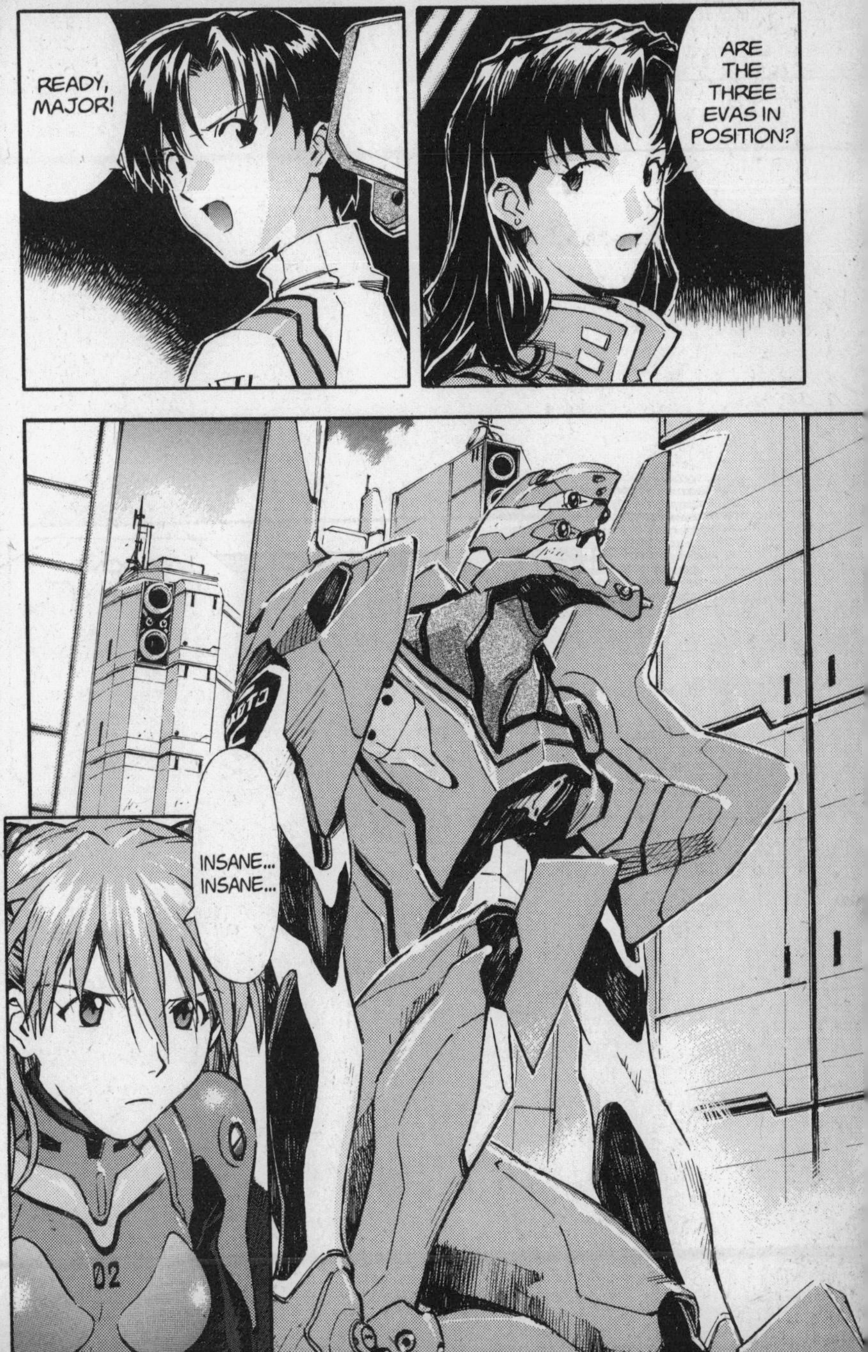
ARE THE THREE EVAS IN POSITION?
READY, MAJOR!
INSANE... INSANE...

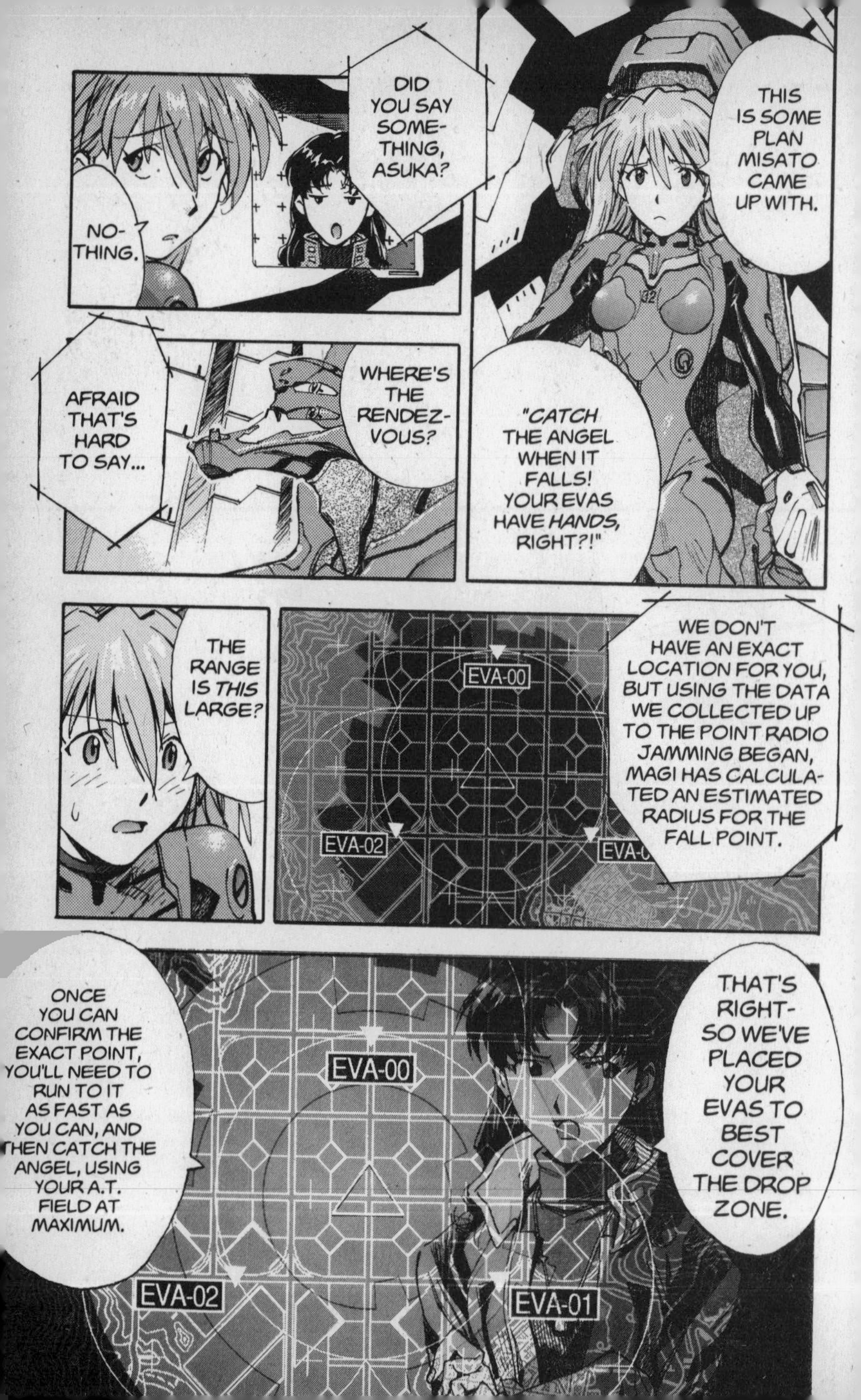
THIS IS SOME PLAN MISATO CAME UP WITH.
"CATCH THE ANGEL WHEN IT FALLS! YOUR EVAS HAVE HANDS, RIGHT?!"
DID YOU SAY SOME-THING, ASUKA?
NO-THING.
WHERE'S THE RENDEZ-VOUS?
AFRAID THAT'S HARD TO SAY...
WE DON'T HAVE AN EXACT LOCATION FOR YOU, BUT USING THE DATA WE COLLECTED UP TO THE POINT RADIO JAMMING BEGAN, MAGI HAS CALCULA-TED AN ESTIMATED RADIUS FOR THE FALL POINT.
EVA-00
EVA-02
THE RANGE IS THIS LARGE?
THAT'S RIGHT- SO WE'VE PLACED YOUR EVAS TO BEST COVER THE DROP ZONE.
ONCE YOU CAN CONFIRM THE EXACT POINT, YOU'LL NEED TO RUN TO IT AS FAST AS YOU CAN, AND THEN CATCH THE ANGEL, USING YOUR A.T. FIELD AT MAXIMUM.
EVA-00
EVA-02
EVA-01

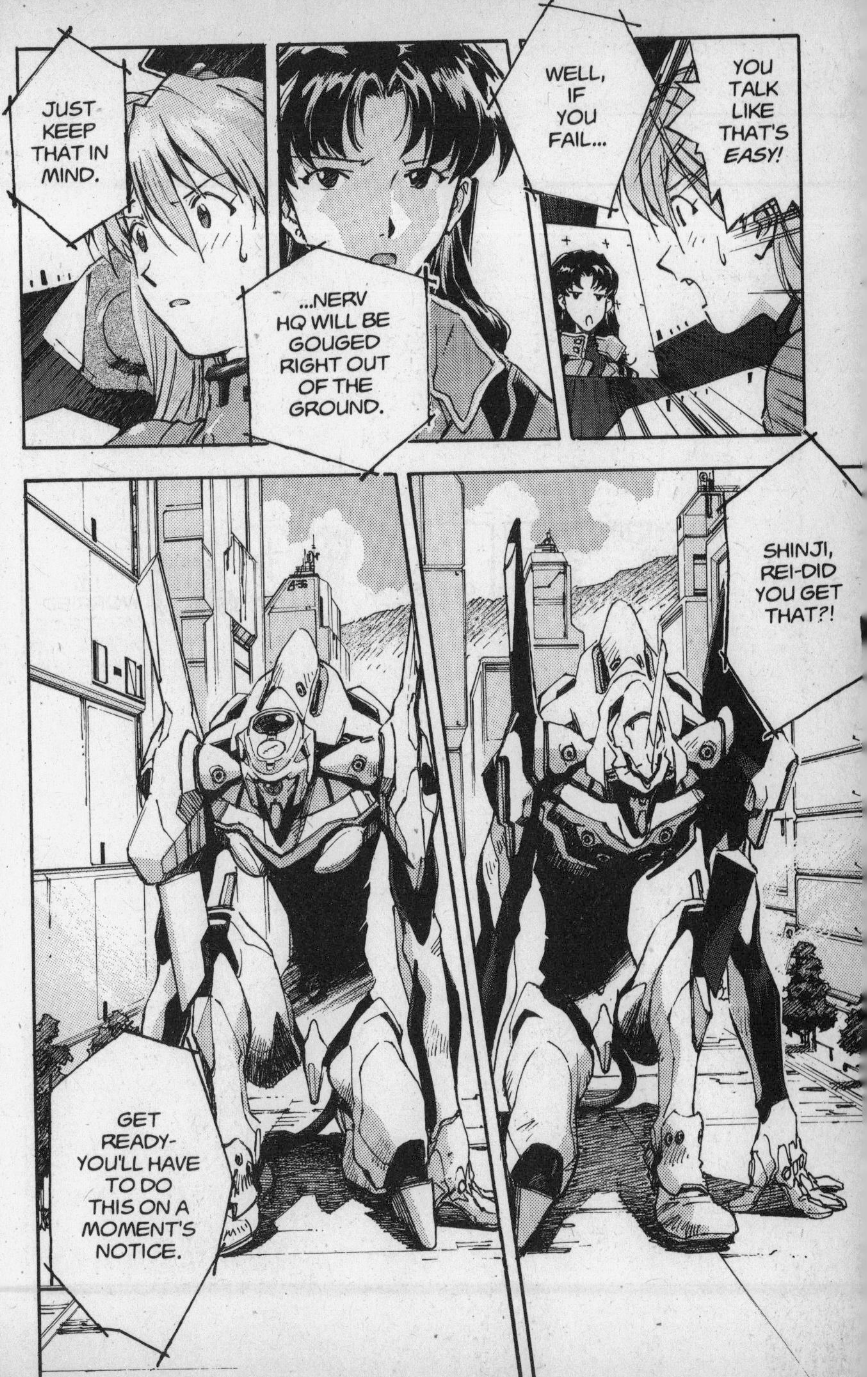
YOU TALK LIKE THAT'S EASY!
WELL, IF YOU FAIL...
...NERV HQ WILL BE GOUGED RIGHT OUT OF THE GROUND.
JUST KEEP THAT IN MIND.
SHINJI, REI-DID YOU GET THAT?!
GET READY- YOU'LL HAVE TO DO THIS ON A MOMENT'S NOTICE.

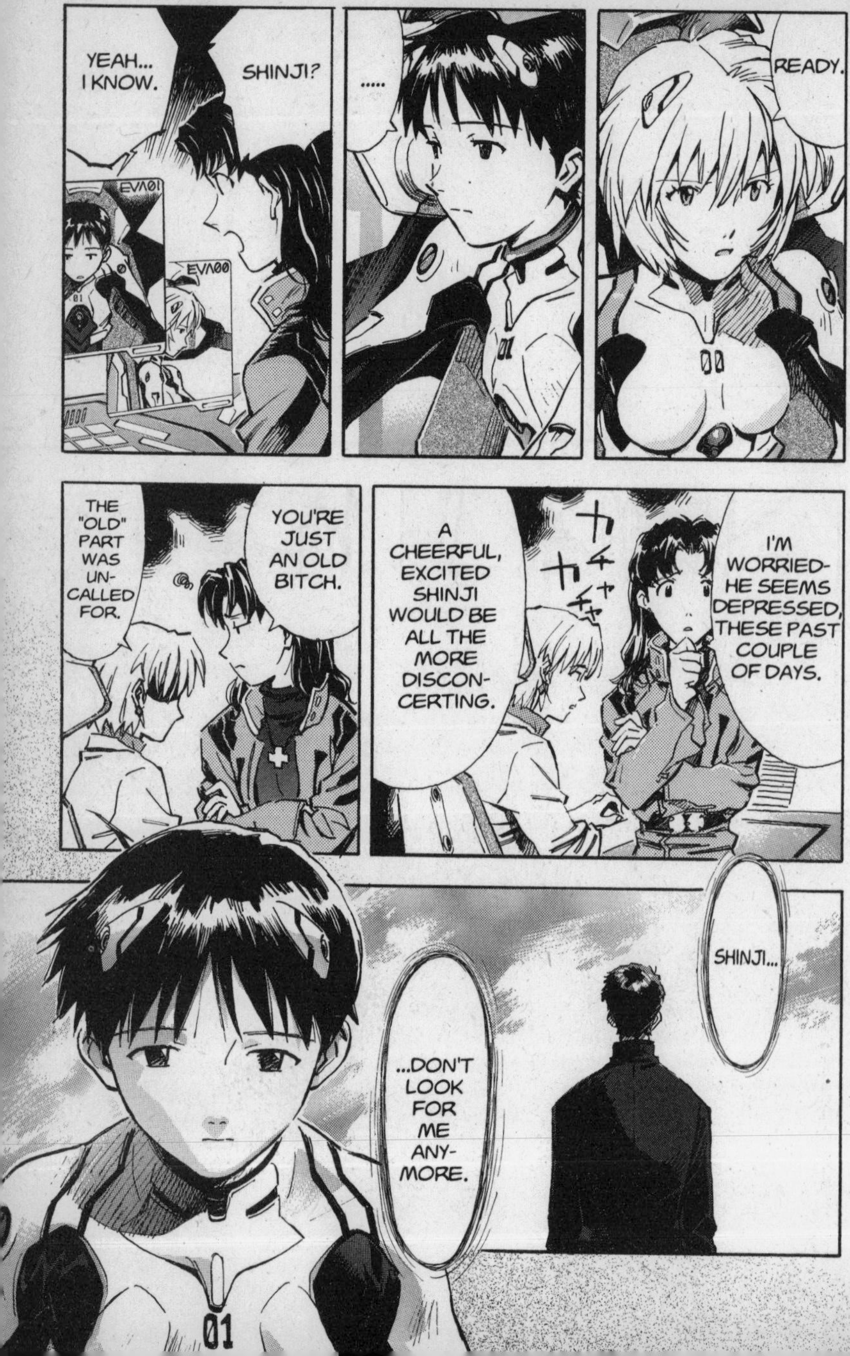
READY.
.....
SHINJI?
YEAH... I KNOW.
EVA01
EVA00
I'M WORRIED- HE SEEMS DEPRESSED, THESE PAST COUPLE OF DAYS.
カチャカチャ
A CHEERFUL, EXCITED SHINJI WOULD BE ALL THE MORE DISCONCERTING.
YOU'RE JUST AN OLD BITCH.
THE "OLD" PART WAS UN-CALLED FOR.
SHINJI...
...DON'T LOOK FOR ME ANY-MORE.

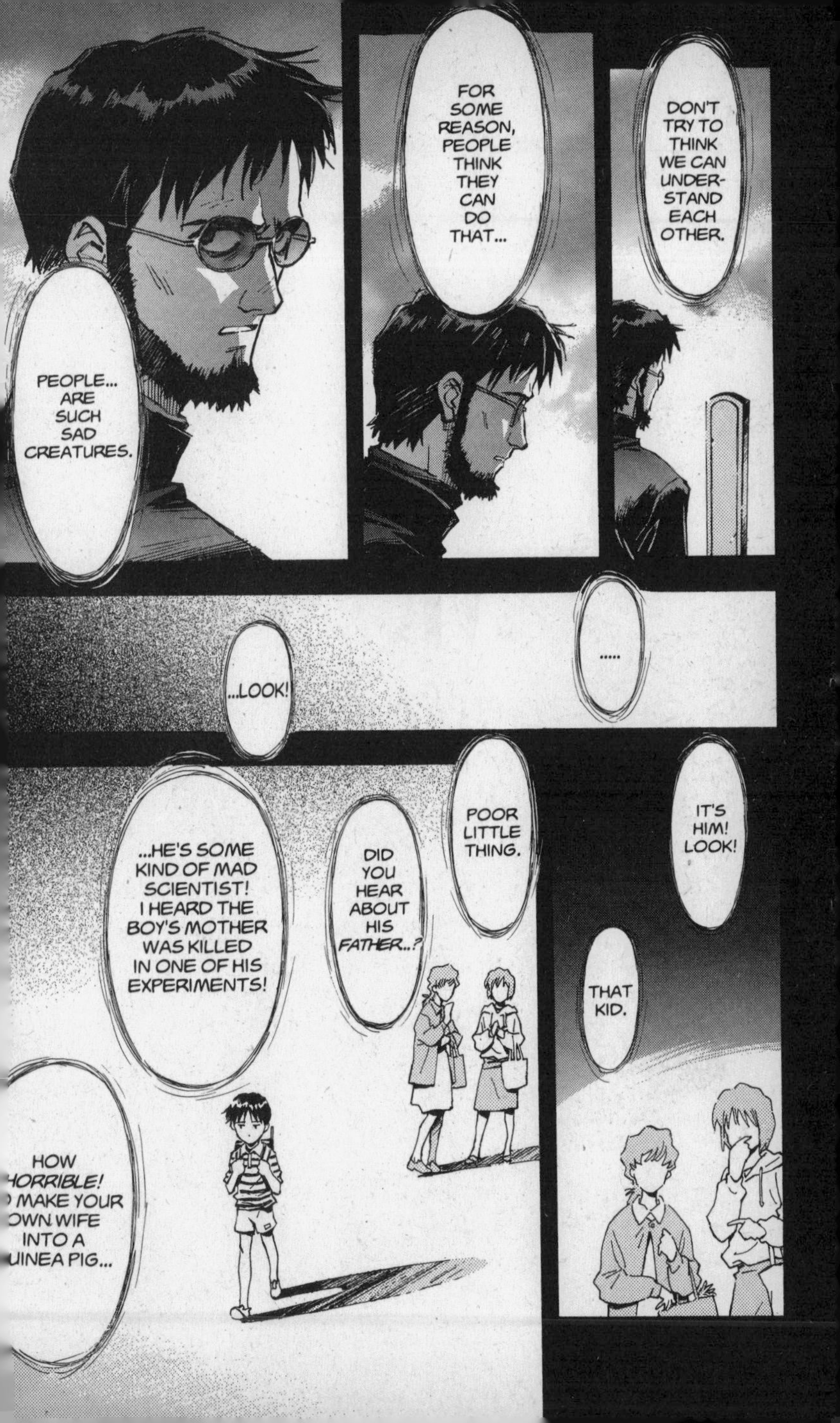
DON'T TRY TO THINK WE CAN UNDER-STAND EACH OTHER.
FOR SOME REASON, PEOPLE THINK THEY CAN DO THAT...
PEOPLE... ARE SUCH SAD CREATURES.
.....
...LOOK!
IT'S HIM! LOOK!
THAT KID.
POOR LITTLE THING.
DID YOU HEAR ABOUT HIS *FATHER...?*
...HE'S SOME KIND OF MAD SCIENTIST! I HEARD THE BOY'S MOTHER WAS KILLED IN ONE OF HIS EXPERIMENTS!
HOW HORRIBLE! D MAKE YOUR OWN WIFE INTO A UINEA PIG...

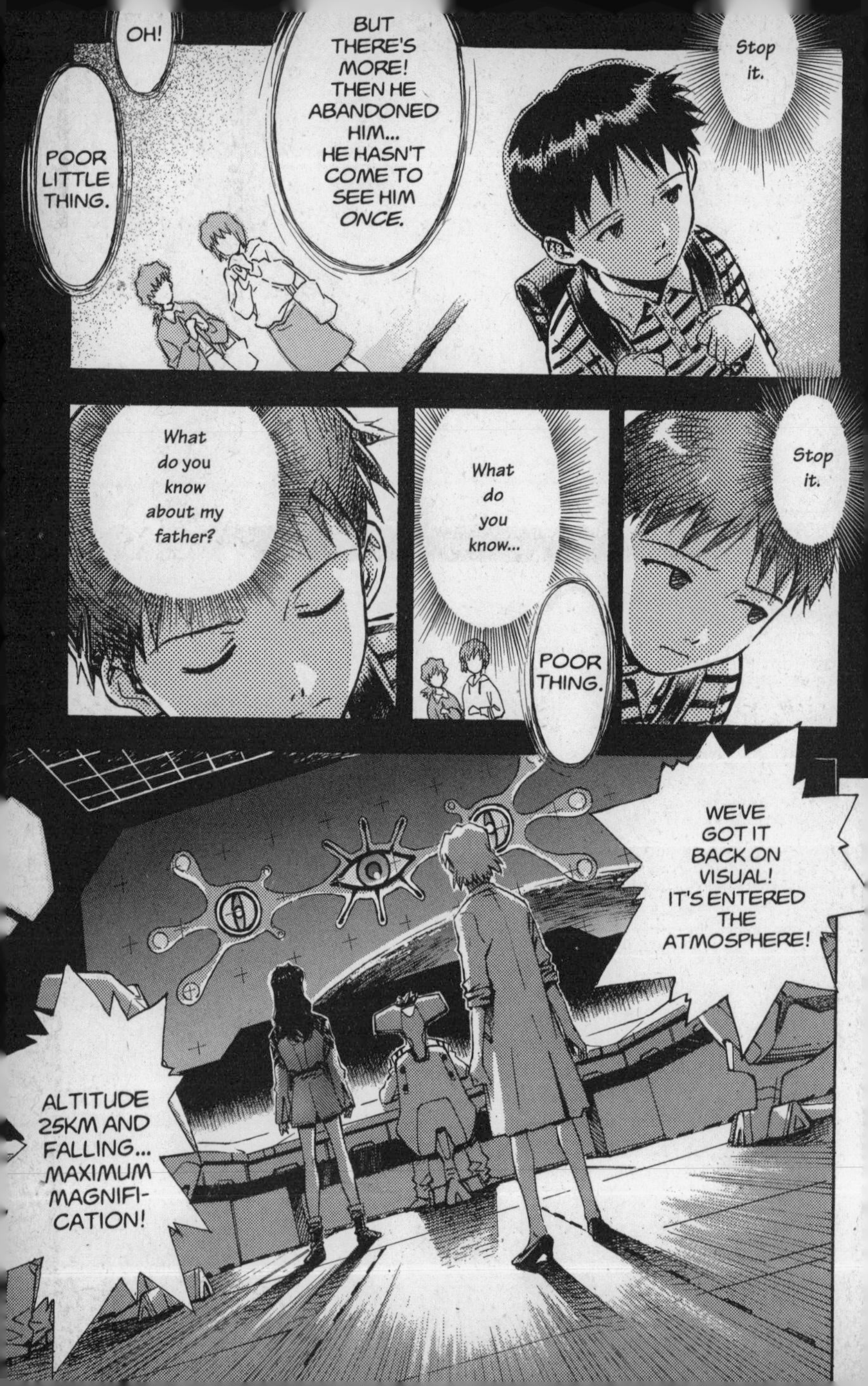
Stop it.
BUT THERE'S MORE! THEN HE ABANDONED HIM... HE HASN'T COME TO SEE HIM ONCE.
OH!
POOR LITTLE THING.
Stop it.
What do you know...
POOR THING.
What do you know about my father?
WE'VE GOT IT BACK ON VISUAL! IT'S ENTERED THE ATMOSPHERE!
ALTITUDE 25KM AND FALLING... MAXIMUM MAGNIFI-CATION!

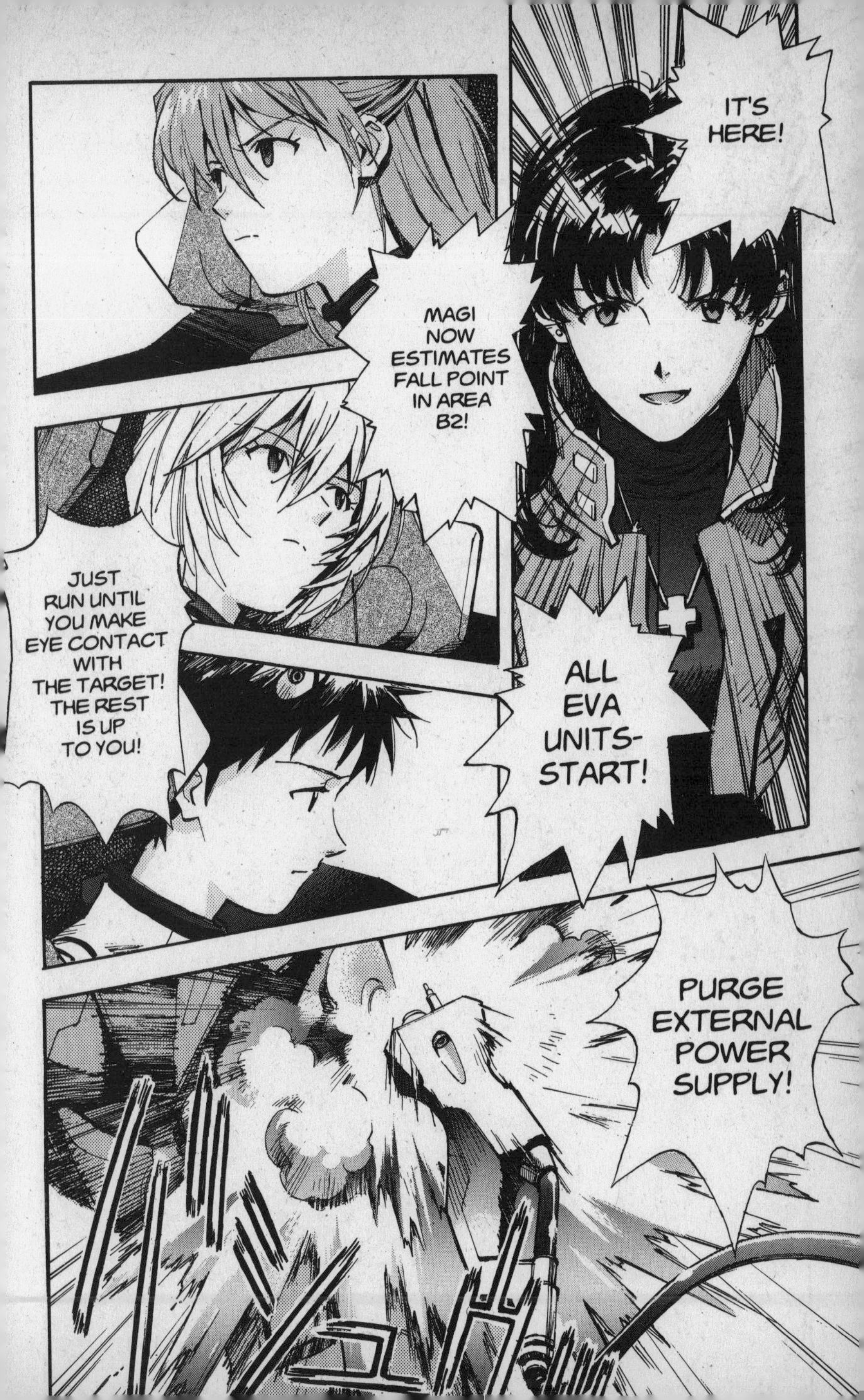
IT'S HERE!
MAGI NOW ESTIMATES FALL POINT IN AREA B2!
ALL EVA UNITS- START!
JUST RUN UNTIL YOU MAKE EYE CONTACT WITH THE TARGET! THE REST IS UP TO YOU!
PURGE EXTERNAL POWER SUPPLY!

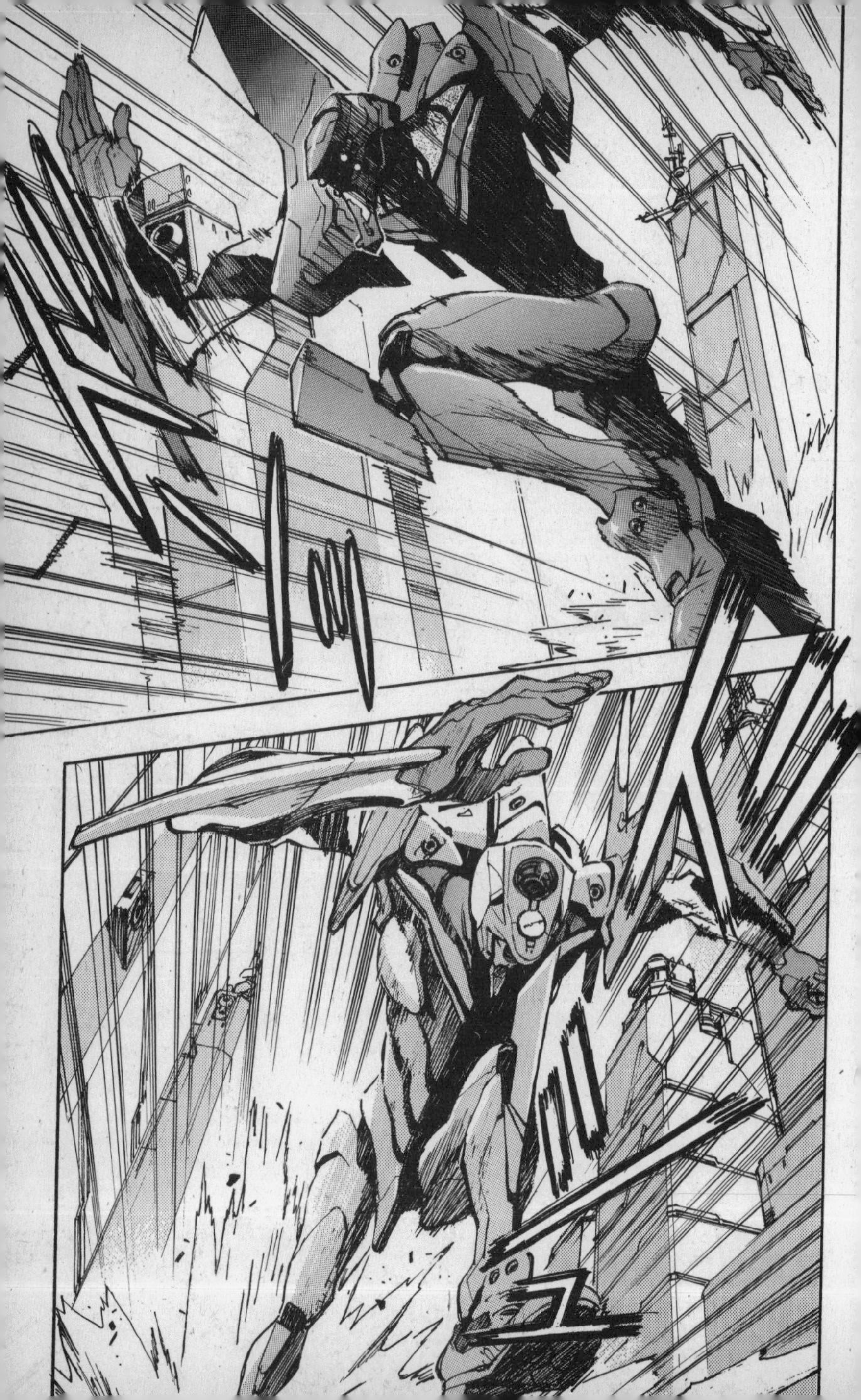

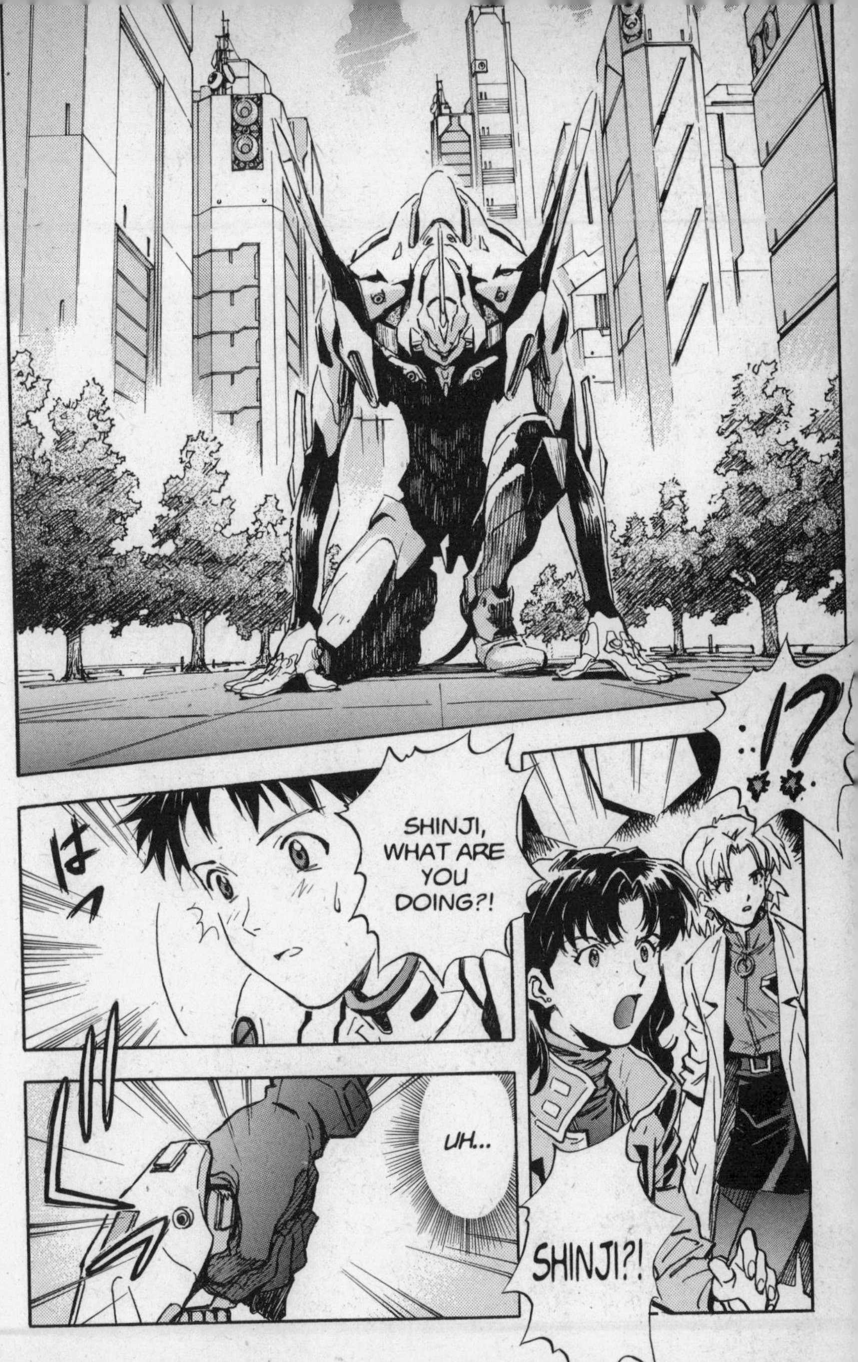
!?
SHINJI, WHAT ARE YOU DOING?!
は
UH...
SHINJI?!

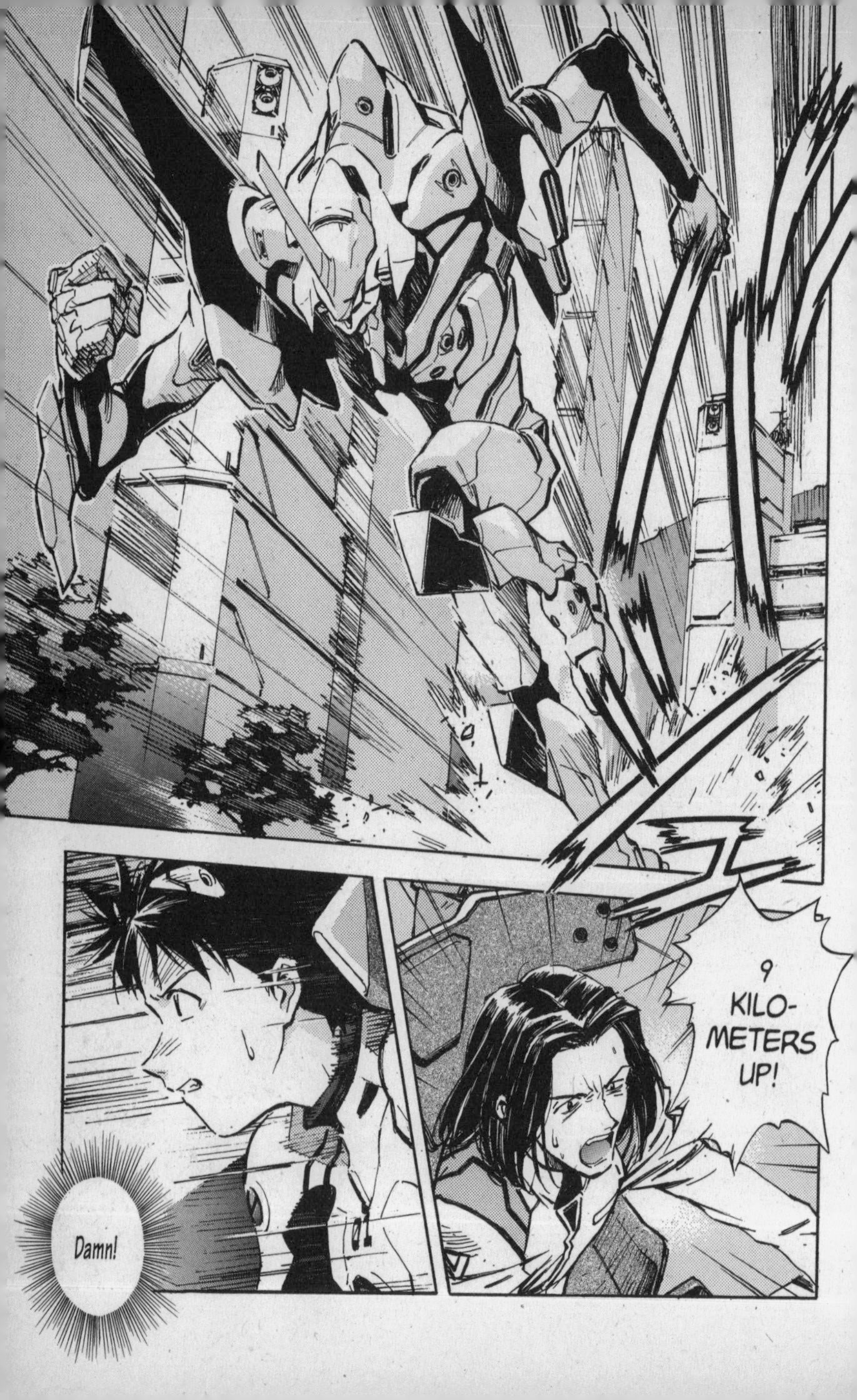
9 KILO-METERS UP!
Damn!

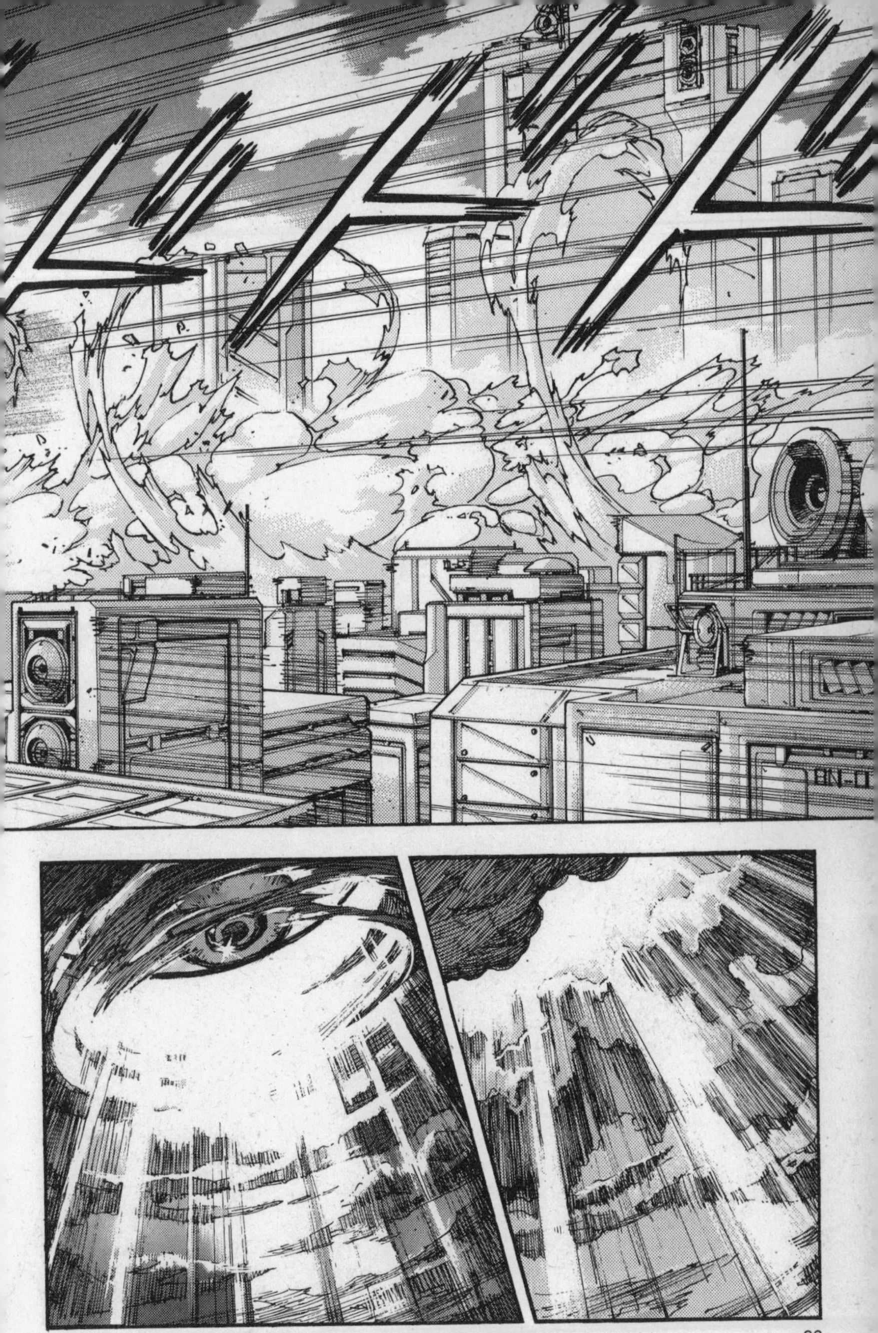

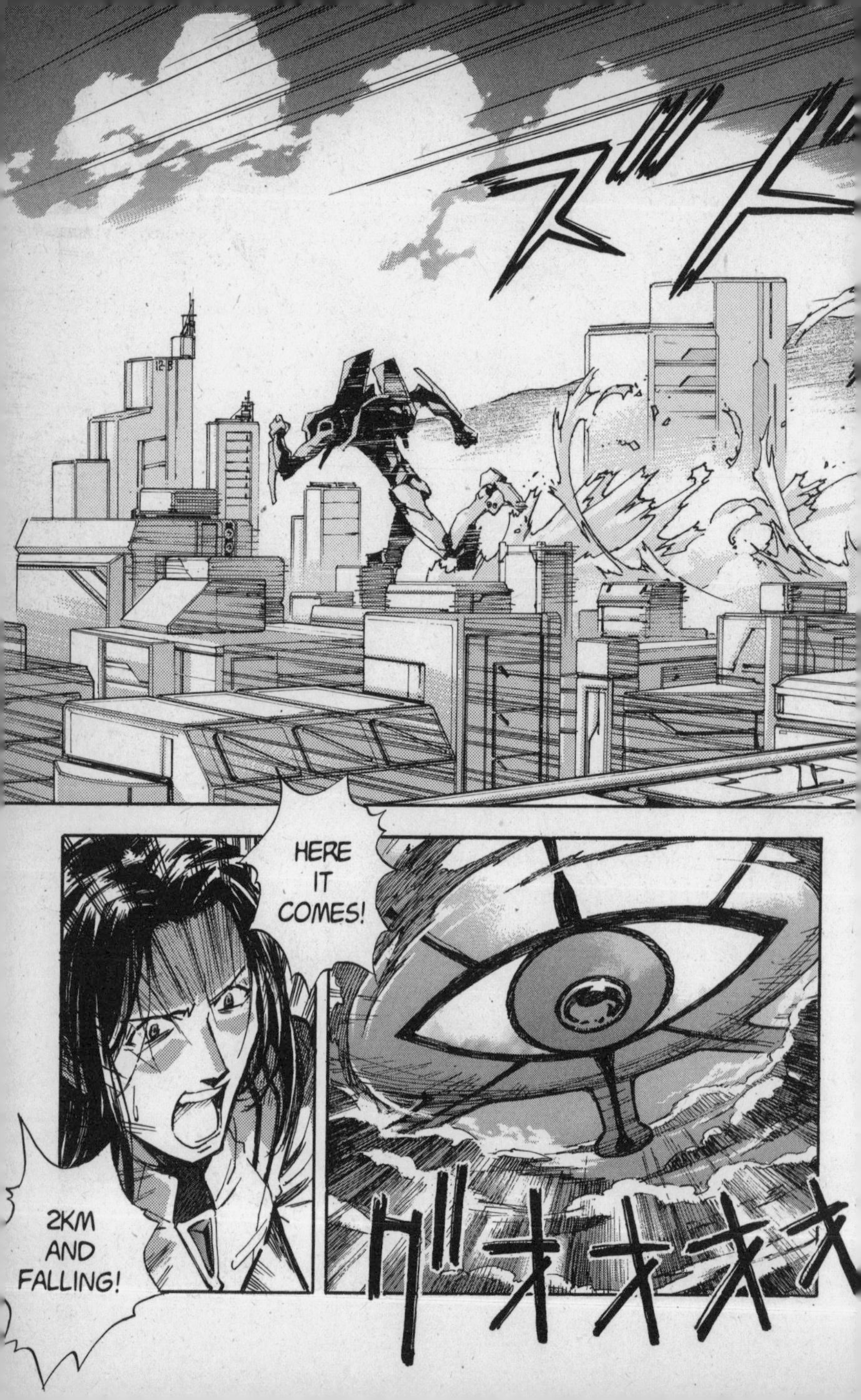
HERE IT COMES!
2KM AND FALLING!

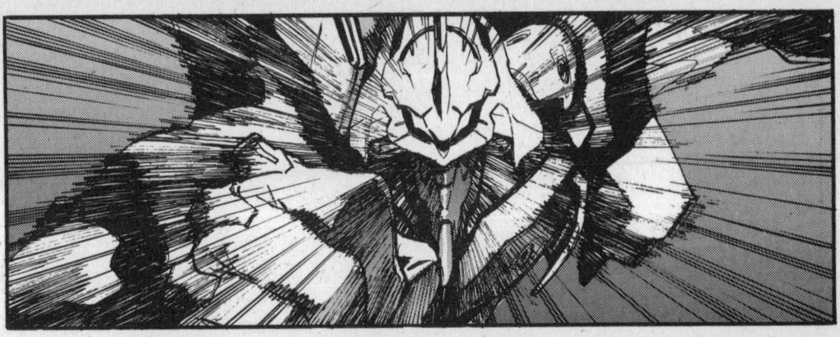
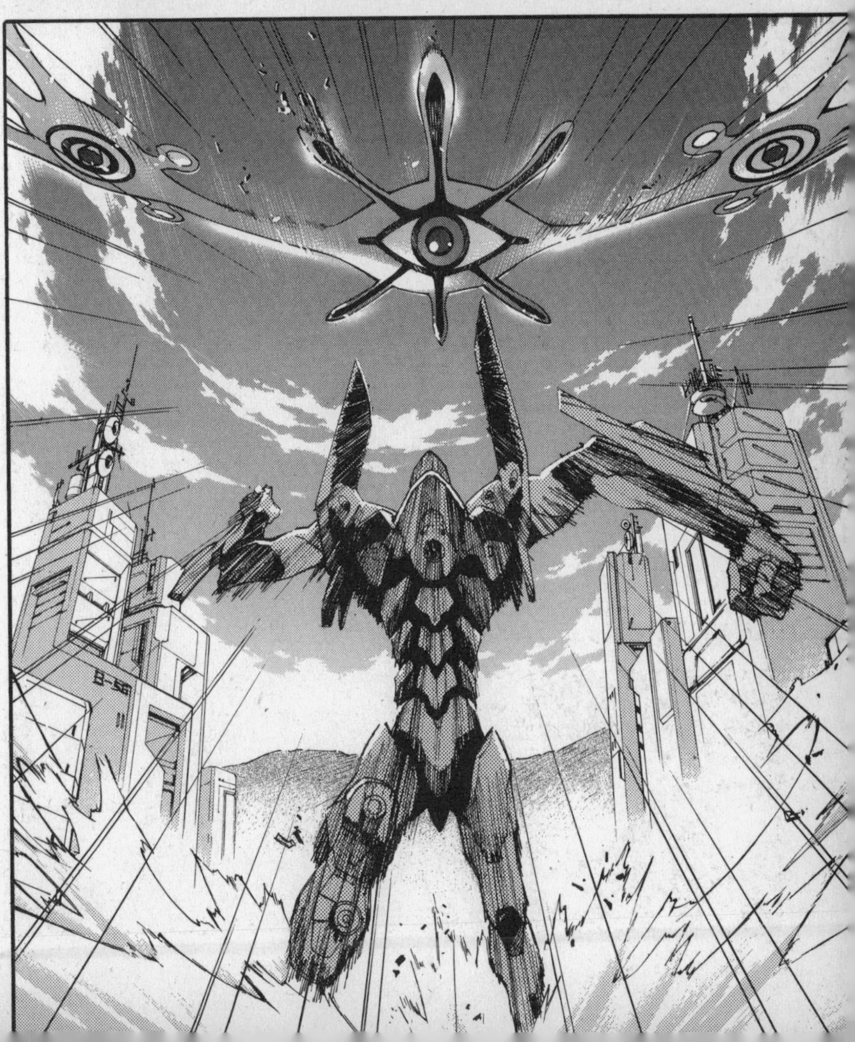

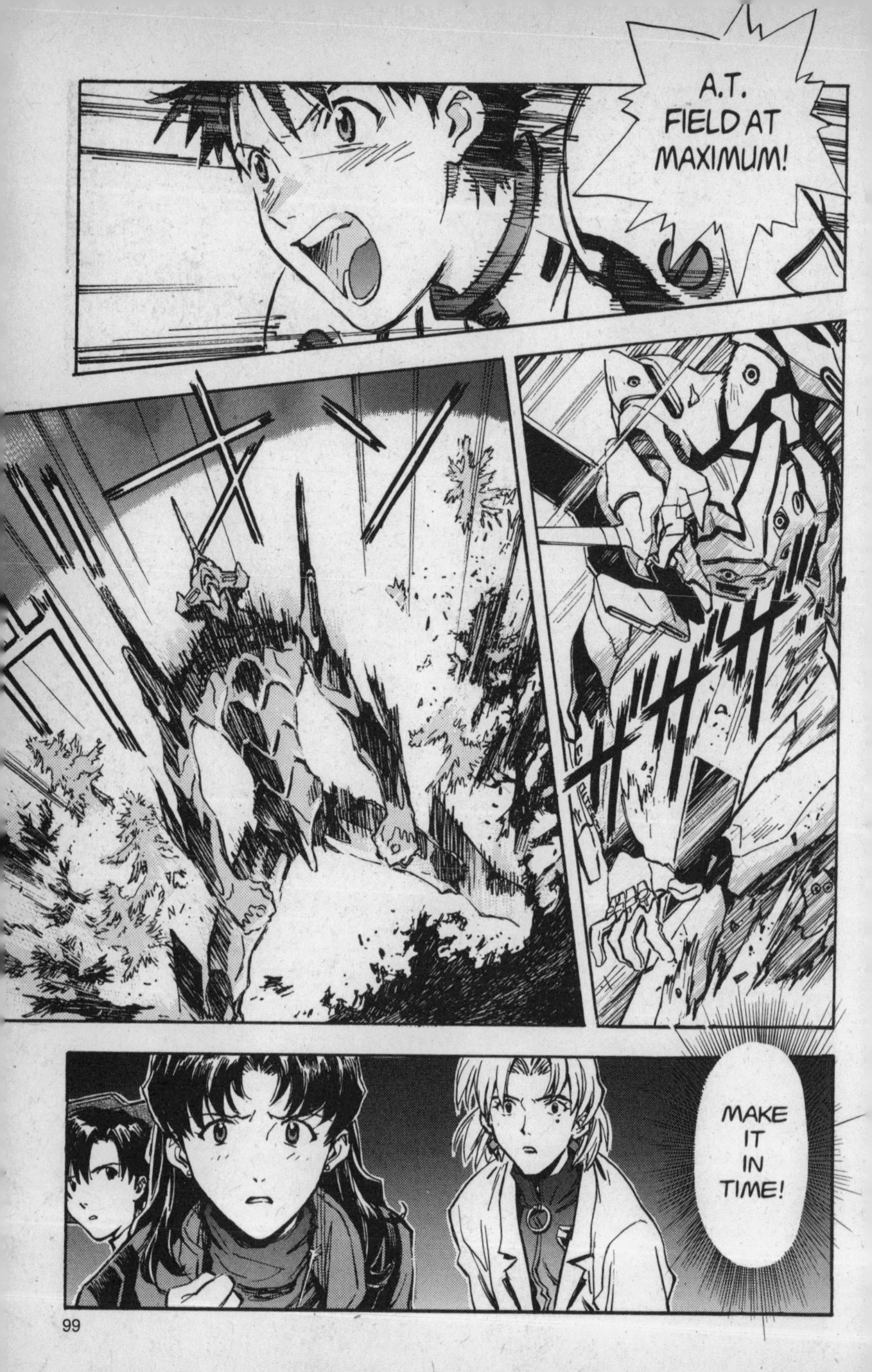
A.T. FIELD AT MAXIMUM!
MAKE IT IN TIME!

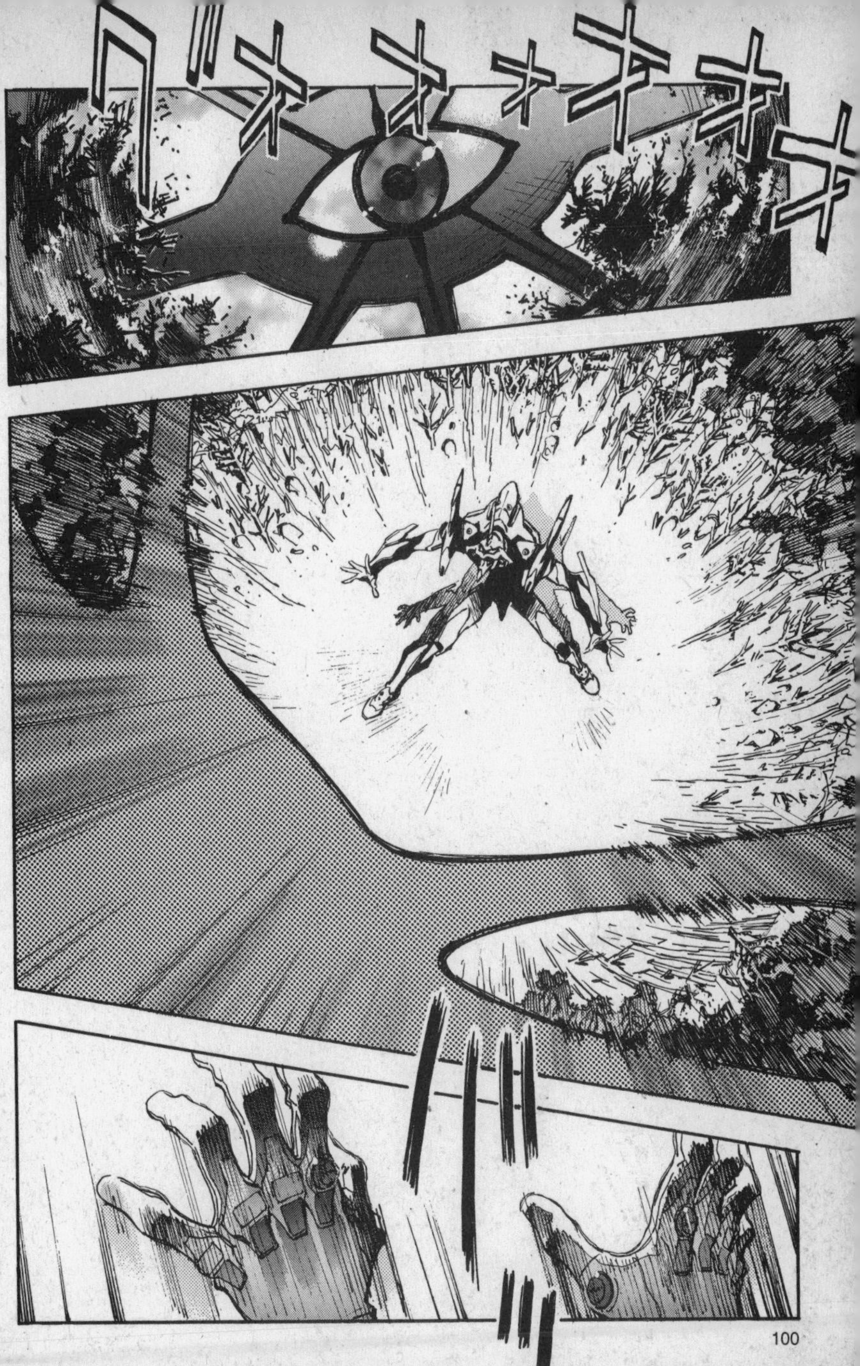
グォオォオオオ

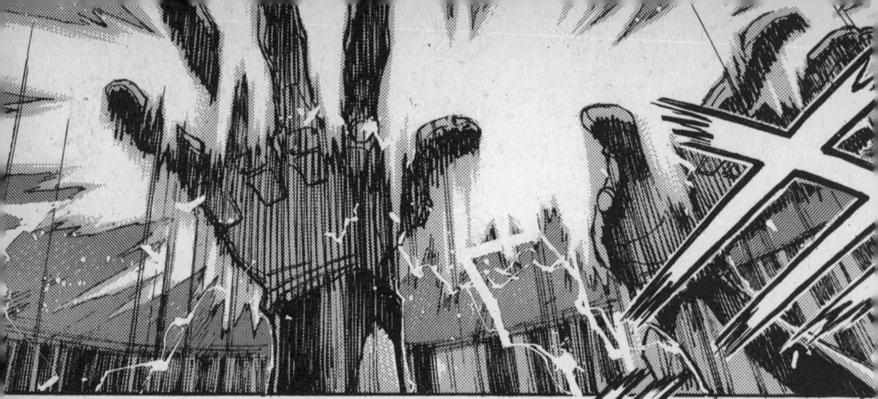

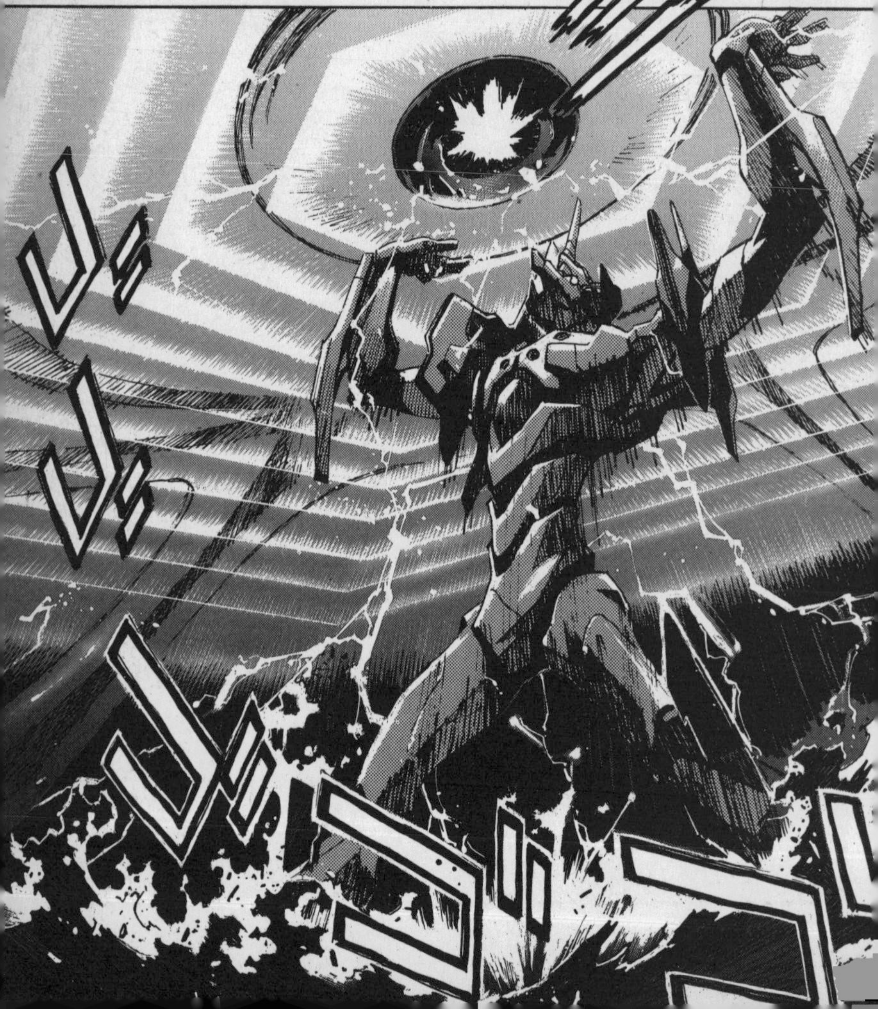

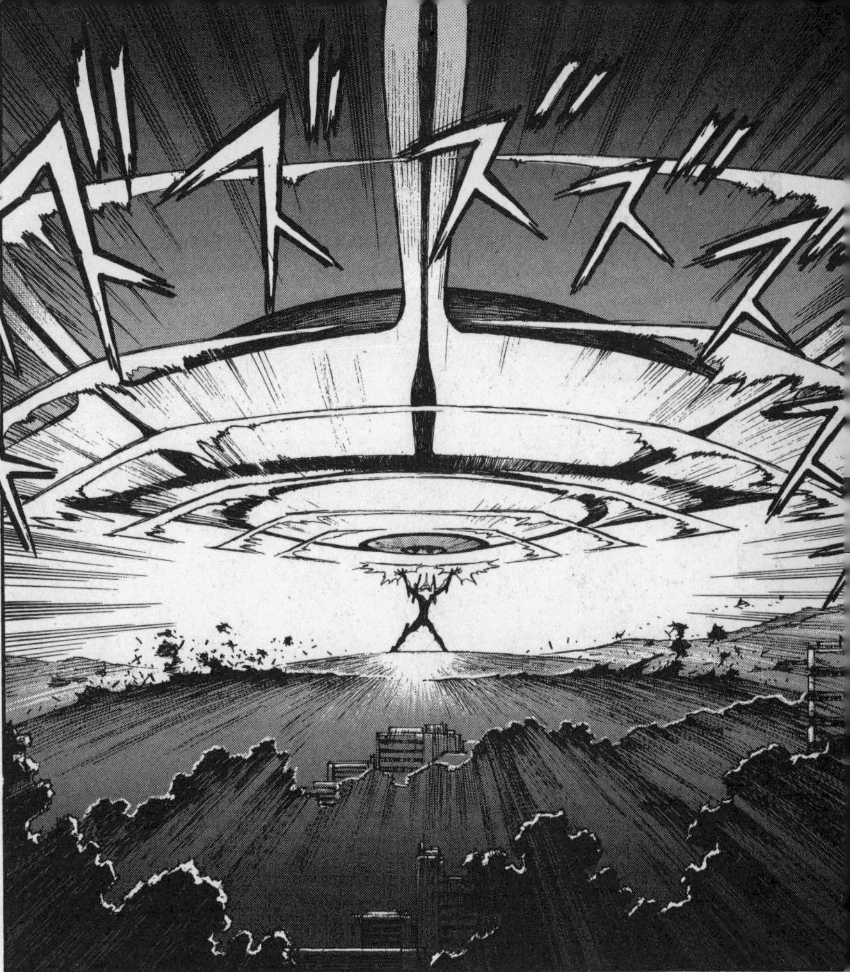

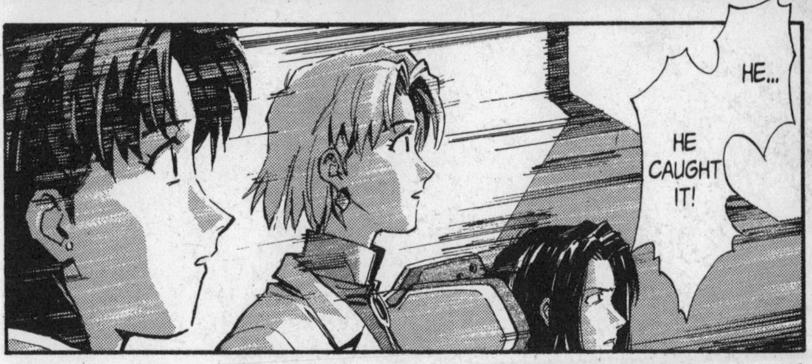
HE...
HE CAUGHT IT!

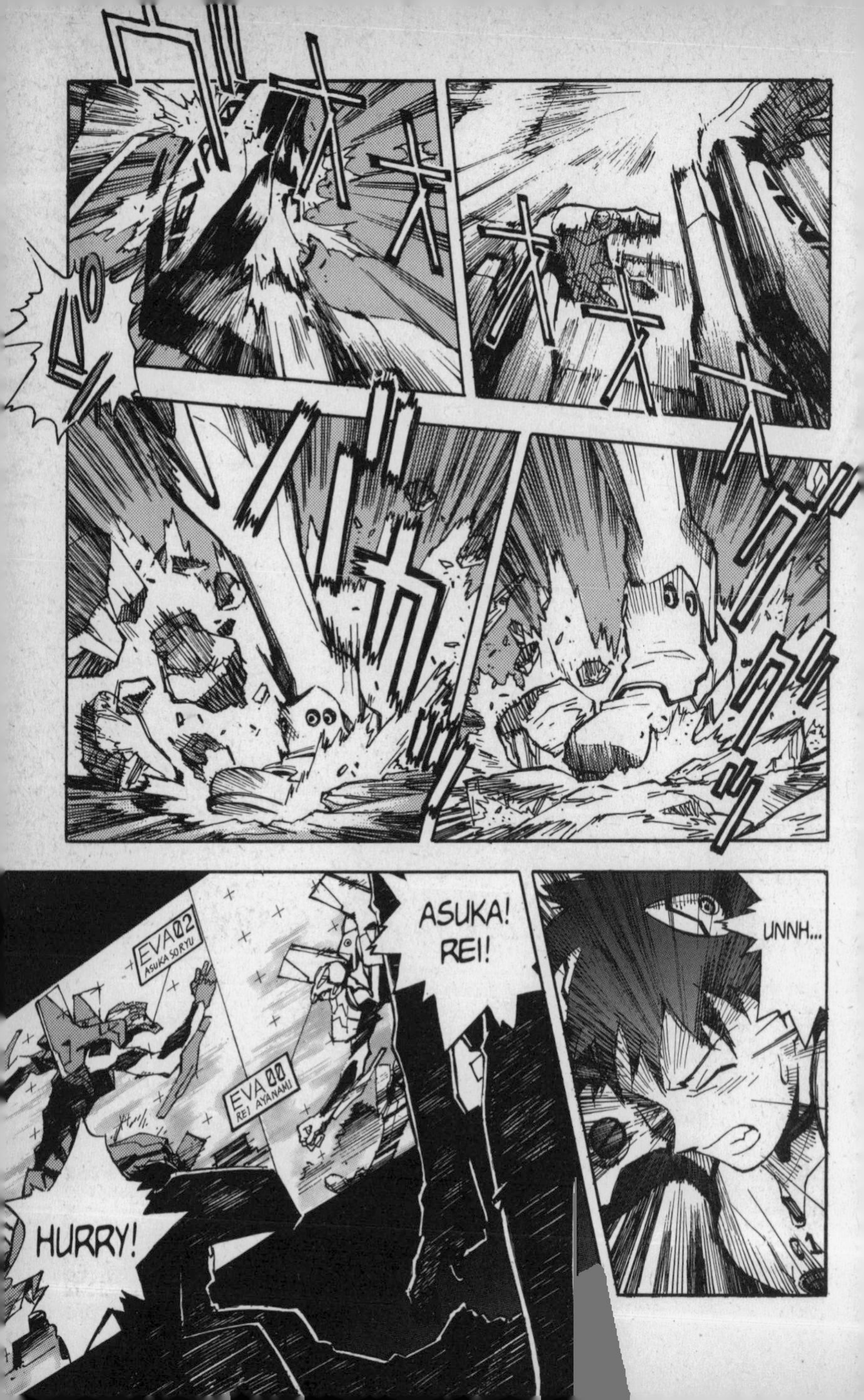
UNNH...
ASUKA! REI!
EVA 02
ASUKA SORYU
EVA 00
REI AYANAMI
HURRY!

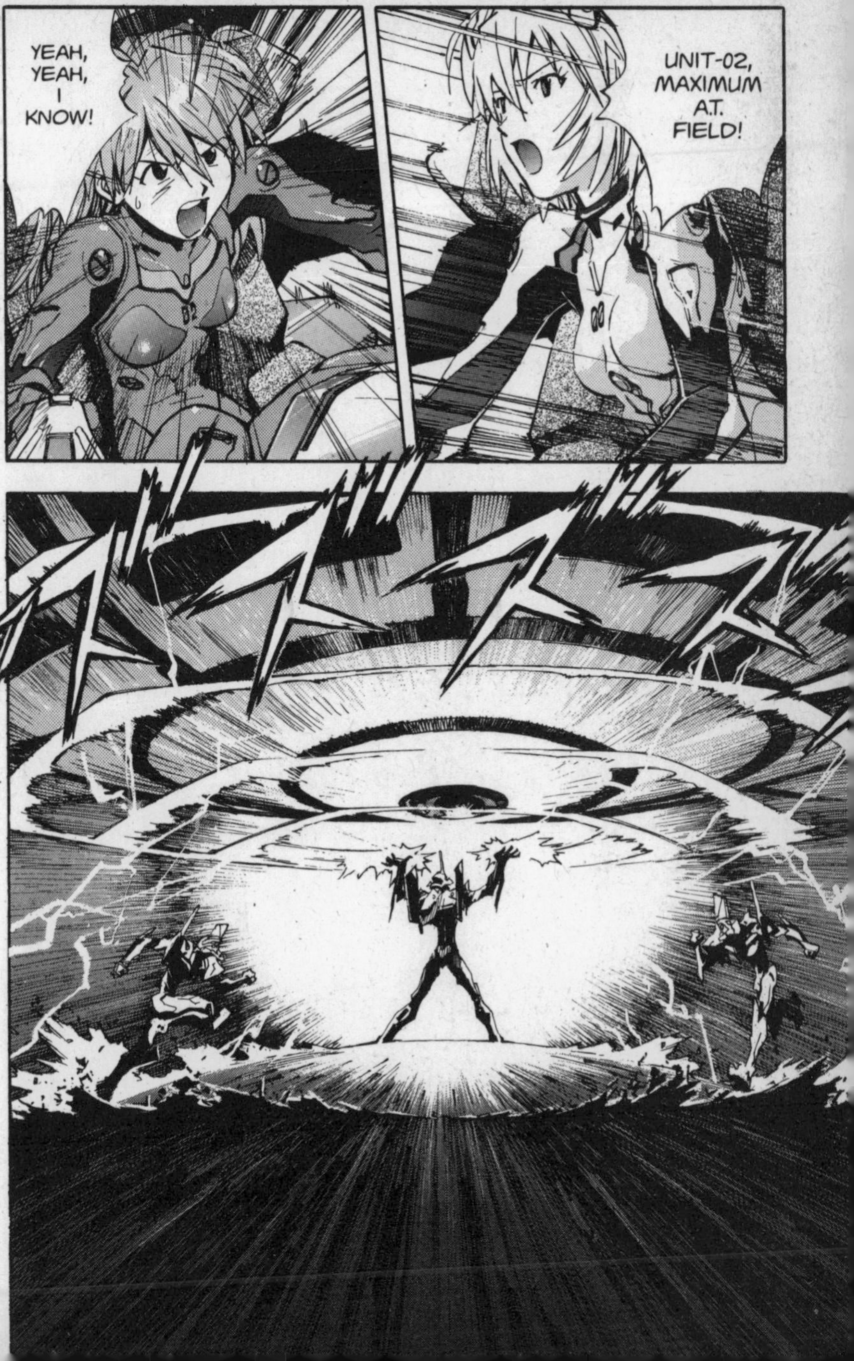
UNIT-02, MAXIMUM A.T. FIELD!
YEAH, YEAH, I KNOW!

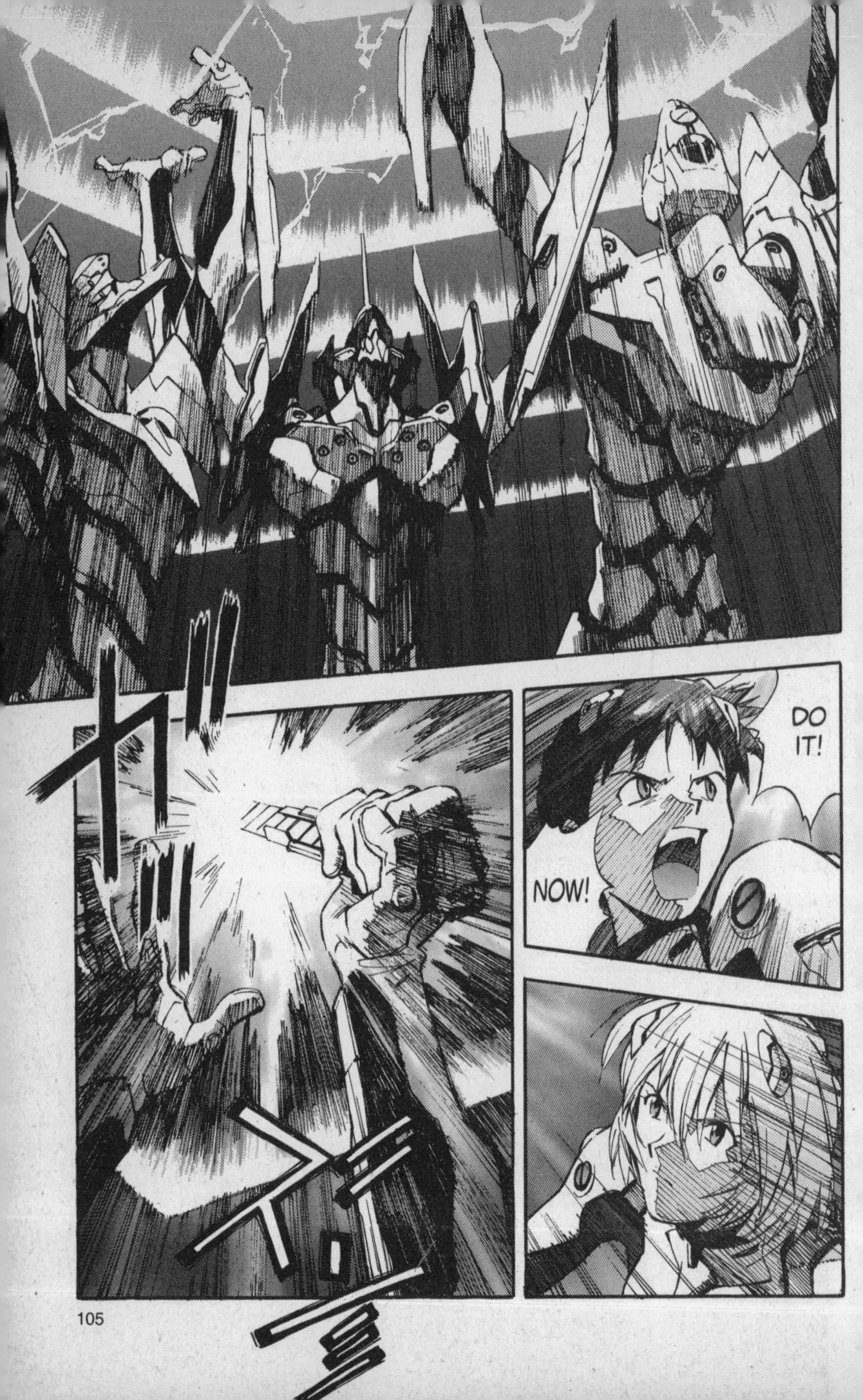
DO IT!
NOW!

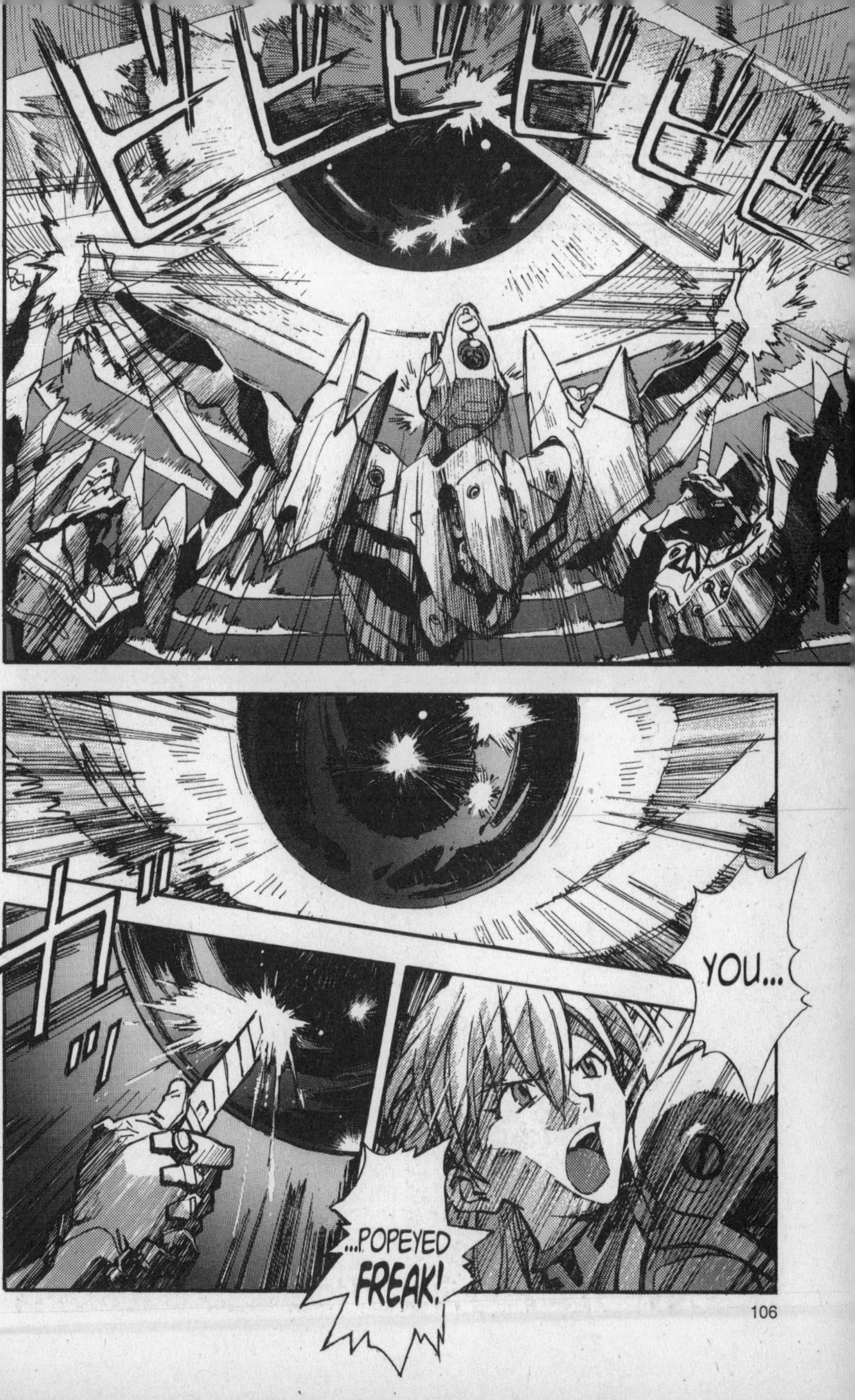
YOU...
...POPEYED FREAK!

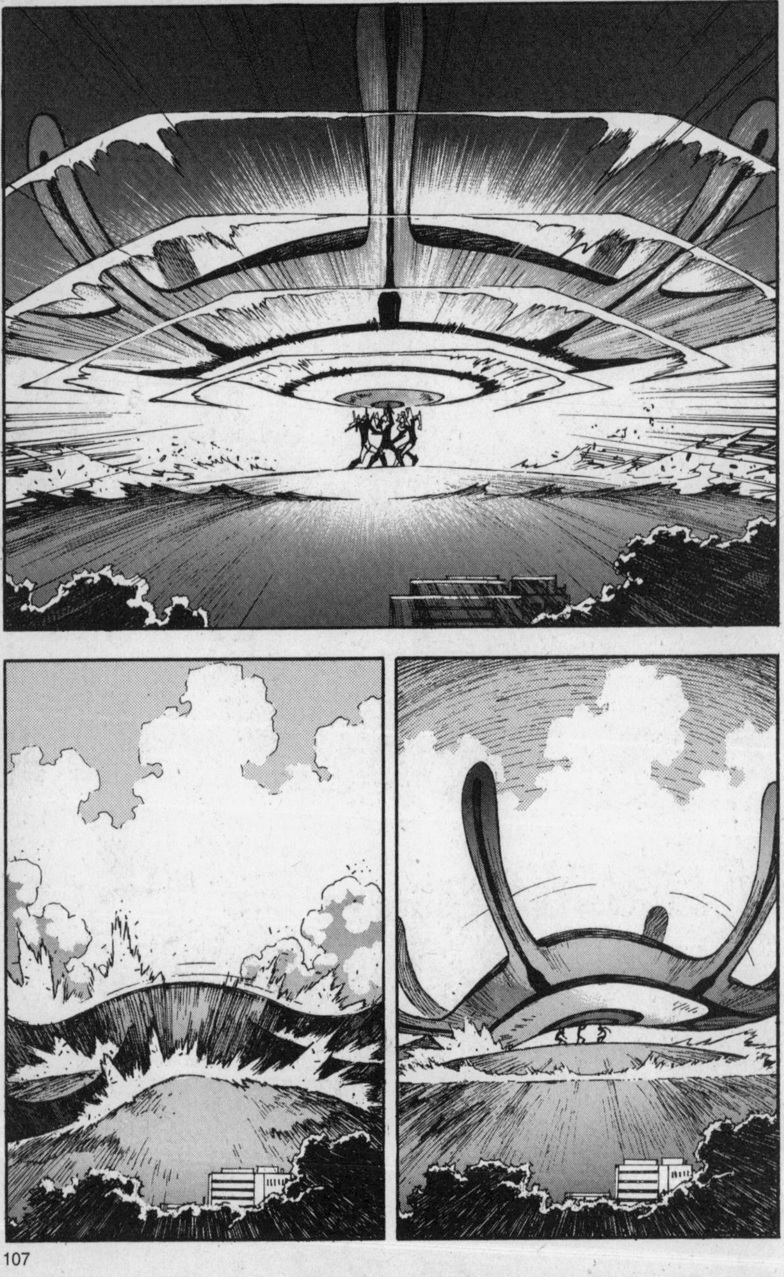

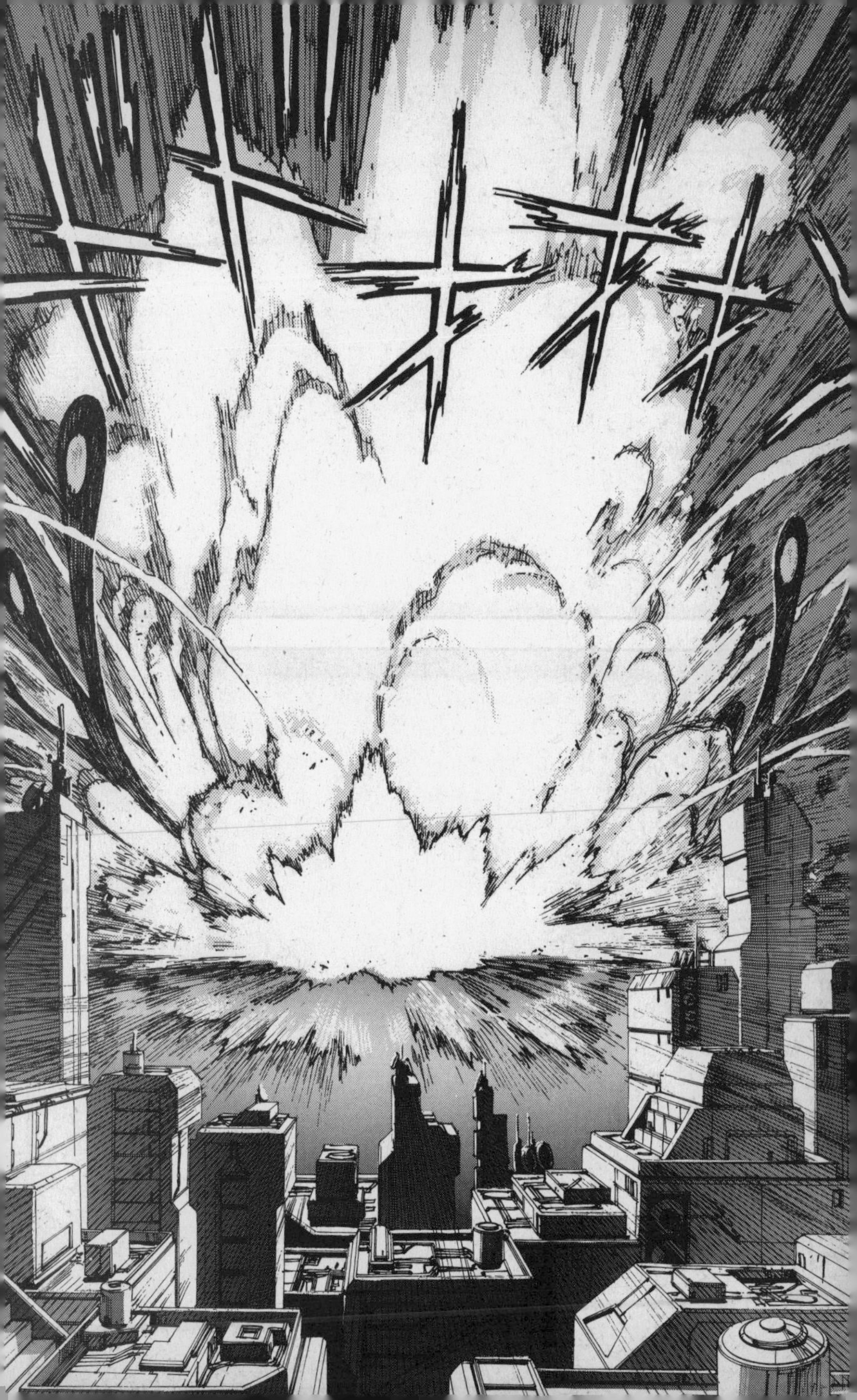

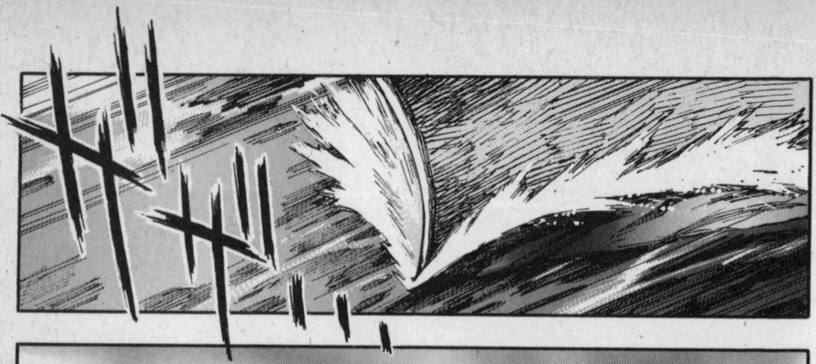

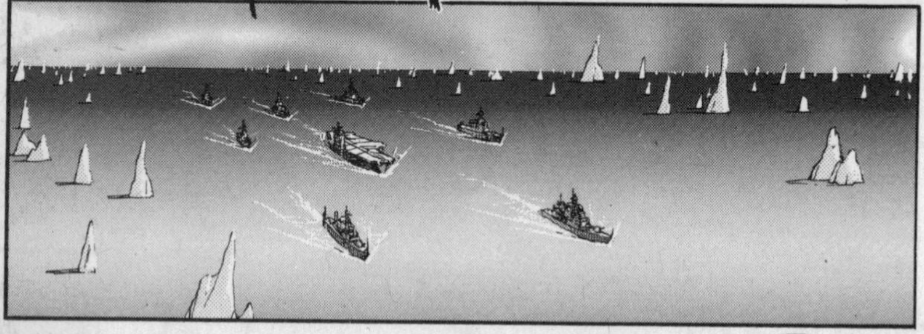

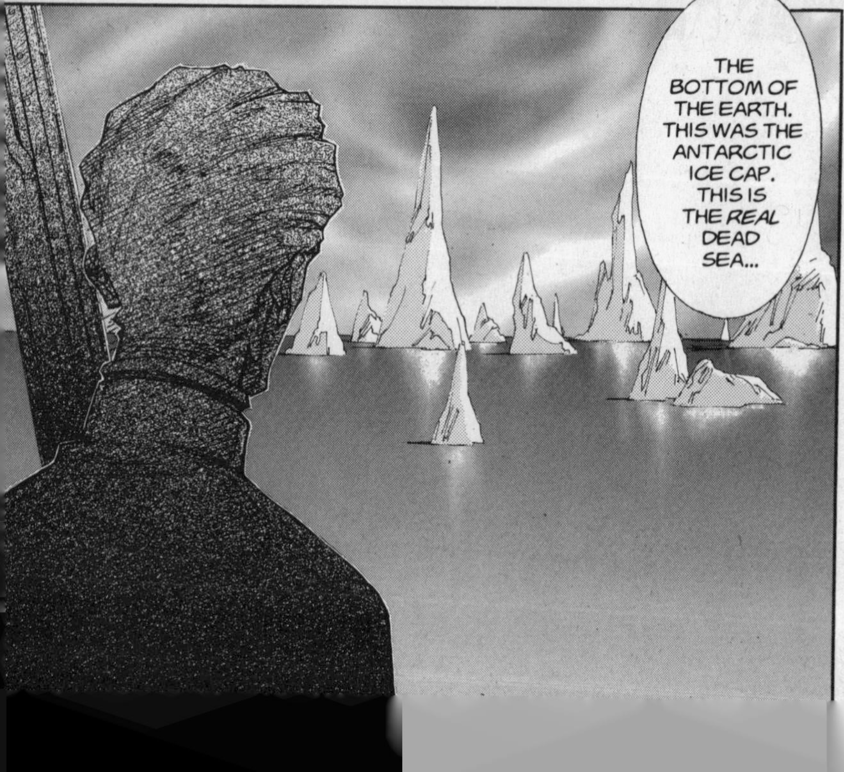
THE BOTTOM OF THE EARTH. THIS WAS THE ANTARCTIC ICE CAP. THIS IS THE *REAL* DEAD SEA...

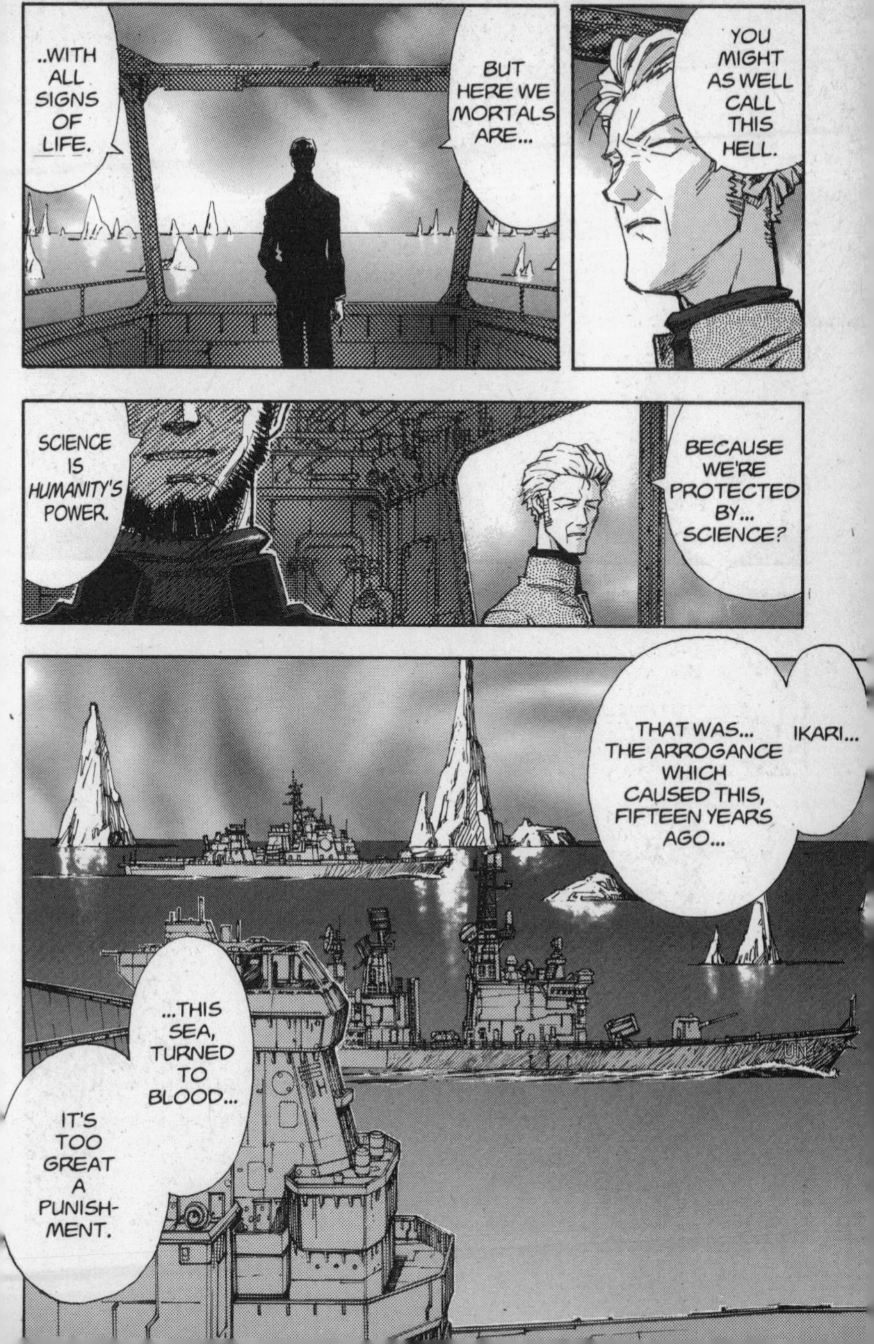
..WITH ALL SIGNS OF LIFE.
BUT HERE WE MORTALS ARE...
YOU MIGHT AS WELL CALL THIS HELL.
BECAUSE WE'RE PROTECTED BY... SCIENCE?
SCIENCE IS HUMANITY'S POWER.
IKARI...
THAT WAS... THE ARROGANCE WHICH CAUSED THIS, FIFTEEN YEARS AGO...
...THIS SEA, TURNED TO BLOOD...
IT'S TOO GREAT A PUNISHMENT.
UN

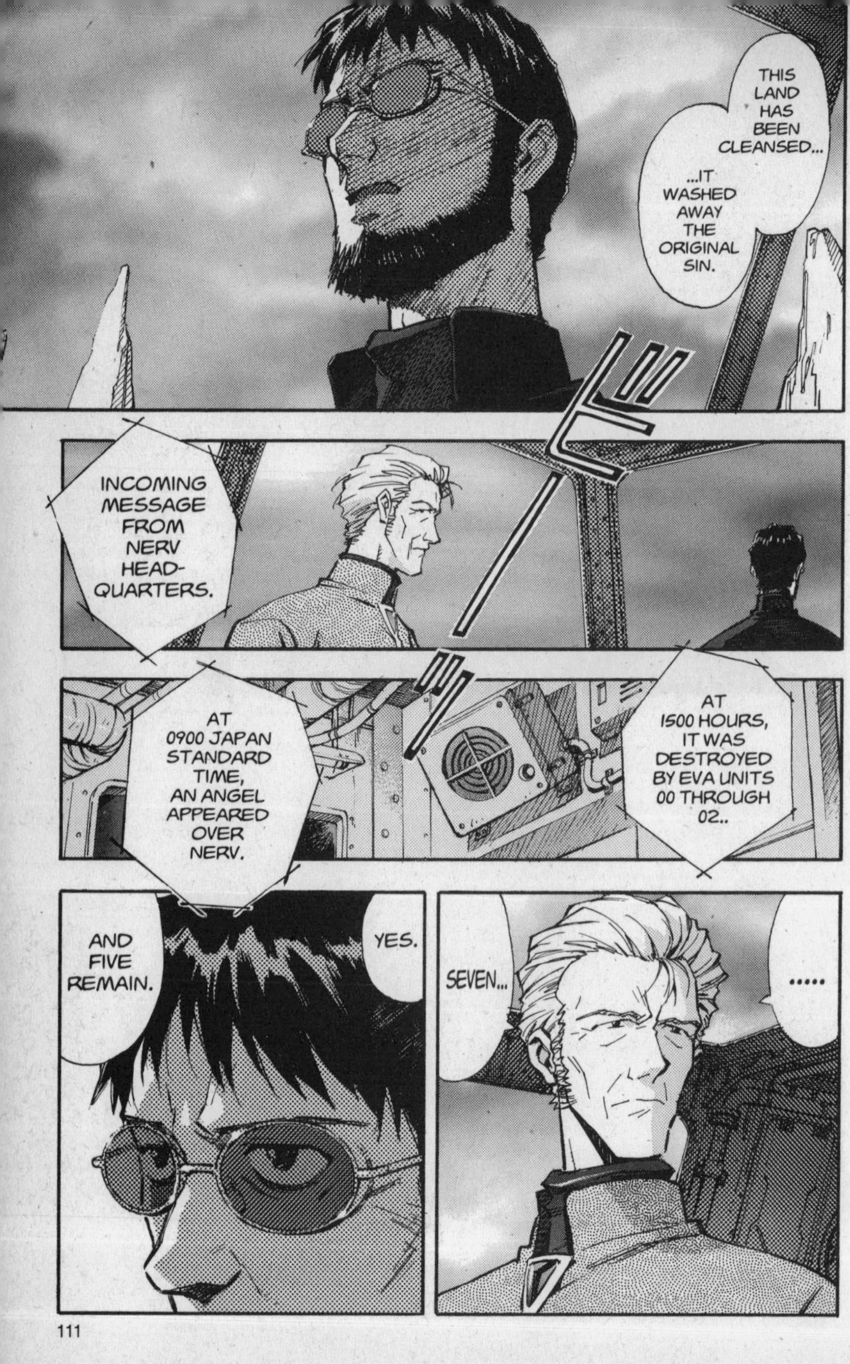
THIS LAND HAS BEEN CLEANSED...
...IT WASHED AWAY THE ORIGINAL SIN.
INCOMING MESSAGE FROM NERV HEAD-QUARTERS.
AT 0900 JAPAN STANDARD TIME, AN ANGEL APPEARED OVER NERV.
AT 1500 HOURS, IT WAS DESTROYED BY EVA UNITS 00 THROUGH 02..
.....
SEVEN...
YES.
AND FIVE REMAIN.

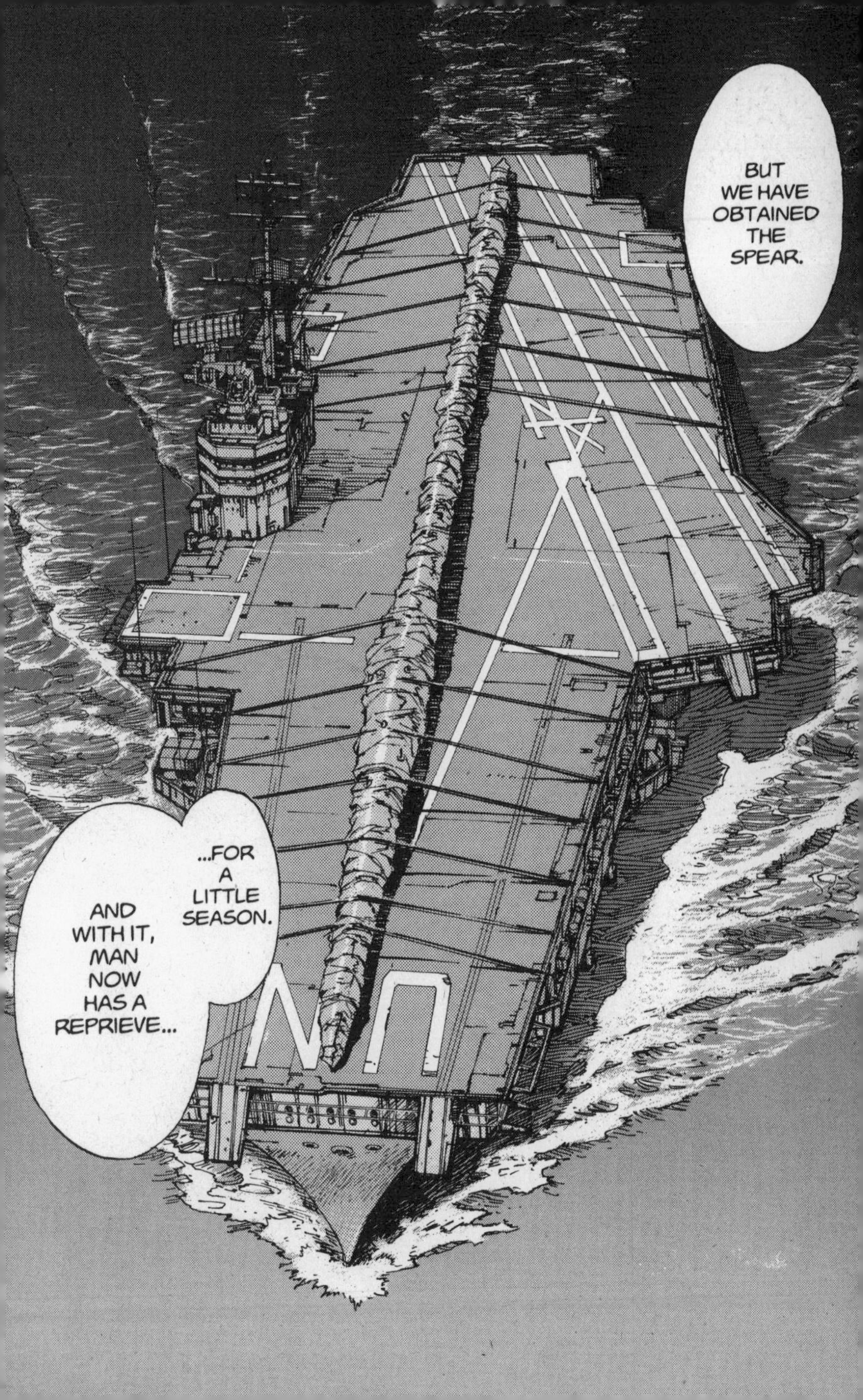
BUT WE HAVE OBTAINED THE SPEAR.
...FOR A LITTLE SEASON.
AND WITH IT, MAN NOW HAS A REPRIEVE...

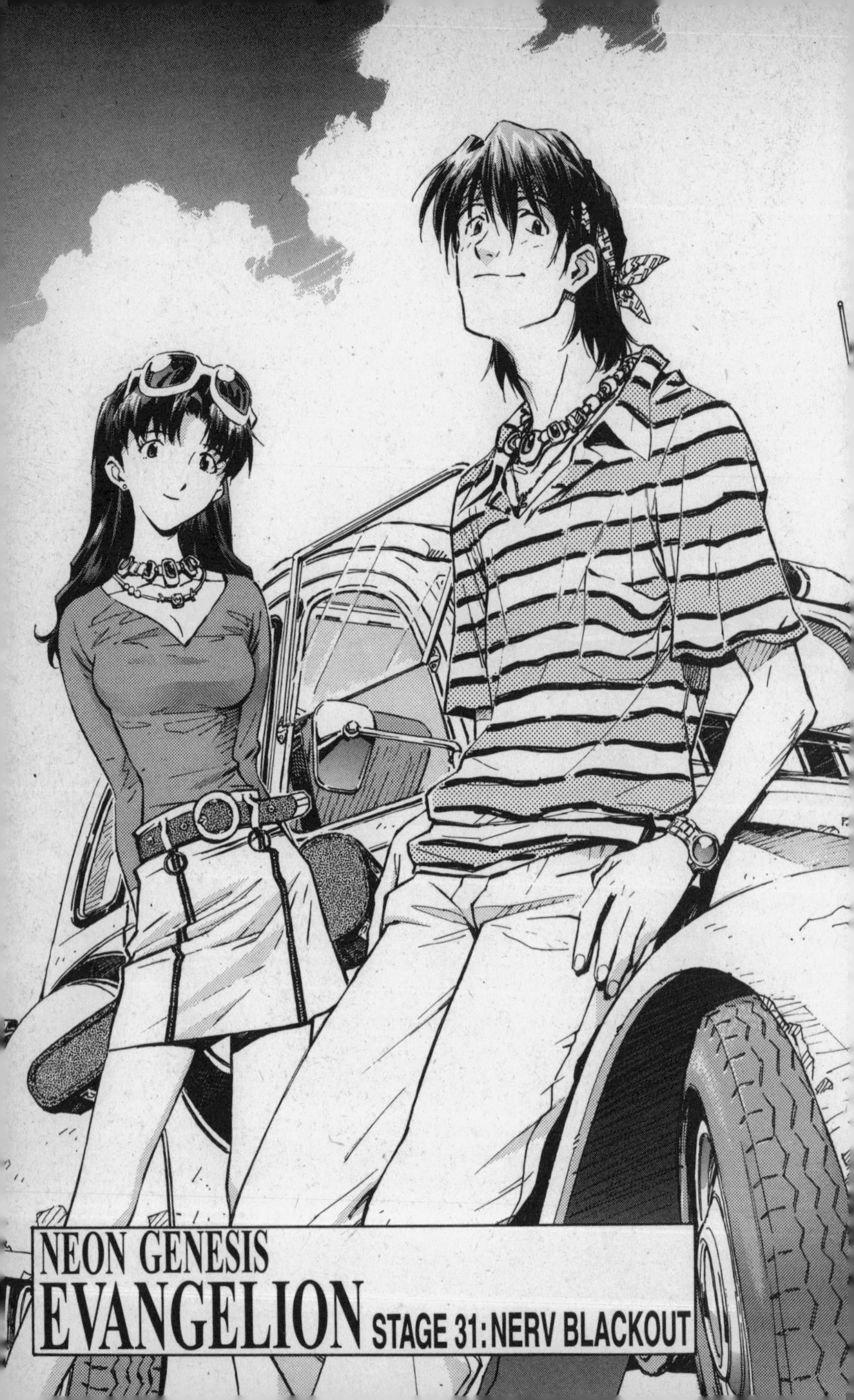
NEON GENESIS
EVANGELION
STAGE 31: NERV BLACKOUT

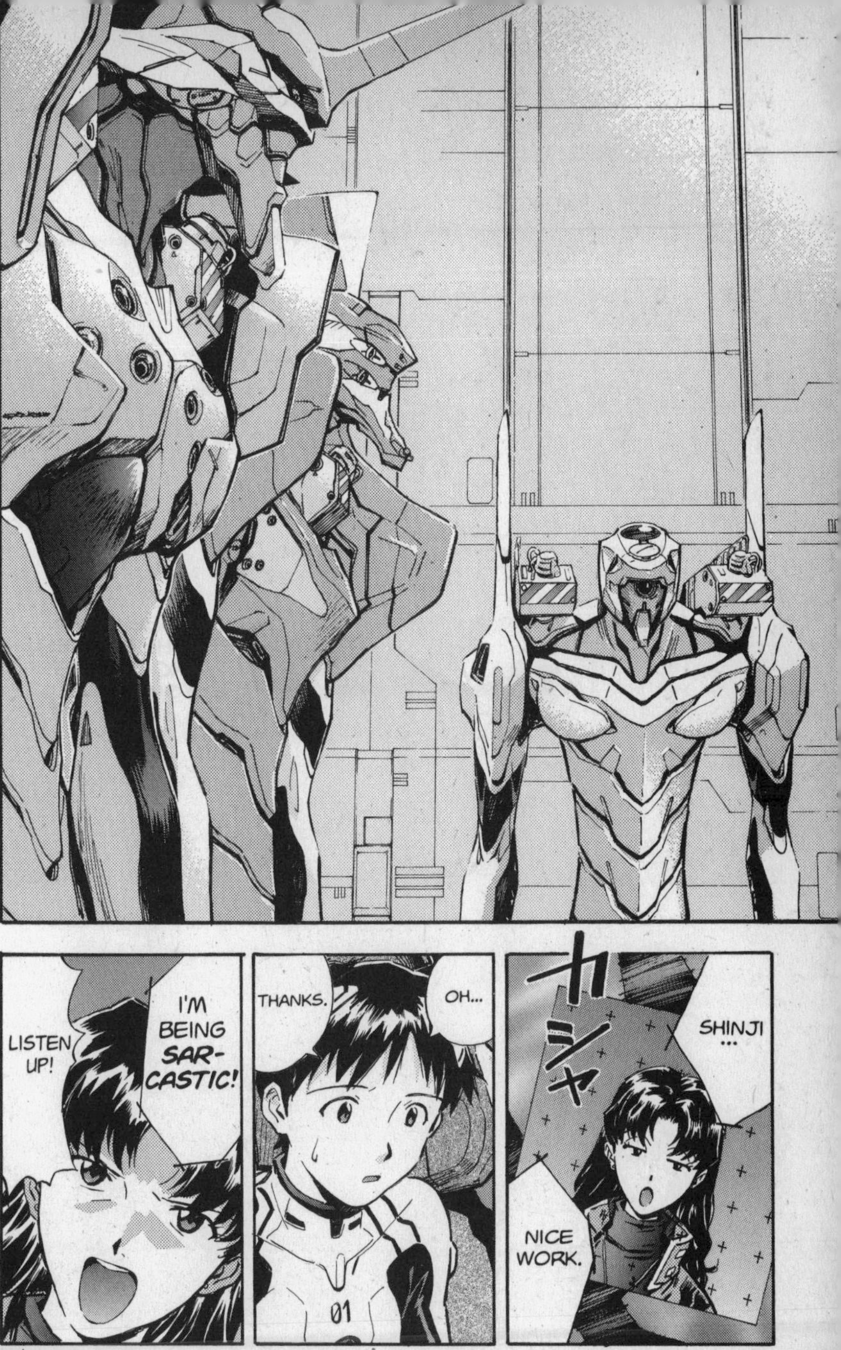
SHINJI
...
カシャ
NICE WORK.
OH...
THANKS.
I'M BEING SAR-CASTIC!
LISTEN UP!

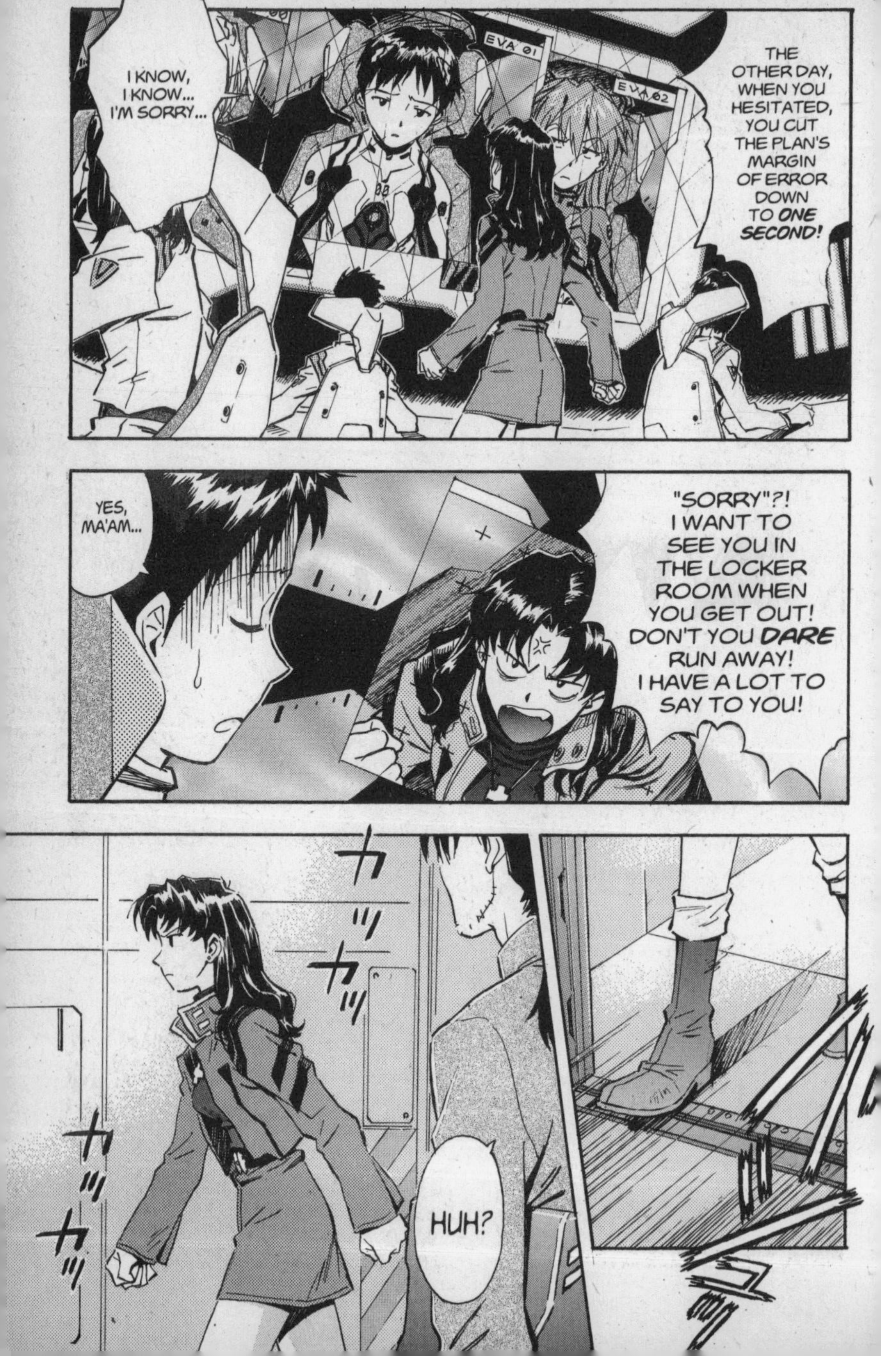
EVA 01
EVA 02
THE OTHER DAY, WHEN YOU HESITATED, YOU CUT THE PLAN'S MARGIN OF ERROR DOWN TO **ONE SECOND!**
I KNOW, I KNOW... I'M SORRY...
"SORRY"?! I WANT TO SEE YOU IN THE LOCKER ROOM WHEN YOU GET OUT! DON'T YOU **DARE** RUN AWAY! I HAVE A LOT TO SAY TO YOU!
YES, MA'AM...
HUH?

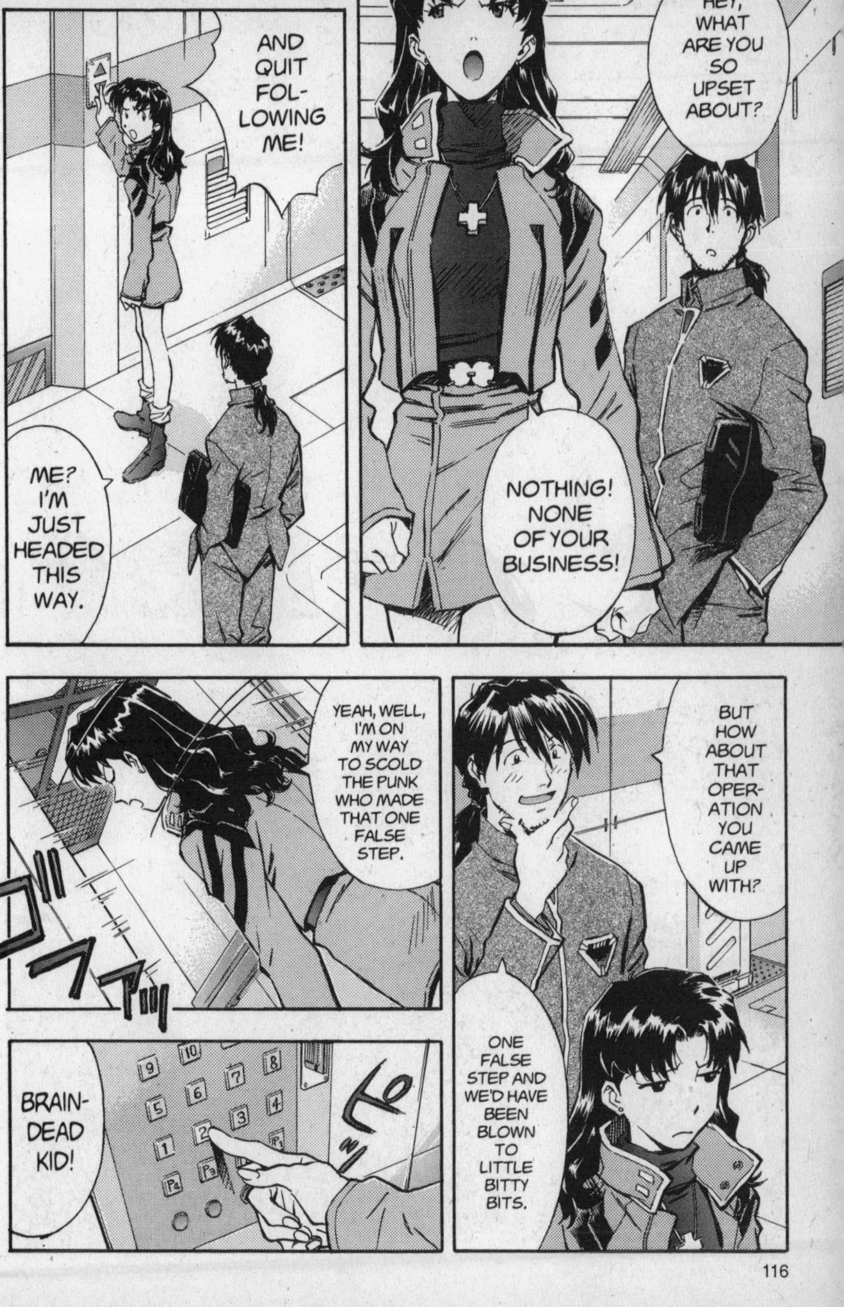
HEY, WHAT ARE YOU SO UPSET ABOUT?
NOTHING! NONE OF YOUR BUSINESS!
AND QUIT FOL-LOWING ME!
ME? I'M JUST HEADED THIS WAY.
BUT HOW ABOUT THAT OPER-ATION YOU CAME UP WITH?
ONE FALSE STEP AND WE'D HAVE BEEN BLOWN TO LITTLE BITTY BITS.
YEAH, WELL, I'M ON MY WAY TO SCOLD THE PUNK WHO MADE THAT ONE FALSE STEP.
BRAIN-DEAD KID!

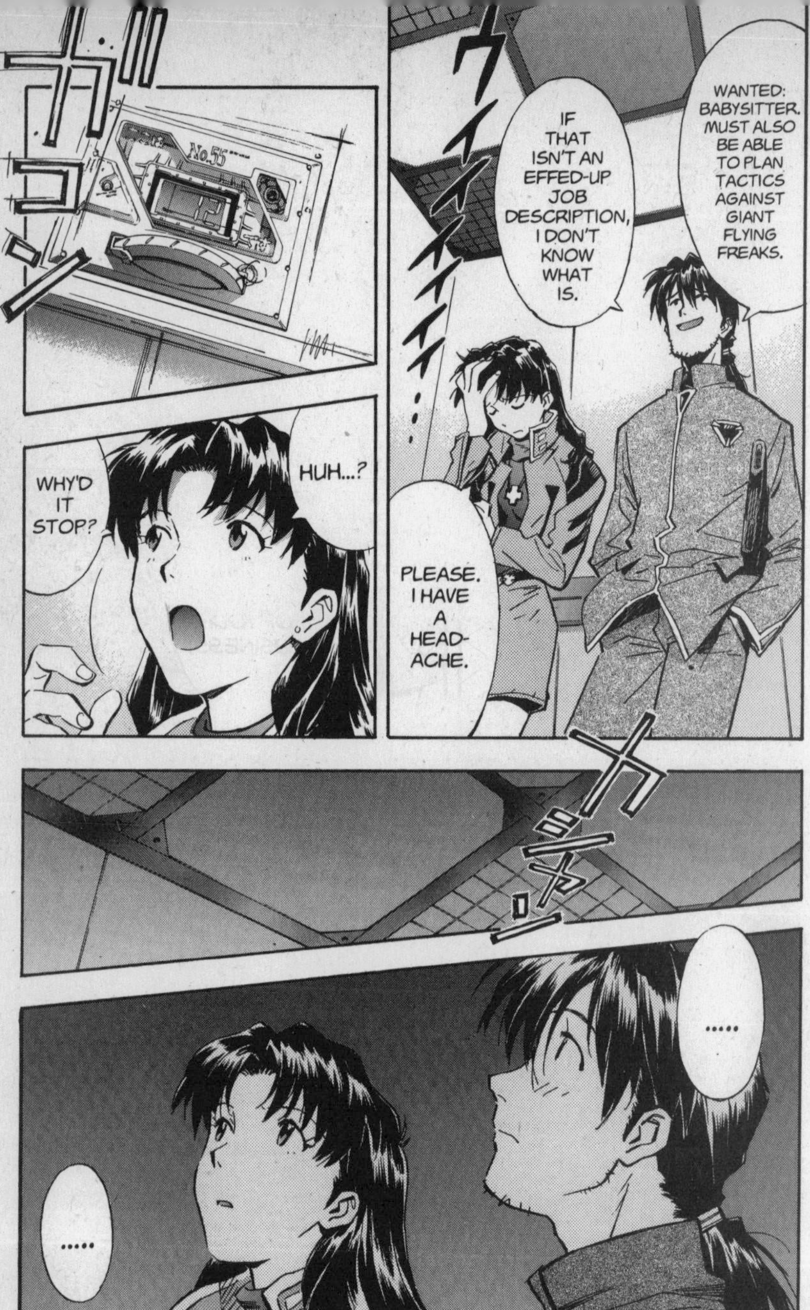
WANTED: BABYSITTER. MUST ALSO BE ABLE TO PLAN TACTICS AGAINST GIANT FLYING FREAKS.
IF THAT ISN'T AN EFFED-UP JOB DESCRIPTION, I DON'T KNOW WHAT IS.
PLEASE. I HAVE A HEADACHE.
No.55
HUH...?
WHY'D IT STOP?
.....
.....

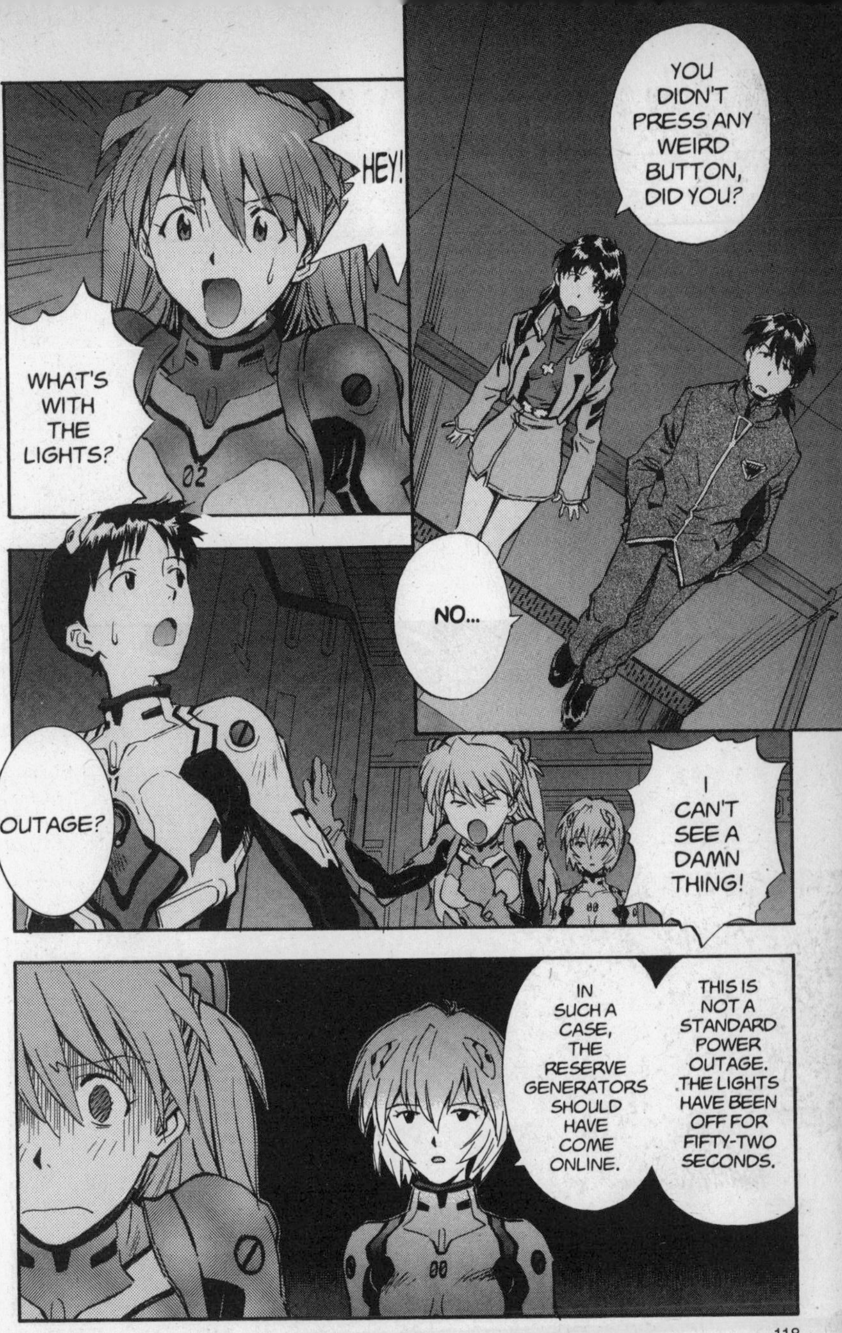
YOU DIDN'T PRESS ANY WEIRD BUTTON, DID YOU?
HEY!
WHAT'S WITH THE LIGHTS?
NO...
OUTAGE?
I CAN'T SEE A DAMN THING!
THIS IS NOT A STANDARD POWER OUTAGE. THE LIGHTS HAVE BEEN OFF FOR FIFTY-TWO SECONDS.
IN SUCH A CASE, THE RESERVE GENERATORS SHOULD HAVE COME ONLINE.

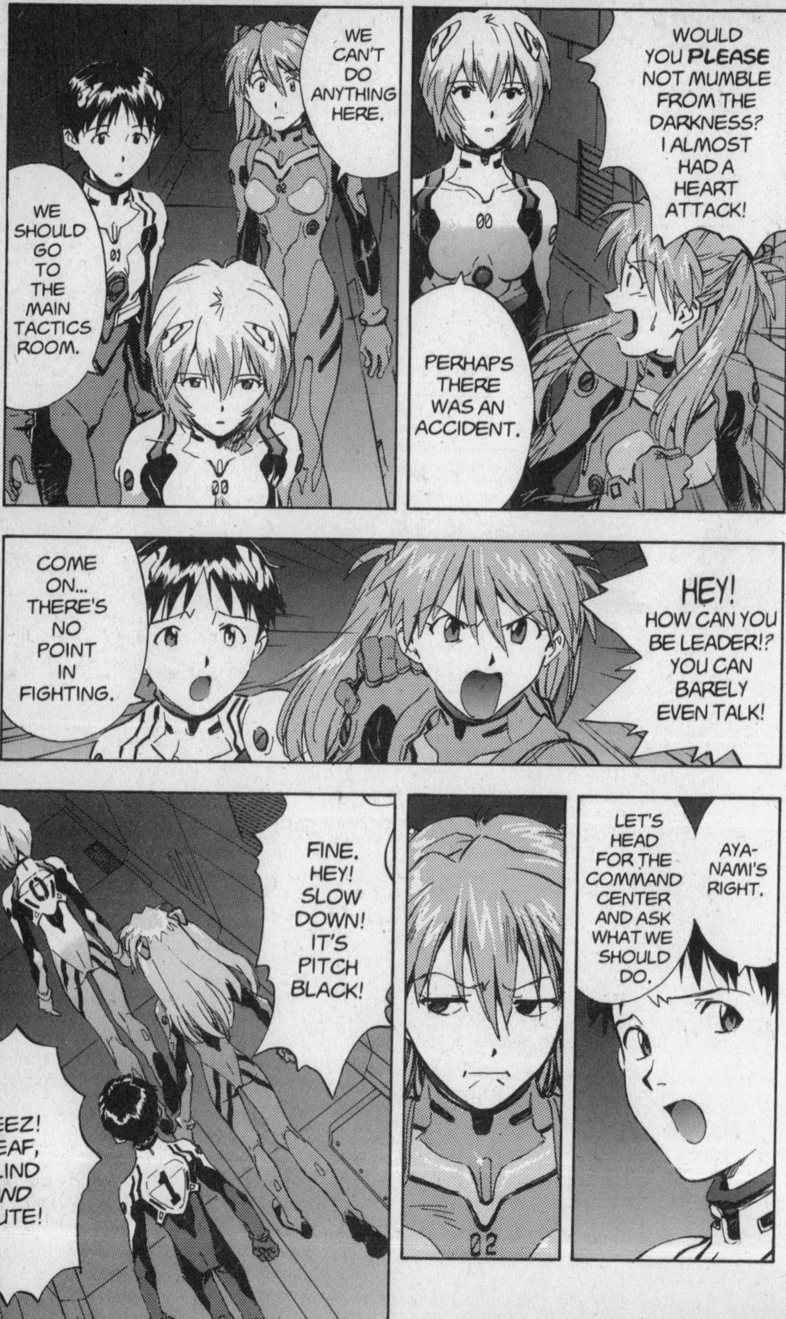
WOULD YOU **PLEASE** NOT MUMBLE FROM THE DARKNESS? I ALMOST HAD A HEART ATTACK!
PERHAPS THERE WAS AN ACCIDENT.
WE CAN'T DO ANYTHING HERE.
WE SHOULD GO TO THE MAIN TACTICS ROOM.
HEY! HOW CAN YOU BE LEADER!? YOU CAN BARELY EVEN TALK!
COME ON... THERE'S NO POINT IN FIGHTING.
AYA-NAMI'S RIGHT.
LET'S HEAD FOR THE COMMAND CENTER AND ASK WHAT WE SHOULD DO.
FINE. HEY! SLOW DOWN! IT'S PITCH BLACK!
GEEZ! DEAF, BLIND AND MUTE!

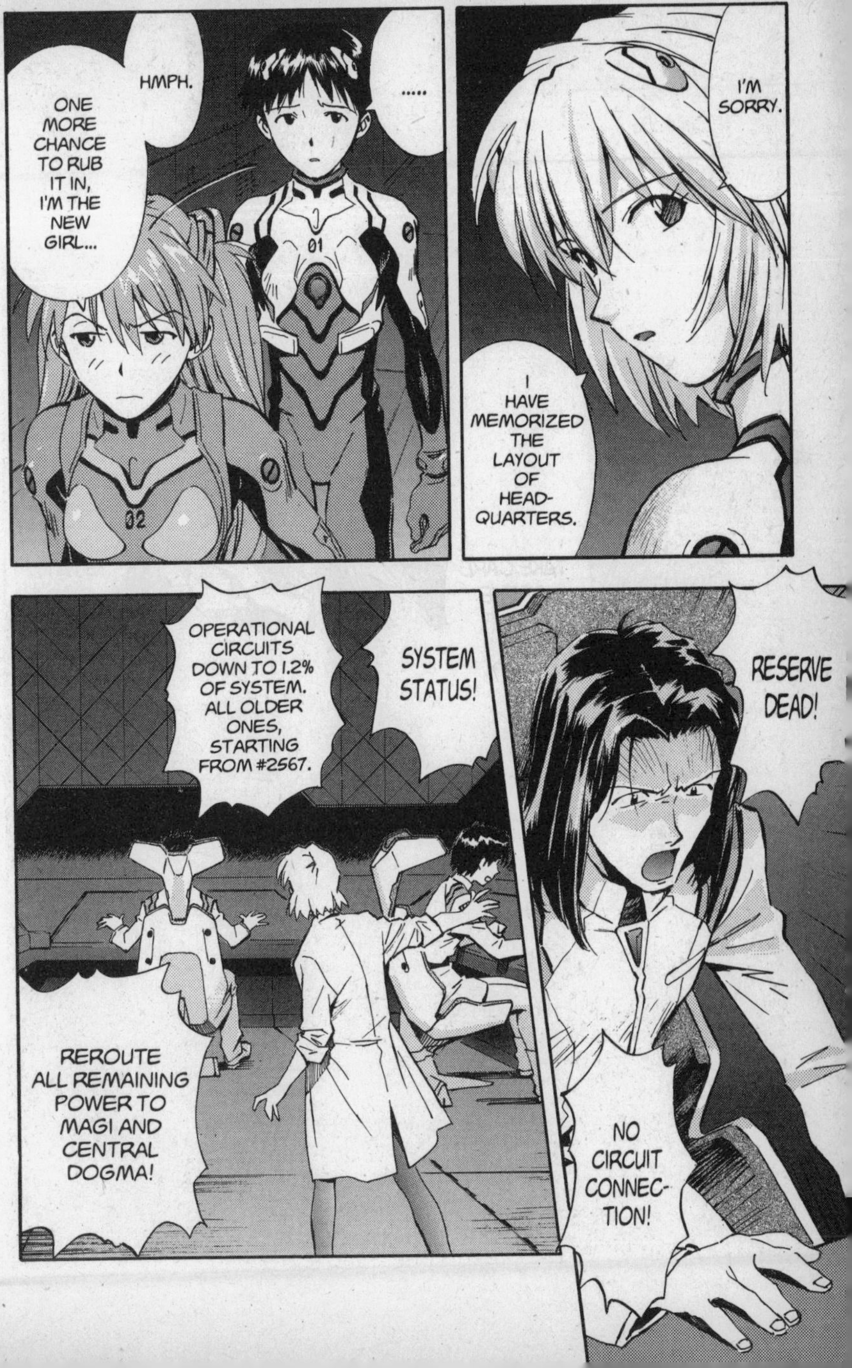
I'M SORRY.
I HAVE MEMORIZED THE LAYOUT OF HEAD-QUARTERS.
.....
HMPH.
ONE MORE CHANCE TO RUB IT IN, I'M THE NEW GIRL...
RESERVE DEAD!
NO CIRCUIT CONNEC-TION!
SYSTEM STATUS!
OPERATIONAL CIRCUITS DOWN TO 1.2% OF SYSTEM. ALL OLDER ONES, STARTING FROM #2567.
REROUTE ALL REMAINING POWER TO MAGI AND CENTRAL DOGMA!

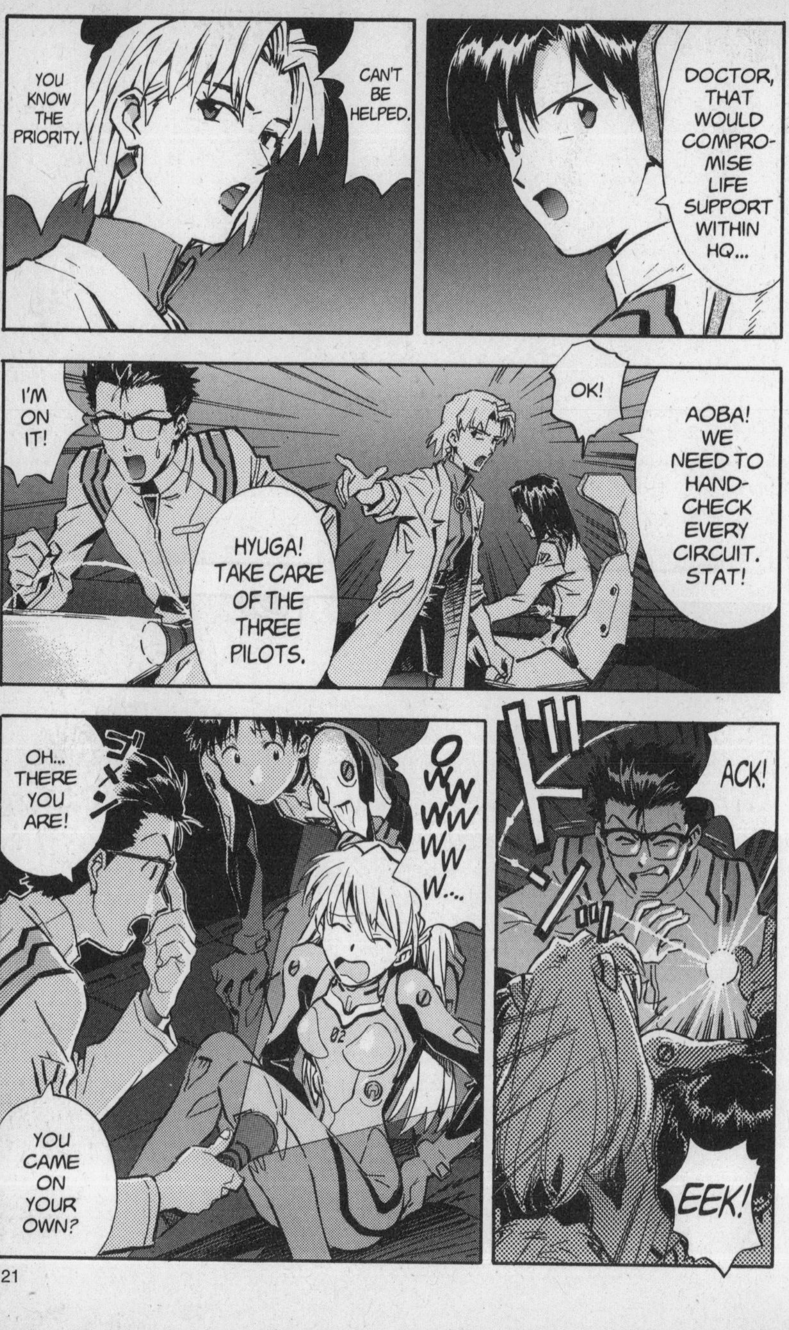
DOCTOR, THAT WOULD COMPROMISE LIFE SUPPORT WITHIN HQ...
CAN'T BE HELPED.
YOU KNOW THE PRIORITY.
AOBA! WE NEED TO HAND-CHECK EVERY CIRCUIT. STAT!
OK!
HYUGA! TAKE CARE OF THE THREE PILOTS.
I'M ON IT!
ACK!
EEK!
OH... THERE YOU ARE!
OWWWWWWWW...
YOU CAME ON YOUR OWN?

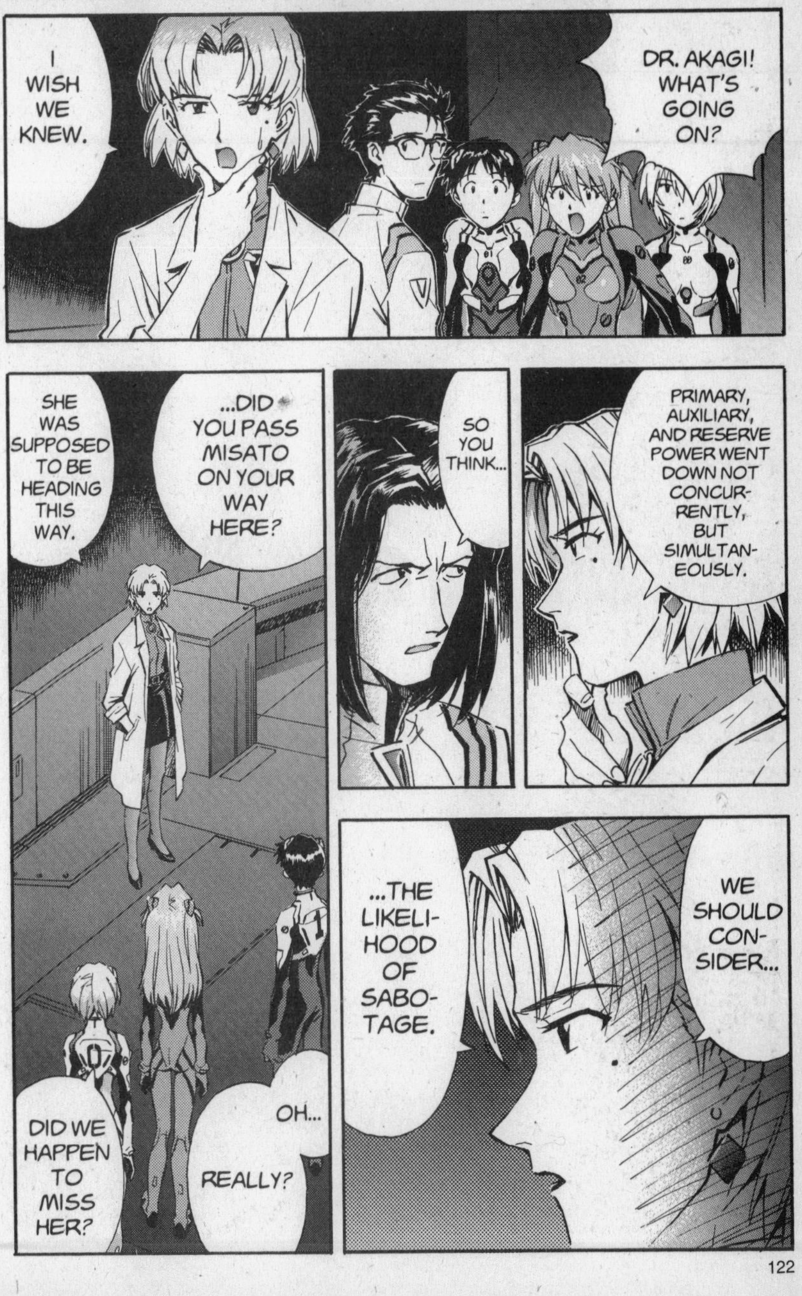
DR. AKAGI! WHAT'S GOING ON?
I WISH WE KNEW.
PRIMARY, AUXILIARY, AND RESERVE POWER WENT DOWN NOT CONCUR-RENTLY, BUT SIMULTAN-EOUSLY.
SO YOU THINK...
WE SHOULD CON-SIDER...
...THE LIKELI-HOOD OF SABO-TAGE.
...DID YOU PASS MISATO ON YOUR WAY HERE?
SHE WAS SUPPOSED TO BE HEADING THIS WAY.
OH...
REALLY?
DID WE HAPPEN TO MISS HER?

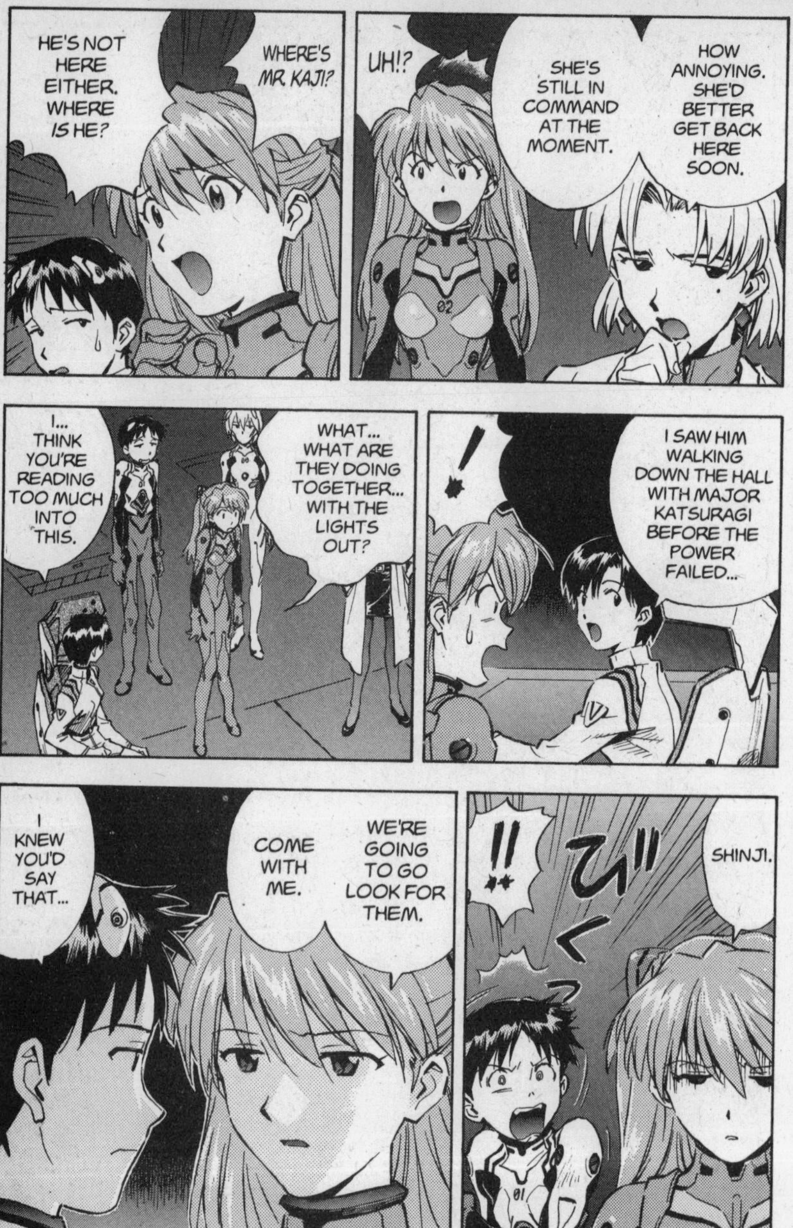
HOW ANNOYING. SHE'D BETTER GET BACK HERE SOON.
SHE'S STILL IN COMMAND AT THE MOMENT.
UH!?
WHERE'S MR. KAJI?
HE'S NOT HERE EITHER. WHERE IS HE?
I SAW HIM WALKING DOWN THE HALL WITH MAJOR KATSURAGI BEFORE THE POWER FAILED...
!
WHAT... WHAT ARE THEY DOING TOGETHER... WITH THE LIGHTS OUT?
I... THINK YOU'RE READING TOO MUCH INTO THIS.
SHINJI.
びくっ
!!
WE'RE GOING TO GO LOOK FOR THEM.
COME WITH ME.
I KNEW YOU'D SAY THAT...

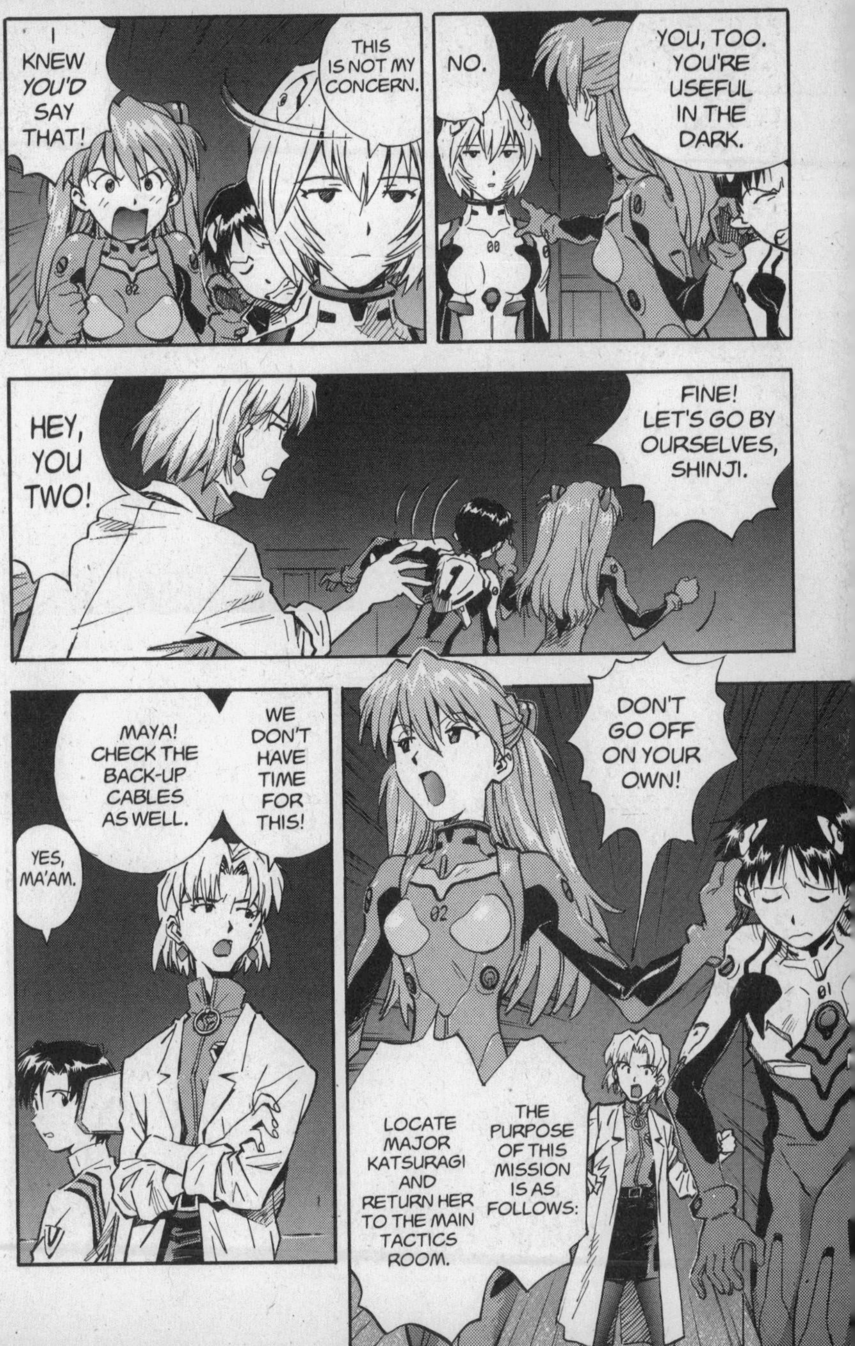
YOU, TOO. YOU'RE USEFUL IN THE DARK.
NO.
THIS IS NOT MY CONCERN.
I KNEW YOU'D SAY THAT!
FINE! LET'S GO BY OURSELVES, SHINJI.
HEY, YOU TWO!
DON'T GO OFF ON YOUR OWN!
THE PURPOSE OF THIS MISSION IS AS FOLLOWS:
LOCATE MAJOR KATSURAGI AND RETURN HER TO THE MAIN TACTICS ROOM.
WE DON'T HAVE TIME FOR THIS!
MAYA! CHECK THE BACK-UP CABLES AS WELL.
YES, MA'AM.

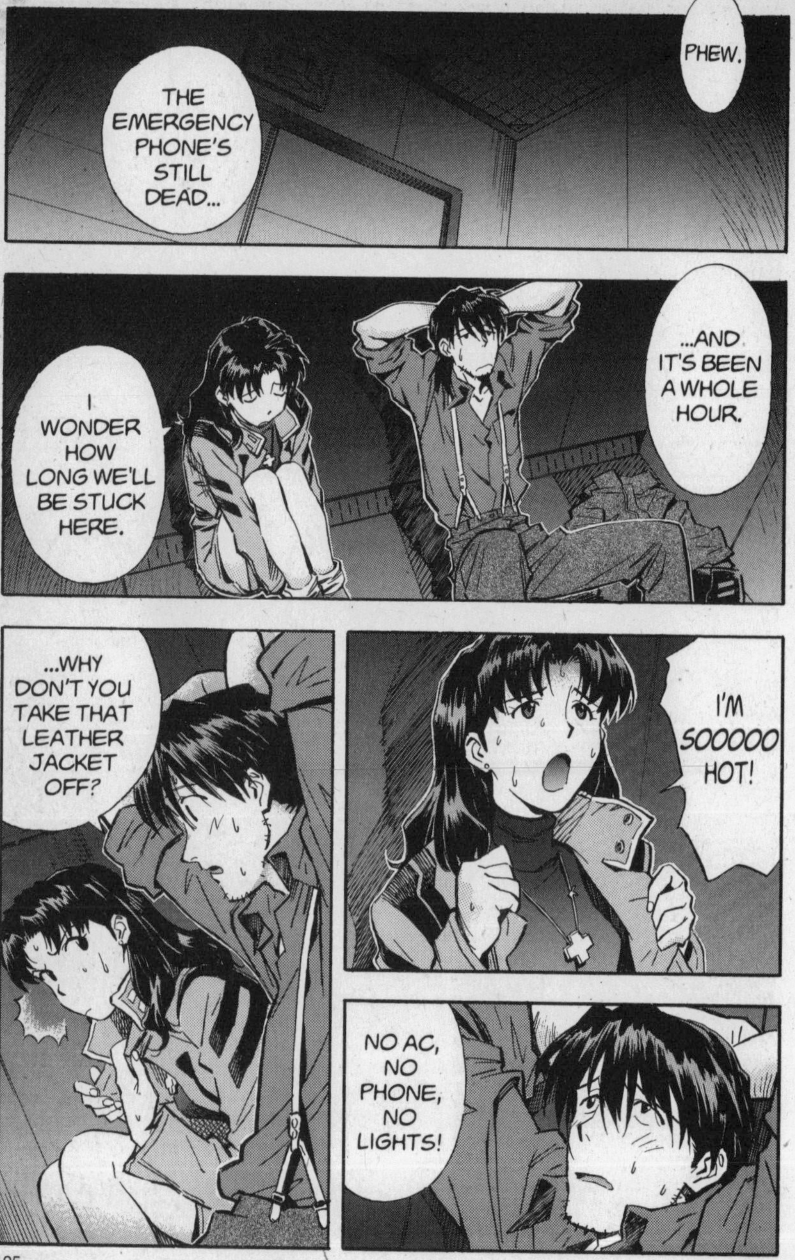
PHEW.
THE EMERGENCY PHONE'S STILL DEAD...
...AND IT'S BEEN A WHOLE HOUR.
I WONDER HOW LONG WE'LL BE STUCK HERE.
I'M SOOOOO HOT!
NO AC, NO PHONE, NO LIGHTS!
...WHY DON'T YOU TAKE THAT LEATHER JACKET OFF?

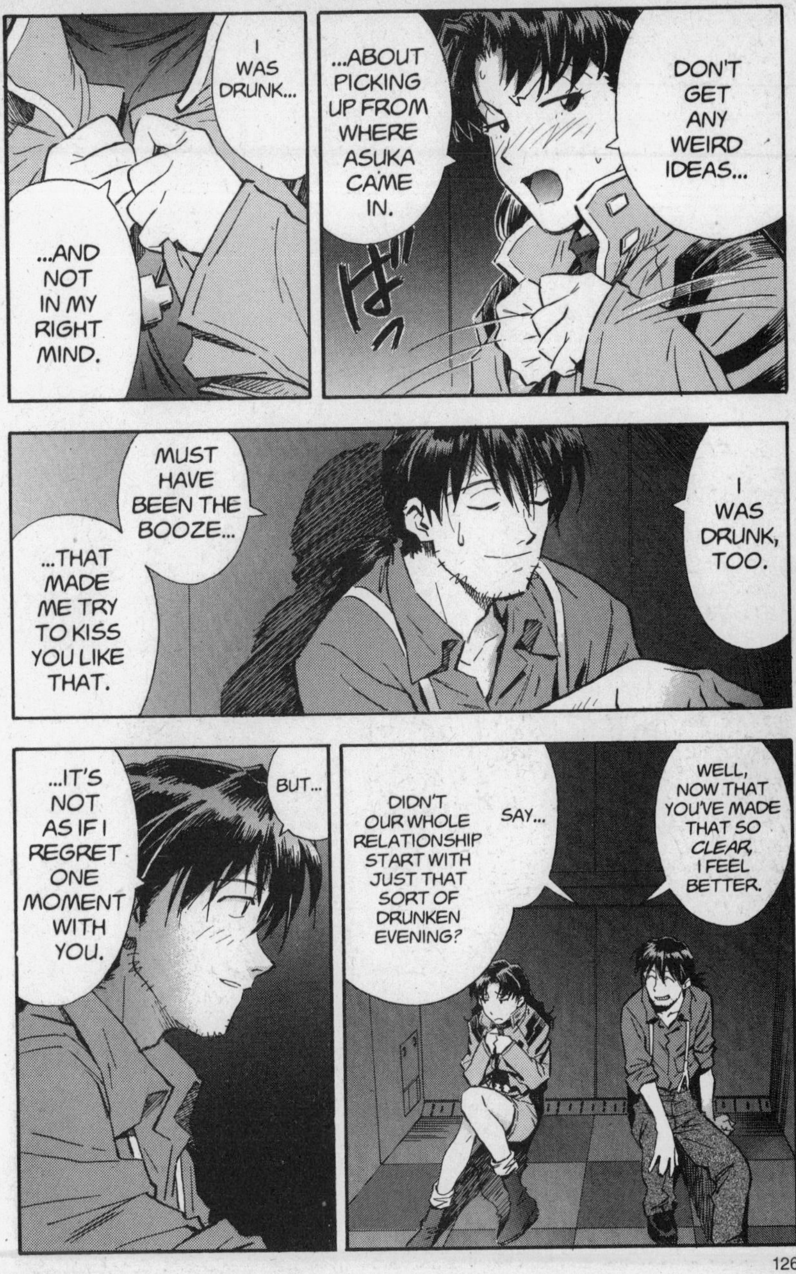
DON'T GET ANY WEIRD IDEAS...
...ABOUT PICKING UP FROM WHERE ASUKA CAME IN.
ばっ
I WAS DRUNK...
...AND NOT IN MY RIGHT MIND.
I WAS DRUNK, TOO.
MUST HAVE BEEN THE BOOZE...
...THAT MADE ME TRY TO KISS YOU LIKE THAT.
WELL, NOW THAT YOU'VE MADE THAT SO *CLEAR*, I FEEL BETTER.
SAY...
DIDN'T OUR WHOLE RELATIONSHIP START WITH JUST THAT SORT OF DRUNKEN EVENING?
BUT...
...IT'S NOT AS IF I REGRET ONE MOMENT WITH YOU.

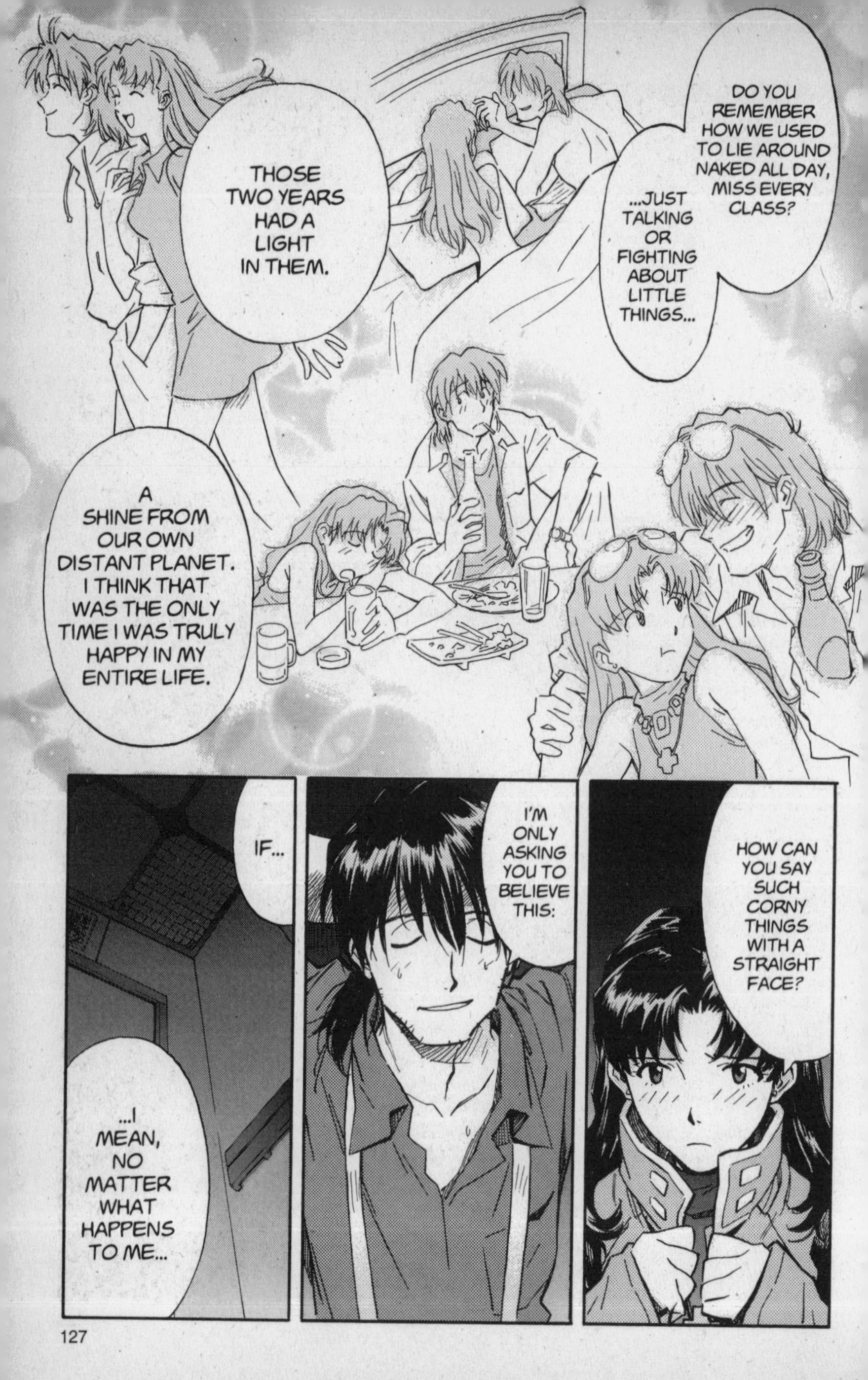
DO YOU REMEMBER HOW WE USED TO LIE AROUND NAKED ALL DAY, MISS EVERY CLASS?
...JUST TALKING OR FIGHTING ABOUT LITTLE THINGS...
THOSE TWO YEARS HAD A LIGHT IN THEM.
A SHINE FROM OUR OWN DISTANT PLANET. I THINK THAT WAS THE ONLY TIME I WAS TRULY HAPPY IN MY ENTIRE LIFE.
HOW CAN YOU SAY SUCH CORNY THINGS WITH A STRAIGHT FACE?
I'M ONLY ASKING YOU TO BELIEVE THIS:
IF...
...I MEAN, NO MATTER WHAT HAPPENS TO ME...

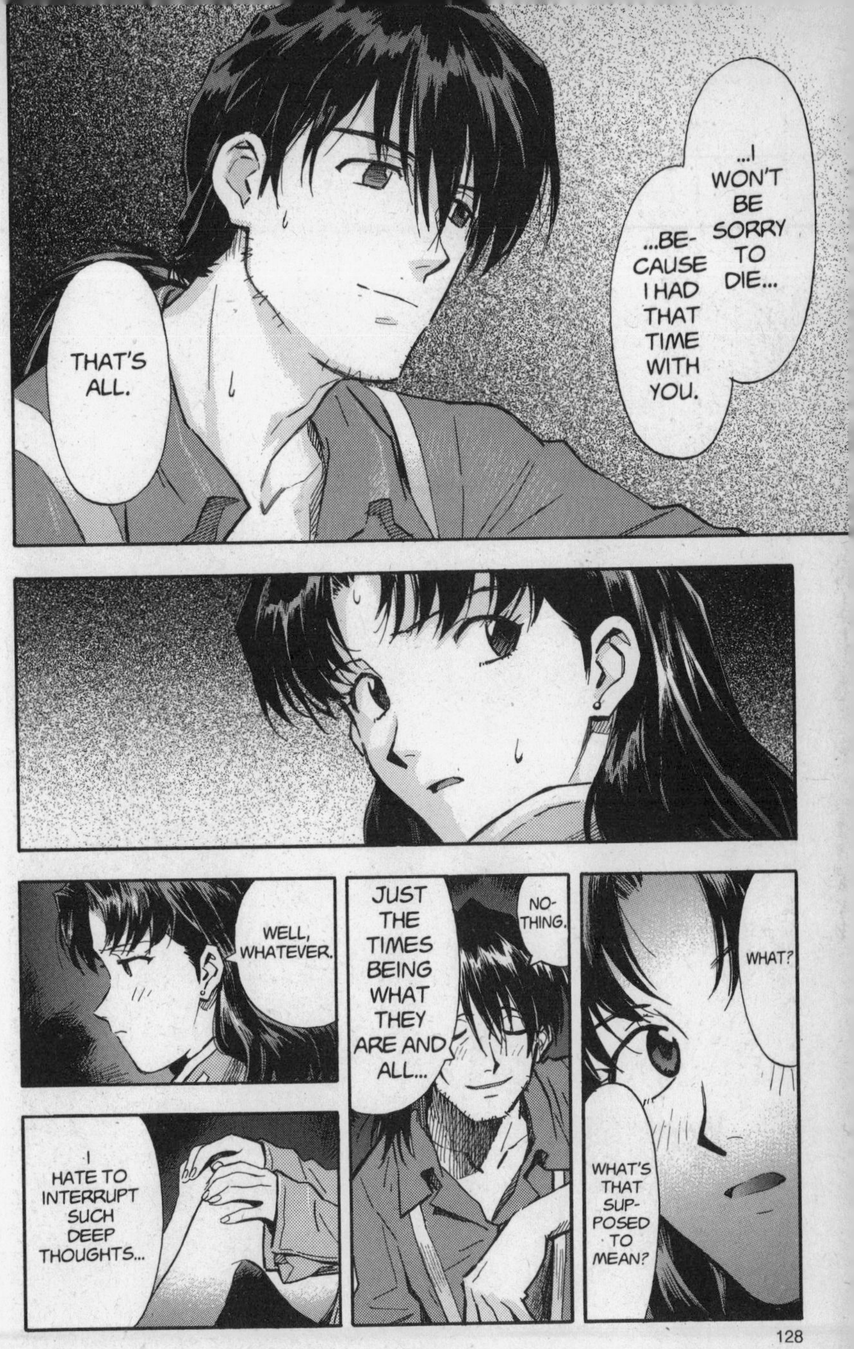
...I WON'T BE SORRY TO DIE...
...BE-CAUSE I HAD THAT TIME WITH YOU.
THAT'S ALL.
WHAT?
WHAT'S THAT SUP-POSED TO MEAN?
NO-THING.
JUST THE TIMES BEING WHAT THEY ARE AND ALL...
WELL, WHATEVER.
I HATE TO INTERRUPT SUCH DEEP THOUGHTS...

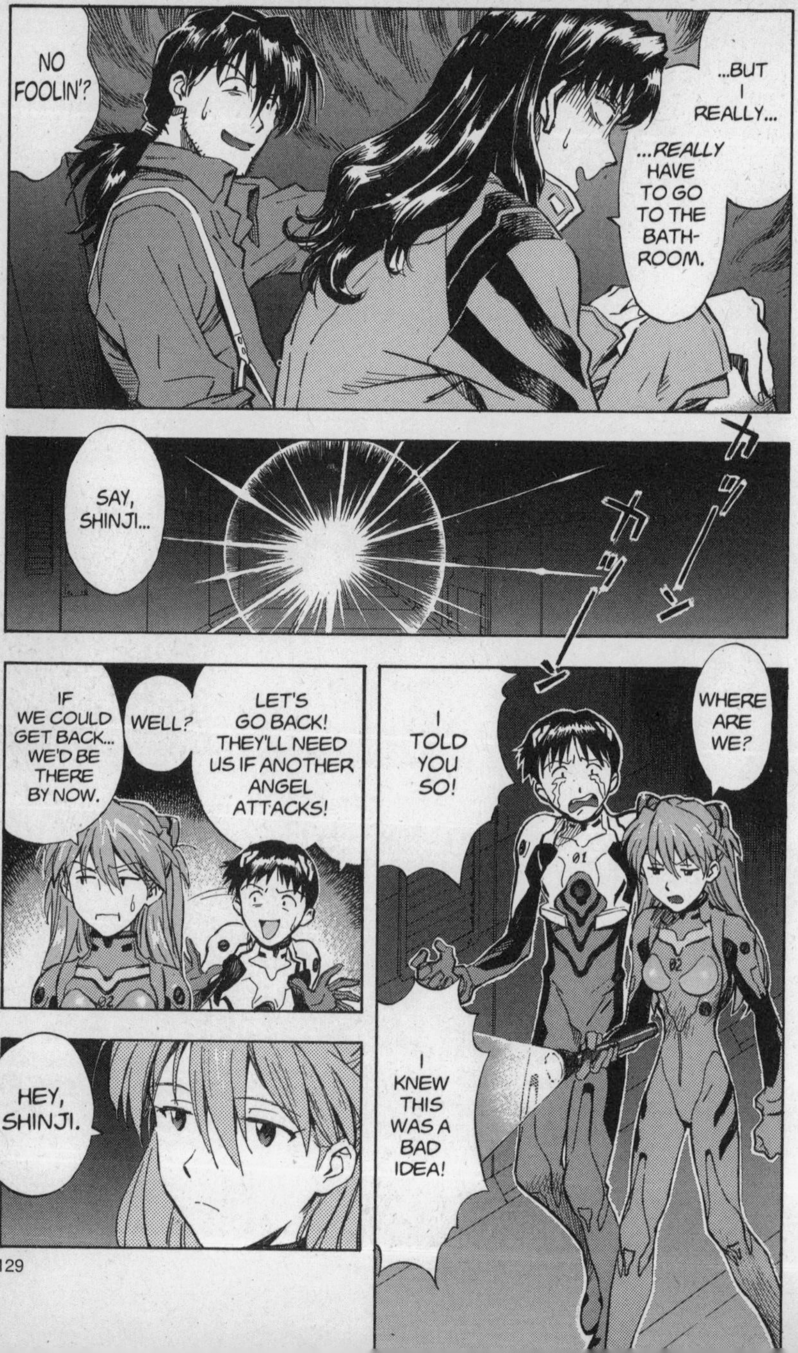
...BUT I REALLY...
...REALLY HAVE TO GO TO THE BATH-ROOM.
NO FOOLIN'?
SAY, SHINJI...
WHERE ARE WE?
I TOLD YOU SO!
I KNEW THIS WAS A BAD IDEA!
LET'S GO BACK! THEY'LL NEED US IF ANOTHER ANGEL ATTACKS!
WELL?
IF WE COULD GET BACK... WE'D BE THERE BY NOW.
HEY, SHINJI.

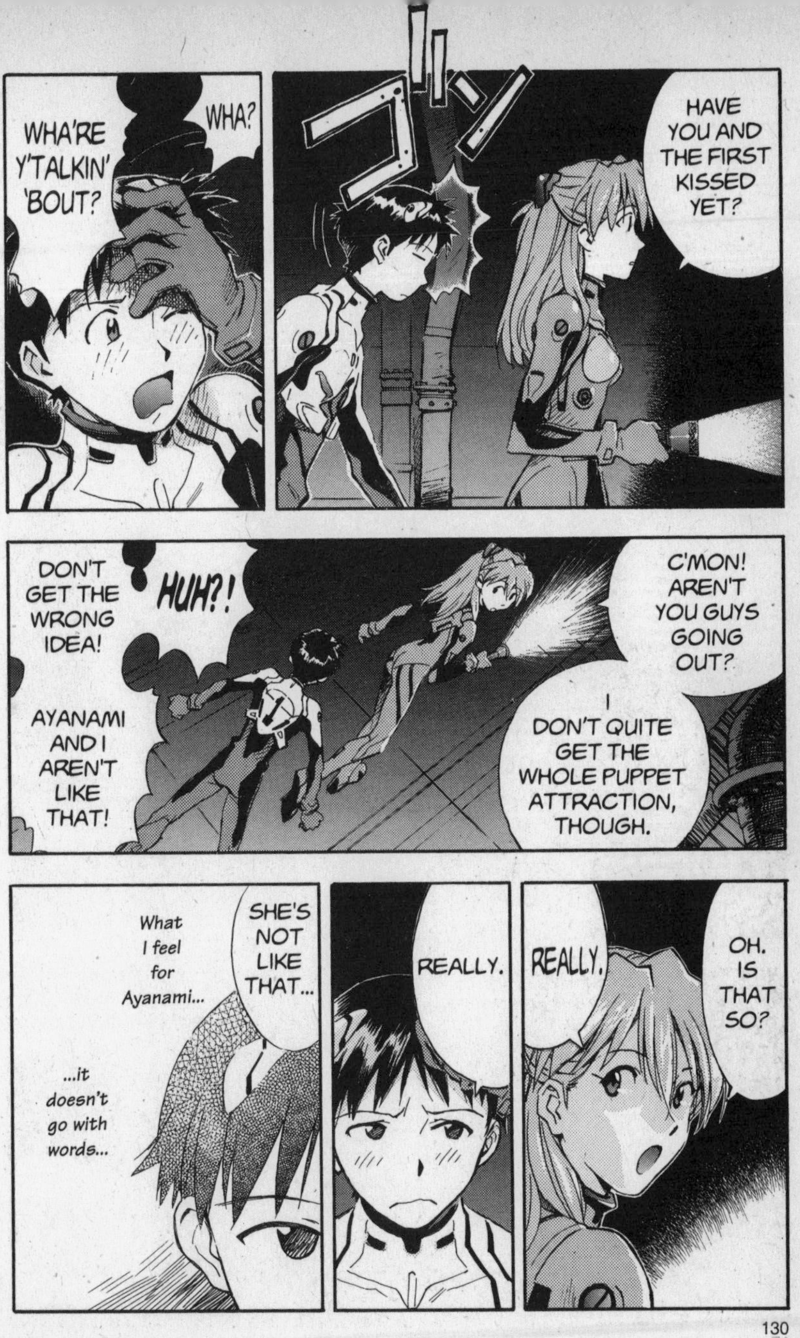
HAVE YOU AND THE FIRST KISSED YET?
WHA?
WHA'RE Y'TALKIN' 'BOUT?
C'MON! AREN'T YOU GUYS GOING OUT?
I DON'T QUITE GET THE WHOLE PUPPET ATTRACTION, THOUGH.
HUH?!
DON'T GET THE WRONG IDEA!
AYANAMI AND I AREN'T LIKE THAT!
OH. IS THAT SO?
REALLY.
REALLY.
SHE'S NOT LIKE THAT...
What I feel for Ayanami...
...it doesn't go with words...

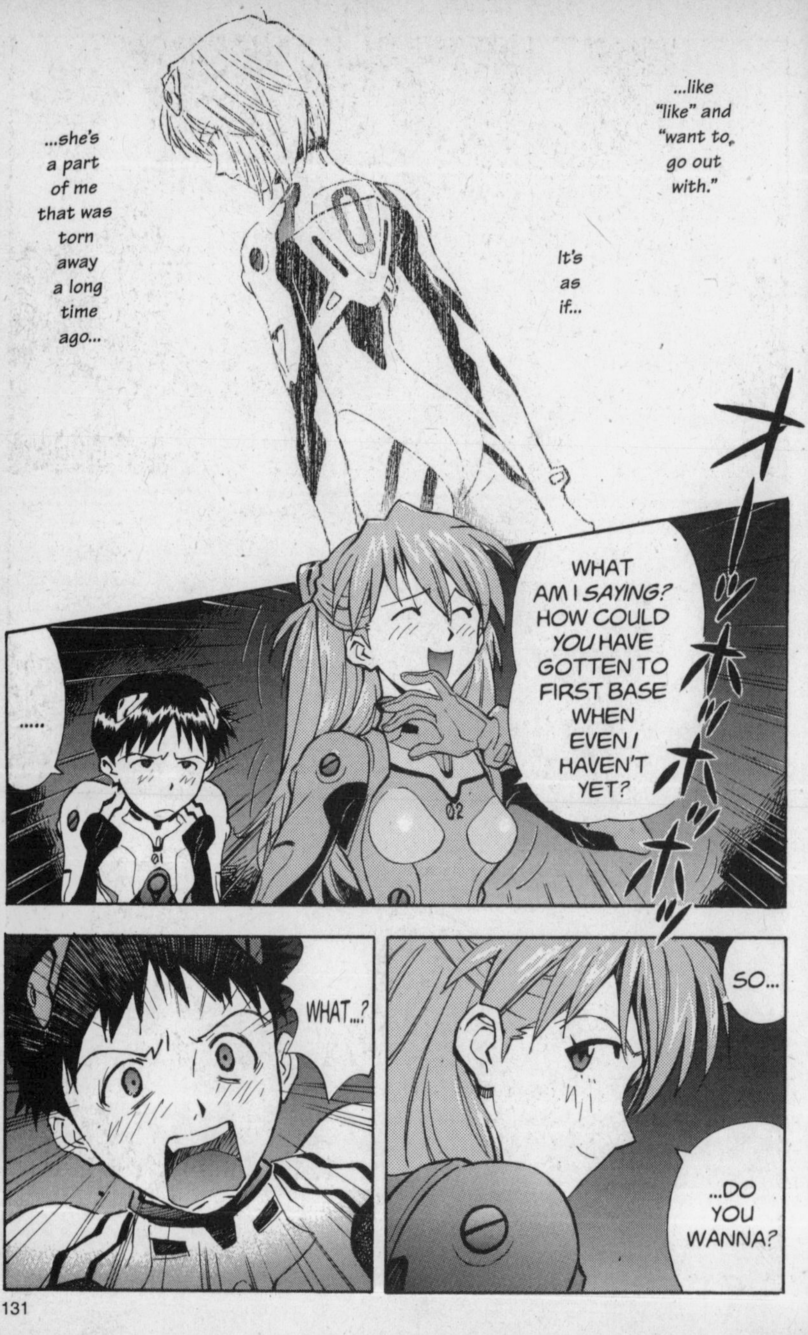
...like "like" and "want to go out with."
It's as if...
...she's a part of me that was torn away a long time ago...
WHAT AM I *SAYING?* HOW COULD *YOU* HAVE GOTTEN TO FIRST BASE WHEN EVEN *I* HAVEN'T YET?
.....
SO...
...DO YOU WANNA?
WHAT...?

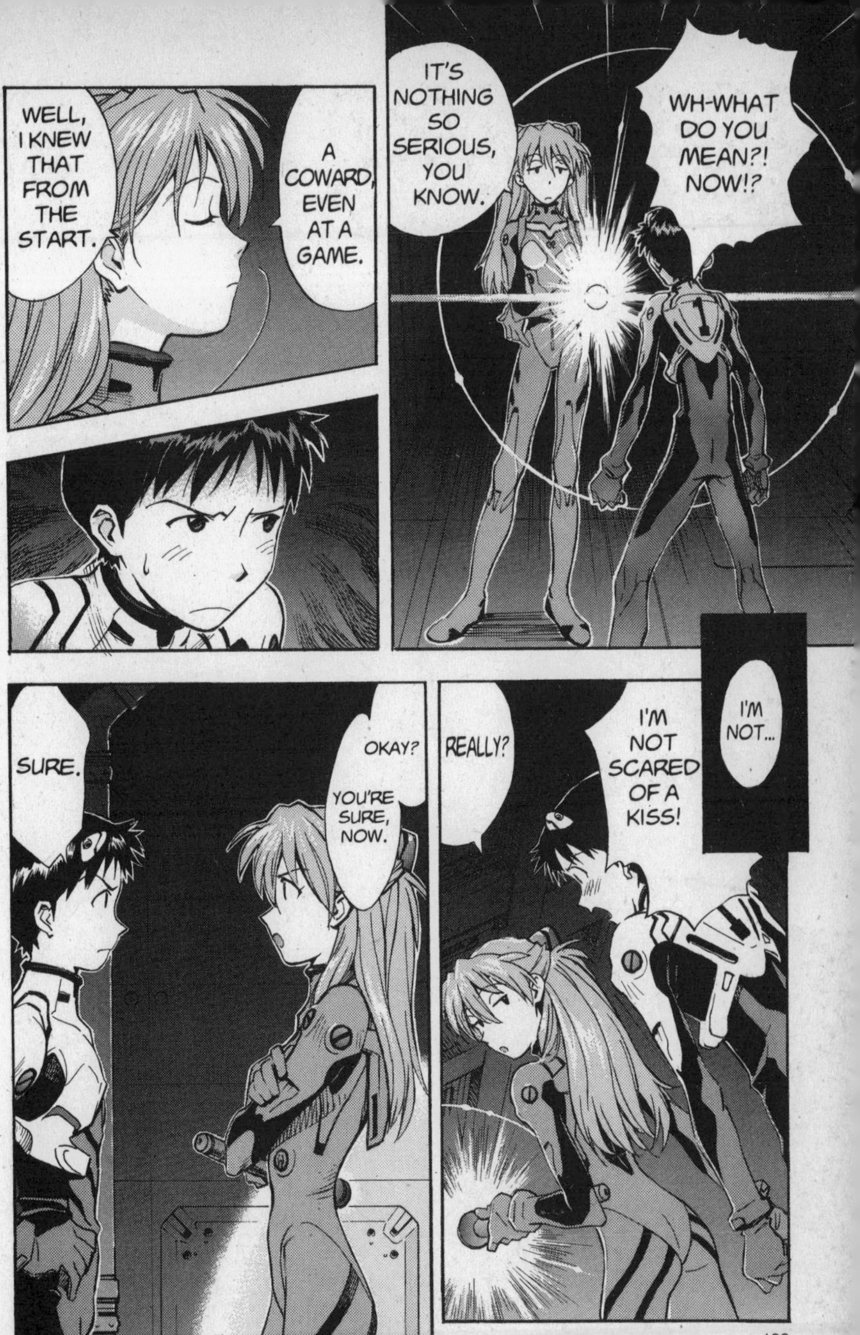
WH-WHAT DO YOU MEAN?! NOW!?
IT'S NOTHING SO SERIOUS, YOU KNOW.
A COWARD, EVEN AT A GAME.
WELL, I KNEW THAT FROM THE START.
I'M NOT...
I'M NOT SCARED OF A KISS!
REALLY?
OKAY?
YOU'RE SURE, NOW.
SURE.

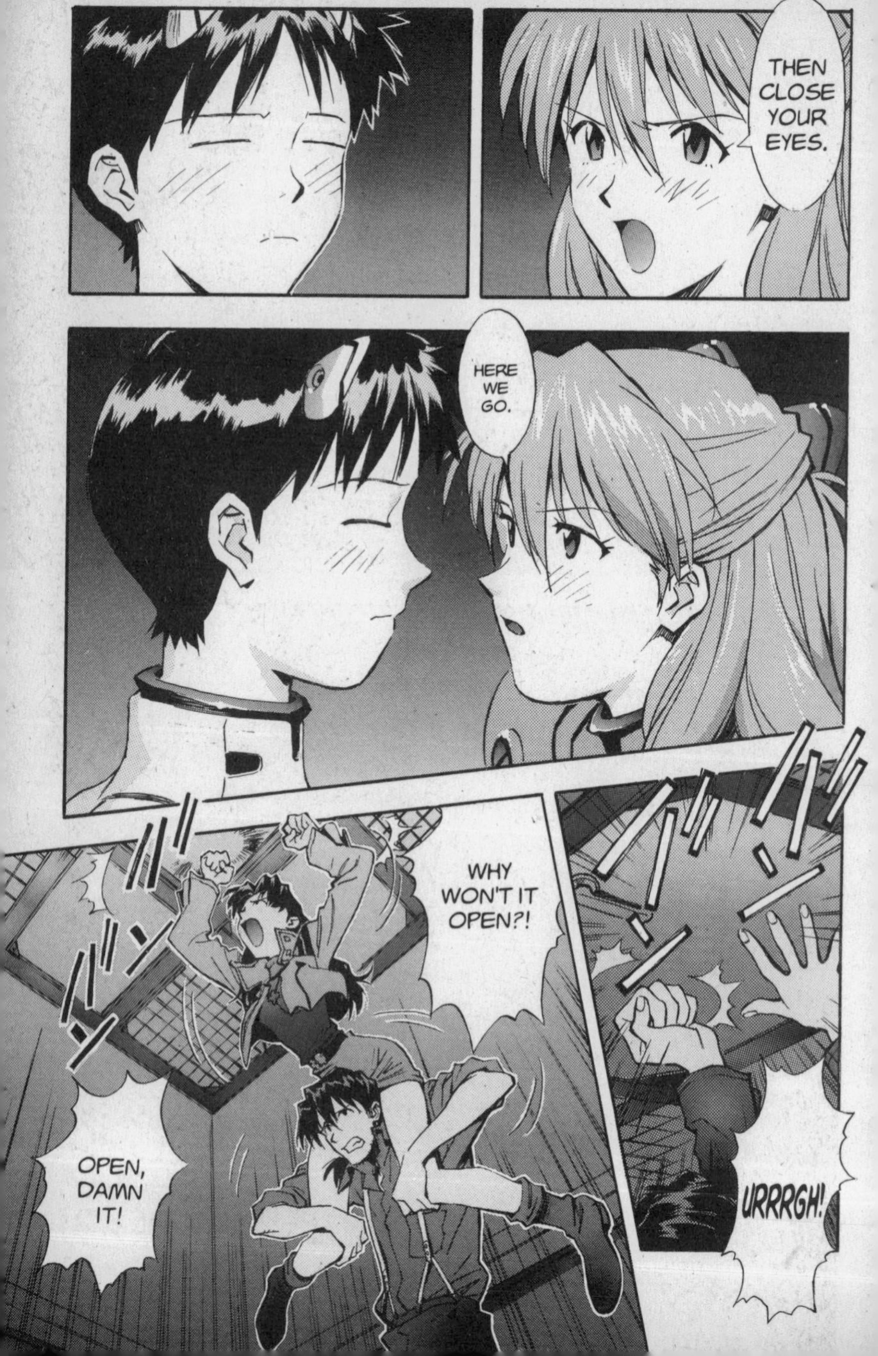
THEN CLOSE YOUR EYES.
HERE WE GO.
URRRGH!
WHY WON'T IT OPEN?!
OPEN, DAMN IT!

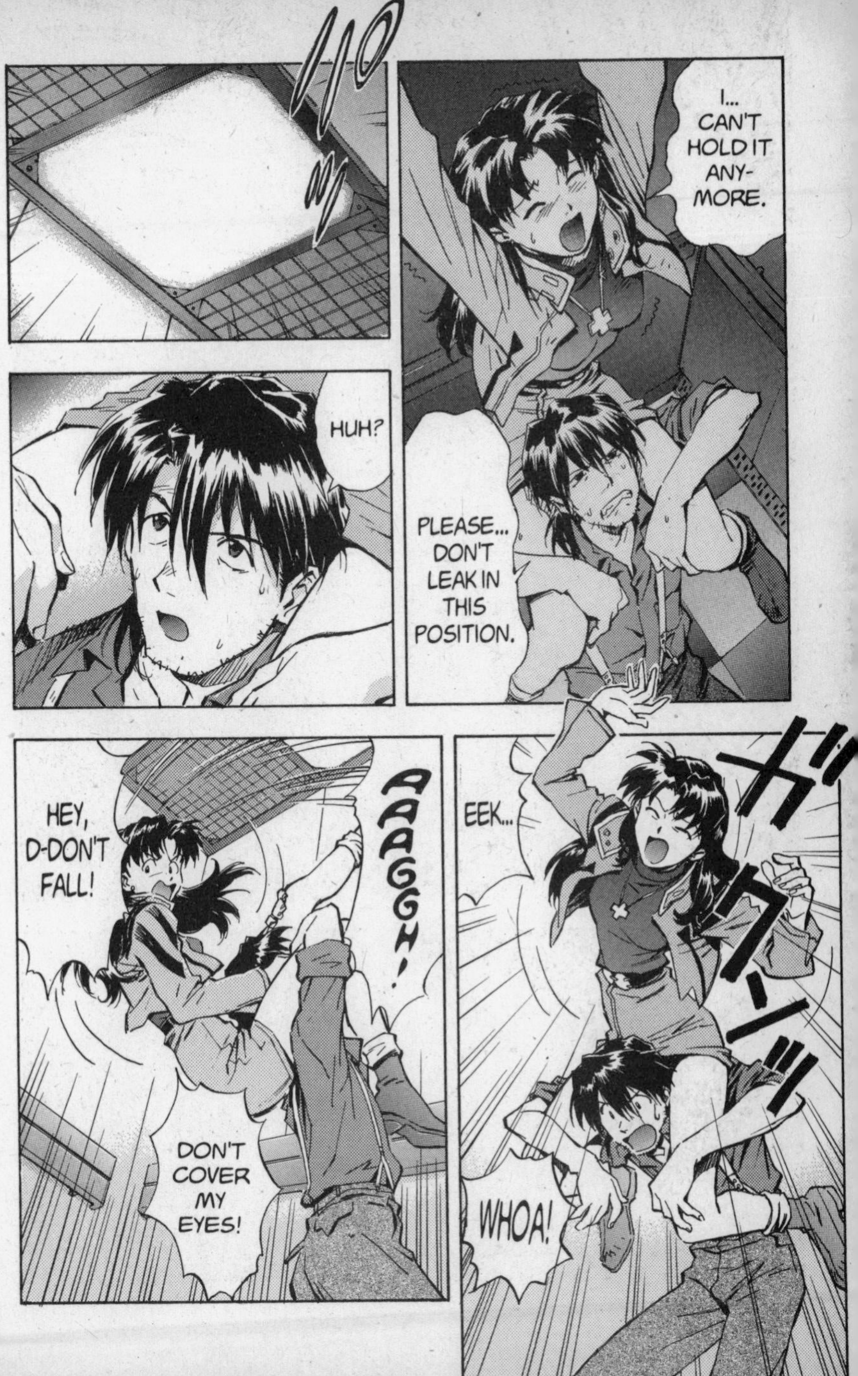
I... CAN'T HOLD IT ANY-MORE.
PLEASE... DON'T LEAK IN THIS POSITION.
HUH?
EEK...
WHOA!
HEY, D-DON'T FALL!
AAAGGH!
DON'T COVER MY EYES!

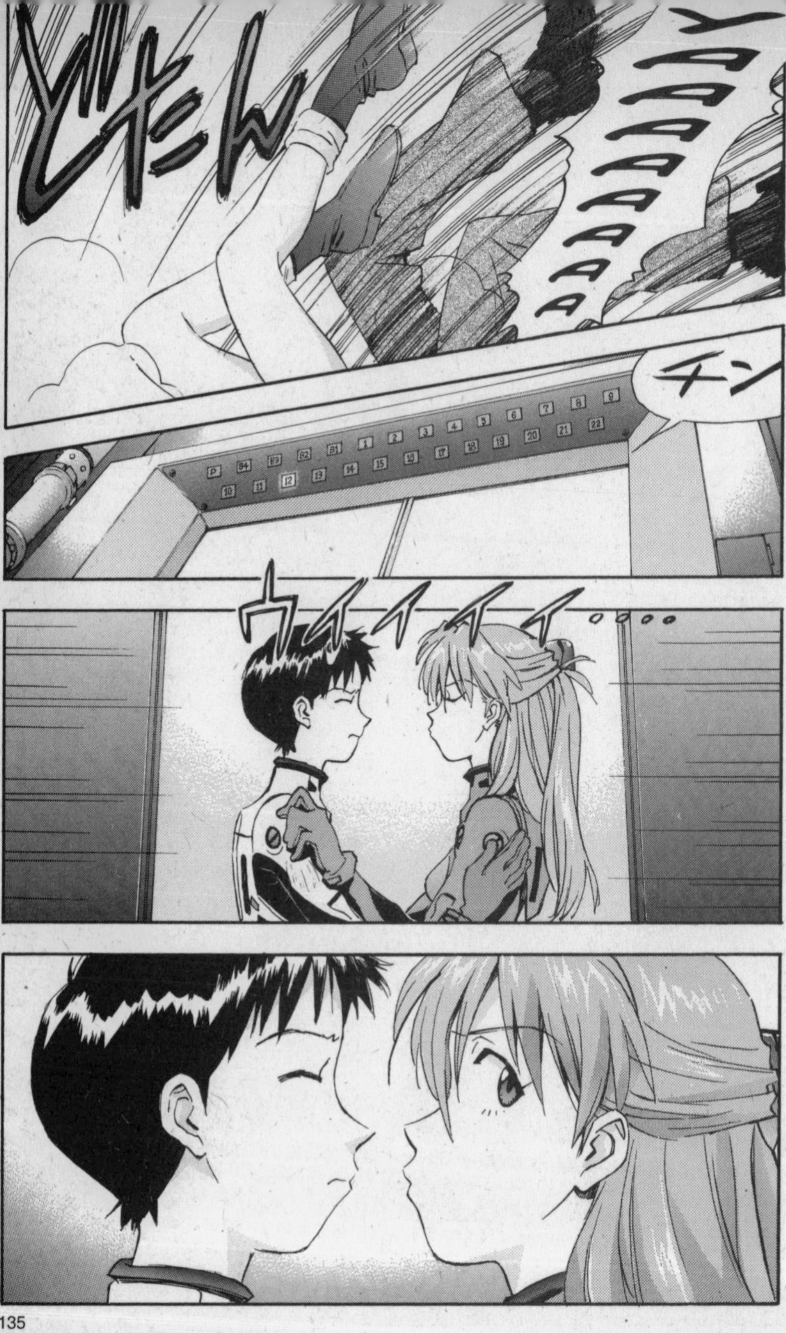
ヤAAAAAAAAA
どたん
チン
P B4 B3 B2 B1 1 2 3 4 5 6 7 8 9
10 11 12 13 14 15 16 17 18 19 20 21 22
ウイイイイ…

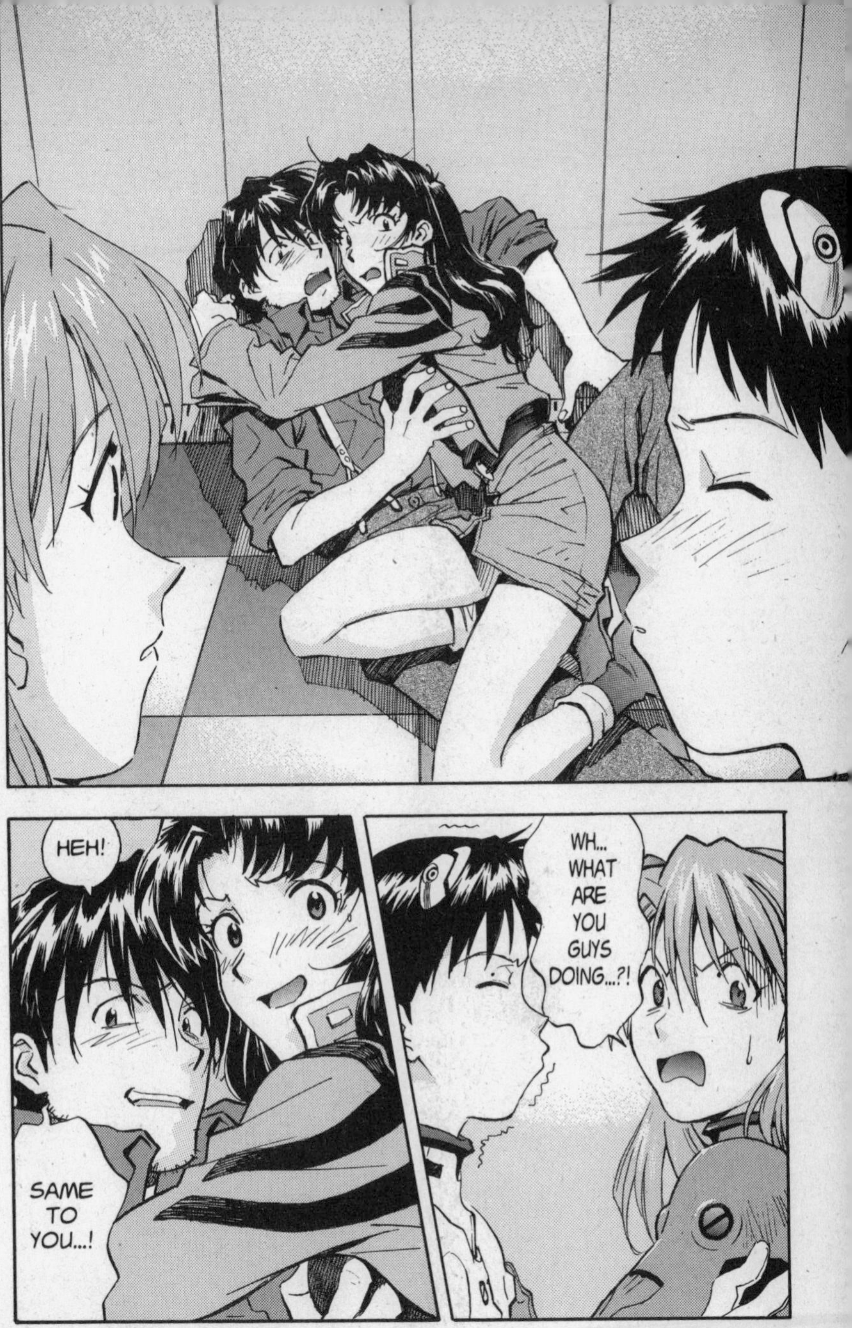
WH... WHAT ARE YOU GUYS DOING...?!
HEH!
SAME TO YOU...!

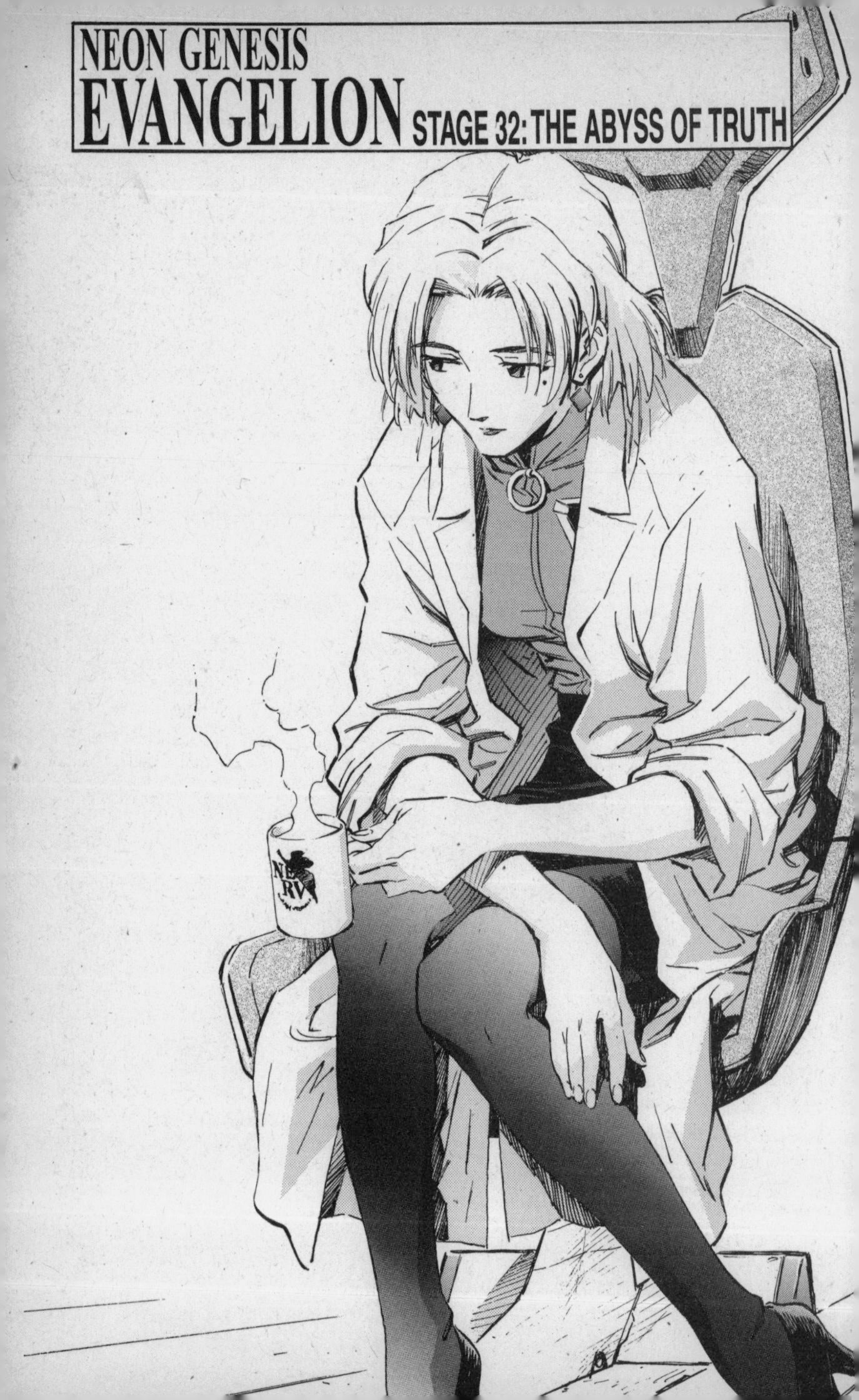
NEON GENESIS
EVANGELION
STAGE 32: THE ABYSS OF TRUTH

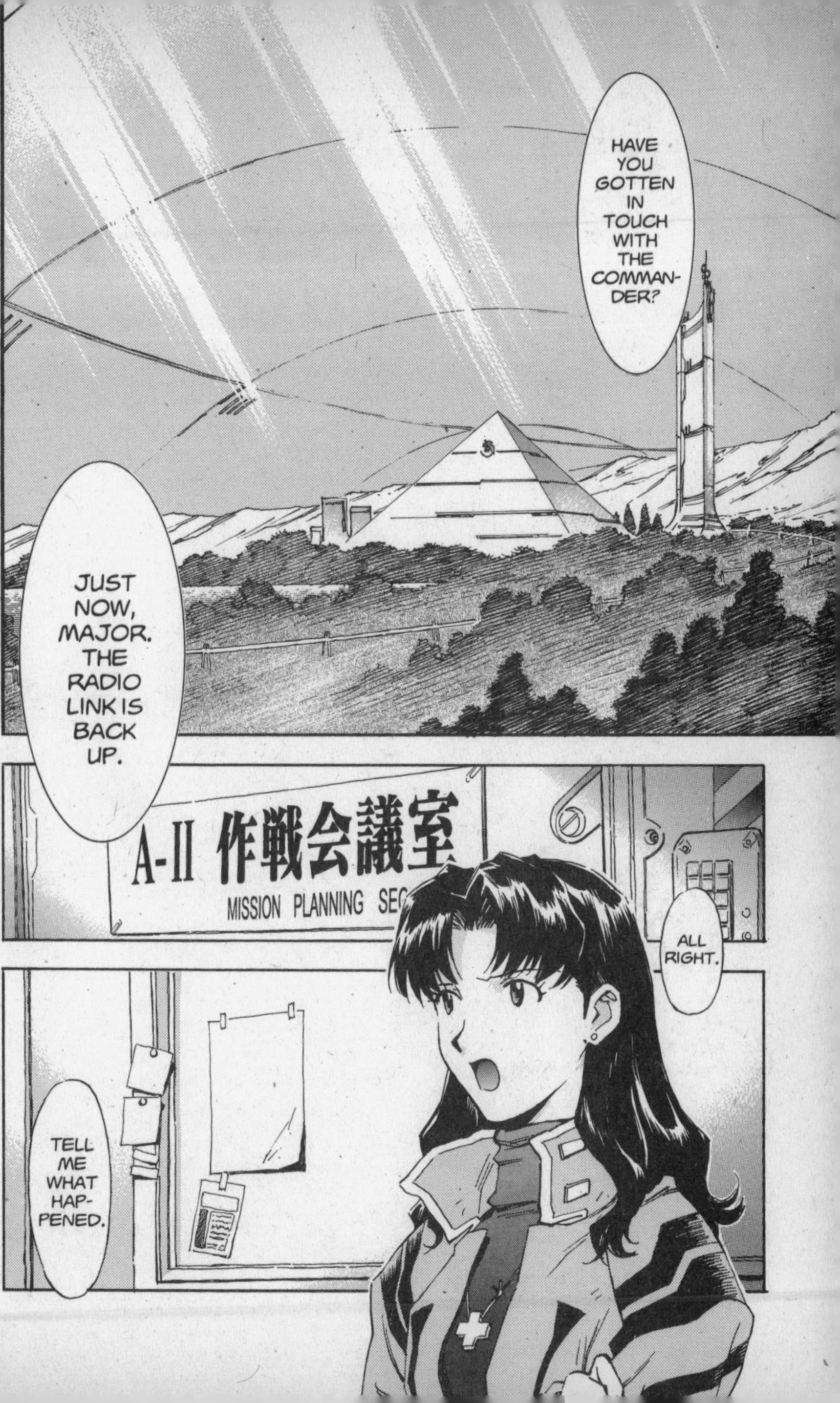
HAVE YOU GOTTEN IN TOUCH WITH THE COMMANDER?
JUST NOW, MAJOR. THE RADIO LINK IS BACK UP.
A-II 作戦会議室
MISSION PLANNING SEC
ALL RIGHT.
TELL ME WHAT HAPPENED.

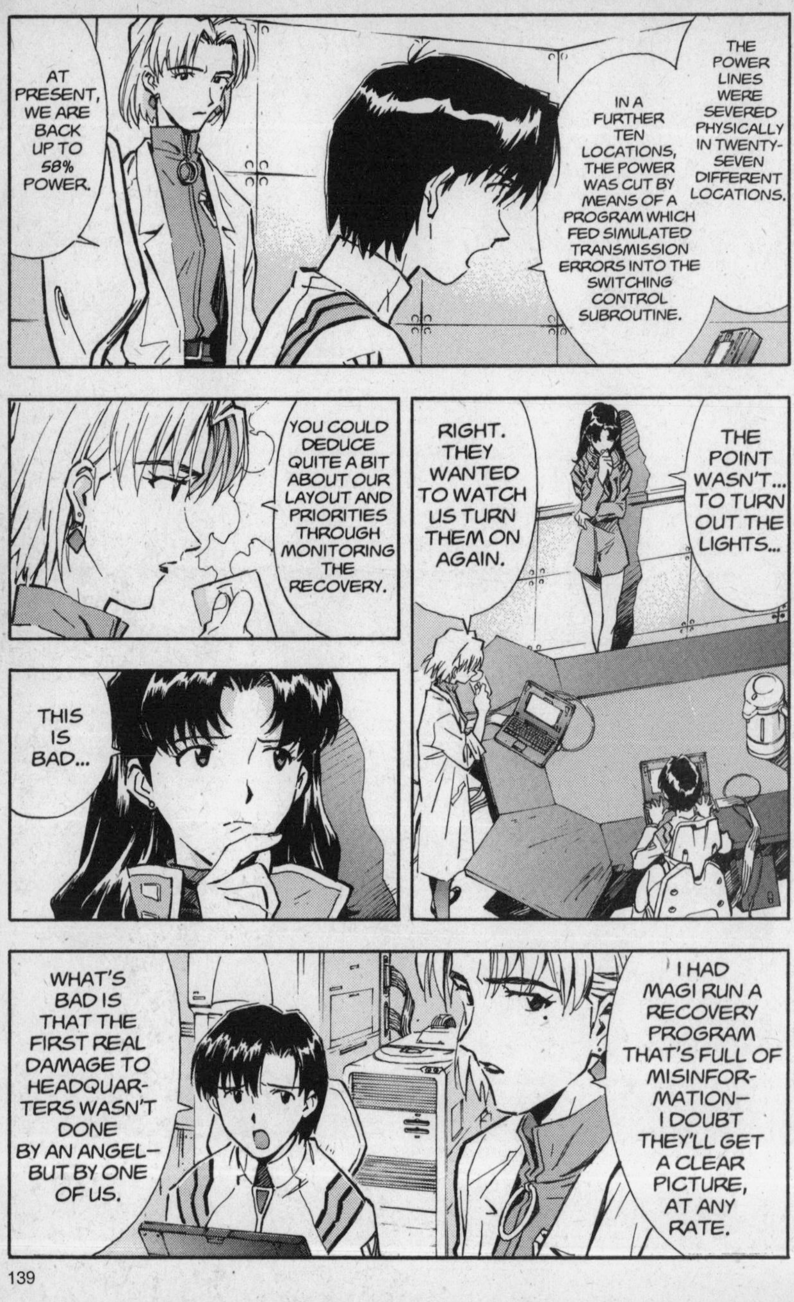
THE POWER LINES WERE SEVERED PHYSICALLY IN TWENTY-SEVEN DIFFERENT LOCATIONS.
IN A FURTHER TEN LOCATIONS, THE POWER WAS CUT BY MEANS OF A PROGRAM WHICH FED SIMULATED TRANSMISSION ERRORS INTO THE SWITCHING CONTROL SUBROUTINE.
AT PRESENT, WE ARE BACK UP TO 58% POWER.
THE POINT WASN'T... TO TURN OUT THE LIGHTS...
RIGHT. THEY WANTED TO WATCH US TURN THEM ON AGAIN.
YOU COULD DEDUCE QUITE A BIT ABOUT OUR LAYOUT AND PRIORITIES THROUGH MONITORING THE RECOVERY.
THIS IS BAD...
I HAD MAGI RUN A RECOVERY PROGRAM THAT'S FULL OF MISINFOR-MATION– I DOUBT THEY'LL GET A CLEAR PICTURE, AT ANY RATE.
WHAT'S BAD IS THAT THE FIRST REAL DAMAGE TO HEADQUAR-TERS WASN'T DONE BY AN ANGEL– BUT BY ONE OF US.

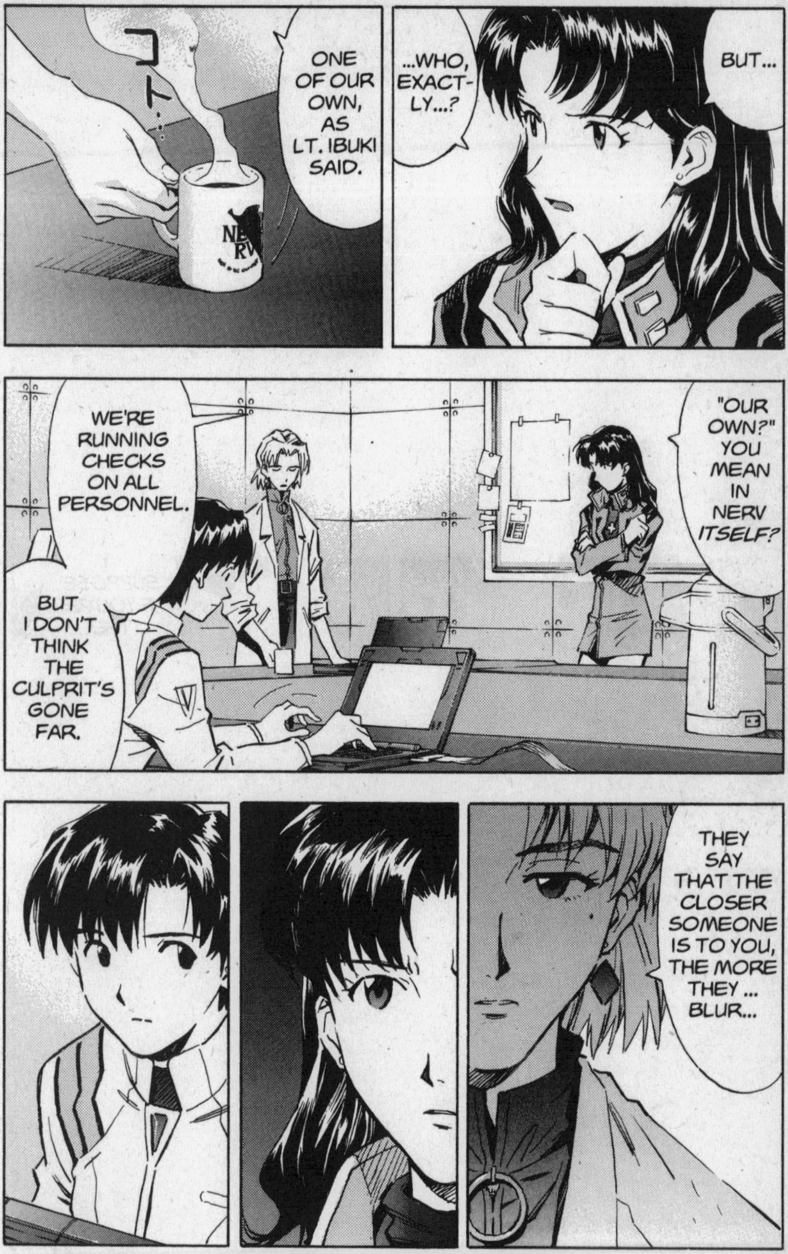
BUT...
...WHO, EXACTLY...?
ONE OF OUR OWN, AS LT. IBUKI SAID.
コト
"OUR OWN?" YOU MEAN IN NERV *ITSELF?*
WE'RE RUNNING CHECKS ON ALL PERSONNEL.
BUT I DON'T THINK THE CULPRIT'S GONE FAR.
THEY SAY THAT THE CLOSER SOMEONE IS TO YOU, THE MORE THEY ... BLUR...

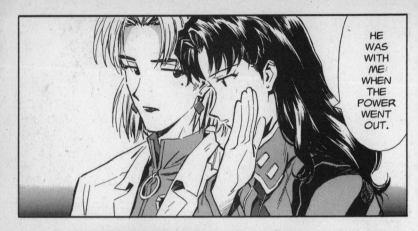

HE WAS WITH ME WHEN THE POWER WENT OUT.

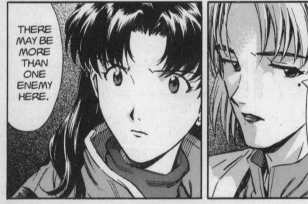

THERE MAY BE MORE THAN ONE ENEMY HERE.

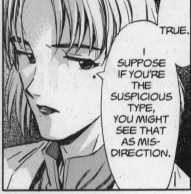

TRUE.

I SUPPOSE IF YOU'RE THE SUSPICIOUS TYPE, YOU MIGHT SEE THAT AS MIS-DIRECTION.

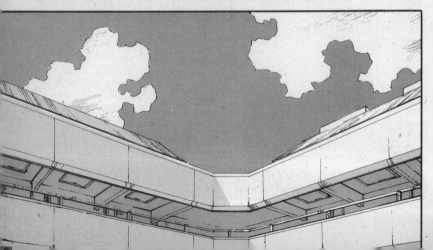

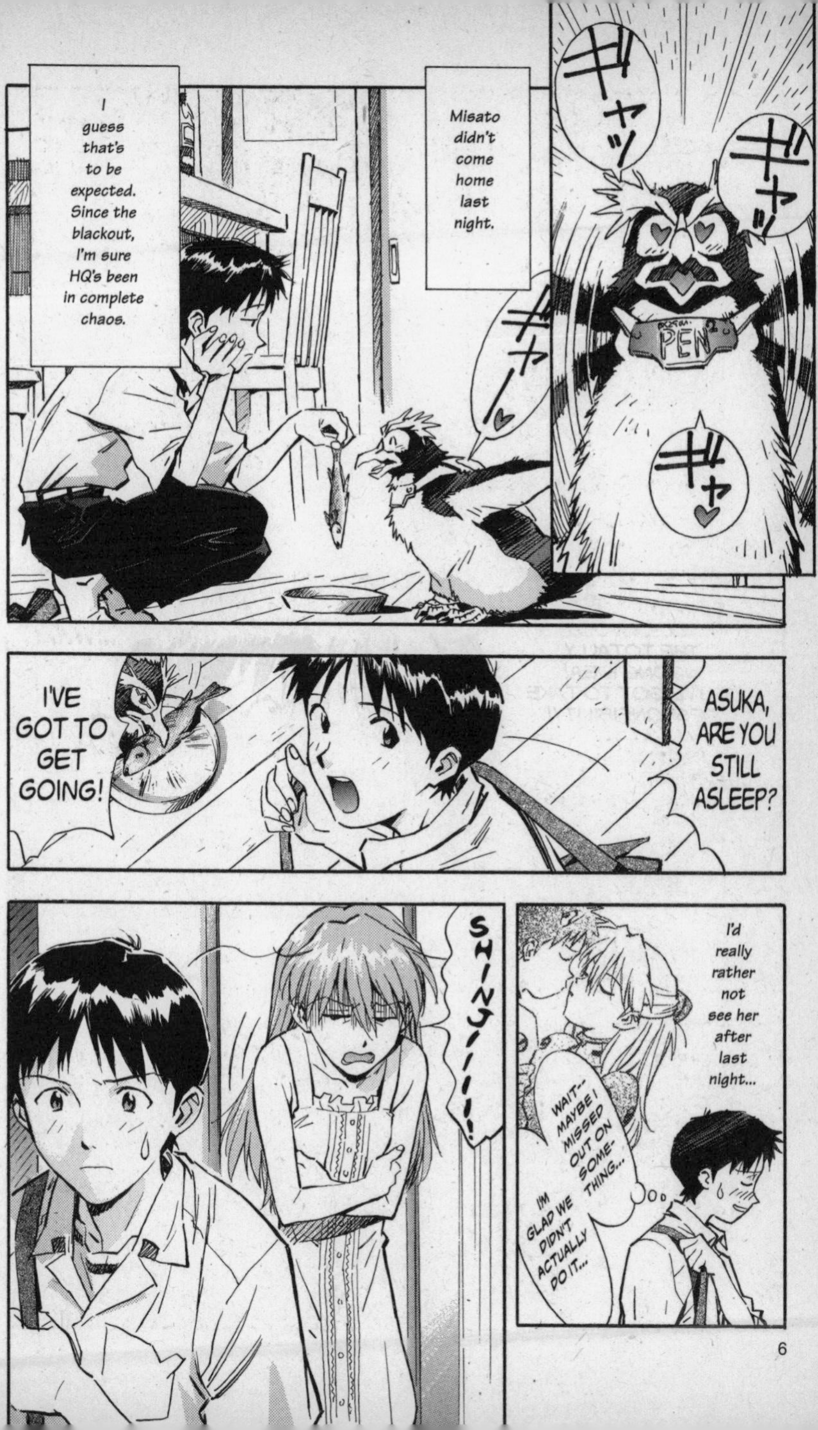
ギャッ
ギャッ
ギャ♥
Misato didn't come home last night.
ギャー♥
I guess that's to be expected. Since the blackout, I'm sure HQ's been in complete chaos.
PEN²
ASUKA, ARE YOU STILL ASLEEP?
I'VE GOT TO GET GOING!
I'd really rather not see her after last night...
WAIT--MAYBE I MISSED OUT ON SOME-THING...
I'M GLAD WE DIDN'T ACTUALLY DO IT...
SHINJI!!!!!!

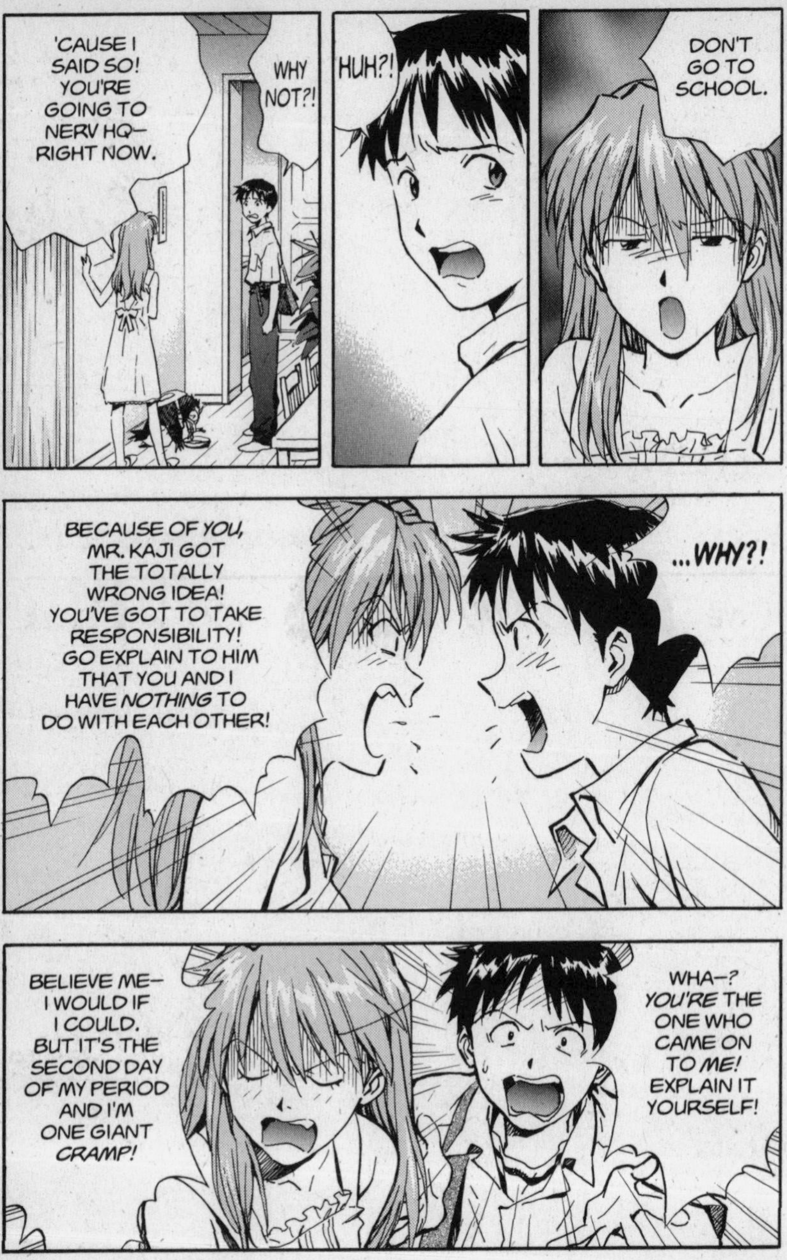
DON'T GO TO SCHOOL.
HUH?!
WHY NOT?!
'CAUSE I SAID SO! YOU'RE GOING TO NERV HQ— RIGHT NOW.
...WHY?!
BECAUSE OF *YOU*, MR. KAJI GOT THE TOTALLY WRONG IDEA! YOU'VE GOT TO TAKE RESPONSIBILITY! GO EXPLAIN TO HIM THAT YOU AND I HAVE *NOTHING* TO DO WITH EACH OTHER!
WHA—? *YOU'RE* THE ONE WHO CAME ON TO *ME!* EXPLAIN IT YOURSELF!
BELIEVE ME— I WOULD IF I COULD. BUT IT'S THE SECOND DAY OF MY PERIOD AND I'M ONE GIANT *CRAMP!*

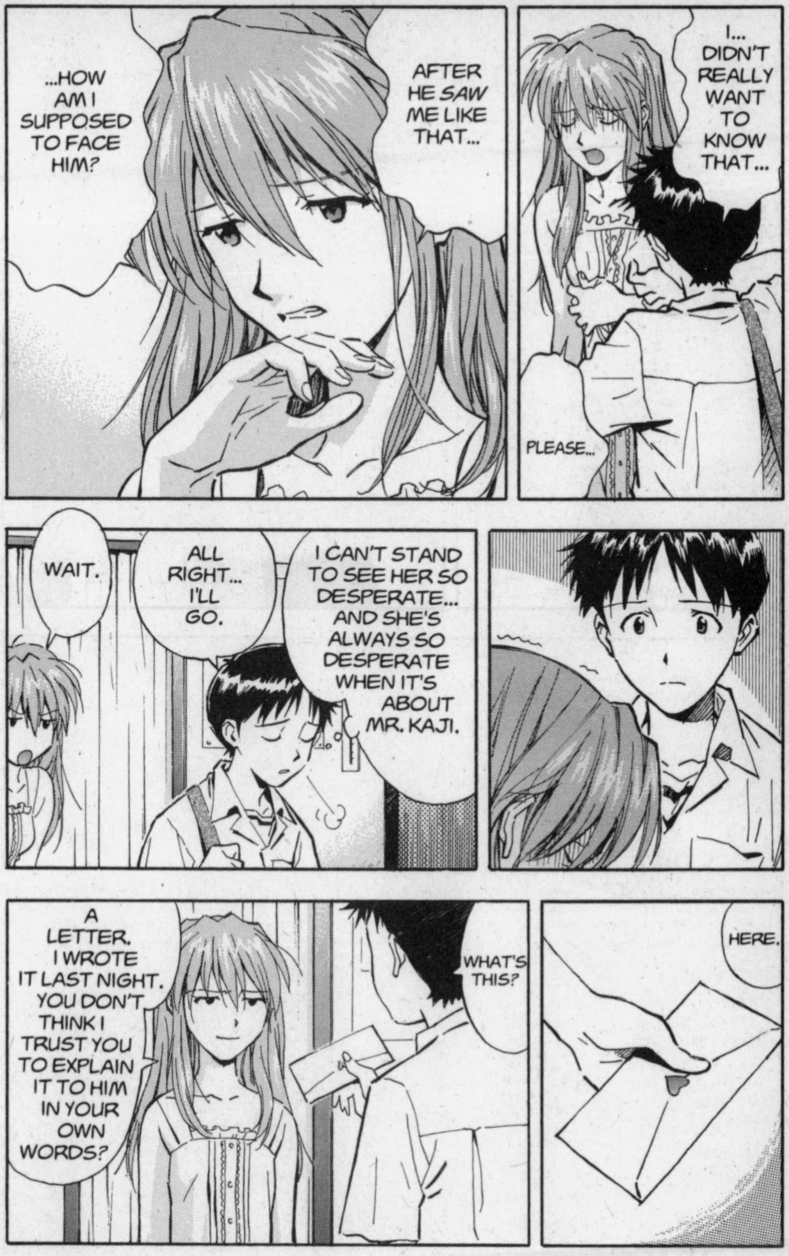
I... DIDN'T REALLY WANT TO KNOW THAT...
PLEASE...
AFTER HE *SAW* ME LIKE THAT...
...HOW AM I SUPPOSED TO FACE HIM?
I CAN'T STAND TO SEE HER SO DESPERATE... AND SHE'S ALWAYS SO DESPERATE WHEN IT'S ABOUT MR. KAJI.
ALL RIGHT... I'LL GO.
WAIT.
HERE.
WHAT'S THIS?
A LETTER. I WROTE IT LAST NIGHT. YOU DON'T THINK I TRUST YOU TO EXPLAIN IT TO HIM IN YOUR OWN WORDS?

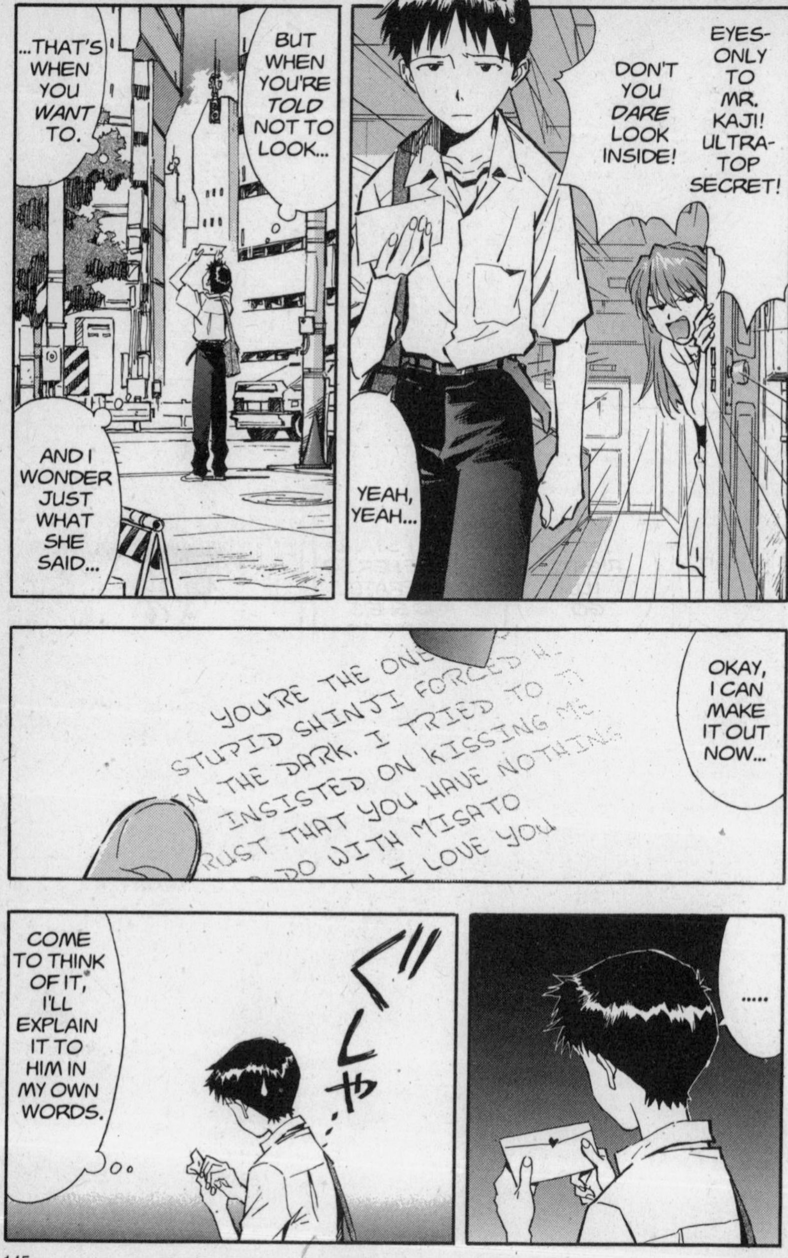
EYES-ONLY TO MR. KAJI! ULTRA-TOP SECRET!
DON'T YOU DARE LOOK INSIDE!
YEAH, YEAH...
BUT WHEN YOU'RE TOLD NOT TO LOOK...
...THAT'S WHEN YOU WANT TO.
AND I WONDER JUST WHAT SHE SAID...
OKAY, I CAN MAKE IT OUT NOW...
YOU'RE THE ONE
STUPID SHINJI FORCED
IN THE DARK. I TRIED TO
INSISTED ON KISSING ME
TRUST THAT YOU HAVE NOTHING
DO WITH MISATO
I LOVE YOU
.....
ぐしゃ
COME TO THINK OF IT, I'LL EXPLAIN IT TO HIM IN MY OWN WORDS.

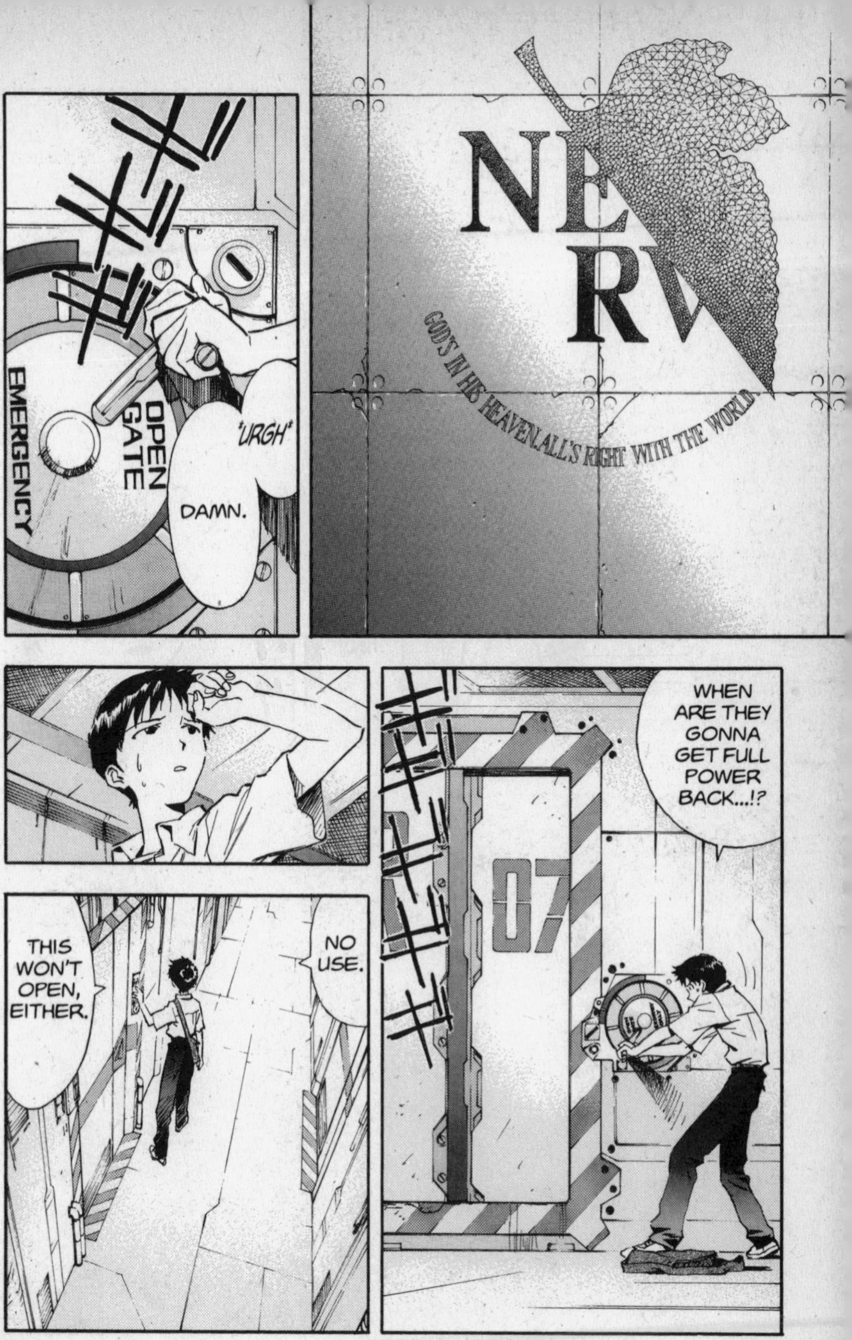
NERV
GOD'S IN HIS HEAVEN. ALL'S RIGHT WITH THE WORLD.
URGH
DAMN.
EMERGENCY
OPEN GATE
WHEN ARE THEY GONNA GET FULL POWER BACK...!?
07
NO USE.
THIS WON'T OPEN, EITHER.

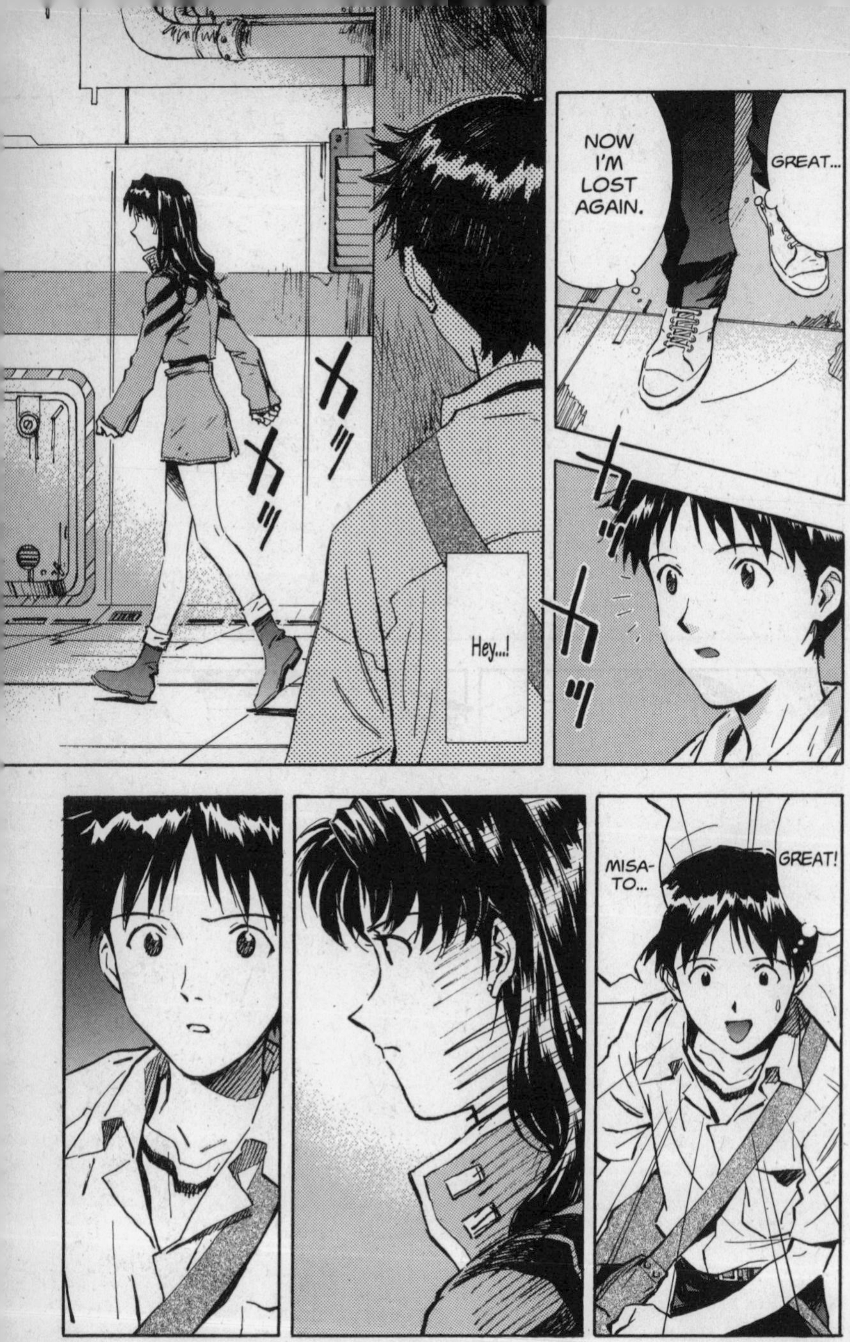
GREAT...
NOW I'M LOST AGAIN.
カッ
カッ
Hey...!
カッ
カッ
GREAT!
MISA-TO...

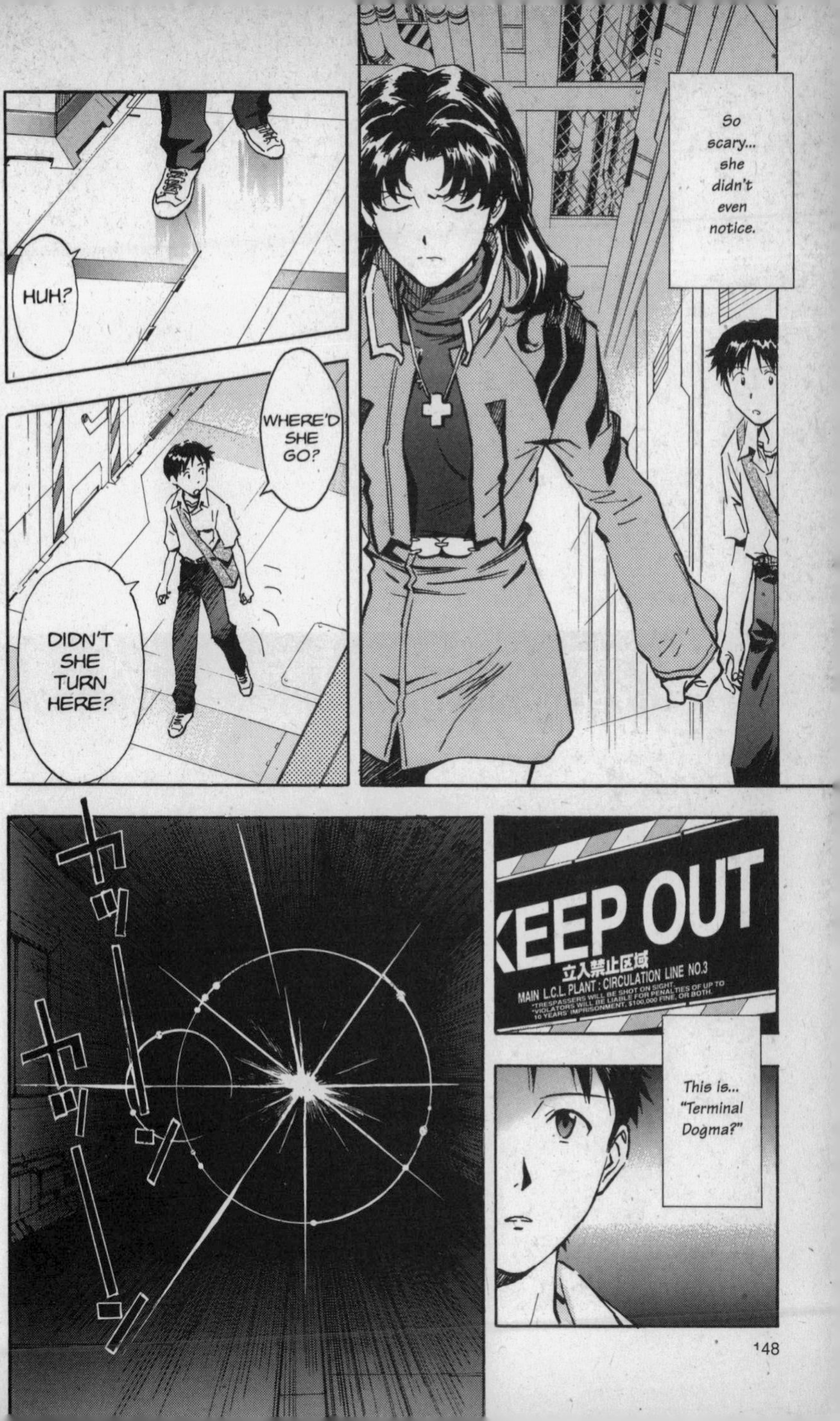
So scary... she didn't even notice.
HUH?
WHERE'D SHE GO?
DIDN'T SHE TURN HERE?
KEEP OUT
立入禁止区域
MAIN L.C.L. PLANT : CIRCULATION LINE NO.3
*TRESPASSERS WILL BE SHOT ON SIGHT.
*VIOLATORS WILL BE LIABLE FOR PENALTIES OF UP TO 10 YEARS' IMPRISONMENT, $100,000 FINE, OR BOTH.
This is... "Terminal Dogma?"

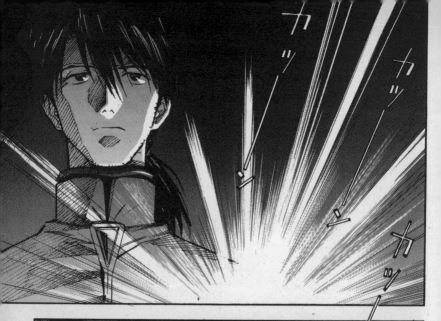

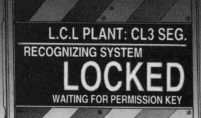

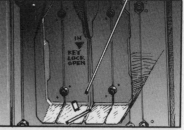

L.C.L PLANT: CL3 SEG.

RECOGNIZING SYSTEM

LOCKED

WAITING FOR PERMISSION KEY

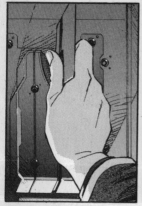

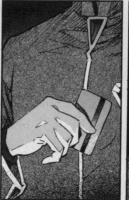

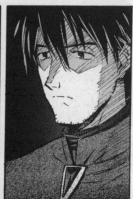

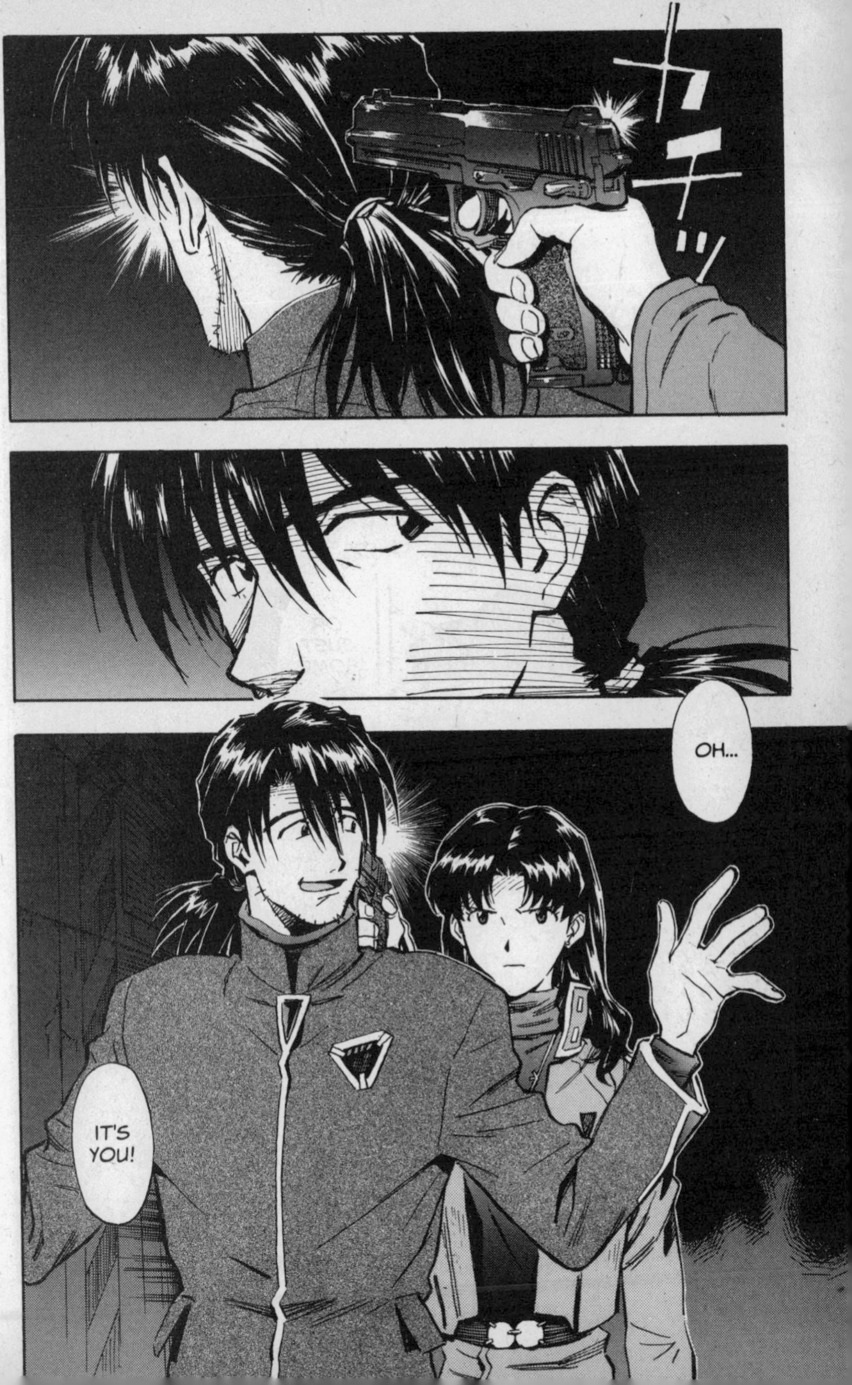
OH...
IT'S YOU!

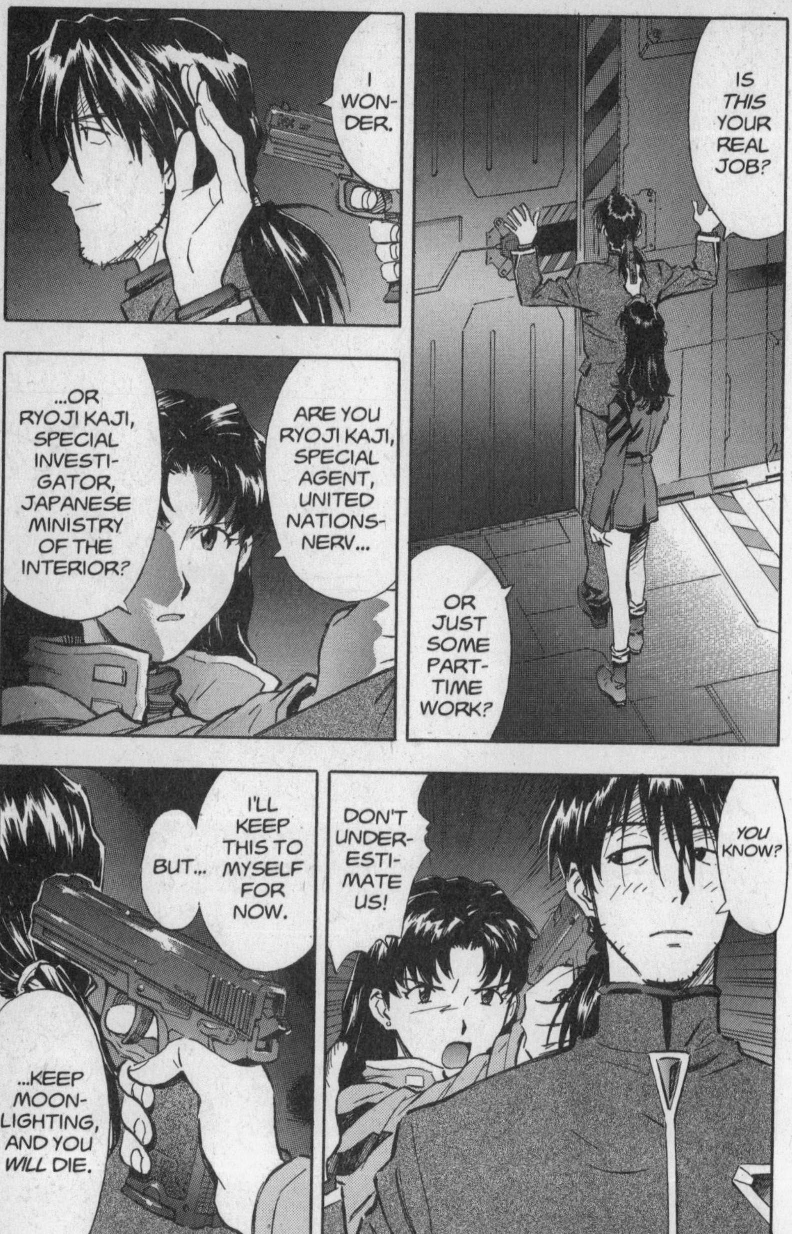
IS THIS YOUR REAL JOB?
OR JUST SOME PART-TIME WORK?
I WONDER.
ARE YOU RYOJI KAJI, SPECIAL AGENT, UNITED NATIONS-NERV...
...OR RYOJI KAJI, SPECIAL INVESTIGATOR, JAPANESE MINISTRY OF THE INTERIOR?
YOU KNOW?
DON'T UNDERESTIMATE US!
I'LL KEEP THIS TO MYSELF FOR NOW.
BUT...
...KEEP MOONLIGHTING, AND YOU WILL DIE.

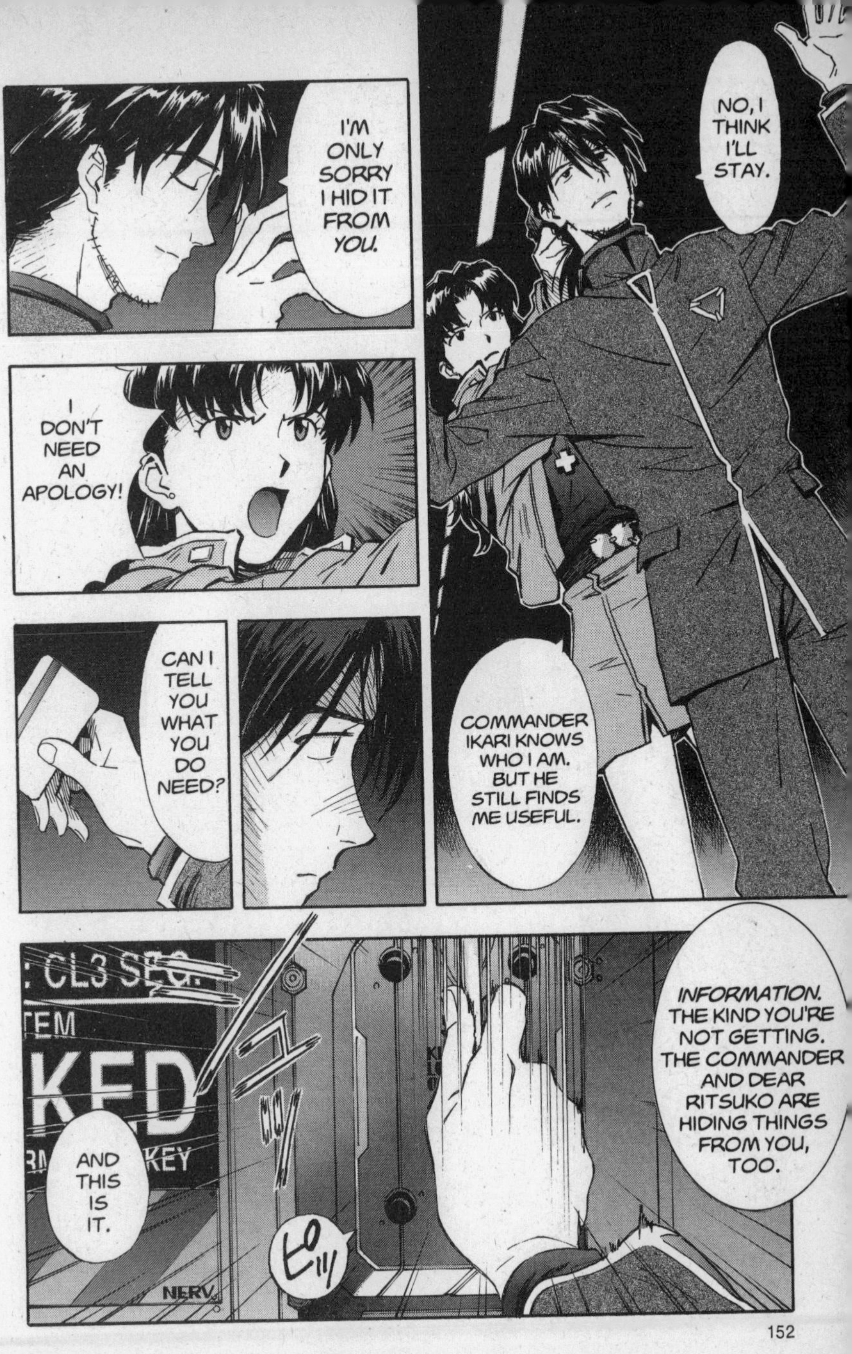
NO, I THINK I'LL STAY.
COMMANDER IKARI KNOWS WHO I AM. BUT HE STILL FINDS ME USEFUL.
I'M ONLY SORRY I HID IT FROM YOU.
I DON'T NEED AN APOLOGY!
CAN I TELL YOU WHAT YOU DO NEED?
INFORMATION. THE KIND YOU'RE NOT GETTING. THE COMMANDER AND DEAR RITSUKO ARE HIDING THINGS FROM YOU, TOO.
AND THIS IS IT.
ピッ
NERV

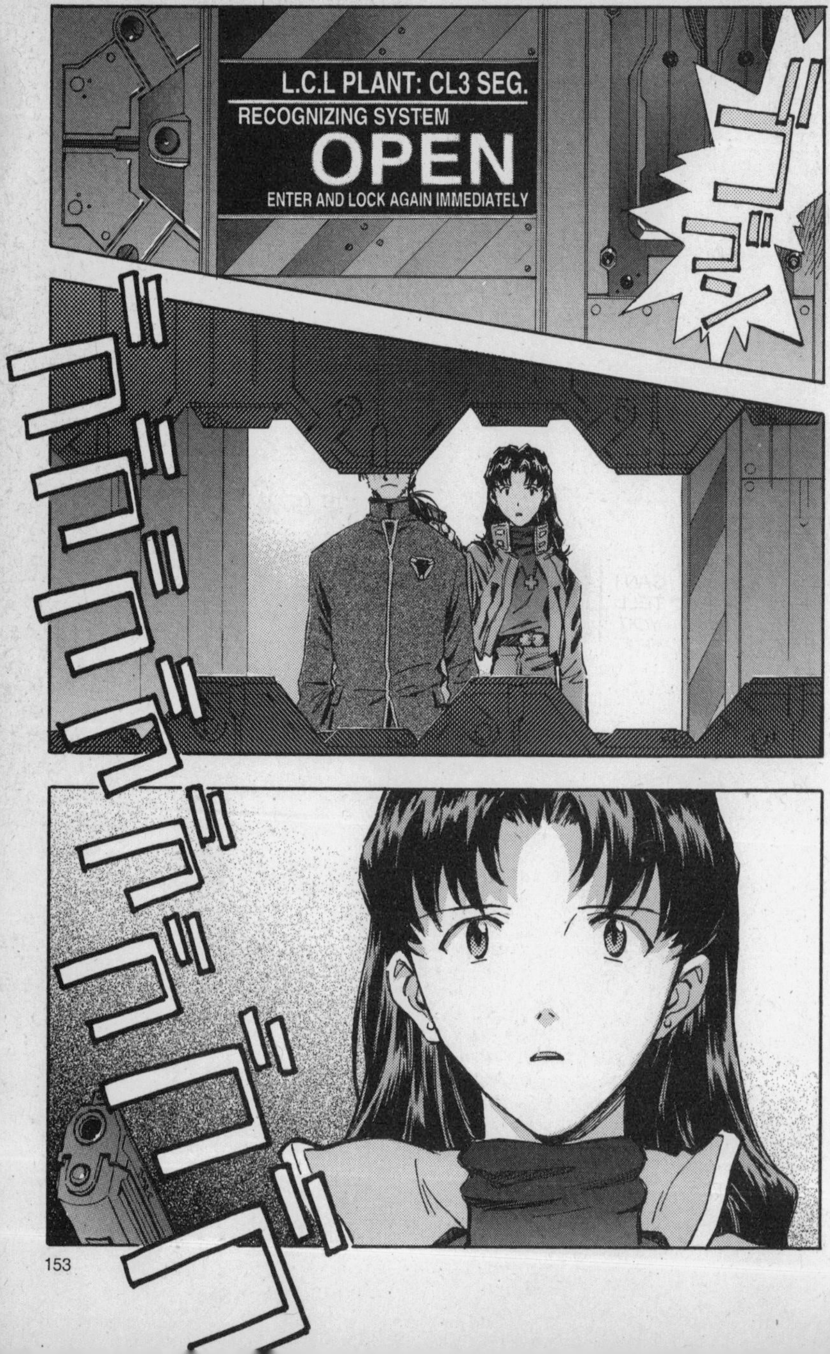
ゴゴン
L.C.L PLANT: CL3 SEG.
RECOGNIZING SYSTEM
OPEN
ENTER AND LOCK AGAIN IMMEDIATELY

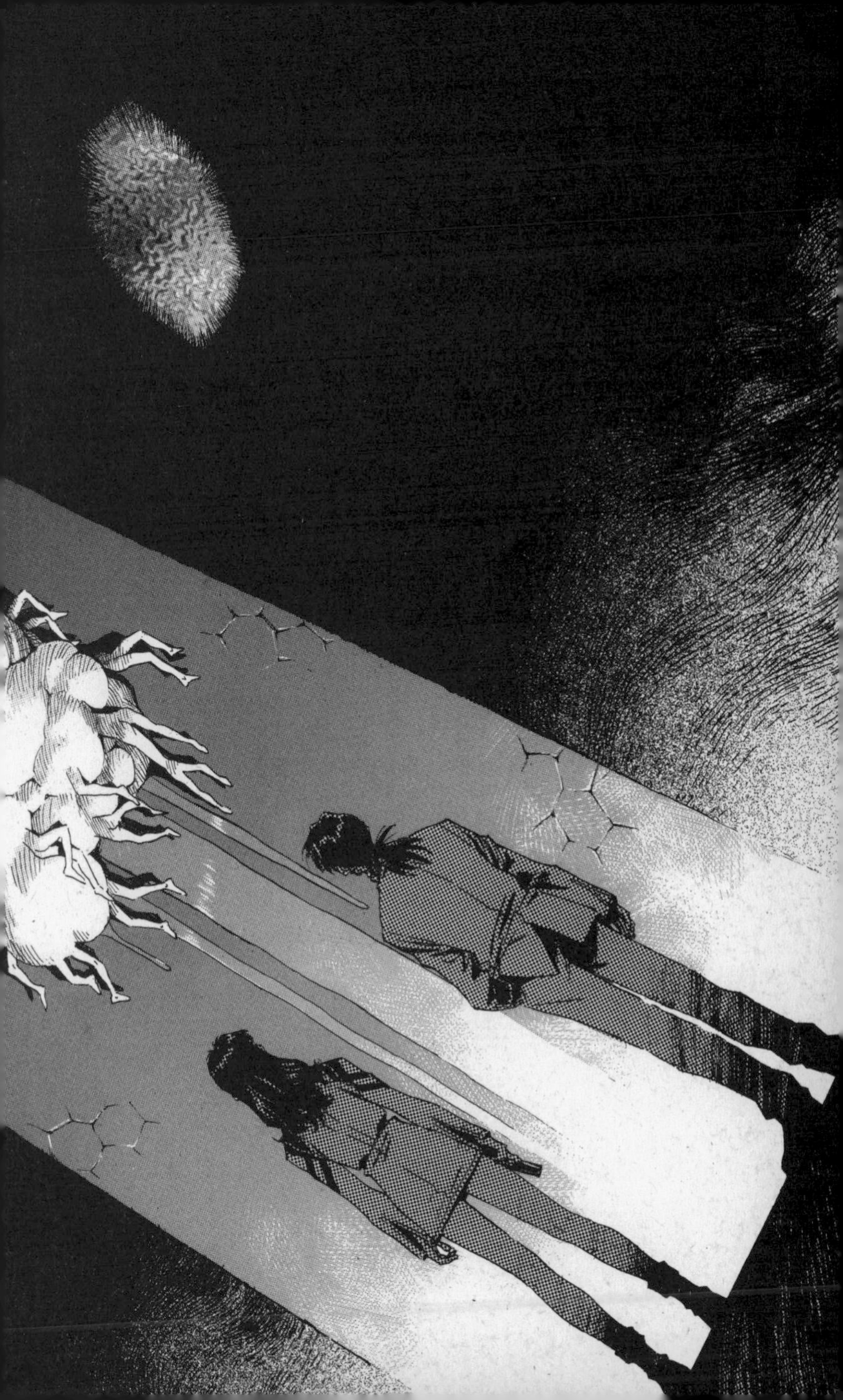

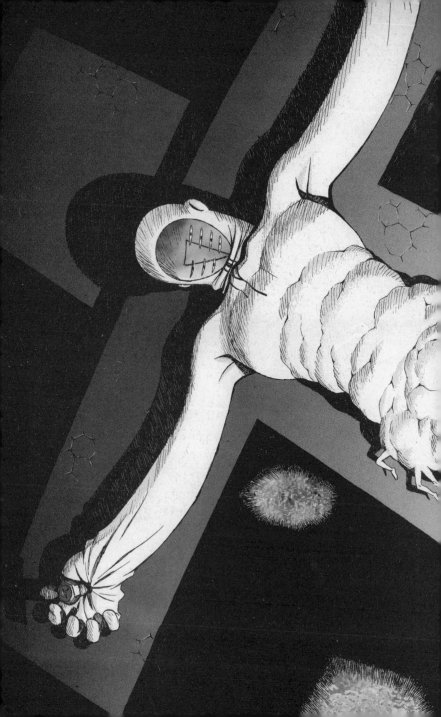

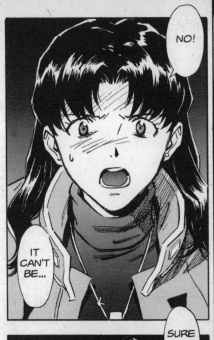

NO!

IT CAN'T BE...

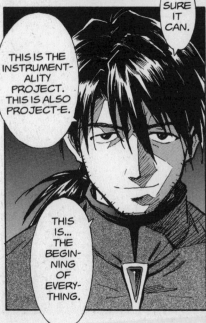

SURE IT CAN.

THIS IS THE INSTRUMENTALITY PROJECT. THIS IS ALSO PROJECT-E.

THIS IS... THE BEGINNING OF EVERYTHING.

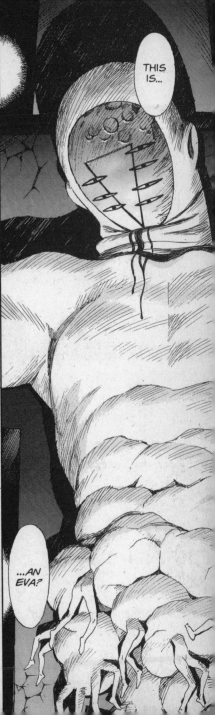

THIS IS...

...AN EVA?

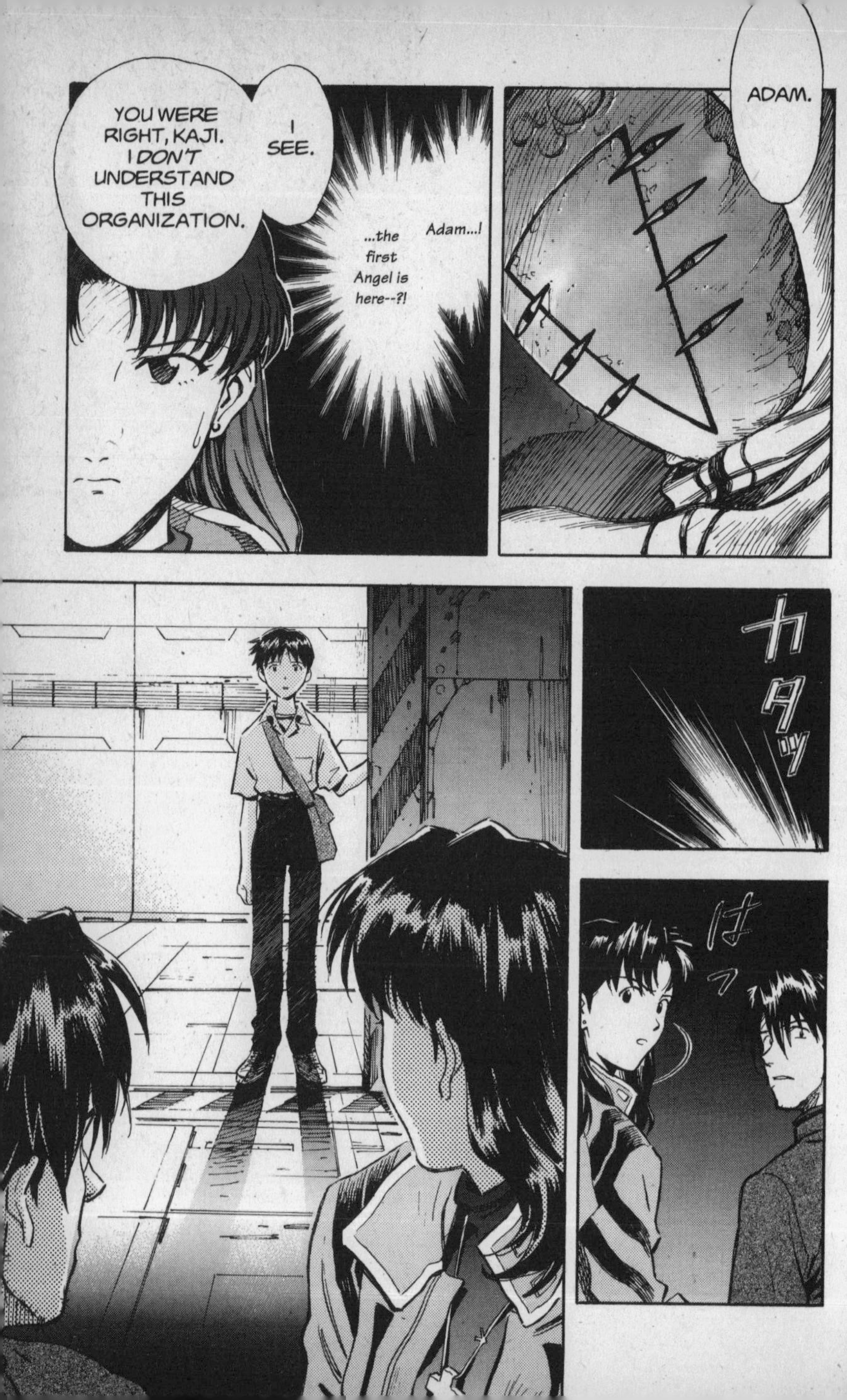
ADAM.
Adam...!
...the first Angel is here--?!
I SEE.
YOU WERE RIGHT, KAJI. I DON'T UNDERSTAND THIS ORGANIZATION.
カタッ
はっ

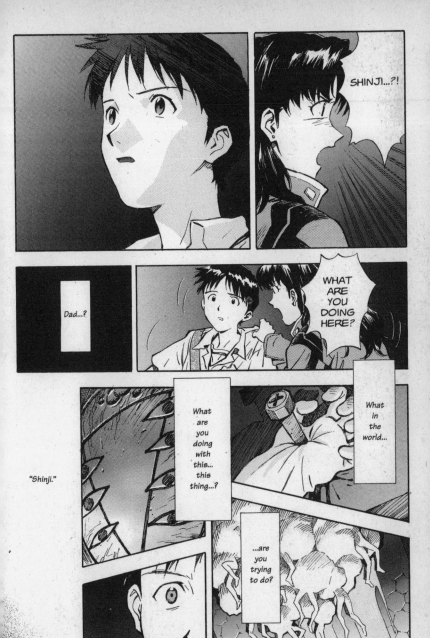

SHINJI...?!

Dad...?

WHAT ARE YOU DOING HERE?

What are you doing with this... this thing...?

What in the world...

"Shinji."

...are you trying to do?

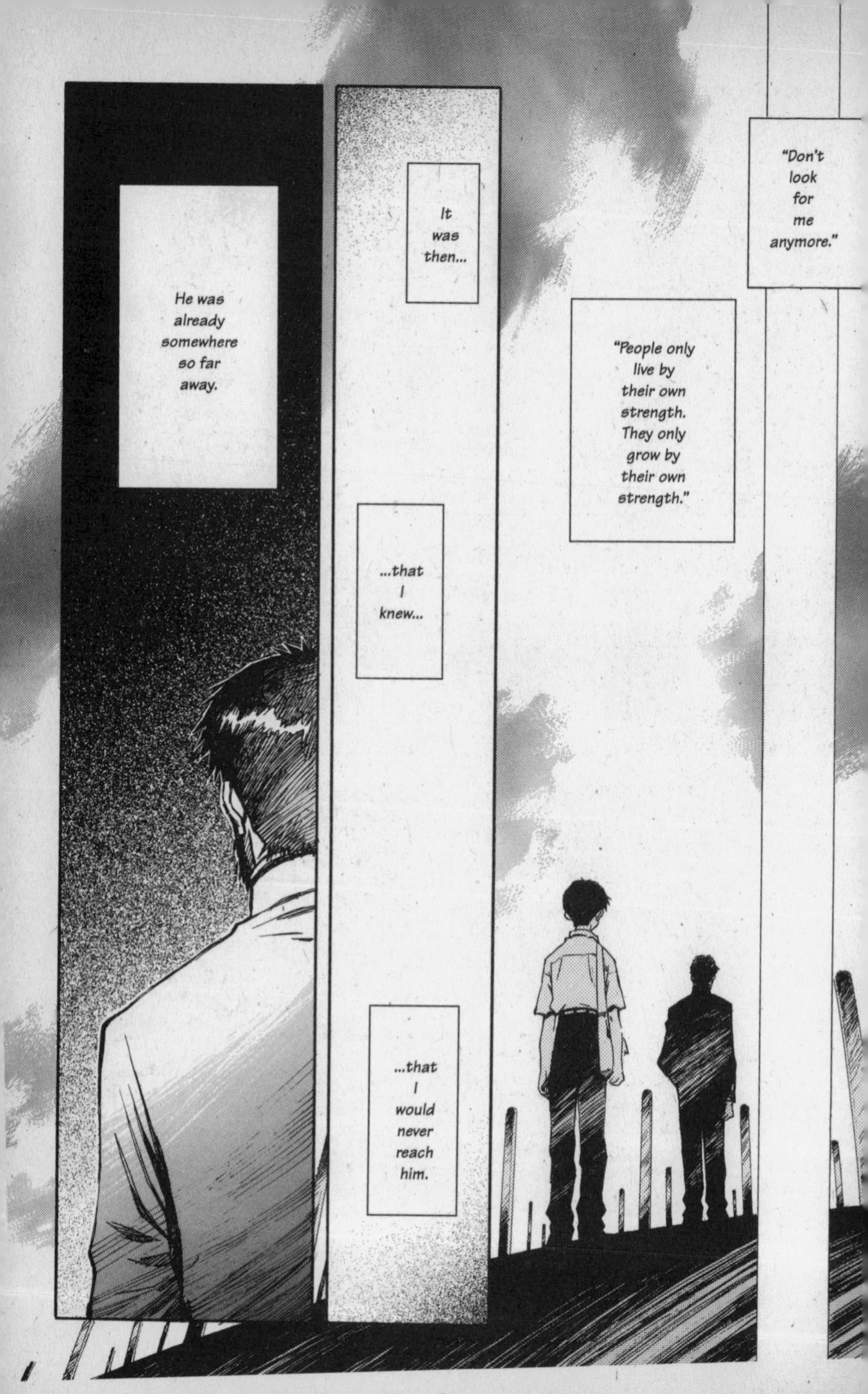
"Don't look for me anymore."
"People only live by their own strength. They only grow by their own strength."
It was then...
...that I knew...
...that I would never reach him.
He was already somewhere so far away.

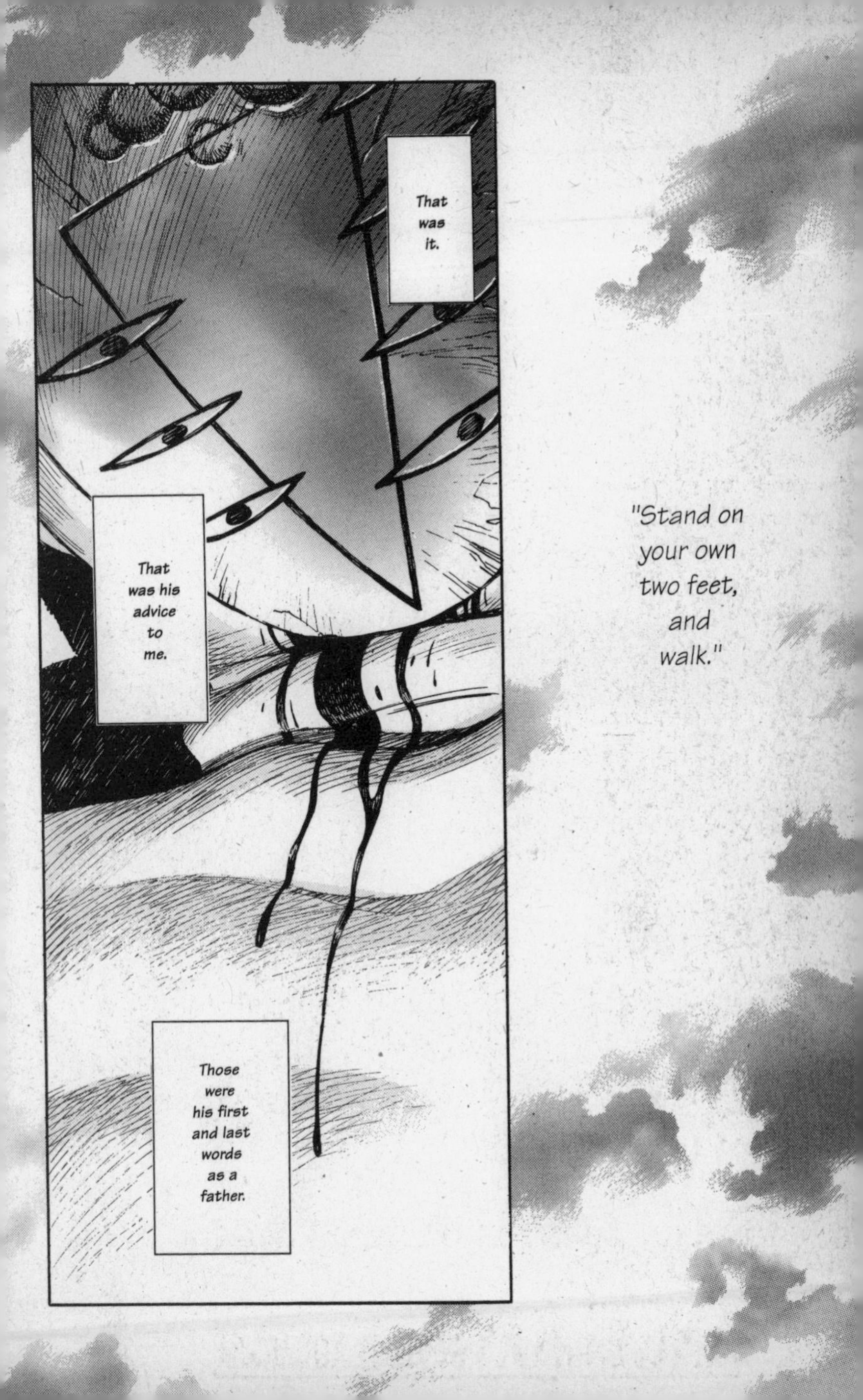
"Stand on your own two feet, and walk."
That was it.
That was his advice to me.
Those were his first and last words as a father.

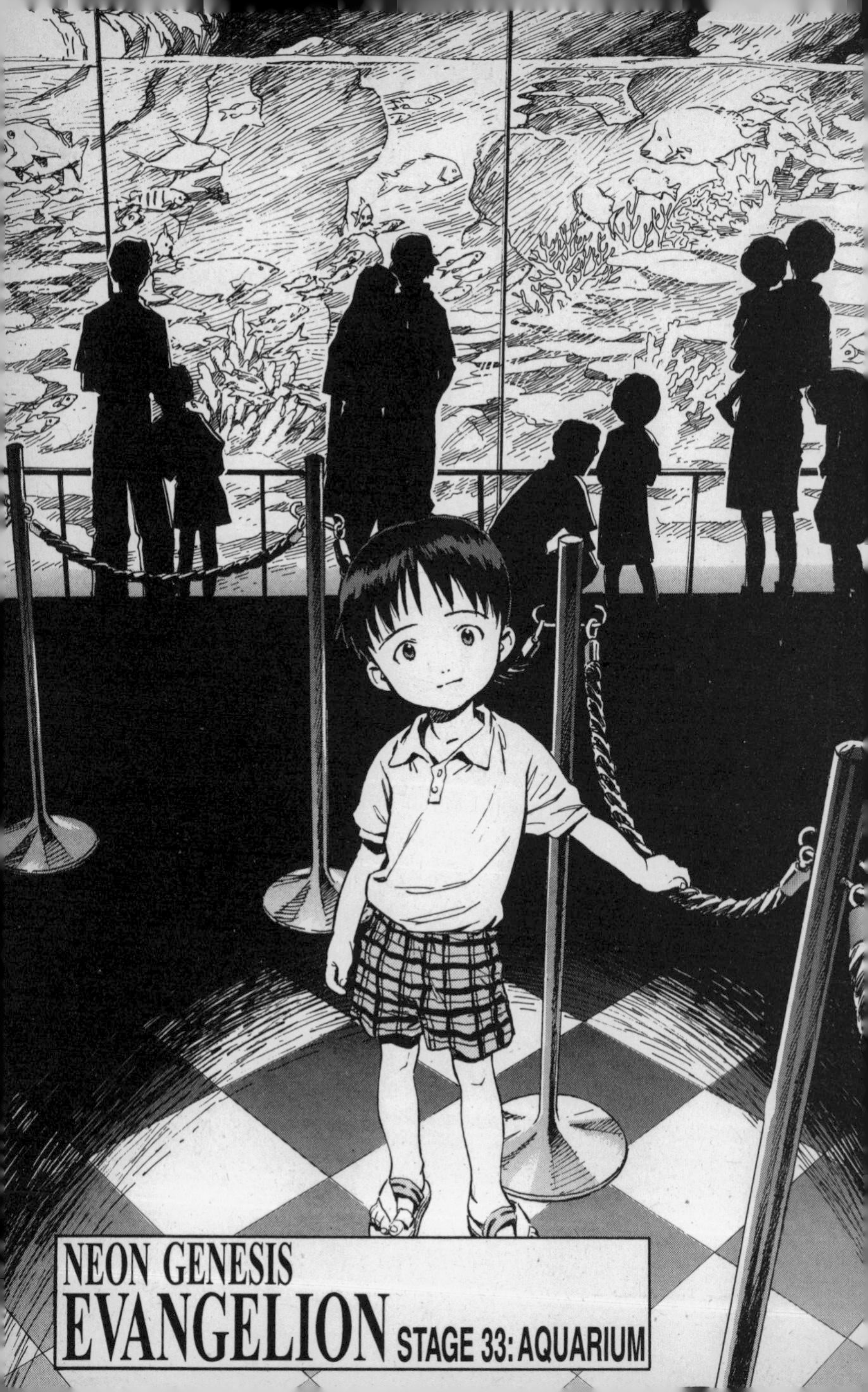
NEON GENESIS
EVANGELION
STAGE 33: AQUARIUM

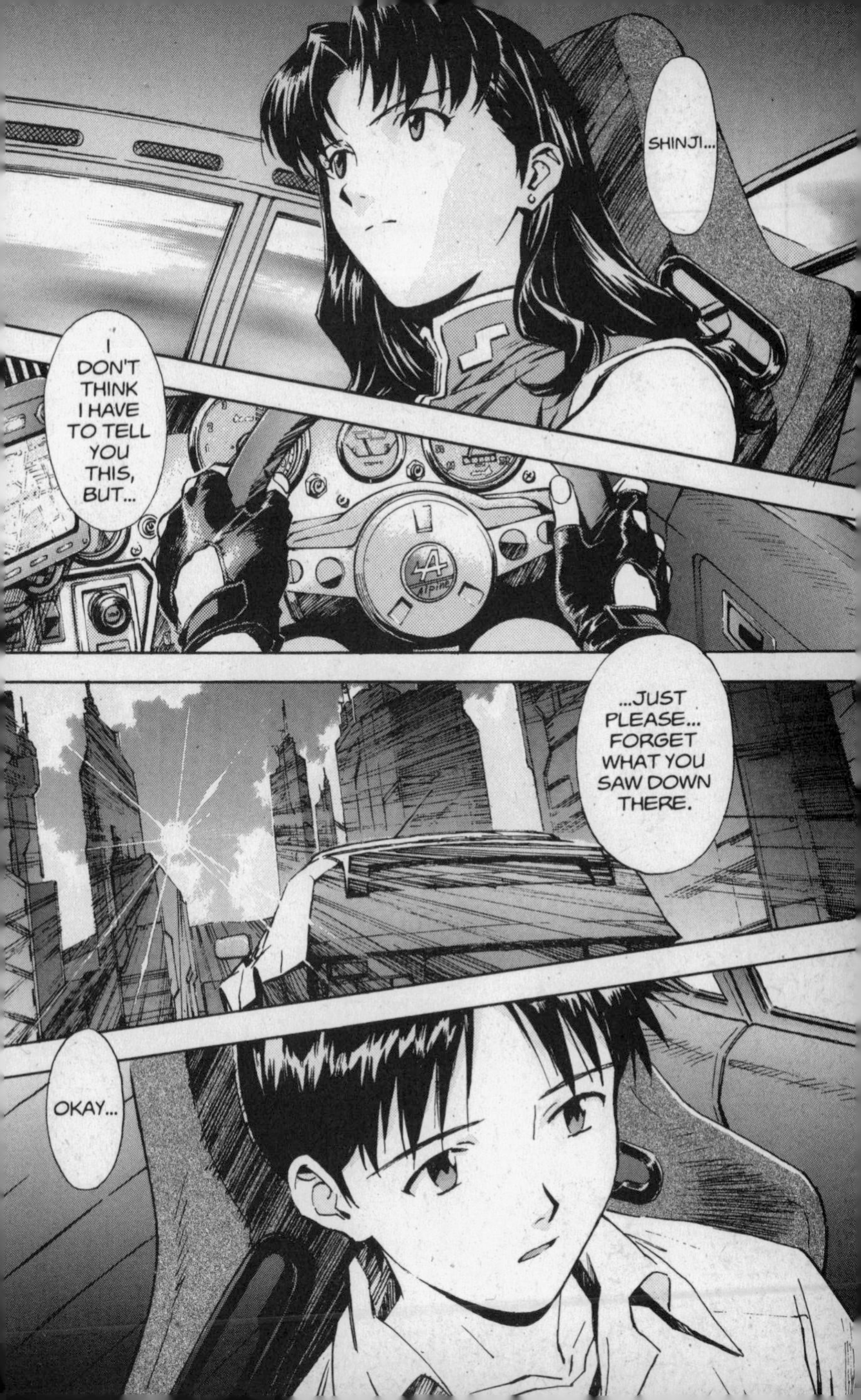
SHINJI...
I DON'T THINK I HAVE TO TELL YOU THIS, BUT...
...JUST PLEASE... FORGET WHAT YOU SAW DOWN THERE.
OKAY...

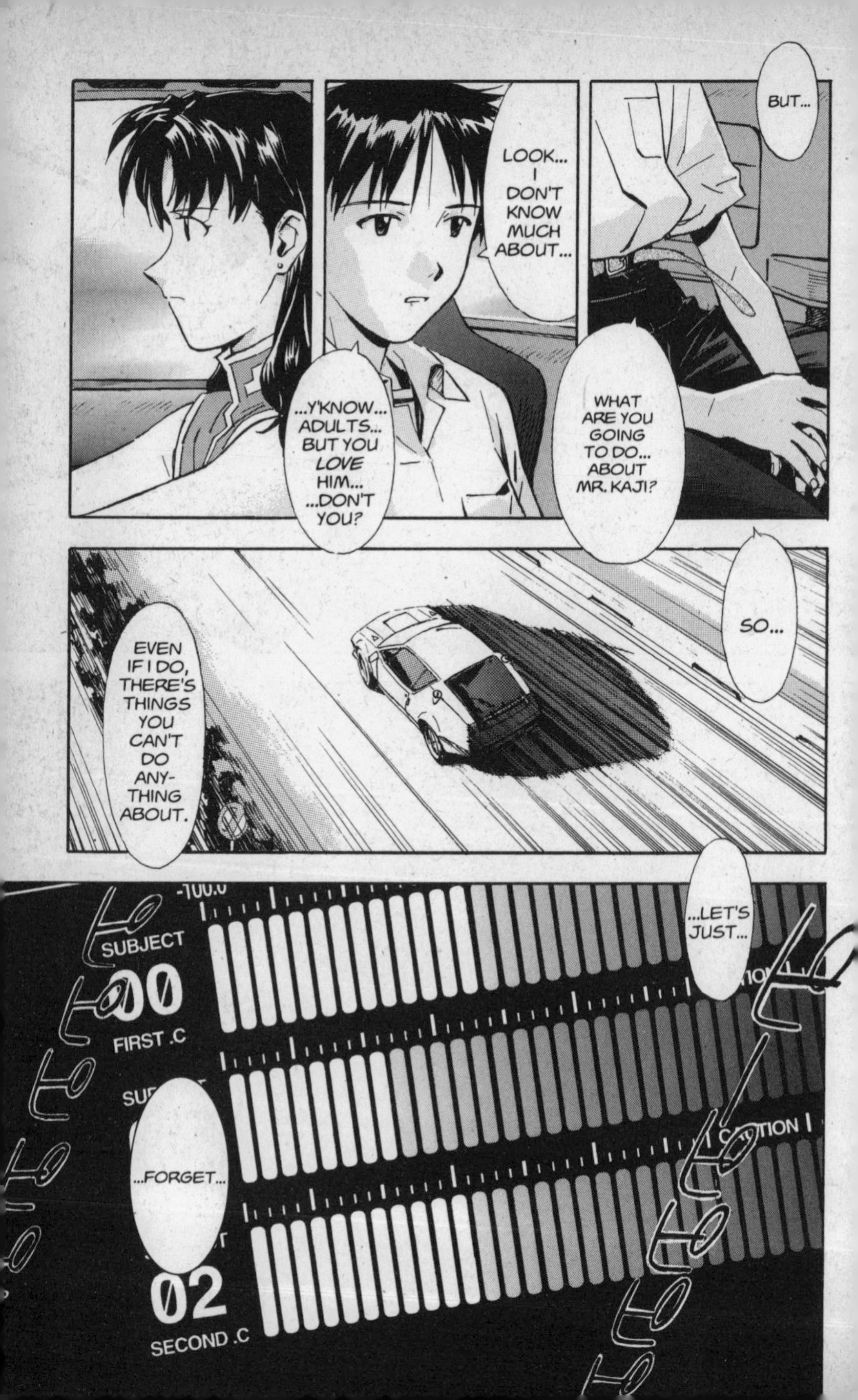
BUT...
LOOK... I DON'T KNOW MUCH ABOUT...
...Y'KNOW... ADULTS... BUT YOU *LOVE* HIM... ...DON'T YOU?
WHAT ARE YOU GOING TO DO... ABOUT MR. KAJI?
SO...
EVEN IF I DO, THERE'S THINGS YOU CAN'T DO ANY-THING ABOUT.
...LET'S JUST...
-100.0
SUBJECT
00
FIRST .C
CAUTION
...FORGET...
02
SECOND .C

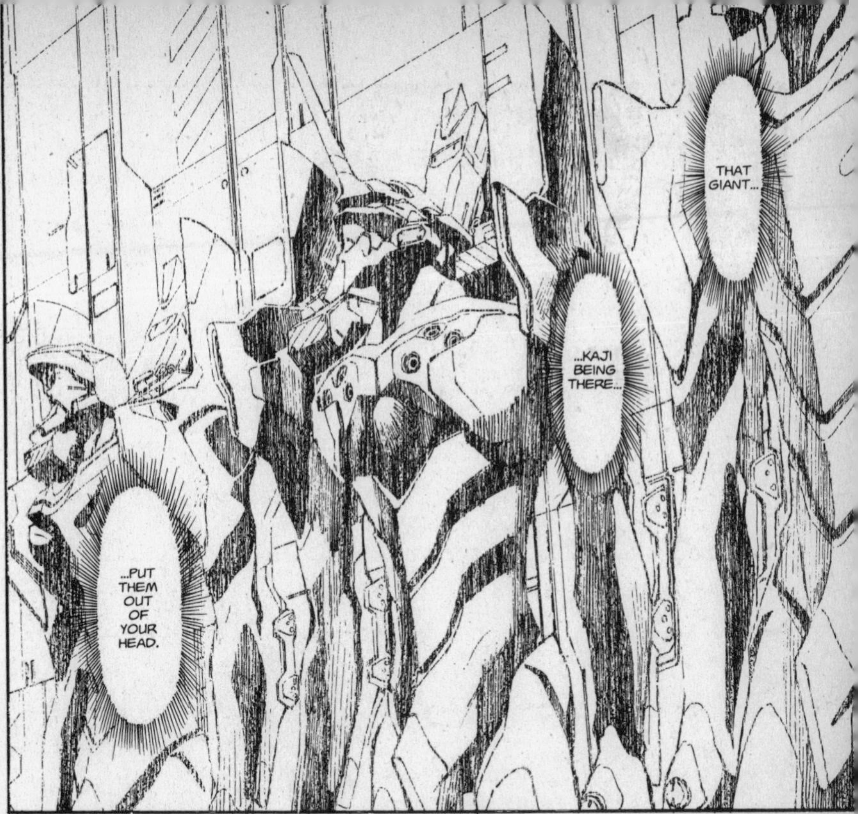
THAT GIANT...
...KAJI BEING THERE...
...PUT THEM OUT OF YOUR HEAD.

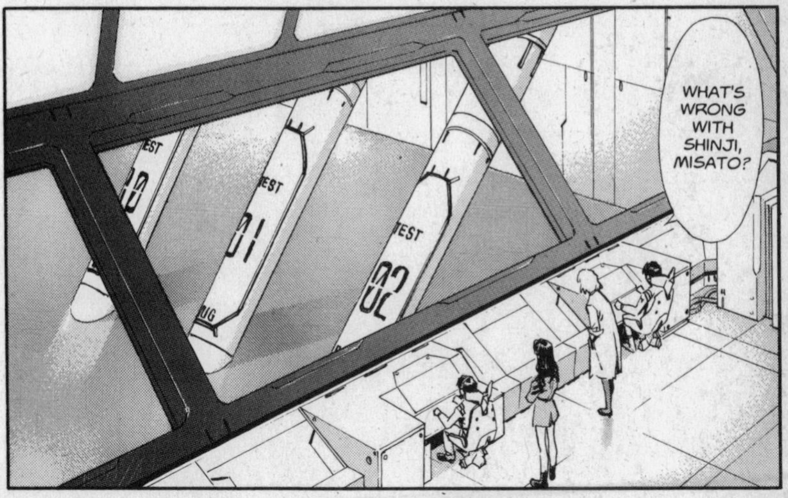
WHAT'S WRONG WITH SHINJI, MISATO?

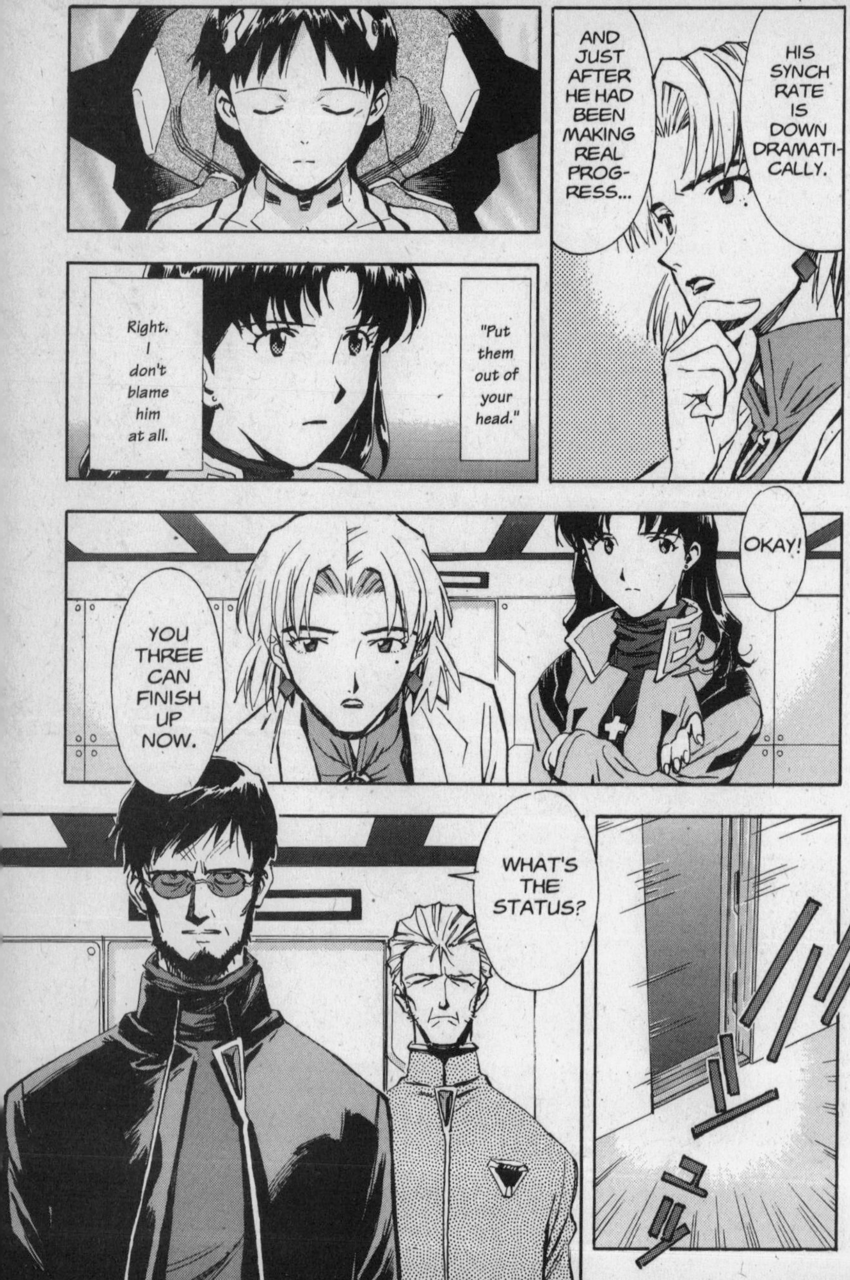
HIS SYNCH RATE IS DOWN DRAMATI-CALLY.
AND JUST AFTER HE HAD BEEN MAKING REAL PROG-RESS...
"Put them out of your head."
Right. I don't blame him at all.
OKAY!
YOU THREE CAN FINISH UP NOW.
WHAT'S THE STATUS?

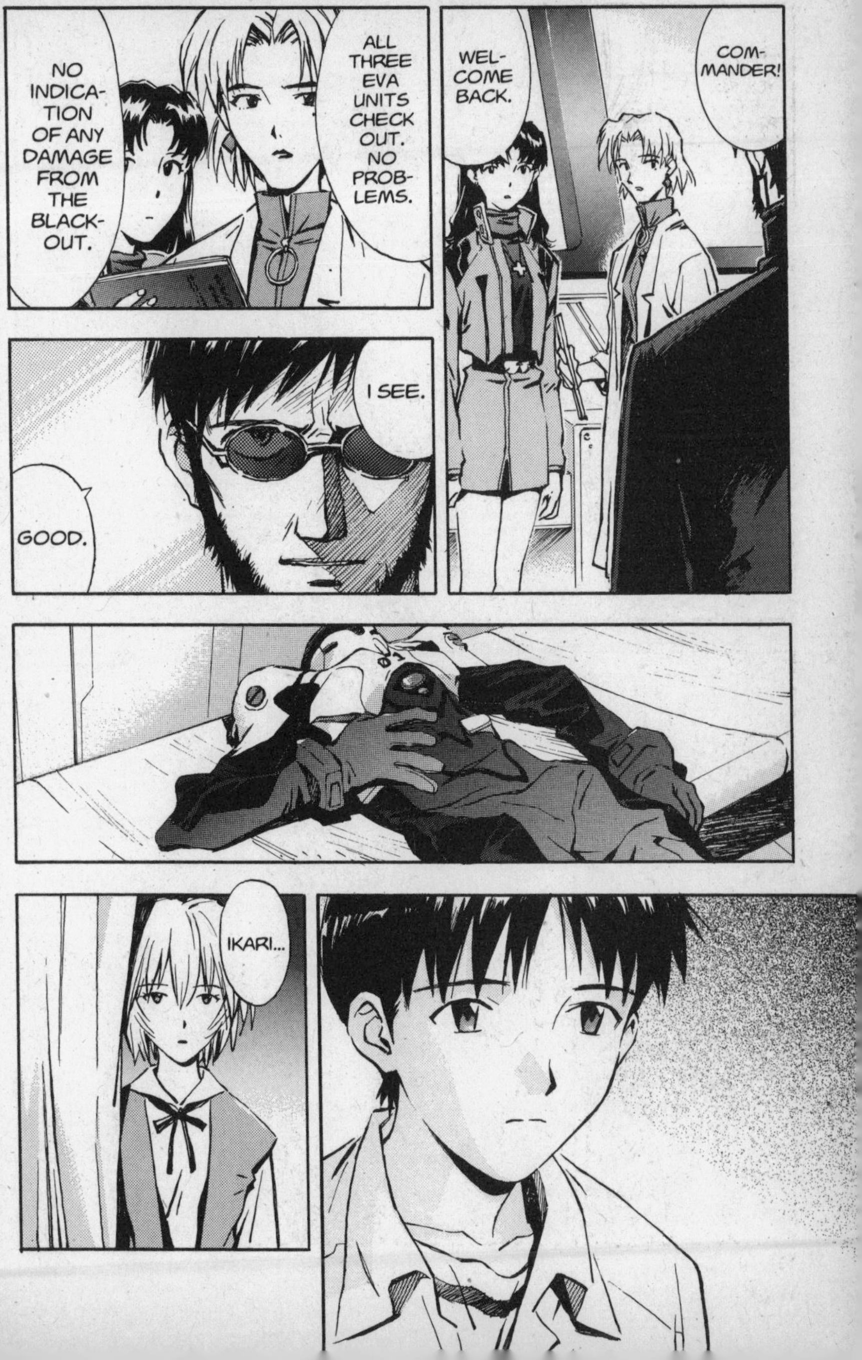
COMMANDER!
WELCOME BACK.
ALL THREE EVA UNITS CHECK OUT. NO PROBLEMS.
NO INDICATION OF ANY DAMAGE FROM THE BLACKOUT.
I SEE.
GOOD.
IKARI...

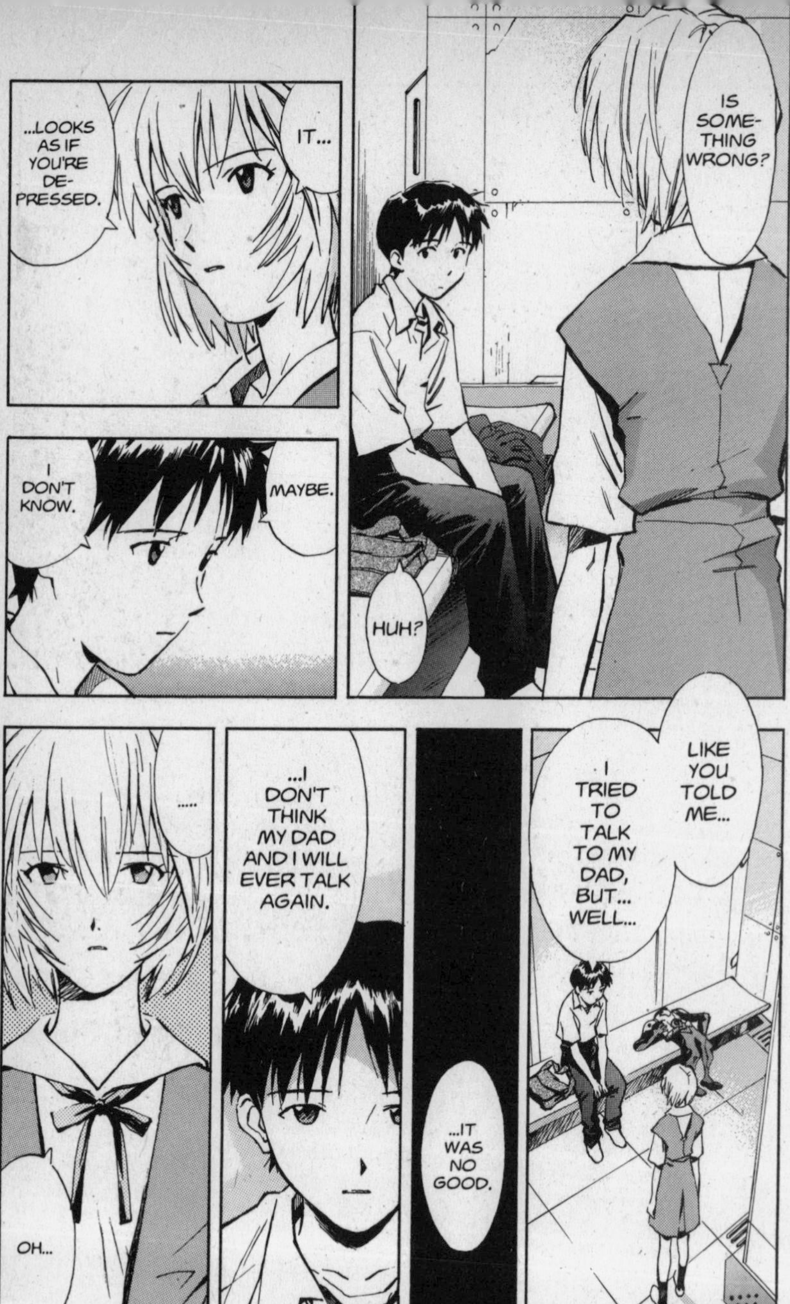
IS SOMETHING WRONG?
HUH?
IT...
...LOOKS AS IF YOU'RE DE-PRESSED.
MAYBE.
I DON'T KNOW.
LIKE YOU TOLD ME...
I TRIED TO TALK TO MY DAD, BUT... WELL...
...IT WAS NO GOOD.
...I DON'T THINK MY DAD AND I WILL EVER TALK AGAIN.
.....
OH...

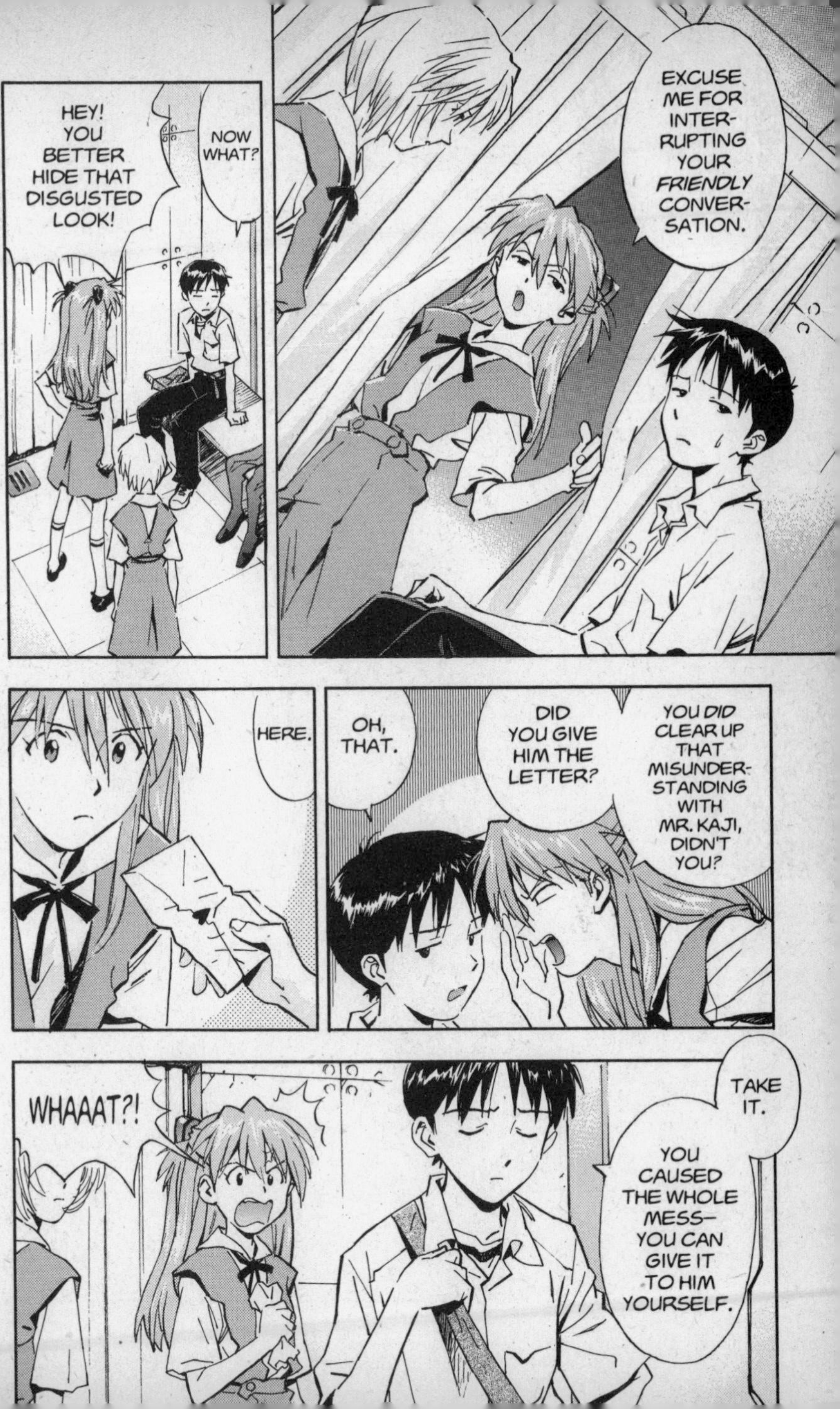
EXCUSE ME FOR INTER-RUPTING YOUR *FRIENDLY* CONVER-SATION.
NOW WHAT?
HEY! YOU BETTER HIDE THAT DISGUSTED LOOK!
YOU *DID* CLEAR UP THAT MISUNDER-STANDING WITH MR. KAJI, DIDN'T YOU?
DID YOU GIVE HIM THE LETTER?
OH, THAT.
HERE.
TAKE IT.
YOU CAUSED THE WHOLE MESS— YOU CAN GIVE IT TO HIM YOURSELF.
WHAAAT?!

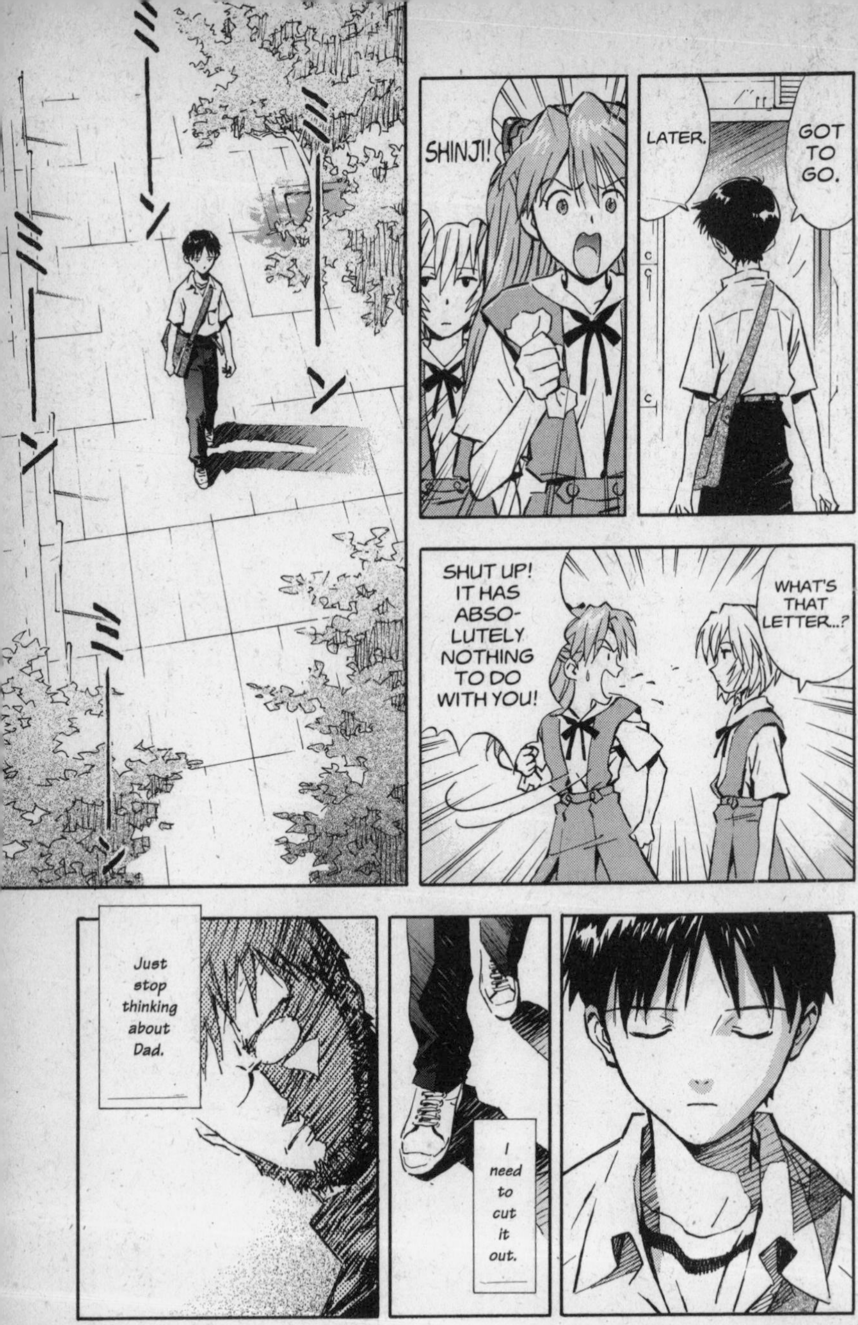
GOT TO GO.
LATER.
SHINJI!
WHAT'S THAT LETTER...?
SHUT UP! IT HAS ABSO-LUTELY NOTHING TO DO WITH YOU!
I need to cut it out.
Just stop thinking about Dad.

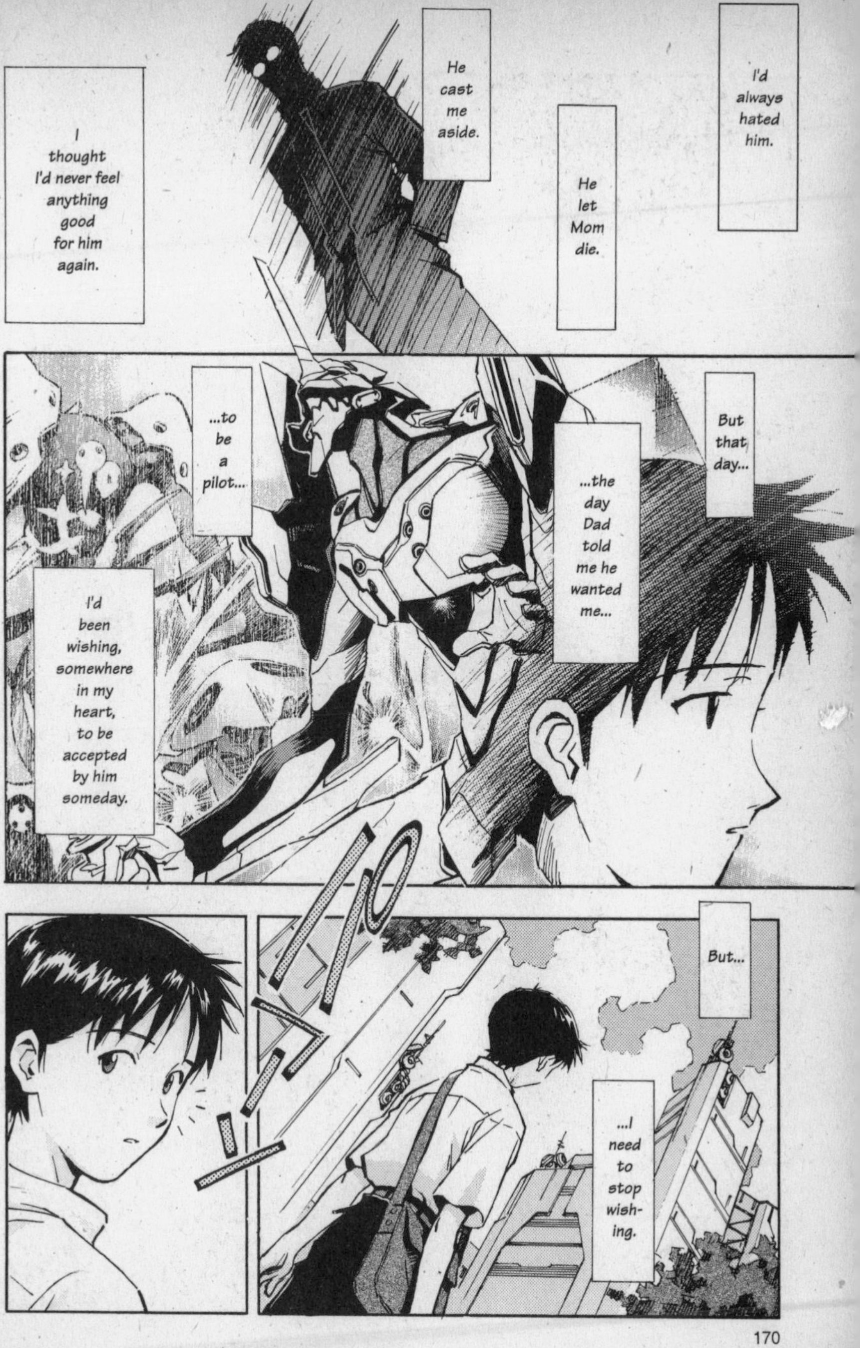
I'd always hated him.
He let Mom die.
He cast me aside.
I thought I'd never feel anything good for him again.
But that day...
...the day Dad told me he wanted me...
...to be a pilot...
I'd been wishing, somewhere in my heart, to be accepted by him someday.
But...
...I need to stop wishing.

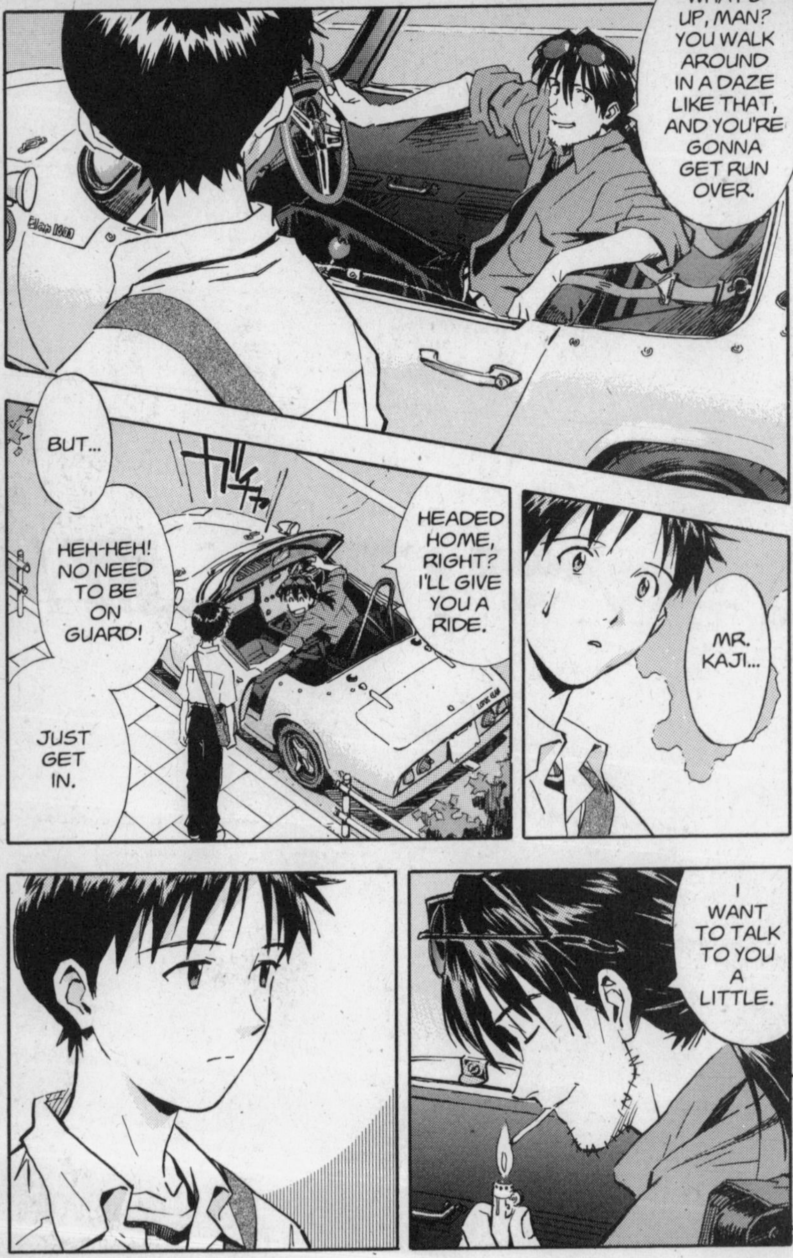
WHAT'S UP, MAN? YOU WALK AROUND IN A DAZE LIKE THAT, AND YOU'RE GONNA GET RUN OVER.
MR. KAJI...
HEADED HOME, RIGHT? I'LL GIVE YOU A RIDE.
BUT...
HEH-HEH! NO NEED TO BE ON GUARD!
JUST GET IN.
I WANT TO TALK TO YOU A LITTLE.

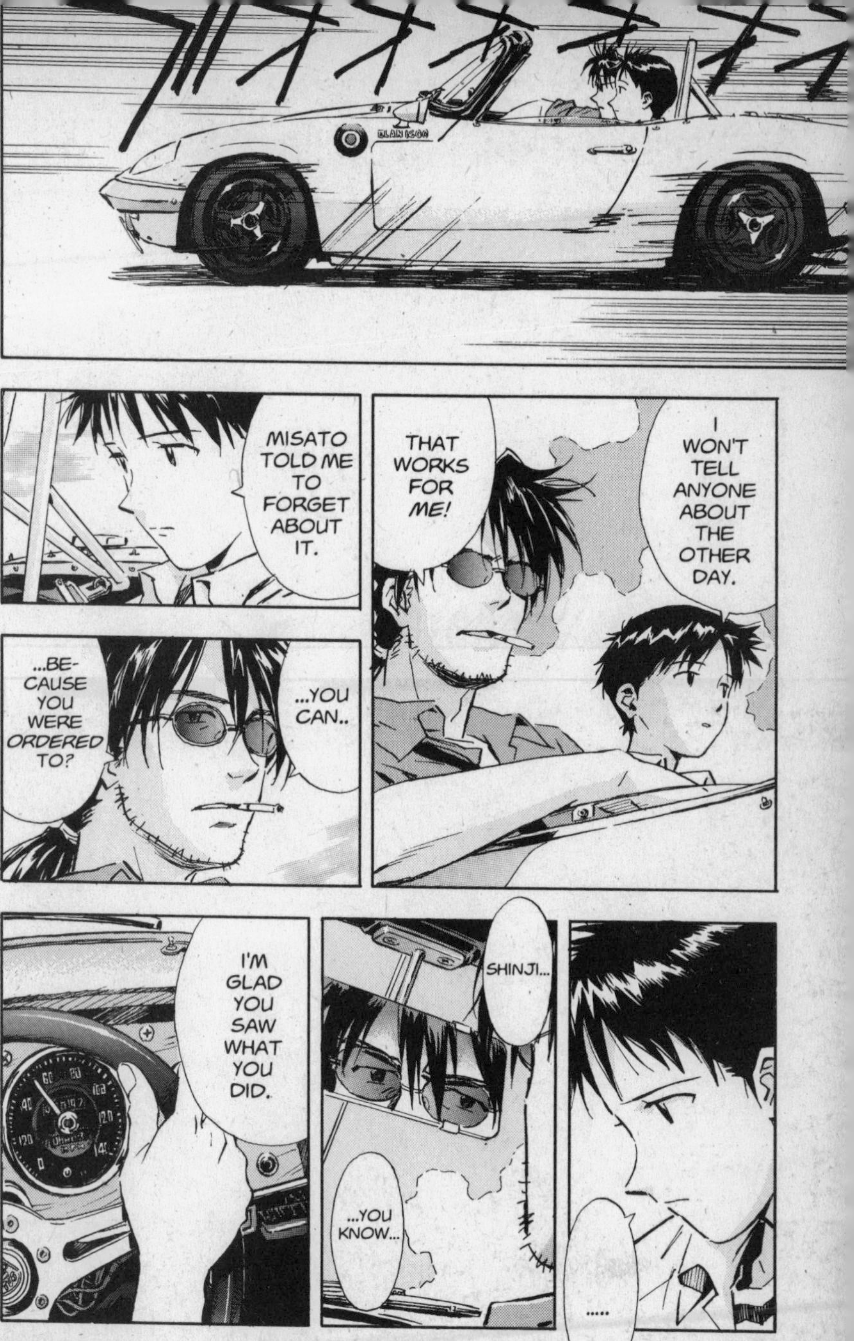
I WON'T TELL ANYONE ABOUT THE OTHER DAY.
THAT WORKS FOR ME!
MISATO TOLD ME TO FORGET ABOUT IT.
...YOU CAN..
...BE-CAUSE YOU WERE ORDERED TO?
.....
SHINJI...
...YOU KNOW...
I'M GLAD YOU SAW WHAT YOU DID.

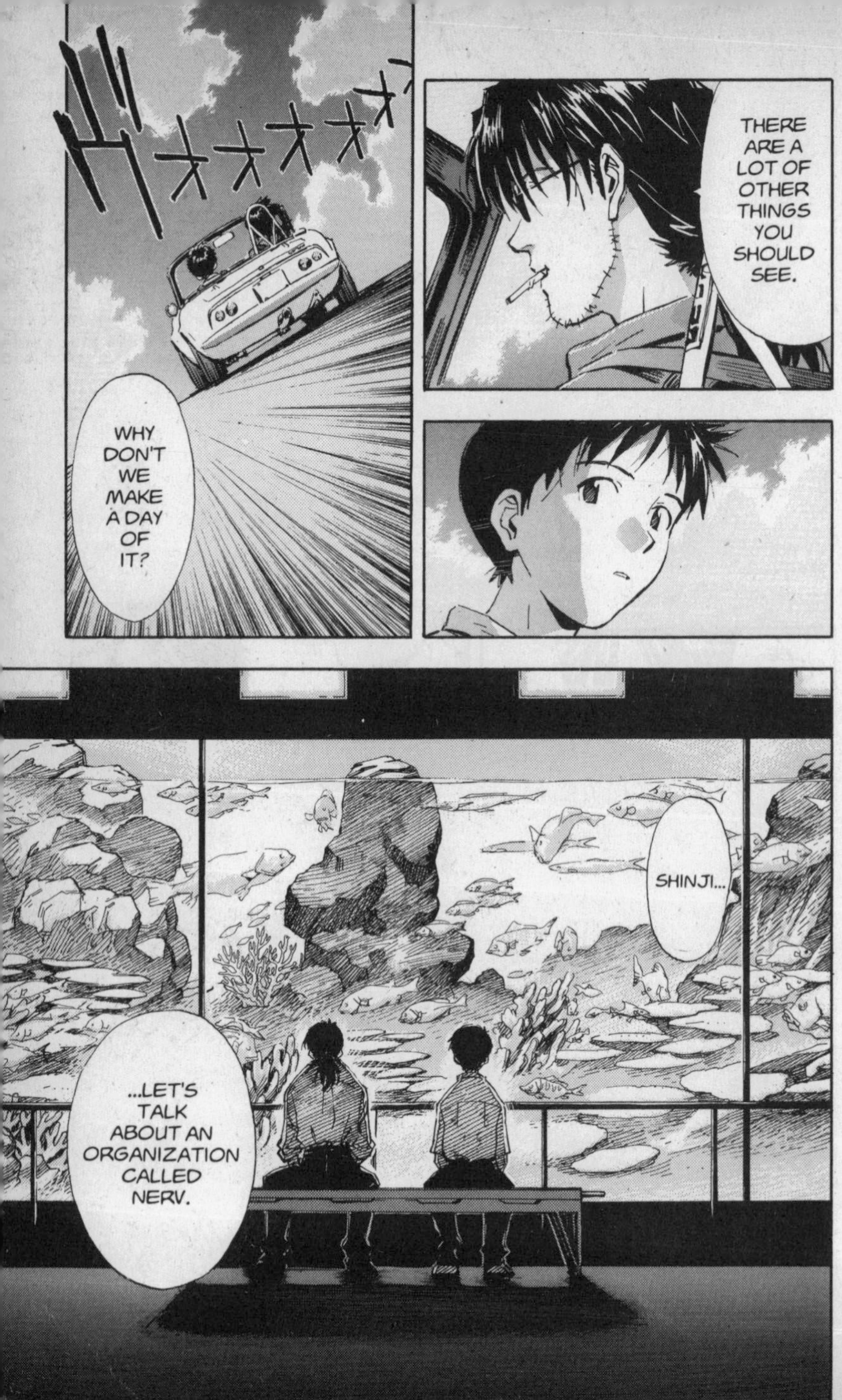
THERE ARE A LOT OF OTHER THINGS YOU SHOULD SEE.
WHY DON'T WE MAKE A DAY OF IT?
SHINJI...
...LET'S TALK ABOUT AN ORGANIZATION CALLED NERV.

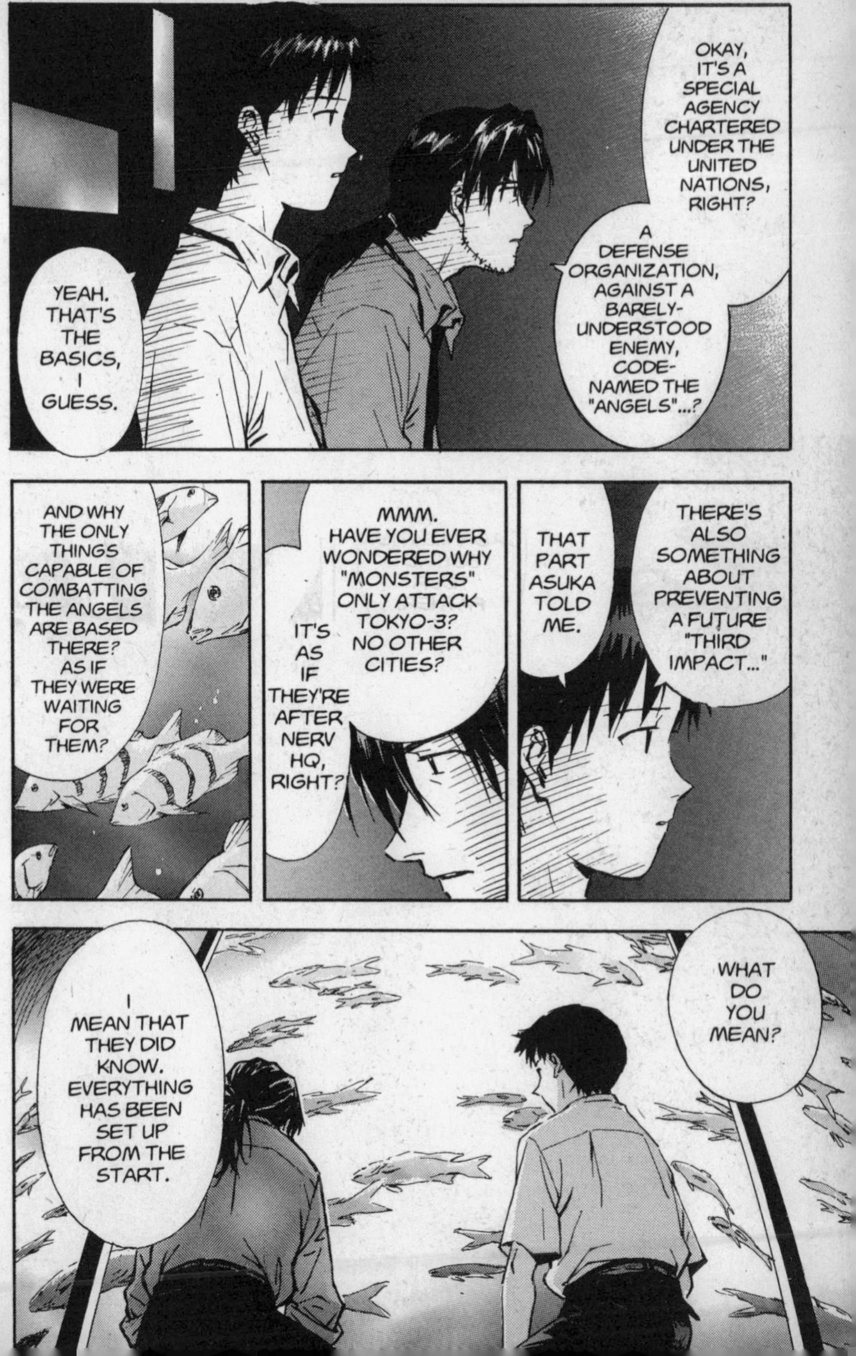
OKAY, IT'S A SPECIAL AGENCY CHARTERED UNDER THE UNITED NATIONS, RIGHT?
A DEFENSE ORGANIZATION, AGAINST A BARELY-UNDERSTOOD ENEMY, CODE-NAMED THE "ANGELS"...?
YEAH. THAT'S THE BASICS, I GUESS.
THERE'S ALSO SOMETHING ABOUT PREVENTING A FUTURE "THIRD IMPACT..."
THAT PART ASUKA TOLD ME.
MMM. HAVE YOU EVER WONDERED WHY "MONSTERS" ONLY ATTACK TOKYO-3? NO OTHER CITIES?
IT'S AS IF THEY'RE AFTER NERV HQ, RIGHT?
AND WHY THE ONLY THINGS CAPABLE OF COMBATTING THE ANGELS ARE BASED THERE? AS IF THEY WERE WAITING FOR THEM?
WHAT DO YOU MEAN?
I MEAN THAT THEY DID KNOW. EVERYTHING HAS BEEN SET UP FROM THE START.

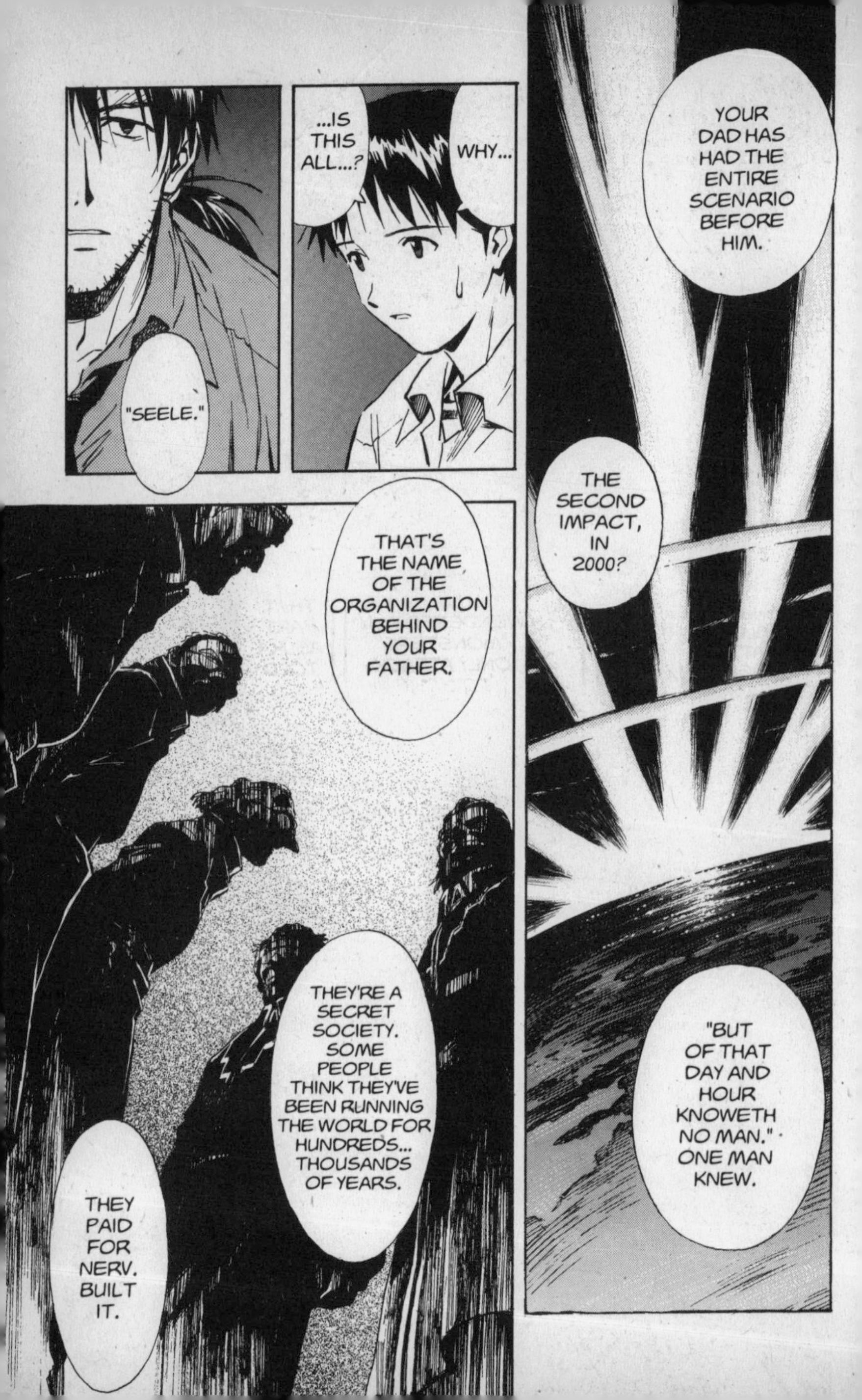
YOUR DAD HAS HAD THE ENTIRE SCENARIO BEFORE HIM.
THE SECOND IMPACT, IN 2000?
"BUT OF THAT DAY AND HOUR KNOWETH NO MAN." ONE MAN KNEW.
WHY...
...IS THIS ALL...?
"SEELE."
THAT'S THE NAME OF THE ORGANIZATION BEHIND YOUR FATHER.
THEY'RE A SECRET SOCIETY. SOME PEOPLE THINK THEY'VE BEEN RUNNING THE WORLD FOR HUNDREDS... THOUSANDS OF YEARS.
THEY PAID FOR NERV. BUILT IT.

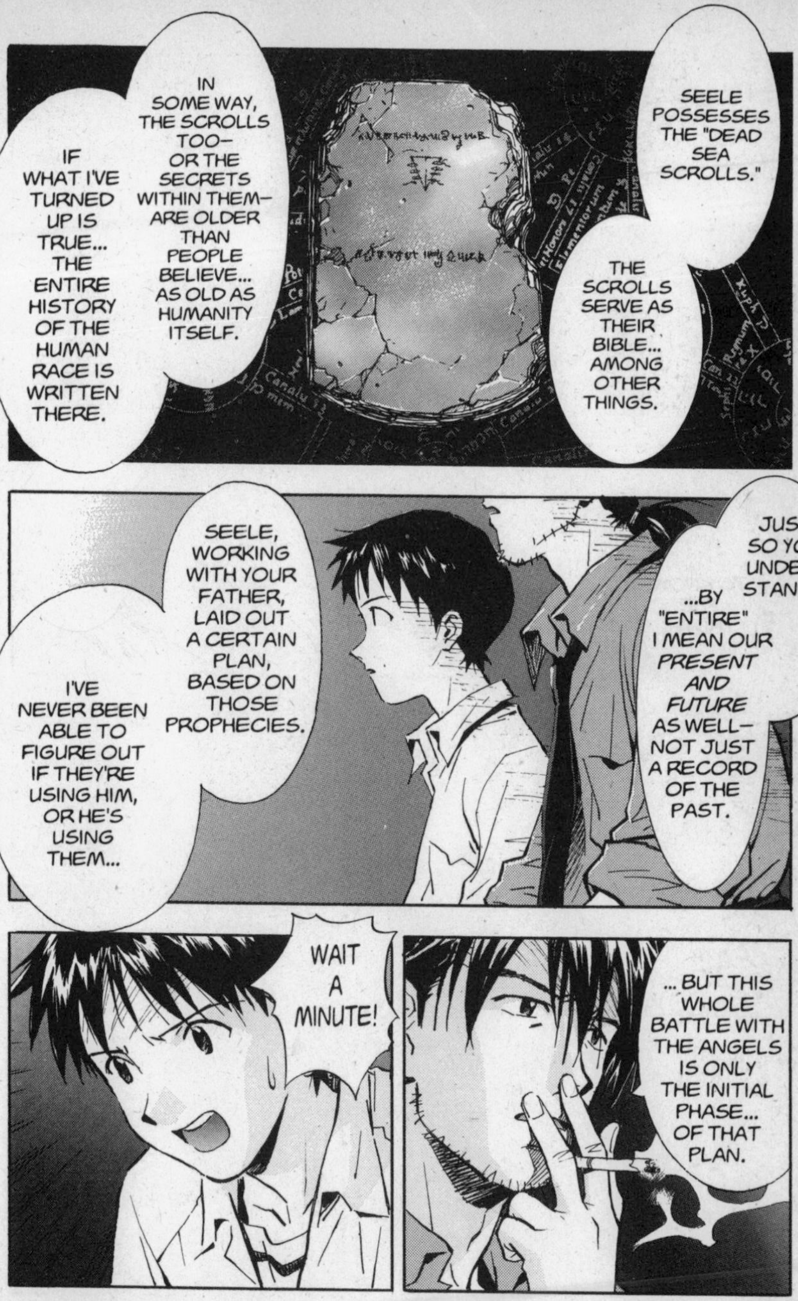
SEELE POSSESSES THE "DEAD SEA SCROLLS."
THE SCROLLS SERVE AS THEIR BIBLE... AMONG OTHER THINGS.
IN SOME WAY, THE SCROLLS TOO— OR THE SECRETS WITHIN THEM— ARE OLDER THAN PEOPLE BELIEVE... AS OLD AS HUMANITY ITSELF.
IF WHAT I'VE TURNED UP IS TRUE... THE ENTIRE HISTORY OF THE HUMAN RACE IS WRITTEN THERE.
JUST SO YOU UNDERSTAND...
...BY "ENTIRE" I MEAN OUR *PRESENT AND FUTURE* AS WELL— NOT JUST A RECORD OF THE PAST.
SEELE, WORKING WITH YOUR FATHER, LAID OUT A CERTAIN PLAN, BASED ON THOSE PROPHECIES.
I'VE NEVER BEEN ABLE TO FIGURE OUT IF THEY'RE USING HIM, OR HE'S USING THEM...
... BUT THIS WHOLE BATTLE WITH THE ANGELS IS ONLY THE INITIAL PHASE... OF THAT PLAN.
WAIT A MINUTE!

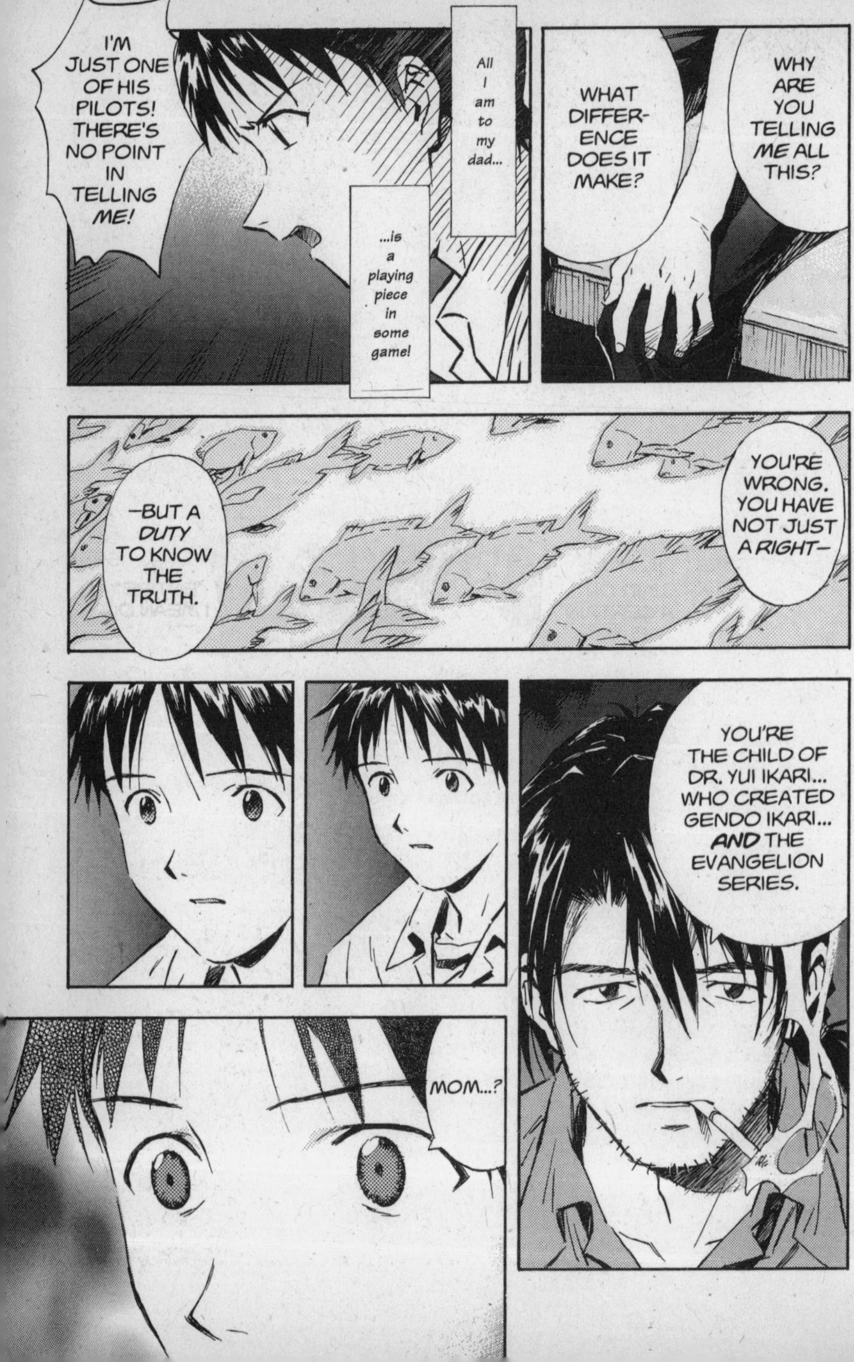
WHY ARE YOU TELLING *ME* ALL THIS?
WHAT DIFFERENCE DOES IT MAKE?
I'M JUST ONE OF HIS PILOTS! THERE'S NO POINT IN TELLING *ME*!
All I am to my dad...
...is a playing piece in some game!
YOU'RE WRONG. YOU HAVE NOT JUST A *RIGHT*—
—BUT A *DUTY* TO KNOW THE TRUTH.
YOU'RE THE CHILD OF DR. YUI IKARI... WHO CREATED GENDO IKARI... ***AND*** THE EVANGELION SERIES.
MOM...?

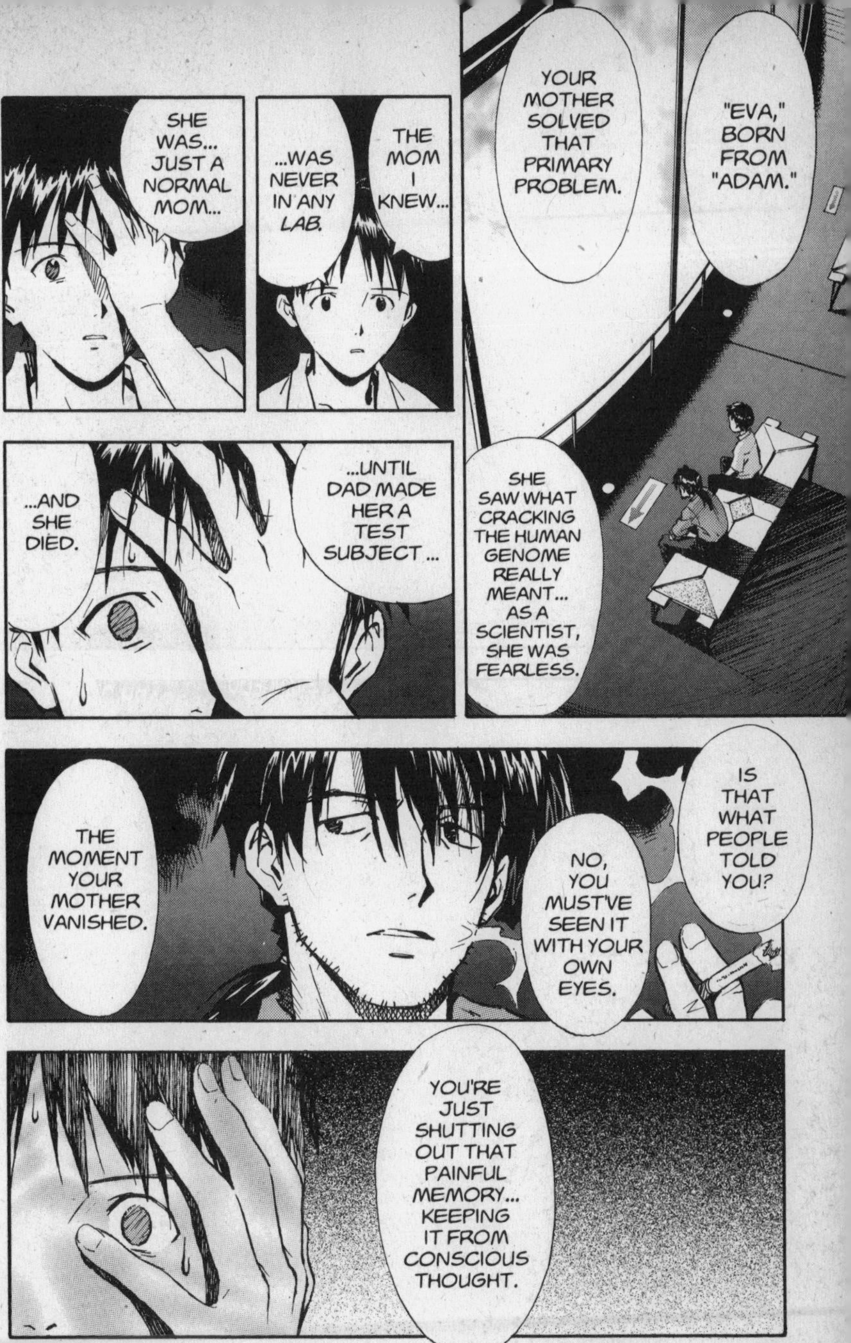
"EVA," BORN FROM "ADAM."
YOUR MOTHER SOLVED THAT PRIMARY PROBLEM.
SHE SAW WHAT CRACKING THE HUMAN GENOME REALLY MEANT... AS A SCIENTIST, SHE WAS FEARLESS.
THE MOM I KNEW...
...WAS NEVER IN ANY *LAB.*
SHE WAS... JUST A NORMAL MOM...
...UNTIL DAD MADE HER A TEST SUBJECT ...
...AND SHE DIED.
IS THAT WHAT PEOPLE TOLD YOU?
NO, YOU MUST'VE SEEN IT WITH YOUR OWN EYES.
THE MOMENT YOUR MOTHER VANISHED.
YOU'RE JUST SHUTTING OUT THAT PAINFUL MEMORY... KEEPING IT FROM CONSCIOUS THOUGHT.

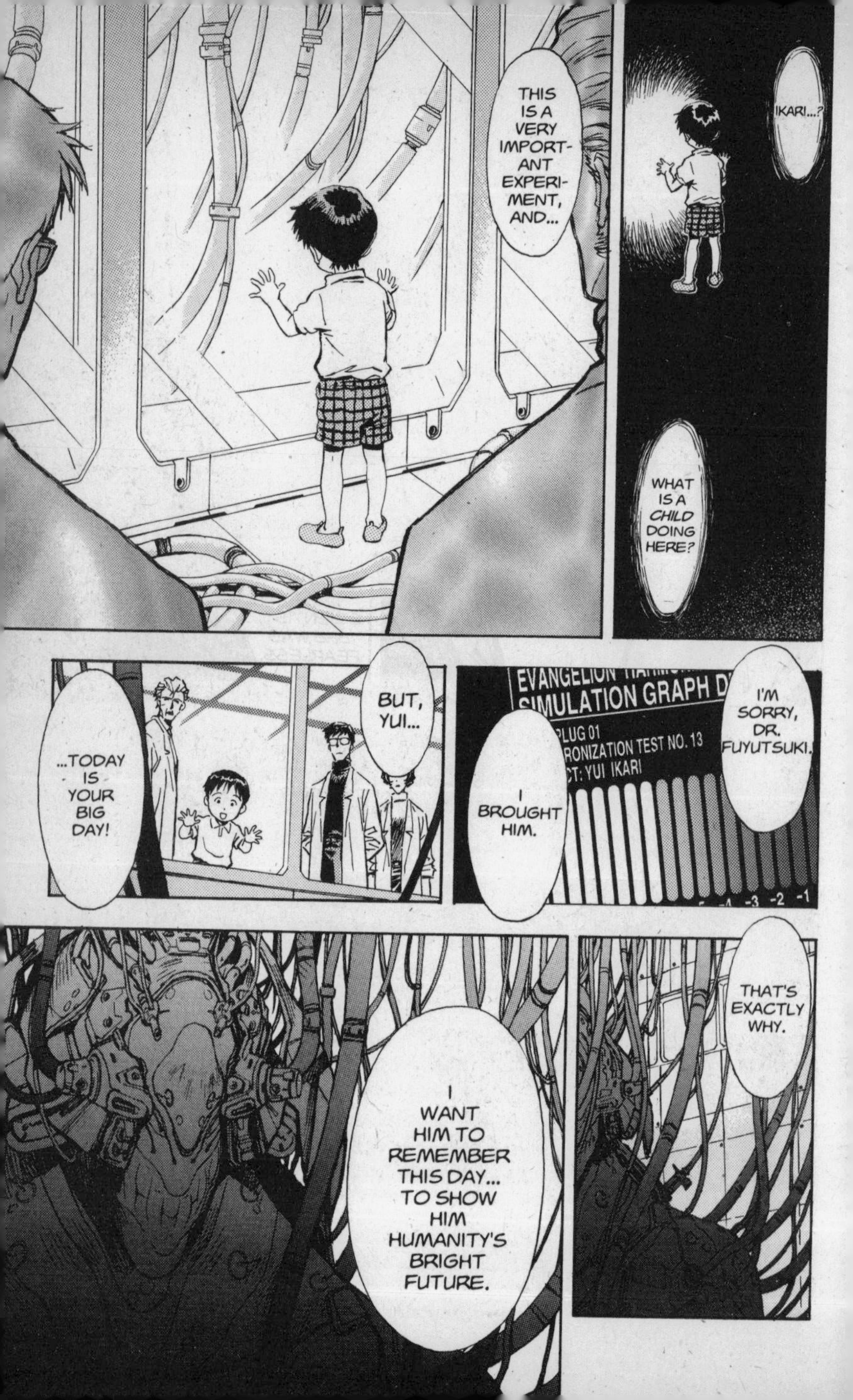
IKARI...?
WHAT IS A CHILD DOING HERE?
THIS IS A VERY IMPORTANT EXPERIMENT, AND...
EVANGELION
SIMULATION GRAPH D
PLUG 01
RONIZATION TEST NO. 13
CT: YUI IKARI
I'M SORRY, DR. FUYUTSUKI.
I BROUGHT HIM.
BUT, YUI...
...TODAY IS YOUR BIG DAY!
THAT'S EXACTLY WHY.
I WANT HIM TO REMEMBER THIS DAY... TO SHOW HIM HUMANITY'S BRIGHT FUTURE.

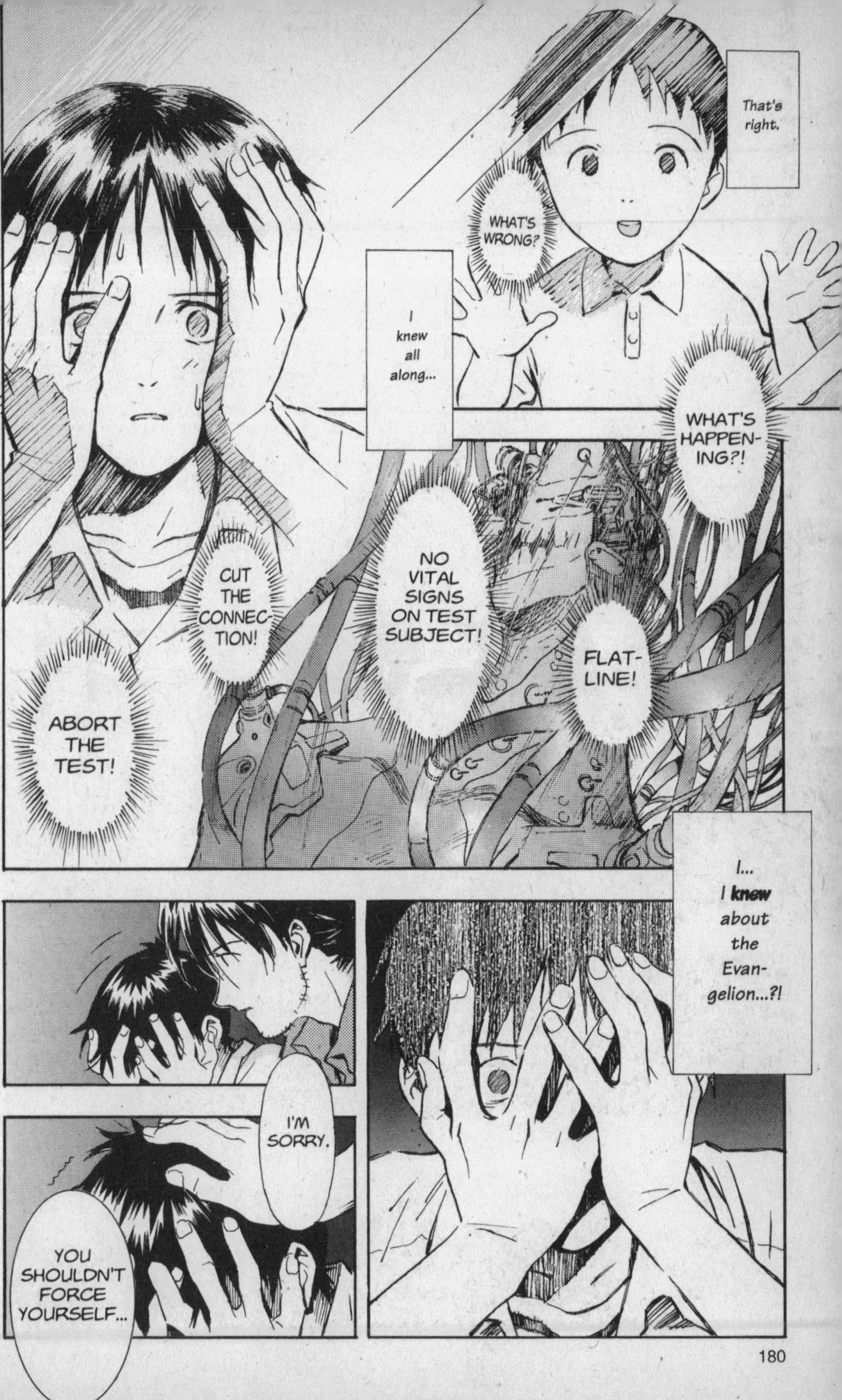
That's right.
WHAT'S WRONG?
I knew all along...
WHAT'S HAPPENING?!
FLAT-LINE!
NO VITAL SIGNS ON TEST SUBJECT!
CUT THE CONNECTION!
ABORT THE TEST!
I... I knew about the Evangelion...?!
I'M SORRY.
YOU SHOULDN'T FORCE YOURSELF...

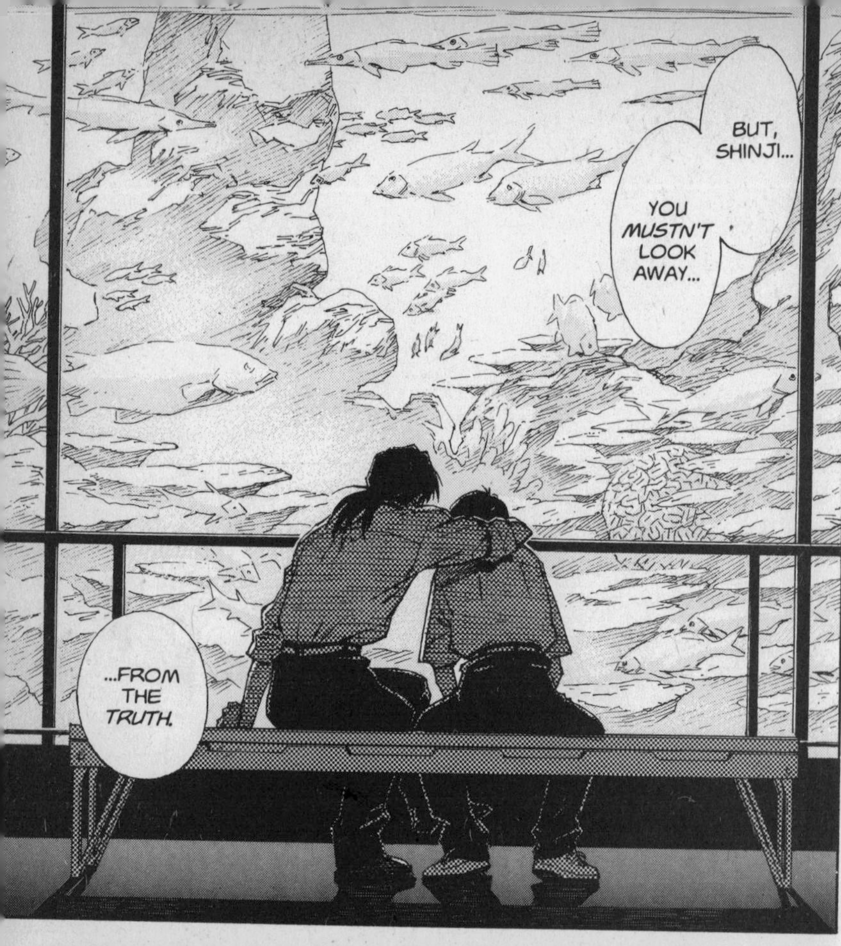
BUT, SHINJI...
YOU MUSTN'T LOOK AWAY...
...FROM THE TRUTH.
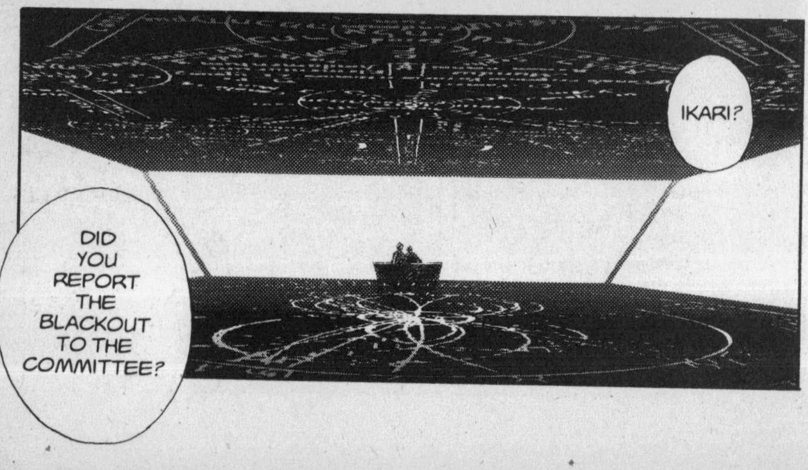
IKARI?
DID YOU REPORT THE BLACKOUT TO THE COMMITTEE?

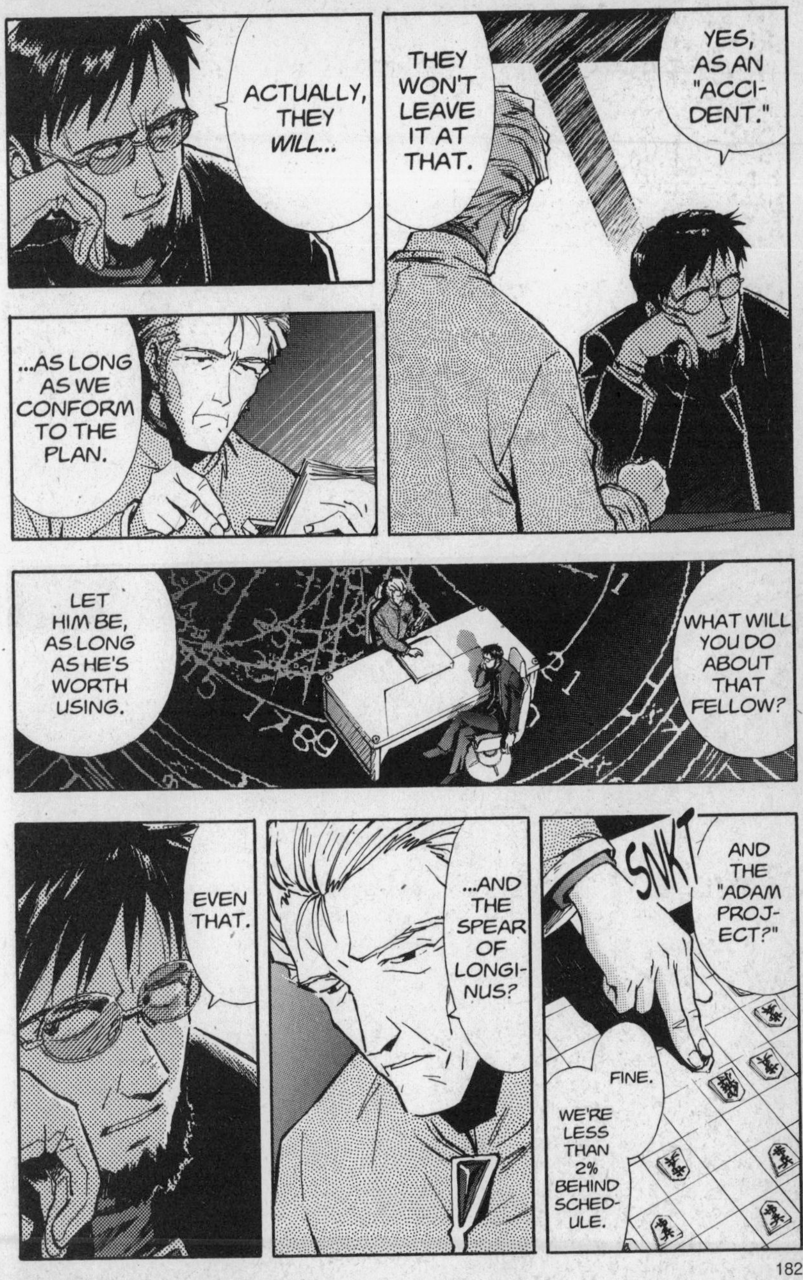
YES, AS AN "ACCI- DENT."
THEY WON'T LEAVE IT AT THAT.
ACTUALLY, THEY *WILL*...
...AS LONG AS WE CONFORM TO THE PLAN.
WHAT WILL YOU DO ABOUT THAT FELLOW?
LET HIM BE, AS LONG AS HE'S WORTH USING.
SNKT
AND THE "ADAM PROJ- ECT?"
FINE.
WE'RE LESS THAN 2% BEHIND SCHED- ULE.
...AND THE SPEAR OF LONGI- NUS?
EVEN THAT.

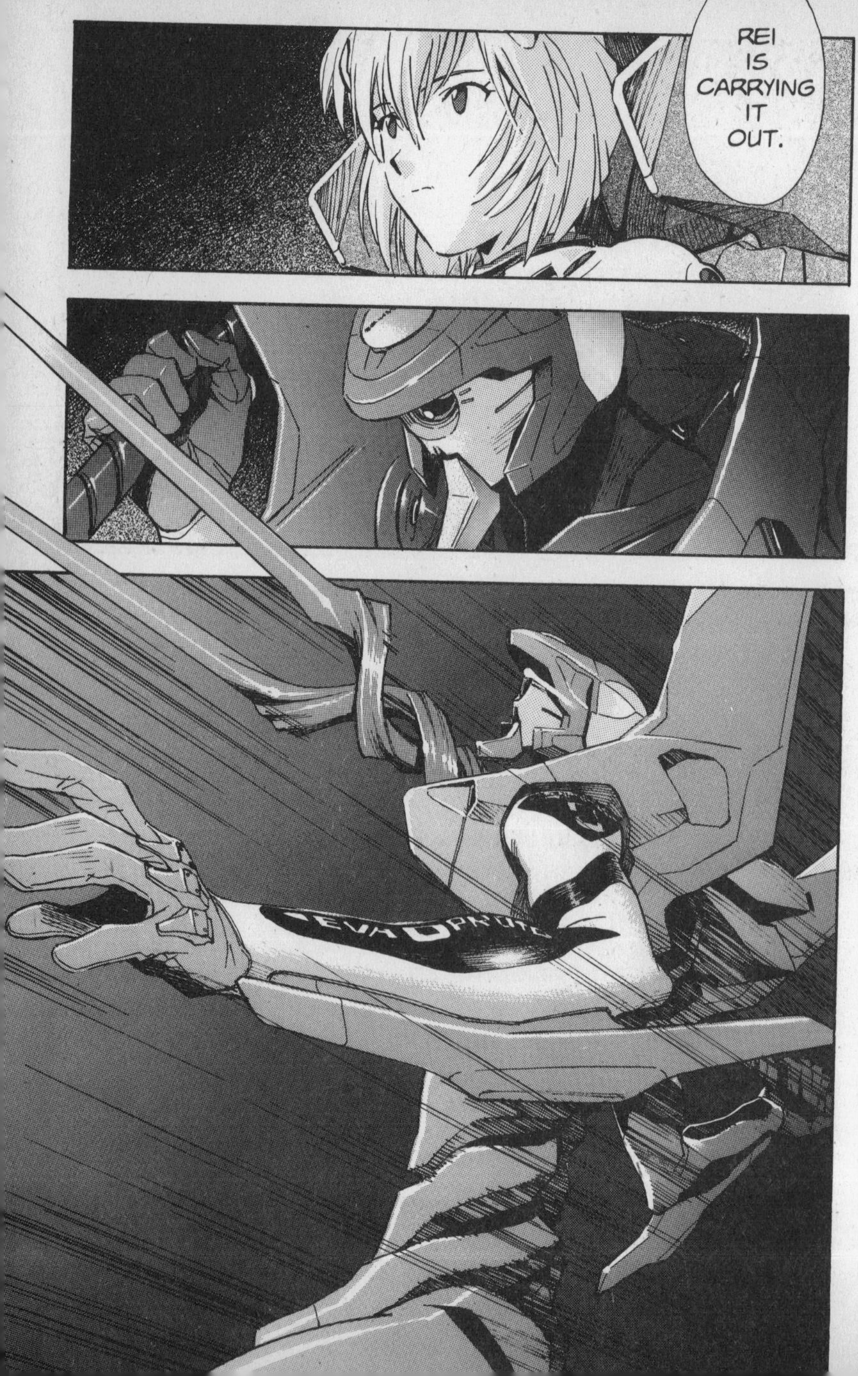
REI IS CARRYING IT OUT.

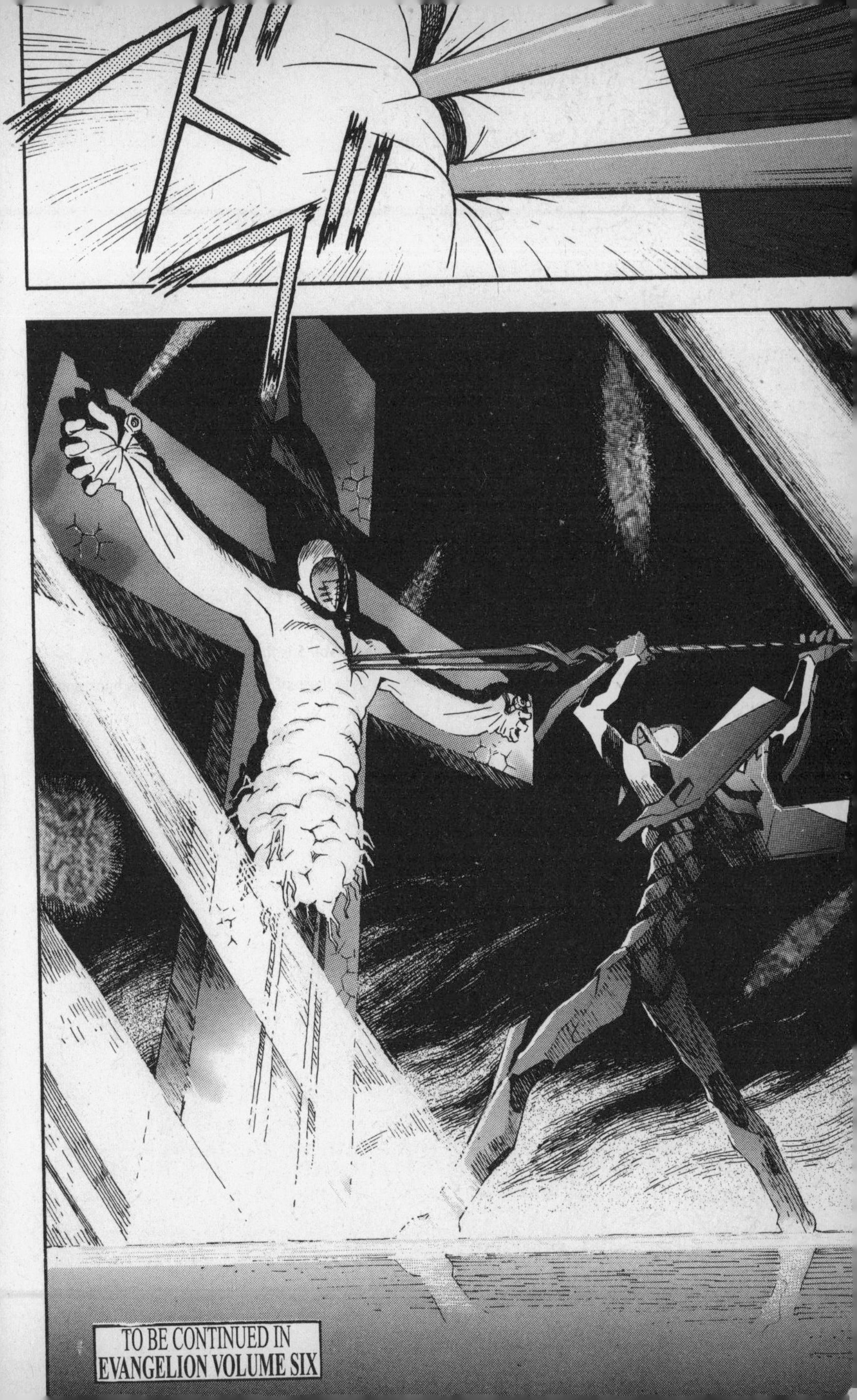
TO BE CONTINUED IN
EVANGELION VOLUME SIX

NEON GENESIS EVANGELION

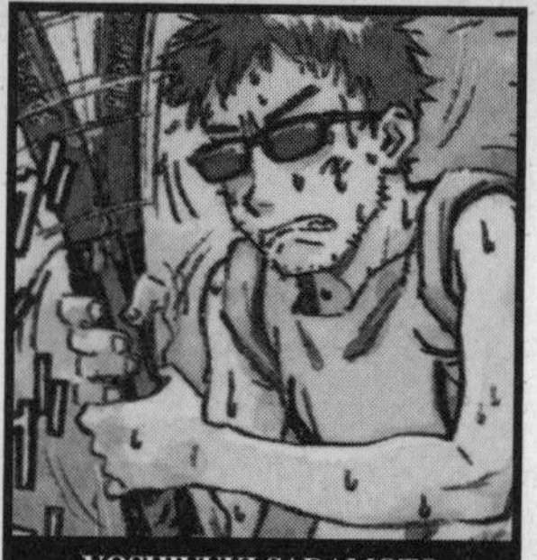

YOSHIYUKI SADAMOTO

YOSHIYUKI SADAMOTO
WRITER AND ARTIST

You've been anxiously waiting for ***two years!*** Vol. 5 is *finally here!*

First, I'd like to give a heartfelt "thank you" to those of you who bought this book and are reading it now. I know you kind souls won't ask any questions about why it's so late, and will wait just as patiently for Vol. 6. Yes...I know you'll wait.

I think you'll wait.

Probably.

I hope.

Pretty please…?

All right! Time to limber up, buff out, and crawl forward! Get going already, me!

EDITOR'S NOTE:

The two years Sadamoto refers to was the wait readers originally had in Japan between Vol. 4 and Vol. 5. Stages 27, 28, and 29 appeared in the January, March, and May 1998 issues of *SHONEN ACE* magazine, followed by more than a year's hiatus before, in an incredible effort, the artist actually managed to produce Stages 30-33 in four consecutive issues between July and October of 1999.

The truant nature of *EVANGELION* is a tradition that has continued well into this very day, with recent issues of *SHONEN ACE* again missing the *EVA* manga but instead featuring increasingly elaborate giveaways such as matching Rei and Asuka cell-phone cleaners and a folding 1/2 scale pasteboard standee of the Second Child possessing a better personality than the actual article.

Thus far these trinkets have bought off mob violence, and Japanese fans are looking forward to the tenth anniversary of the *EVANGELION* manga itself in February 2005. Sadamoto may be celebrate it in *SHONEN ACE* with a special event; perhaps, it is even rumored, an actual new installment of the story.

-Carl Gustav Horn

SOUND EFFECTS GLOSSARY

Welcome to the sound effects glossary for Volume Five of **Neon Genesis Evangelion**! Japanese is written with a combination of *kanji*—Chinese ideograms, borrowed and modified—and *kana*, phonetic characters. There are two kinds of *kana*: *katakana* and *hiragana*. *Hiragana*, written in a cursive style, is very important in indicating grammar in Japanese.

However, when it comes to manga sound FX, we're mostly concerned with *katakana*. These are written in a more angular style, and their uses include spelling out foreign words, and giving emphasis in ads and signs (sort of like writing in block letters). It's in this role of emphasis that *katakana* are used as sound FX, and almost all of **Evangelion's** FX (and manga in general) so use it. Sometimes, however, *hiragana* is used instead—in cases where, for some reason, it would seem more "natural" to a Japanese speaker to write out that particular FX in *hiragana*.

Here's how this glossary works: 8-2 simply means the sound FX that's on page 8 in panel 2; when a third number gets added—as in 105-4-1 for instance—it means there's more than one FX in the panel. The order all FX are listed, of course, is the Japanese reading order, right-to-left: so 4-1 is the upper right (not upper left) panel of page 105: and 105-4-2 is to the left (not the right) of 105-4-1. In situations where you have multiple FX in a panel, but they're at different heights, the numbering goes clockwise. Note that a tilde (~) is sometimes used in such instances as 96.1~97.1 where an FX is perceived to stretch over more than one panel or page.

After each line's number and FX, you get the literal *kana* reading followed by the description of what the FX stands for in brackets. Sometimes this will be symbolized by an attempt to give an English equivalent of the sound FX, and sometimes just a description of the sound will be given.

Note, however, that some of the FX the artist draws in **Evangelion** aren't literally representing sounds; instead they represent the "sound" Japanese sometimes give to things that don't really have sounds—attitudes, emotional states. In the West the difference between these two kinds of FX is described by the words *onomatopoeia* vs. *mimesis*; in Japan, the equivalent concepts are *giseigo* and *gitaigo*.

One last note: Japanese vowels (they learn them as "AIUEO" rather than "AEIOU") have a regular pronunciation, like those in Spanish. "A" is said *ah*, "I" is *eee*, "U" is *ooh*, "E" is *eh*, and "O" is *oh*.

8.2—FX: jari (shk)
9.5—FX: kii (creak)
11.3—FX: gata (clunk)
13.2—FX: miin miin (cicadas)
18.4—FX: dadada (tump tump)
22.5—FX: koso (whisper)
24.1—FX: pin poon (ding dong)
26.4—FX: doka (kapow)
26.6—FX: do (thud)
27.1—FX: ha (ahhh)
50.6—FX: don (thud)
51.3—FX: hai ("yes," meaning in this instance "here you are")
51.6—FX: kakoon kakoon (ktong ktong)
52.1—FX: kaan kaan (ktong ktong)
52.4—FX: kachi kachi (clik clik)
52.5—FX: gon gon (bang bang- metallic)
52.6—FX: gacha (chk)
56.1—FX: shun shun shun (boiling water)
57.3—FX: gachan (clunk)
57.5—FX: gui (tug)
57.6.1—FX: kyu (squeak)
57.6.2—FX: jaa (fssshh)
58.1—FX: zaa (fshh)
58.2—FX: zaa (fshh)
59.2—FX: ko (tunk)
61.2—FX: kyu (squeak)
65.6—FX: pi pi pi (beep bip beep)
66.2—FX: goku (gulp)
66.3—FX: biku (urk)
67.4—FX: putsu (clik)
67.5—FX: tsu tsu tsu (dial tone)
67.6—FX: tsu tsu tsu (dial tone)
76.3—FX: hiii (wheeen)
76.4—FX: kii (shwoo)
77.1—FX: hiii (wheeen)
77.5—FX: kiii (shwoo)
78.1—FX: kiii (shwoo)
78.3—FX: iii (whee)
89.4—FX: kacha kacha (clickety clack)
92.5—FX: bashuu (bsht)
93.1—FX: don (boom)
93.2—FX: doshu (dash)
94.3—FX: haa (startled)
94.4—FX: guu (grip)
95.1—FX: bashu (dash)
96.1~97.1 FX: zudododo (whoosh)
97.2—FX: guoo (whoo)
99.2—FX: zaza (shkk)
99.3—FX: guon (vmm)
100.1—FX: guoo (whoo)
100.3—FX: ba (whap)
101.1—FX: ga (glom)
101.2—FX: gogogo (rumble)
102.1—FX: zuzuzu (rumble)
103.1~2—FX: guooo (wooo)
103.2—FX: pashi (crack)
103.3—FX: gugu (rumble)
103.4—FX: baka (crash)
104.3—FX: zuzuzu (rumble)
105.4.1—FX: ga (glom)
105.4.2—FX: zun (stab)
106.1—FX: bibibi (rrrip)
106.4—FX: ga (stab)

149.1-2 —FX: katsuun katsuun (same)

150.1 —FX: kachi (chk

152.6.1 —FX: shu (swipe)

152.6.2 —FX: pi (eep)

153.1 —FX: gogon (clank)

153.2-3 —FX: gogogo (rumble)

157.3 —FX: kata (clunk)

157.4 —FX: ha (ah!)

163.5 —FX: pii pipipi (eep eep)

165.5 —FX: bashu (fsht)

169.4 —FX: miin miin (cicadas)

170.3 —FX: paan (beep-car horn)

171.3 —FX: gacha (chk)

172.1 —FX: buoo (vroom)

173.3 —FX: guoo (vroom)

182.5 —FX: pachi (snap)

184.1 —FX: zubu (thbp-fleshy sinking sound)

185 —FX: bun bun [whiff whiff]

108.1 —FX: dodoon (kaboom)

109.1 —FX: zaza (sloosh)

111.1~3 —FX: bii (beep)

114.2 —FX: kasha (klik)

115.3 —FX: bashu (fsht)

115.4 —FX: ka ka ka (clop clop)

116.4 —FX: gofa (woosh)

116.5 —FX: pi (beep)

117.1 —FX: wiii (whirr)

117.2 —FX: gakon (clunk)

117.4 —FX: kashan (click)

121.4 —FX: don (thud)

123.5 —FX: biku (urk)

126.1 —FX: ba (fwap)

129.2 —FX: katsuun katsuun (clop clop- echoing footsteps)

130.1 —FX: gon (bonk)

131.2 —FX: ho ho ho

133.4 —FX: ban ban (bang bang)

133.5 —FX: ban ban (bang bang)

134.2 —FX: pa (clik- turning on)

134.4 —FX: gakun (thunk)

135.1 —FX: dotan (thud)

135.2 —FX: chin (ping)

135.3 —FX: wii (whirr)

140.2 —FX: koto (clunk)

145.5 —FX: gusha (crumple)

146.2 —FX: gigigi (crank)

146.3 —FX: gigigi (creeeak)

147.2 —FX: ka ka (clop clop)

147.3 —FX: ka ka (clop clop)

148.6 —FX: katsuun katsuun (echoing footsteps)

SECRETS OF EVANGELION

SPECIAL DOSSIER

BONUS SECTION

NEON GENESIS EVANGELION

VOLUME FIVE

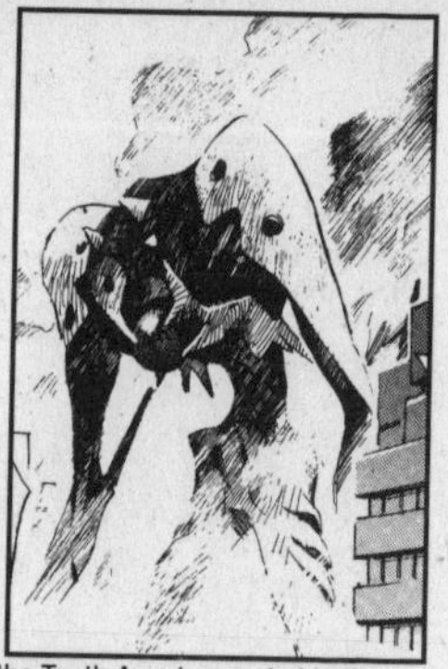

ANGELS:

Recent remarks by Gendo and Fuyutsuki of NERV seem intriguingly to confirm that certain details of the Angels differ in this version of events. Although the first Angel to appear, Sachiel [in Stages 1-5], had been previously assumed to be the Third Angel as so coded in the anime, it is now suggested that in this version of events it was actually the Second. Fuyutsuki commented that the Angel Sahaquiel [Stage 30]—the Tenth Angel as coded in the anime—was actually "[number] seven," to which Gendo replied, "Yes. And five remain." According to this differing classification, then, the Third Angel would be Shamshel [Stages 9-10], the Fourth, Ramiel [Stages 15-19], the Fifth, Gaghiel [Stage 20], and the Sixth, Israfel [Stage 22-26]. Note that the Angels Sandalphon and Matarael—the Eighth and Ninth respectively—have not appeared in this version of events, as they did in the anime where they followed Israfel and preceded Sahaquiel.

The Angels appear to vary in size, shape, offensive and defensive strength, and tactics, but as a rule they are immense, uncommunicative, enigmatic, and ultra-powerful entities. The nigh-invulnerability of the Angels derives from both their **A.T. Fields** [see below] and their own physical makeup. Dr. Ritsuko Akagi has observed that the composition of the Angels appears to have both wave and particle properties [as do, for example, the photons through which the electromagnetic spectrum is expressed] and that the waveform pattern of the Angels is 99.89% expresses information similar to that of the human genome. Major [then Captain] Misato Katsuragi, remarked that that the Evangelion Units had an identical degree of similarity, suggesting an affinity between the Eva Units and the Angels.

As the Eva Units were designed to defeat the Angels, this similarity is perhaps not surprising. While it has also been demonstrated as possible to delay or damage Angels through the use of weapons of mass destruction [and therefore in theory a multi-megaton weapon of sufficient strength could destroy one entirely] the tendency of the Angels to be sighted only when closing on target has raised the considerable issue of collateral damage accompanying the use of **N^2 bombs** [see below]. Previous to the orbital manifestation of the Angel Sahaquiel, the Angels had always first appeared in the environs of Tokyo-3 and immediately moved to attack NERV HQ. The exception was an incident involving the transshipment by the UN aircraft carrier *Over The Rainbow* (possibly the former U.S. ship *Theodore Roosevelt*) of Eva Unit-02 and the then-embryonic First Angel, Adam, which was attacked in mid-ocean by the Angel Gaghiel.

Of the Angels, the Kabbalist Z'ev ben Shimon Halevi remarks, "those who would not concede human superiority...were relegated to the task of leading the chaotic forces that plague the universe and man in particular...[the] risk of deviation from the cosmic plan was corrected, legend tells us, by the attachment of the Divine Name EL [from 'elohim'] to the functional name of each angelic being, so that it could never exert more of its power than God wished. Thus each celestial being was confined to its task, like the angel Shalgiel who dealt only with snow." According to this Kabbalistic view, then, it is incorrect to think of the Angels attacking NERV as "invaders" from "outside;" it would be more accurate to speak of them having been present among/in certain aspects of creation and of having recently "awakened."

SPECIAL BONUS DOSSIER SECTION

NEON GENESIS EVANGELION

VOLUME FIVE

SECRETS OF EVANGELION

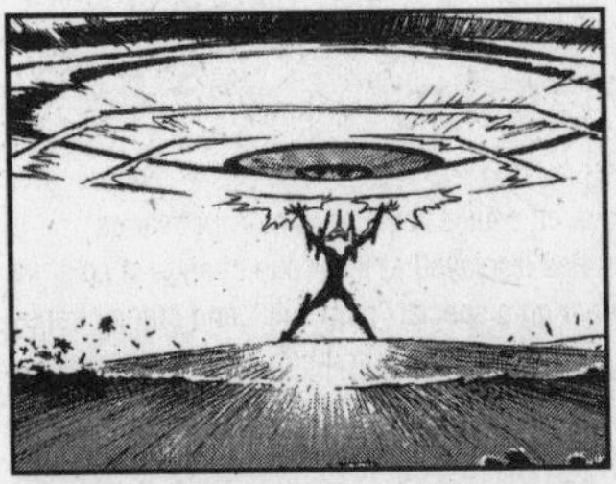

A.T. FIELD:

Named for the "absolute terror" it inspires—a directional field with the visual manifestation of concentric hexagons—a shield theoretically almost invulnerable to physical attack. The "A.T. Field" is understood not to exert physical force per se, but instead to warp normal three-dimensional space in a manner that serves to deflect attack. Only Angels and the Evangelion Units are known to be capable of generating an A.T. Field; by generating one in close proximity to that of an Angel, an Eva Unit can effectively cancel its usefulness to the Angel as a defense, and then close for hand-to-hand combat. Some quantitative sense of the defensive value of the A.T. Field can be appreciated by the estimate of NERV's Magi System that it would require a narrow-focused positron beam of at least 180 GW in strength [comparable to the combined output of 20 major power generating complexes such as Grand Coulee, U.S.A.] to disrupt and penetrate the Angel Ramiel's A.T. Field. The offensive value of the field was illustrated by its use by the Angel Sahaquiel to hurl pieces of itself at ultra-high velocity from orbit, striking with the force of a nuclear warhead. The A.T. Field is inadequately understood and remains a subject of ongoing research at NERV.

N2 BOMB:

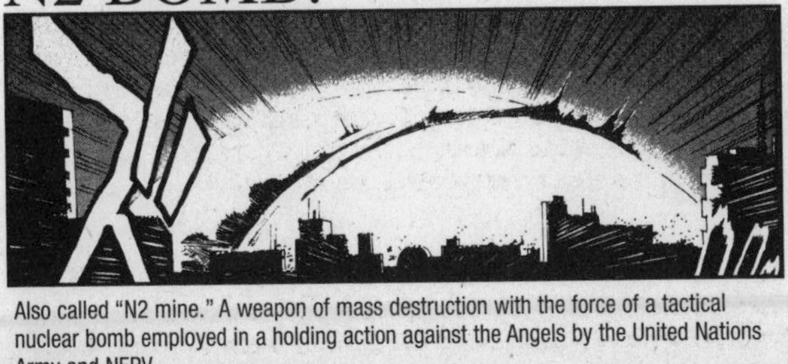

Also called "N2 mine." A weapon of mass destruction with the force of a tactical nuclear bomb employed in a holding action against the Angels by the United Nations Army and NERV.

SECRETS OF EVANGELION

SPECIAL DOSSIER

BONUS SECTION

NEON GENESIS EVANGELION

VOLUME FIVE

EVANGELION:

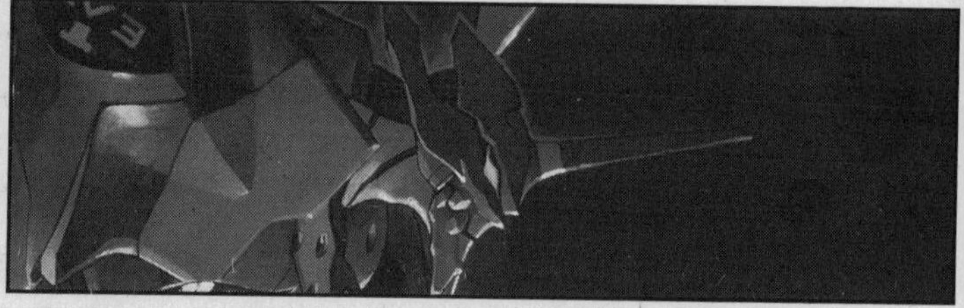

A.K.A. "Eva Units" or "Eva." The Eva, which is approx. 40m tall, is humanoid in shape and biomechanical in construction, an organic being covered with articulated armor that varies according to the individual unit [and Eva Unit-00 has displayed at least one change of color in its armor scheme]. The pilot—normally, while wearing a special "plug suit," and cranial transmitters attached to his or her hair—boards the Eva first through sitting down in a control seat located inside the "entry plug," a long cylinder with rounded ends. The entry plug, with the pilot inside, is then inserted via mechanical servos into the upper back of the Eva, slanting downwards at approximately a 45-degree angle. The plug is then filled with LCL [Link Connect Liquid], an oxygenated, semi-transparent fluid which the pilots "breathe," and which provides a necessary transmission medium between the cranial transmitters and the Eva.

Although there are physical controls within the entry plug, these appear to be merely assistive somatic foci; it is necessary for the pilot to achieve a mental "synchronization" with the Eva in order to pilot. The higher the sync-rate, the more effective the piloting. The Eva has the full range of human articulation and can punch or kick, as well as fight with a wide range of scaled hand or projectile weapons. Eva Unit-01 has also been observed to apparently—with its pilot Shinji Ikari unconscious—pilot itself, with a high degree of skill.

The Eva Series [as of Stage 33] numbers five, having been constructed—at very great expense—in various NERV facilities throughout the world. Ryoji Kaji's investigation has revealed that Dr. Yui Ikari vanished in 2004 during the first, failed attempt to construct a working Eva Unit. A functional Evangelion, the "prototype" Unit Zero, was not realized until ten years later in 2014. It however went out of control during the initial attempt at activation with pilot Rei Ayanami. and had to be chemically "frozen" using a quick-setting plastic until its reactivation in Stage 15. In this version of events, Rei subsequently became the first pilot of the Eva Unit-01, with which she was presumably able to achieve a satisfactory synchronization. Unit-01, however, was later transferred to the "Third Child," Shinji Ikari, upon his arrival in Tokyo-3.

Unit-00 and 01 were manufactured in Japan; Unit-02, piloted by Soryu Asuka Langley, was the first "production model," manufactured in Germany. Eva Units-03 are 04 were under construction and testing at the two NERV facilities in the United States, in Massachusetts and Nevada respectively.

SECRETS OF EVANGELION

SPECIAL BONUS DOSSIER SECTION

NEON GENESIS EVANGELION

VOLUME FIVE

LCL:

An acronym for Link Connect Liquid, the amber fluid which fills the cylindrical "entry plugs" in which the Eva pilots sit while piloting. As the name implies, LCL is a transmission medium designed to convey the thought impressions of the pilot to the Eva Unit, allowing pilot and unit to "synch" and thus operate. LCL also provides oxygen to the lungs of the pilot; it is a liquid that can be "breathed," suggesting it may be a descendant of 20th-century U.S. Navy research into such breathable liquids to replace gaseous oxygen for deep-sea divers. As liquid cannot be compressed as can gas, such a medium provides protection from high-pressure environments. This implies that LCL may also serve to protect EVA pilots from physical shock in combat. LCL may have additional properties which remain classified.

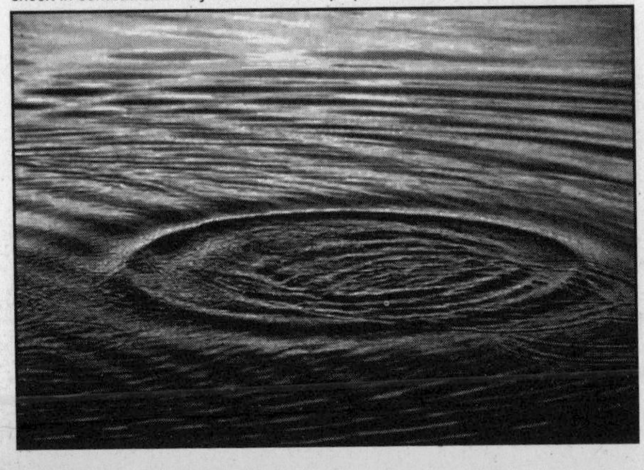

SECRETS OF EVANGELION

SPECIAL BONUS DOSSIER SECTION

NEON GENESIS EVANGELION VOLUME FIVE

GEOFRONT:

A neologism developed to refer to deep underground construction developments, [the term "geofront" was also used in the manga GHOST IN THE SHELL and the first PATLABOR anime movie]. The geofront in which NERV headquarters is located is directly below the city of Tokyo-3, and is a massive dome-shaped vault 6 km wide and 900 meters high, lit by sunlight reflected down from the surface by a system of mirror-faced skyscrapers. Vehicles and personnel enter and leave the Geofront via trains that spiral up and down the curved walls. Many of Tokyo-3's above-ground skyscraper blocks are designed to be retracted below the surface and lock into a position from the roof of the Geofront dome; while this was designed to remove them from the possibility of damage in case of an attack on the city, the system has proved only partially effective against the Angels. The NERV HQ building rests on the floor below the dome, surrounded by a terraced and forested landscape. NERV HQ has a "mirror" architecture as unusual as the rest of the Geofront: it has the shape of a pyramid which appears half-buried at ground level, excepting the southeastern face, which descends down the side of a trench in the shape of an inverted pyramid. NERV HQ possesses a sealed-environment system; sub-basements of the building extend for at least one km below the surface of the Geofront.

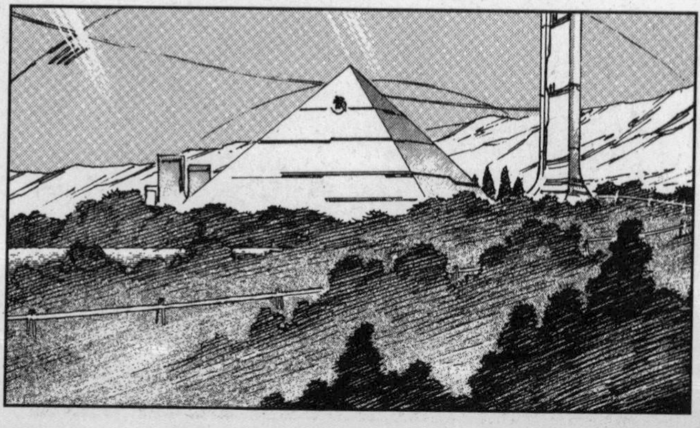

SPECIAL BONUS DOSSIER SECTION

NEON GENESIS EVANGELION

VOLUME FIVE

SECRETS OF EVANGELION

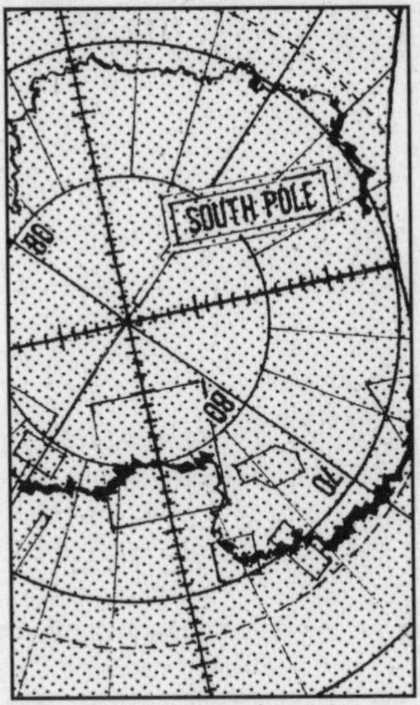
SOUTH POLE

SECOND IMPACT:

Internal NERV references to the Second Impact and its actual origins remain classified. The official report of the United Nations states that at on Sept. 13, 2000, a small meteorite, estimated at no more than several centimeters in size, impacted Mt. Markham on the Shackleton Coast of the Ross Ice Shelf, Antarctica. The tremendous speed of the meteorite, only marginally less than that of light, gave the resulting explosion an energy equivalent to that of an object several miles across, vaporizing the Antarctic ice cap. What is not contested are the results: two billion people died as a result of immediate tsunami and flooding; the Southern Hemisphere was virtually wiped clean of life. On Sept. 15, conflict between refugees on the India-Pakistan border sparked the first of a series of wars that raged worldwide until the Valentine Cease-Fire of Feb. 14, 2001. The "Second Impact" was so-named after the theory of lunar formation which states that the moon and earth were one body during the very early history of the solar system, but were split apart by a massive object in the First, or "Great" Impact.

SECRETS OF EVANGELION

SPECIAL BONUS DOSSIER SECTION

NEON GENESIS EVANGELION

VOLUME FIVE

NERV

GOD'S IN HIS HEAVEN. ALL'S RIGHT WITH THE WORLD.

NERV:

German for "nerve" (pronounced "nehrf"). Commanded by Gendo Ikari, NERV is a paramilitary research organization under the United Nations ceded provisional authority to assist in the war against the Angels; however objections to NERV from the conventional UN armed forces are frequent. In addition to its Tokyo-3 headquarters on Lake Ashino, NERV is believed to have six other branches: at Matsushiro in Nagano Prefecture (approx. 50 km NNE of Tokyo-2), in Beijing (People's Republic of China), in Massachusetts and Nevada (United States—exact locations unknown), and in Hamburg and Berlin (Federal Republic of Germany). NERV's origins lie in an earlier group, GEHIRN (German for "brain"), also headed by Gendo Ikari, that dates to at least 2003—at which time Ikari was Chief of Research of the U.N. Artificial Evolution Laboratory at Hakone (now Tokyo-3). By 2010, GEHIRN had become reorganized as NERV, following the death of Dr. Naoko Akagi, mother of NERV's current head scientist, Dr. Ritsuko Akagi. NERV and its ultra-expensive Evangelion Series are regarded with controversy and suspicion by a number of UN member governments, and it is the subject of clandestine investigation by at least one national intelligence service. Further information is unavailable at this time.

SECRETS OF EVANGELION

SPECIAL BONUS DOSSIER SECTION

NEON GENESIS EVANGELION

VOLUME FIVE

TOKYO-2:

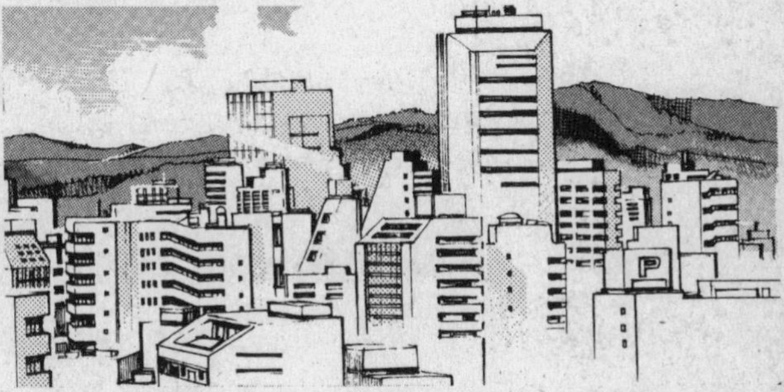

On September 20, 2000, the city of Tokyo fell victim to the rising world chaos when it was hit by what is believed to have been a nuclear weapon of unknown origin, resulting in the death of approximately 500,000 people. The Provisional Government of Japan at first made efforts towards reconstruction, but soon decided to relocate the capital inland to the high ground of Matsumoto City in Nagano Prefecture, renamed Tokyo-2.

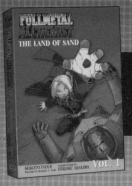
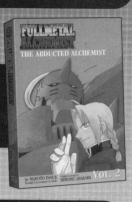
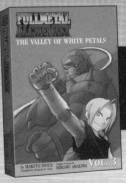

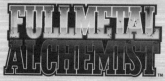

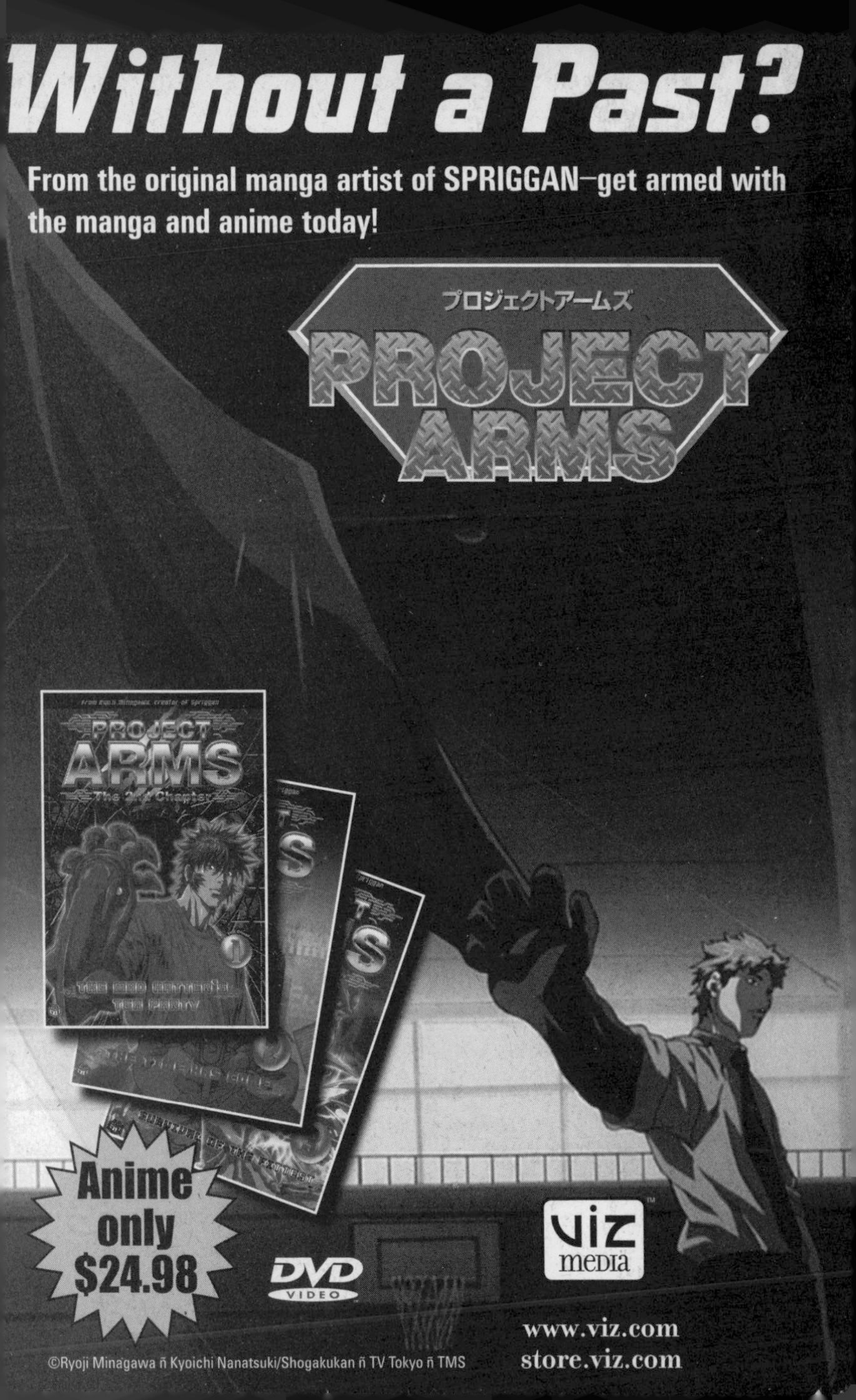
Without a Past?
From the original manga artist of SPRIGGAN—get armed with the manga and anime today!
プロジェクトアームズ
PROJECT ARMS
PROJECT ARMS The 2nd Chapter
Anime only $24.98
DVD VIDEO
viz media
www.viz.com
store.viz.com
©Ryoji Minagawa ñ Kyoichi Nanatsuki/Shogakukan ñ TV Tokyo ñ TMS

What's a Future

Ryo thought he was normal until he learned his arm was secretly replaced with a powerful weapon. But he soon learns that there are others—teens like him—with mechanical limbs and no idea how the weapons were implanted. Now a secret organization is after the only living samples of this technology and wants to obtain their power by any means possible...

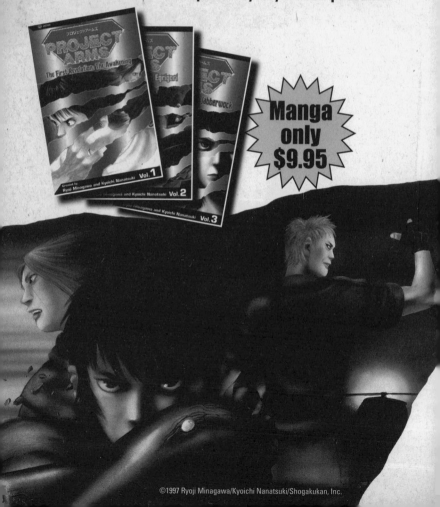

Manga only $9.95

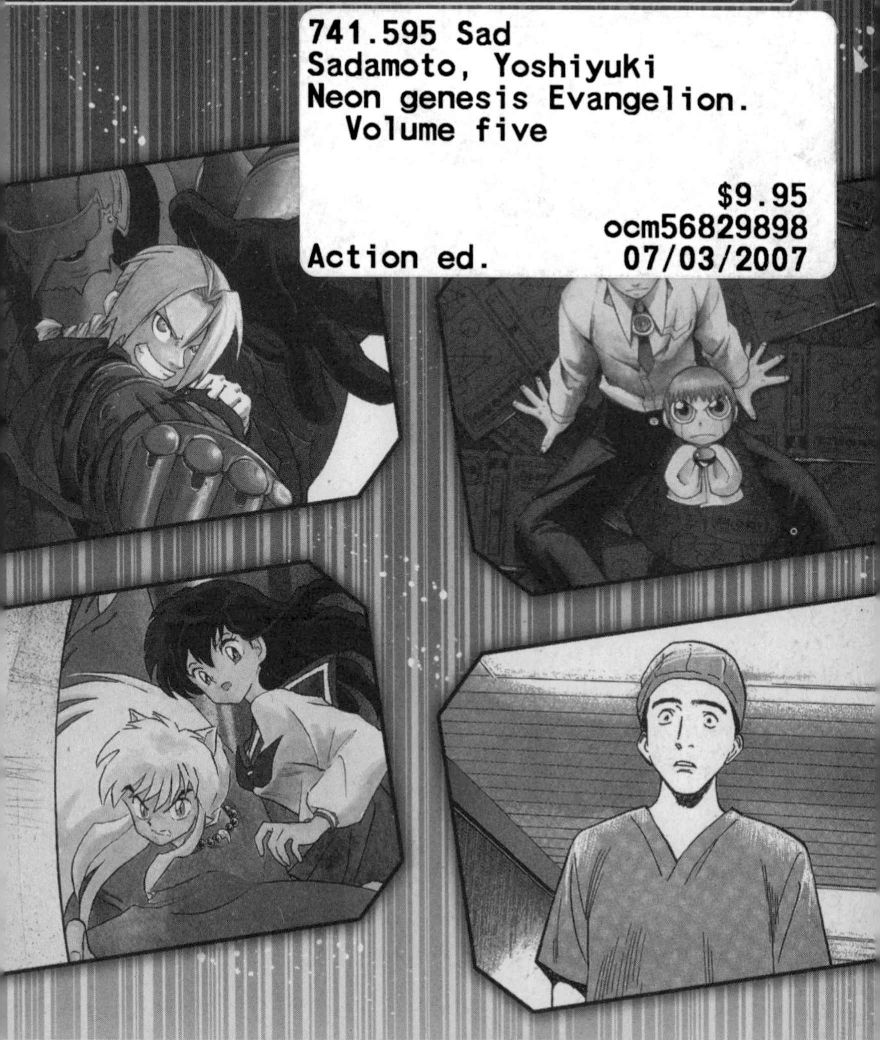